Humanism in Business Series

Series Editors
Ernst von Kimakowitz
Humanistic Management Network
Humanistic Management Center
Geneva, Switzerland

Wolfgang Amann
HEC Paris in Qatar
Doha, Qatar

Pingping Fu
University of Nottingham Ningbo China
Ningbo, China

Carlos Largacha-Martínez
Fundación Universitaria del Área Andina
School of Management
Bogotá, Colombia

Kemi Ogunyemi
Lagos Business School
Pan-Atlantic University
Lagos, Nigeria

Agata Stachowicz-Stanusch
Canadian University of Dubai
Dubai, United Arab Emirates

Shiv S. Tripathi
IIHMR University Campus
Jaipur, India

Since its inception in the year 2011, the Humanism in Business book Series is brought to you by a dedicated editorial board representing the Humanistic Management Network (www.humanisticmanagement. network). The Humanistic Management Network is a global network registered as a Swiss association that lives, works and acts through chapters and collaborations in many countries around the globe. Its purpose is to encourage, promote and support economic activities and business conduct that demonstrate unconditional respect for the dignity of life.

* * *

Following the purpose of the Humanistic Management Network this book series serves to enhance and consolidate the body of knowledge on Humanistic Management and surrounding topics such as business ethics, leadership, CSR, corporate citizenship, sustainability, executive education, impact investing or purpose driven organizations to name but a few.

The books in this series all view Humanistic Management through their own lens, focusing on different aspects and highlighting different dimensions of humanism in business. What unites the books in this series is that they are all aligned to the three stepped approach which defines how we view Humanistic Management. It is based on the unconditional respect for the dignity of life, the integration of ethical reflection in managerial decision making and the active and ongoing engagement with stakeholders.

Furthermore the volumes in the series are an open invitation to join our efforts to make impact towards a more equitable and a more sustainable planet.

Christian Hauser • Wolfgang Amann
Editors

The Future of Responsible Management Education

University Leadership and the Digital Transformation Challenge

Editors
Christian Hauser
PRME Business Integrity Action Center
University of Applied Sciences of
the Grisons
Chur, Switzerland

Wolfgang Amann
HEC Paris in Qatar
Doha, Qatar

ISSN 2662-124X   ISSN 2662-1258   (electronic)
Humanism in Business Series
ISBN 978-3-031-15631-1   ISBN 978-3-031-15632-8   (eBook)
https://doi.org/10.1007/978-3-031-15632-8

This Palgrave Macmillan imprint is published by the registered company Springer Nature Switzerland AG.
The registered company address is: Gewerbestrasse 11, 6330 Cham, Switzerland

Acknowledgments

This book would not have been possible without the vibrant UN-backed Principles for Responsible Management Education (PRME) community globally and all the educationists in all types of higher education institutions. Business schools have been criticized for several things, such as relevance, a too weak ethics orientation, commercialization, and so on. Simultaneously, there has been much positive change and accelerated dynamics toward building future-ready institutions. This book outlines key thoughts based on a group of international experts in their field. We are grateful for their unique contributions on how responsible management education can successfully cope with the digital transformation challenge.

We want to reserve a special place in this acknowledgments section for two dear colleagues who unfortunately left us during the finalization of this book project: Consuelo Garcia De la Torre and Mark Meaney were tremendous contributors to both the academic community and practice. They are lost, but never forgotten.

Contents

About the Authors

Wolfgang Amann, Dr. oec. EdD D.Ed.Psy. D.Litt. (hon.) graduated from the University of St. Gallen in Switzerland with a doctorate in international strategy. He added further qualifications in educational leadership and learning psychology. He is a graduate of key faculty development programs, such as Harvard University's Institute for Management and Leadership in Education, IESE's IFP, IMD's ITP, the EFMD International Deans Program, and CEEMAN's IMTA. He won numerous awards for his teaching, case and book writing, and academic impact initiatives. He serves as professor of strategy and leadership as well as academic director of degree, certificate, open enrollment, and custom programs at HEC Paris.

Osmar Arandia is the postgraduate program director of Organizational Development and the Health management program at UDEM Business School. Previously, he was part of the digital transformation team, collaborated in the same university as director of postgraduate courses in management, and was also the chair of the administration department at the same university. Dr. Arandia teaches courses in Social Responsibility and Strategic Management in undergraduate and postgraduate degrees. He has occupied the position of the vice president of strategic development at Cristóbal Colón University in Veracruz, México, where he also serves as professor of marketing undergraduate and graduate programs in business administration, marketing as well as a doctorate in management science of the university. Dr. Arandia is also the coordinator of linking in the Academy of Administrative Sciences ACACIA. Dr. Arandia has several publications in both academic journals and chapters in books. The topics of interest of Dr. Arandia are humanistic management, welfare, social responsibility, sustainability, and strategy.

Walter Baets is Professor Emeritus at the University of Cape Town (South Africa), professor at the Rotterdam University of Applied Sciences, and Learning Officer at Eindhoven Engine. He is a renowned international speaker and teacher in the areas of complexity and the quantum interpretation of innovation and transformation, an area in which he specialized over his academic career. At the University of Cape Town, he was Dean/Director of the Graduate School of Business and the Allan Gray Chair in Values Based Leadership. He graduated in econometrics and operations research at the University of Antwerp in Belgium. After a corporate career in financial modeling and strategic consulting, he obtained a PhD (at Warwick Business School) and a Senior Doctorate (HDR, Aix-Marseilles). He has then developed an academic career which brought him in seven countries on two continents. His key publications include *Complexity, Organisations and Learning: A Quantum Interpretation of Business* (2006), *Rethinking Growth: Social Intrapreneurship for Sustainable Performance* (Palgrave, 2009 coauthor Erna Oldenboom), *Values Based Leadership in Business Model Innovation* (2013, coauthor Erna Oldenboom), and *Une Interprétation Quantique de l'Innovation* (2017). He is the Past Chair of the Association of African Business Schools (AABS). He is an astute photographer, and his life goal is to become a flamenco guitarist.

Luciana Cezarino is scientific researcher in the field of Applied Social Sciences in the field of Organizational Management. Its main research topics are corporate sustainability, in particular the systemic link between business strategy, socioemotional skills, and cleaner operations. She is a researcher at the Ca' Foscari University in Venice, Italy. In terms of professional training, she has a postdoctoral degree at the Polytechnic of Milan, Italy, for the Erasmus Smart-2 Program, a PhD and a Master's in Business Administration from the Faculty of Economics, Administration and Accounting (FEA) of the University of São Paulo (USP). She worked during her PhD period at Luigi Bocconi University in Milan, Italy, under the supervision of Professor Maurizio Zollo. She also has a degree in Economic Sciences from the State University of Londrina (UEL). The research groups that it acts as coordinator are SSYSD Social Systems and Sustainable Development (SSYSD). As a member, she is part of the Golden for Sustainability hosted by the Bocconi University and ISSS (Brazilian Chapter)-International Society for the System Sciences at FEARP-USP. She is editor-in-chief of the *Latin American Journal of Management for Sustainable Development* (inderscience). She is master's and doctoral advisor at the Graduate Program in Organizational Administration (PPGAO) at FEARP/USP.

Xiao Chen PhD, is part of the faculty of business, University of Prince Edward Island, Canada. His primary research interests include the effects of goal setting/priming in organizational behavior and human resource management and cross-cultural management. His scholarly work has appeared in Organizational Behavior & Human Decision Processes, Applied Psychology: An International Review, and conferences of the Academy of Management, European Group for Organizational Studies, and others. Xiao was the sole recipient of the 2013 'Innovative Teaching Award' from the Academy of Management Human Resources Division.

Paul Dale is the LLB Programme Director and a Lecturer in Law at Aston University. He has previously lectured in law at the University of Birmingham, The Open University, and the Institute of Law, Jersey (CI). Paul's research interests and teaching portfolio include Technology and Law, International Human Rights Law, and Jurisprudence. He is a Fellow of the Higher Education Academy.

Arindam Das is Professor of Strategy and International Business at T A Pai Management Institute, Manipal, India, one of the premier, AACSB-accredited business schools in India, and an advanced signatory of UN PRME. Prior to this academic position, Prof. Das worked for more than two decades in the technology consulting domain, working with global businesses operating in the manufacturing industry sector. His research interests include technology-led business model innovation and internationalization of emerging market firms. Prof. Das is a member of the Strategic Management Society, Academy of International Business, and Association for Information Systems.

Gary Evans prior to embarking on an academic career was Senior Partner and CEO for KPMG Consulting for Central Eastern Europe and prior to that appointment was Partner in Charge of Chemicals, Pharmaceuticals and Energy for the London, UK office of KPMG for tax, audit, and consulting. As a partner in a professional firm, Dr. Evans spent substantial amount of time with corporate boards and the executive management of major international corporations. After retiring from professional practice, Dr. Evans has dedicated his time to research and teaching at the University of Prince Edward Island and completed his PhD in Corporate Governance at Liverpool John Moores University. Dr. Evans continues researching corporate boards globally and is on the editorial board of three academic journals, has been the guest editor for special corporate governance journal publications, and is considered a leading author within the field of corporate governance. Dr. Evans developed the Board Culture Theory using CGT. An active international speaker, he has given presentation on technology, diversity, and other key governance issues across Europe. Dr. Evans is an active member of the indigenous community and holds dual British/Canadian Citizenship.

Consuelo García de la Torre was a full-time research professor at EGADE Business School Monterrey, member of the SNI National Research System of Mexico (SNI1), and researcher at the Strategic Research Group in Social Innovation. Her fields of expertise included Sustainability; Ethics and Corporate Governance; Entrepreneurship; Social Responsibility; Consumer Behavior; Marketing Strategy and International Marketing; Social Marketing; Global Management; Industrial Psychology; Management and Humanism; Intercultural Negotiations.

Mary C. Gentile PhD, is Creator and Director of *Giving Voice to Values* (www.GivingVoiceToValuesTheBook.com), launched with The Aspen Institute and Yale School of Management and hosted at Babson College for 6 years, now based at University of Virginia-Darden School of

Business. This pioneering curriculum for values-driven leadership has been piloted and/or presented at well over 1300 sites globally and has been featured in *Financial Times, Harvard Business Review, Stanford Social Innovation Review, McKinsey Quarterly,* and so on. Gentile, Richard M. Waitzer Bicentennial Professor of Ethics at UVA Darden and educational consultant, was previously at Harvard Business School. She holds a BA from The College of William and Mary and PhD from State University of New York-Buffalo.Gentile's publications include *Giving Voice to Values: How To Speak Your Mind When You Know What's Right; Can Ethics Be Taught? Perspectives, Challenges, and Approaches at Harvard Business School* (with Thomas Piper & Sharon Parks); *Differences That Work: Organizational Excellence through Diversity; Managerial Excellence Through Diversity: Text and Cases,* as well as cases and articles in *Harvard Business Review, Stanford Social Innovation Review, Academy of Management Learning and Education, Risk Management, CFO, BizEd, Strategy+Business,* and so on. Gentile was Content Expert for the award-winning CD-ROM, *Managing Across Differences.* Among numerous honors, Gentile was named a 'Top Mind 2017' by *Compliance Weekly* and has been shortlisted for the Thinkers 50 2017 'Ideas into Practice' Award.

Jose Godinez is Assistant Professor of Management at the Robert J. Manning School of Business, University of Massachusetts Lowell. His work lays at the intersection of the strategy, international business, entrepreneurship, and business ethics disciplines, and he focuses on strategies for firms to operate ethically in locations characterized by high corruption levels. He holds a PhD from the University of Edinburgh Business School.

Jorge F. S. Gomes is Full Professor in Organisational Behaviour and Human Resource Management at the Lisbon School of Economics and Management, University of Lisbon, and researcher at Advance/CSG. Dr. Gomes's research interests cover the HRM process view and alternative perspectives on leadership. He has written articles in *Technovation, International Journal of HRM, Human Resource Management, British Journal of Political Science, European Management Review,* and *Journal of Organizational Change Management.* He holds a PhD degree from the Alliance Manchester Business School (2001); an MSc in Statistics and

Information Systems Management from the Higher Institute of Statistics and Information Systems Management, Lisbon Nova University, Portugal (1995); and a BSc in Social and Organisational Psychology from the Higher Institute of Applied Psychology, Portugal (1992).

Alessandro Goulart is CEO of Bandtec Digital School. He holds Master in Business Administration from the University of São Paulo (2018). He has also done MBA and Bachelor of Business Administration from Fundação Getúlio Vargas (1993). He is creator of Bandtec's business model that brings together three pillars: pedagogical leadership, symbiosis with employers, and socioemotional training in technology graduation.

Ishwar Haritas is the head of TAPMI Centre for Inclusive Growth and Competitiveness at T A Pai Management Institute, Manipal, India. He heads sustainability initiatives at TAPMI and teaches strategy, sustainability, and international business courses to graduate students. In a career spanning over 20 years, Prof. Haritas has worked in diverse capacities as an advisor, consultant, and subject matter expert across industries—for-profit and not-for-profit organizations—as well as for intergovernmental agencies, in over 15 countries, across 3 continents, on scores of strategy design and execution projects and programs. Prof. Haritas obtained an MBA degree from HHL Leipzig Graduate School of Management. In his professional engagements, he actively collaborated across the UN system, with partner countries and with transnational organizations.

Christian Hauser is Professor of Business Economics and International Management at the University of Applied Sciences of the Grisons and visiting scholar at the Digital Society Initiative of the University of Zurich, Switzerland. He studied Latin American Studies at the Universities of Cologne, Germany, Lisbon, Portugal, and Fortaleza, Brazil, and earned his doctorate in Economics at the University of Cologne. He is a member of the topical platform Ethics of the Swiss Academy of Engineering Sciences (SATW), member of the United Nations Principles for Responsible Management Education (PRME) Working Group on Anti-Corruption, and head of the first PRME Business Integrity Action Centre in Europe. His research interests include international entrepreneurship, SME and private sector development, corporate responsibility, business integrity, and data ethics.

Adriana Krasniansky is a technology researcher and ethicist with a specific focus on digital healthcare. Adriana has published research and led projects related to digital ethics, telemedicine ethics, and the digital divide in the United States. She has collaborated with the Petrie-Flom Center for Health Law Policy, Biotechnology, and Bioethics, the Massachusetts State Government, and other organizing bodies. Adriana holds a B.S. from Fordham University and an M.T.S. from Harvard University.

Dušan Kučera graduated from the Protestant Theological Faculty of Charles University in Prague. He completed additional semesters at the College in Friedensau, Germany, and Andrews University, MI, USA. He worked for 7 years as a pastor, editor, and teacher. After that, he changed to secular positions and worked for 15 years in some international companies as an HR manager, most of the years in the automotive company Škoda Auto/Volkswagen. During this time, he finished an international study of the MBA program at the Institute for Financial and Industrial Management in Prague in cooperation with Pfeiffer University, NC. He did PhD from the University of Economics, Prague, focusing on the spirit of capitalism as the potential of spirituality for managers and entrepreneurs. At the Faculty of Business Administration, he works as the Head of the Centre for Business Ethics and Sustainability Management. As an Assistant Professor for Managerial Responsibility and Business ethics, he teaches international master's courses, international MBA programs, and executive education. He is a member of the Steering Committee CEE chapter of PRME and Head of the Ethical Committee of the Institute of Physics, Academy of Sciences, Czech Republic.

Lara Liboni, Postdoctoral Scholarship Abroad 2019–2020—University of Western Ontario (UWO), Ivey Business School, is Associate Professor at the Department of Administration, FEARP/USP. She graduated in Business Administration from FEARP/USP (2002) and holds Master's (2005) and PhD (2009) in Business Administration from FEA—Faculty of Economics, Administration and Accounting of USP—University of São Paulo. She did postdoctorate at UNESP (FEB-Bauru). She serves as Associate Professor at FEARP/USP Faculty of Economics, Administration and Accounting of Ribeirão Preto, University of São Paulo. Lines of research developed: sustainability and education for sustainability; green supply chain; dynamic capabilities and competences; and systemic view. She coordinates the Center on Innovation, Systems and Sustainability and participates in the NEB/USP and Inint Low Carbon Economics Center Research group on Internationalization at FEARP. Research group on Internationalization at FEARP. She is vice president of the Latin American Society for Systems and Sustainability. She is a referee for international conferences and journals, in addition to serving as a member of the editorial board of journals. She is executive editor of the *Latin American Journal of Management for Sustainable Development.*

Florencia Librizzi is a sustainability and education professional and international attorney licensed to practice law in Argentina and New York. As Head of Program and Partnerships, she leads the SDG Academy, flagship education initiative of the UN Sustainable Development Solutions Network (UNSDSN). She was appointed the Co-Chair of the UN Higher Education for Sustainability Initiative (HESI), where she aims to scale up the impact of higher education on the SDGs by bringing together and mobilizing key stakeholders. Previously, she devoted over 6 years to building the Principles for Responsible Management Education (PRME) initiative, United Nations Global Compact Office, reaching 730+ participants in 90+ countries under her strategic leadership. She also served as a research consultant for the International Center for Transitional Justice (ICTJ), advising on issues of postconflict societies and addressing human rights violations through truth, memory, reparations, justice, and other measures. Florencia has practiced law since 2006 as a sole practitioner, mediator, and an attorney at a law firm advising business and non-business clients on a wide range of legal and sustainability issues. Florencia has taught several courses and seminars at Universidad Empresarial Siglo 21, Universidad Nacional de Córdoba (UNC), NYU School of Law, and Columbia Institute for Study of Human Rights and actively contributed as a member of the UNC Institute for Environmental Law and Policy.

She graduated from the Conservatory of Music as a Professor of Piano and received her first law degree magna cum laude from Universidad Nacional de Córdoba, School of Law. She earned her Masters of Laws (LL.M.) at NYU School of Law, where she was granted the Dean's Award and distinguished as a Transitional Justice Scholar. Florencia served as a graduate editor for the *NYU Journal of International Law and Politics*, has written several articles, book chapters, and expert reports (for NGOs and UN), and is a PhD candidate at UNC. Florencia has addressed issues of education, policy, and leadership for sustainable development to diverse audiences on all continents around the world.

Simon Linacre is a marketing director at Cabells with almost 20 years of experience in academic publishing. He is a Trustee of the Committee on Publication Ethics (COPE) and Tutor at the Association of Learned and Professional Society Publishers (ALPSP). His background is in journalism, and Simon has written on the topics of bibliometrics, publication ethics, and knowledge transfer. He holds a master's degree in philosophy and international business and has global experience lecturing to researchers on publishing strategies.

Daniela Ludin has held the Chair of General Business Administration at Heilbronn University in the Faculty of Management and Sales at the Schwäbisch Hall campus since 2015. For her, it is part of her self-image to anchor the principle of sustainability as a central moment in her courses. Since 2017, Prof. Dr. Daniela Ludin has been head of the B. A. Management & Procurement, MAP; since 2019, head of the B. A. Sustainable Procurement Management, SPM. Since 2015, Prof. Dr. Daniela Ludin has also been a member of the Council for Sustainable Development of Heilbronn University, which she has also chaired as the Sustainability Officer of Heilbronn University since 2019. In addition, Prof. Dr. Daniela Ludin is also a member of the University Council. Prof. Dr. Daniela Ludin's research focuses on sustainable procurement management, sustainable consumption, and sustainable innovations.

Abiola Makinwa, LL. B (Ife), LL. M (Lagos), LL. M (Rotterdam), PhD (Rotterdam), is a Principal Lecturer in Commercial Law at the Hague University of Applied Sciences in the Netherlands. She is a professional member of the International Compliance Association and served as Chair of the International Bar Association, Structured Criminal Settlements Subcommittee from 2016 to 2018. In 2020, Abiola served as Consultant to the UN Financial, Accountability Transparency and Integrity (FACTI) Panel as author of the background paper on 'Current Developments in Foreign Bribery Investigations and Prosecutions.' Abiola is the creator of the Integrity Digital Training Module (IntegrityDLM https://integrity-dlm.net/), which she developed under the auspices of a Comenius Senior Fellow Grant from the Netherlands Initiative for Educational Research. Abiola is a well-published and frequent speaker on anti-corruption law and policy, as well as integrity training.

Bartosz Makowicz is university professor at the Faculty of Law, European University Viadrina in Frankfurt (O.), Germany. He is director of the Viadrina Compliance Center, which is an interdisciplinary research center and a think-tank for Governance, Ethics, Compliance & Integrity (ECI). He has been the Head of Delegation of Germany and an international expert to ISO TC 309. Bartosz is author of over 100 publications on ethics, compliance, and integrity and gave over 100 speeches on ECI in past years.

Tânia M. G. Marques is an assistant professor at Polytechnic Institute of Leiria, Portugal, and researcher at CARME—Centre of Applied Research in Management and Economics. Dr. Marques holds a PhD's degree in Management ('Nuevas Tendencias en Dirección de Empresas') from University of Salamanca, Spain. She is former Director of the Master in International Business. Dr. Marques's research interests include organizational behavior, human resources management, downsizing, academic ethics, and cross-cultural studies, with a particular focus on responsible leadership.

Flavio Martins is a PhD candidate in Business Administration at the Faculty of Economics, Administration and Accounting of Ribeirão Preto, FEA-RP/USP. He holds Bachelor's and Master's in Business Administration from the same institution. He was also Diffusion and Innovation Manager at the Research Center for Inflammatory Diseases (CRID), a CEPID supported by FAPESP and linked to the Ribeirão Preto School of

Medicine (FMRP/USP). He is the scientific coordinator of the Latin American Society for Systems and Sustainability (Latin2s), educational consultant for the Ribeirão -3°C Program. He works in the research groups 'Social Systems and Sustainable Development (SSYSD)' at FEA-RP/USP and 'Laboratory for Research and Integration in Technology, Psychology, and Education (ConectaLab)' at FFCLRP/USP. His research interests are Education for Sustainable Development, Interdisciplinary, Public Policies for Sustainable Development, Education for Responsible Management, and Scientific Dissemination. He has professional experience in the area of public tenders and contracts.

Erika Müller holds a Master of Science in Forestry and has 10 years of professional experience with a nongovernmental organization. She works as a sustainability officer at Heilbronn University and is doing her PhD in sustainability and innovation at both Heilbronn University and Tallinn University of Technology.

Carole Parkes is Professor of Responsible Management at Winchester University Business School in the UK—a UN-backed PRME (Principles for Responsible Management Education) Champion School—and has both a business and an academic background. Carole was a member (and Acting Chair) of the PRME Global Advisory Committee and a former Chair of the PRME Chapter UK & Ireland. At the PRME 10th Anniversary Global Forum, Carole was presented with a PRME Pioneer Award 'for her leadership and commitment to the development of PRME' and appointed a Global PRME Special Advisor. As an *International Journal of Management Education* (IJME) Associate Editor, Carole edited the PRME 10th Anniversary Special Issue (2017) and the Implementing Sustainable Development Goals (SDGs) Special Issue (2020). Carole is an editor of Fighting Poverty as a Challenge for Management Education PRME Working Group publications and a coeditor of the Sage Handbook of Responsible Management Learning and Education (2020). She is also an Inaugural Fellow of the Environmental Association of Universities and Colleges (EAUC) and on the editorial board of Society and Business Review (SBR). Carole was previously Director of Social Responsibility & Sustainability at Aston University, where she developed and led ethics, responsibility, and sustainability, first in the Business School, the Aston

MBA, and for the MSc Social Responsibility and Sustainability then across all schools in the University. In 2012–2013, Carole was invited to be the Christopher Chair in Business Ethics at Dominican University in Chicago, and in 2015, a 'Researcher in Residence' at PRME in New York. Carole regularly speaks, publishes, and participates in academic and practitioner events locally and globally and works with a range of business and community groups.

Al Rosenbloom is Professor Emeritus and was the first John and Jeanne Rowe Distinguished Professor at Dominican University. His research interests include case writing, the application of the case method in management education, global branding, marketing in countries with emerging and subsistence markets, and the challenge of integrating the topic of poverty into management education. Al coleads the Anti-Poverty Working Group, Principles of Responsible Management Education (PRME), and participates broadly within PRME. He was a Fulbright Scholar in Nepal and Bulgaria and was honored twice with the Teaching Excellence Award from Brennan School of Business students.

Sreerupa Sengupta is Assistant Professor in Healthcare Management at the Goa Institute of Management (GIM). Her teaching and research interests are in the spheres of gender and governance, public policy, health, media, and qualitative research. Sreerupa is also associated with the Centre for Social Sensitivity and Action (CSSA) at GIM. She enjoys working on community-based projects and projects related to social action and sustainable development. She is the coeditor of a quarterly newsletter on SDGs published by CSSA known as SDG Samvaad. Sreerupa holds a PhD in Women's Studies and a Masters in Sociology. She received the Sasakawa Young Leaders Fellowship Fund from the Tokyo Foundation for Policy Research, Japan, for her doctoral research on AIDS communication, gender, and human rights. She has been a Visiting Fellow at Howard University, Washington D.C., USA, and the American University of Cairo, Egypt. She is also an alumnus of the German Development Institute, Bonn, Germany.

Ana Simaens lectures at the Iscte Business School on the topics of Strategic Management and Sustainability, Ethics and Social Responsibility.

Ana holds a PhD in Management from Tilburg University in The Netherlands and is the Director of the MBA in Sustainable Management at Iscte Executive Education. As an integrated researcher at the Business Research Unit (BRU-Iscte), her work has appeared in various publication outlets, including the *Journal of Business Ethics*, *Public Management Review*, and *Sustainability* and is Associate Editor of the *International Journal of Sustainability in Higher Education* and Topic Editor of *Sustainability*. She is the Deputy Director of the Department of Marketing, Operations, and General Management and a member of the Scientific Committee of BRU-Iscte. Ana is collaborating as an Expert in the ISO TC323—Circular Economy, as Guardian of the GRLI Council (Globally Responsible Leadership Initiative), and Head of Programmatic Work at PRME Chapter Iberia. Ana was Executive Director of the Sustainability Knowledge Lab (SKL) at INDEG-ISCTE, and she coordinates the Prosperity dimension of Sustainability at Iscte and is the Interlocutor of Quality and Sustainability at the Iscte Business School. Finally, Ana has complemented her academic training with various professional training, including certifications such as Advanced Chief Sustainability Officer (CSO) Professional, GRI Certified Training Program, and Sustainable Business Strategy from the Harvard Business School online. Ana is a Certified facilitator of the LEGO®SERIOUS PLAY® method and materials, a Certified facilitator of Pro.play® with Playmobil®.pro, and Certified Reinvention Practitioner.

Divya Singhal is a professor at the Goa Institute of Management (GIM) and Chairperson of Centre for Social Sensitivity and Action (CSSA) at GIM. Applied aspects of the subject and learning-centric pedagogy are at the center of her teaching philosophy. She is passionate about teaching and research, sustainability, and pluralism. She holds a PhD in the humanities and social sciences and a master's in economics and journalism. She received an Indian Council for Social Science Research (ICSSR) Doctoral Fellowship for her thesis work on Human Development and role of Education in Rajasthan. She was recently awarded the United Nations Principle for Responsible Management (UN-PRME) to recognize achievements in integrating the SDGs into business schools in the period January 2020 to December 2020 that exemplifies one or more of the six principles of PRME. Divya led the Indian component of the AHRC/PEC-funded project exploring the impacts of the COVID Pandemic on Indian Supply Chains (2020–2021) and British Academy and DFID-funded project Tackling Slavery, Human Trafficking, and Child Labor in Modern Business (2017–2019) with University of Leeds, UK.

David Steingard, PhD, is Director of the *SDG Dashboard* initiative and Associate Professor of Leadership, Ethics, & Organizational Sustainability at the Haub School of Business, Saint Joseph's University, USA. The *SDG Dashboard* is a collaborative, online platform that empowers higher education institutions to report and share their best United Nations Sustainable Development Goals (SDGs) impact practices. He also leads a partnership with Cabells to produce the *SDG Impact Intensity* academic journal rating system powered by artificial intelligence and data analytics.

Andrea Herterich Suzana studied International Cultural and Business Studies (BA) at the University of Passau and has been working at Heilbronn University as a program coordinator since 2019.

Lauren Traczykowski is a senior lecturer in law (Ethics) and director of external engagement for the CRISIS Centre at Aston University. Additionally, at Aston, Lauren serves on the Decolonizing the Curriculum Working Group (DCWG). She is a Board Director of the Birmingham Food Council CIC. Lauren's broad areas of research are disaster ethics and pedagogy, particularly playful learning. Lauren teaches (Global) Business Ethics and Ethics in a Crisis and is a Senior Fellow of the Higher Education Academy (now AdvanceHE).

Wanja Wellbrock holds the Chair of General Business Administration and Procurement Management at Heilbronn University. His main research areas are supply chain management, strategic procurement management, sustainability management, and big data applications in cross-company value chains. He is an author of several English and German publications and a project leader of several practice-oriented research projects in these areas. Prof. Dr. Wanja Wellbrock gained practical experience in management positions in the automotive and aviation industries as well as in management consulting.

Liang Yu works at Duke Kunshan University to oversee its executive education business. He partners with the leading companies to grow their leadership and organizational capability and enjoys the process of designing transformational learning journeys for leaders from around the world. Prior to Duke Kunshan, Liang worked for Deloitte Consulting in organizational change practice and Duke Corporate Education in senior executive development. Liang is passionate about developing future leaders in the digital age in a responsible and sustainable manner. His research focuses on developing purposeful and rooted global leaders in the digital age. Liang holds an MBA degree from Fuqua School of Business at Duke University, where he served as a COLE Leadership Fellow during 2012–2013. He lives in Kunshan, China, with his family.

List of Figures

List of Figures

List of Tables

1

Introduction to the Problems and Opportunities

Wolfgang Amann and Christian Hauser

1.1 Motivation for This Volume and Scoping the Issue

Back in 2007, the United Nations supported a new initiative to emphasize sustainability in business schools around the world. The Principles of
Responsible Management Education (PRME) as a platform rests on the
logic that it is in business schools where current and future leaders learn
on the normative, strategic and functional level. Equipped with the right
values and skills to cope with even complex sustainability challenges,
graduates should be in a much better position to add value. Up until
now, 800+ signatories worldwide have joined the movement, and PRME

W. Amann (✉)
HEC Paris in Qatar, Doha, Qatar
e-mail: amann@hec.fr

C. Hauser (✉)
PRME Business Integrity Action Center, University of Applied Sciences of the
Grisons, Chur, Switzerland
e-mail: christian.hauser@fhgr.ch

© The Author(s), under exclusive license to Springer Nature Switzerland AG 2023
C. Hauser, W. Amann (eds.), *The Future of Responsible Management Education*,
Humanism in Business Series, https://doi.org/10.1007/978-3-031-15632-8_1

offers a rich variety of resources to design, train for, direct and report on initiatives (cf. https://www.unprme.org/about). Regional and national chapters help boost localization beyond numerous initiatives at a global level.

PRME represents a forward-looking movement, working constructively on taking management education and business schools as institutions. In the past, business schools came under fire (cf. Amann et al., 2011) as industry experts voiced concerns over insufficient ethics education. Swanson and Frederick (2011) went as far as saying business schools were silent partners in crime. Mintzberg (2004) questions the relevance of both teaching and research. Beyond the question of relevance, Ghoshal (2005) labelled many theory and models as simply bad. Spender and Locke (2011) saw institutions hijacked by elites. Many authors, however, overemphasized criticism while underdelivering on constructive advice on the way forward. This is where the PRME movement adds value. Central initiatives and resources join forces with decentral, bottom-up initiatives, tapping into a truly divers pool of ideas and experts globally in order to make progress.

This book is best understood in this spirit of (1) these constructive efforts to better business schools both from a deliverables point of view and as institutions, and (2) as a reflection of international, diverse ideas. Management education is done throughout the entire world. Therefore, we should search globally for inspiring ideas and experts in order to give them a platform to voice their insights. In a way, we apply a distinct way of research for this book in line with the Frascati definition—we embarked on a process of investigation targeting new insights and bearing an effective way of dissemination in mind.

At the same time, business schools as institutions cover a myriad of processes for several stakeholders. Management as well as educating on it addresses an overwhelmingly large field. Therefore, this book must adopt a specific hook in order to guarantee a strong enough focus. We have chosen digital transformation as this hook. We deem it one of the meta-challenges for both corporations as well as business schools. We agree with Chamorro-Premuzic (2021) stating that the digital revolution is forcing companies to question established solutions and work towards reinventing themselves. He forecasts investments of almost $7 trillion by

2023. Yet, simply buying technologies from an increasingly non-transparent pool of suppliers does not ensure sound integration. In many cases, a clear definition of what digital transformation means is missing and unique success stories, such as Amazon or Google, are hard to reproduce. He envisages five key components which have to be aligned as part of digital transformation: People, which include staff, clients, and consumers, data, insights, action and results management. Not only experts in change management would easily recognize that a holistic understanding, let alone transformation of such heterogeneous areas and sustaining success can be a challenge. True, not all change has to be systemic and could be more contained. The speed of change does not always have to be revolutionary but could be more evolutionary and, indeed, in some cases, change could be really more about technical adaptations than foundational disruption. In either scenario, demands will be high.

We reviewed initial studies-of-studies and what emerged is rather straightforward. Companies do not master digital transformation. For example, Forth et al. (2020) measure and reveal that 70% of digital transformations do not meet the expectations—with substantial repercussions. Equally, Shooter (2021) clarifies that digital transformations fail in more than 70% of the cases—only 7% were initially bringing about intended change, which could not be sustained versus. The author warns that only 16% of sample companies in a global study indicated that change was positive and lasting.

If it is a challenge for companies, it is one for business schools. After all, this is where leaders and managers not only can go to a character gym but learn the knowledge and skills to better cope with expectations later on. Business schools have a responsibility to help course participants become more critical thinkers and job market ready. Employability is a key deliverable.

Some might argue that digital transformation is still a moving target. How can we educate in business schools if neither companies nor professors have fully understood what it takes to have success? We as editors and together with our chapter authors, however, realized we have already created substantial insights and endeavour to offer a rich and attractive buffet of ideas with the help of this book. Do we arrogantly claim to have the one-size-fits-all framework, field-tested across all types of organizations, markets and cultures? Did we arrive at a crystal-clear mid-range or even grand theory of digital transformation as of 2022? Certainly not. Yet, based on a Responsible Management Education Research Conference on the topic and in-depth discussions with international experts, we see more clearly what the current status quo is and which answers to core questions we already worked out. We have assembled them in a careful global editing and chapter review process.

What makes our book unique is its view on digital transformation from a responsible management education point of view. Articles on heuristics and at times cookie-cutter type of advice on mastering digital transformation abound. They are often well-written, but their empirical evidence is weak and anecdotal at best. What we aspired to accomplish with the book is the fact that all chapters in our volume are written by true educationists. They embrace the Principles of Responsible Management Education and equally aim for improvement practices in business schools. Of course, when we speak of business schools, we include related types of institutions in which management formation and education take place.

How to best use this book? As mentioned above, it is a buffet of ideas. Like food buffets, it is a collection of hopefully as appealing ideas as possible. Yet, not all items will be to your liking. Therefore, we encourage you to read selectively, and the chapter titles will give you a solid point of orientation what to expect in each of the chapters. The following Sect. 1.2 will provide a summary of all what is to follow for a more convenient preview. We do encourage you as the reader to apply a holistic approach to problem-solving, which requires three key questions as outlined by Borton (1970). The first question addresses the WHAT? What is the issue identified by the chapter author? The next question elaborates on the SO WHAT? So what does it mean for your setting and usually chapter authors prepared elaborations helping you in the reflection process. Finally, spend energy on the NOW WHAT? What should you do now? Any new idea requires local adaptation as the solutions provided by chapter authors cannot be copied and pasted too blindly to any setting globally. The subsequent section provides an overview of learning nuggets the chapter authors and we as editors compiled for you.

1.2 Structure of the Book

After our editor's introduction in Chap. 1, Gary Evans and Xiao Chen clarify in Chap. 2 that we may well live in a world where disruptive technologies will change the core of each and every industry and beyond that basically any organization's business model at least in some way. Educational institutions are not spared the onslaught of new technological change and its impact on how and what business educators teach. Their chapter highlights the importance of building creativity as part of the core curriculum combined with disruptive technologies. Technological change occurs exponentially, but we still train business leaders to use linear thinking. The chapter authors argue that teaching strategy, leadership and various disciplines using outdated modelling tools create a false sense of security in managing the change. It does not allow the leader the agility necessary in a changing technological world. The chapter continues with suggestion of new models as content for courses as well as mindsets as learning outcomes.

In Chap. 3, Dušan Kučera responds to enormous optimism and belief in the future importance of scientific and technological development, which the public and schools consider evidence of scientific progress. Students naturally also take over the high expectations of investors, industry and state administration. According to current research, the technological spirit of our times is also an expression of an unavoidable lack of contextual knowledge of minimal historical lessons and social, anthropological and environmental consequences for the future development of digital transformation. The question is whether educators are aware of the holistic impact of all forms of robotics, automation and artificial intelligence (AI). The preparation of the young generation for responsible management faces considerable challenges, which must include a critical evaluation of technological visions. Thus, business schools react with some delay to the outdated conception of capitalism, neoliberal economics, the fragmented concept of managerial responsibility and reduced assessment of business results. The originality of the approach includes fundamental philosophical and anthropological challenges that translate into the transformation of the life and work of future generations. The chapter aims to enter school syllabuses and executive education of managers with the essential elements of responsibility.

In their contribution and Chap. 4, Consuelo García de La Torre and Osmar Arandia argue that despite that digital transformation being a much-mentioned term in the business context nowadays, it is still a rather emerging topic for academia. At the same time, organizations are already experiencing extraordinary challenges, not only because the COVID-19 pandemic, but also because of the rapid environmental changes, and the quick adoption of digital processes. These two features are stressing the organizations and the people within them. From fortune 500 firms to SMEs around the world, firms are facing different dilemmas when they consider enter into the digital transformation world. Some of these dilemmas are related to the ethical implications of using personal data, specifically form the customers and collaborators. Another kind of implications are related to the respect for the human dignity of the peoples within the firm, and the possibly repercussions for the labour force when a firm adopts a digital transformation strategy. In this regard, PRME principles may help business school to address the above-mentioned implications, by providing a general framework for a theoretical and empirical analysis of the conflicts that may occur in the organization when adopting a digital transformation strategy. Considering the aforementioned, a question emerges—how are digitalization and disruptive innovations linked to responsible management education? The objective of this chapter is to present a theoretical model of the PRME's six principles, and how each of them may well give business schools more insights on how executives and firms can address the ethical implications of adopting a digital transformation strategy.

In Chap. 5, Liang Yu continues with the following logic. Currently, machine learning algorithms sweep through the world to train machines to learn and make decisions like a human. These algorithms provide recommendations and sometimes make judgments on behalf of a human. However, machine learning creates a disconnect between the intention of human beings and results from machine learning algorithms, which is defined as the 'alignment problem' (Christian, 2020). This chapter aims to understand what is required for future leaders to address the alignment program and how a new higher education institution such as Duke

Kunshan University innovates to prepare responsible leaders for the digital future.

In Chap. 6, Jorge Gomes and Tania Marques elaborate on The Principles of Responsible Management Education (PRME), which have been in place since 2007. Their aim is to stimulate the thinking of responsibility and sustainability in business and management schools around the world so that current and future business leaders will acquire the necessary skills and knowledge to implement the 17 Sustainable Development Goals (SDGs). Business and management schools have started and reported several initiatives that show commitment to the PRME, but few such documents show how lecturers and educators change to bring change in others. The current chapter examines the role of higher-education (HE) lecturers in educating according to the PRME framework, in general, and to both the responsible management and responsible leadership movements, in particular. Furthermore, the text explores digital teaching and its use by HE lecturers with regard to responsible management practices. Business and management schools might enthusiastically adhere to SDGs and responsible management. However, if academic staff does not bring such individual commitment into play in classes, then it is likely that the whole purpose of the PRME fails at the most fundamental level: the individual encounters education providers and education receivers.

Al Rosenbloom continues our learning journey in Chap. 7 by illustrating how responsible management education and artificial intelligence can inform changes to marketing education. He will refer to AI as a large, disruptive force that is transforming society. As such, management educators have obligations to teach students about AI from a decision-making perspective (both operational and strategic) because one of management education's central purposes is to develop the skills graduates need to make informed, analytical decisions that advance entities. As noted above, management education is not without its criticisms, not the least of which is that management education must move beyond its relentless focus on profit maximization as its sole theory of the firm to include intentional discussions of corporate purpose, stakeholder theory and ethics as many authors have argued. Indeed, and as the author will outline, all organizations are increasingly being called beyond their spreadsheets to tackle society's grand challenges, and while digital transformation is often discussed in terms of technology and process, digital transformation, especially AI, raises important ethical and societal questions for all emerging and current business leaders. Responsible management education can guide this discussion, as it specifically asks educators to integrate ethics, sustainability and responsibility throughout the curriculum and to embed these three elements into courses they teach. The responsible management education perspective can therefore guide discussions of AI and marketing. On the one hand, marketing managers are already using AI in marketing tactics and strategy. On the other hand, to date, there has been no discussion of how to apply a responsible management education framework to marketing education with specific reference to AI. This chapter's focus is on marketing education as a means for developing morally mature, socially responsive marketing managers who understand the challenges that AI presents in terms of ethics, sustainability and responsibility. The chapter makes contributions to (1) the marketing education literature by applying a responsible management education framework; (2) the RME literature by using a specific discipline, marketing, to illustrate RME principles and perspectives; and (3) the digital transformation literature through discussion of AI as applied in marketing education.

In Chap. 8, Jose Godinez argues that firms are increasingly implementing programs to prevent engaging in corruption. These programs are characterized by a set of rules and procedures aimed at preventing improper conduct and promoting adherence to legal standards. Recently, scholarship has acknowledged that digitalization has the potential to help firms with their anti-corruption agendas. Nevertheless, digitalization can also be utilized to allow companies to misbehave. Hence, it is necessary to understand how digitalization can be used by firms to enhance their anti-corruption measures. In the study presented in Chap. 8, we focus on blockchain technologies to help firms in their compliance programs when operating in developing countries to create trust among different stakeholders. We also analyse how blockchain can be used to collaborate with possible business partners and/or clients, access foreign funds and gain relief funds when fighting against corruption.

In Chap. 9, Bartosz Makowicz continues our train of thought that the educational sector represents a substantial part of our society. Due to

scientific inventions, followed by science transfer into practice and proper education of young generations it builds the foundation for the quality of life, the economics and social progress and the whole welfare. In the recent years, more and more educational and scientific processes have been conducted with the support of digitalized tools, especially the pandemic age caused an immense acceleration of the digitalization of educational sector. At the same time, however, digitalization entails new risks, while most academic institutions have neither the proper tools to address them, nor the awareness of those risks. Digitalization could therefore be compared with a double-edged sword: on the one hand, it creates new chances and possibilities; on the other hand, it causes new risks like breaches of personal data, fakes news, unethical manipulation of scientific results, cyber-attacks just to mention few of them. In other sectors, for example in the private industry, companies have developed robust systematic approaches to address this kind of risks, to strengthen and support the awareness and—by implementing adequate procedures and processes—to create a sustainable compliance culture and promote individual and corporate integrity. In this contribution, the author investigates if and how far those so-called Integrity and Compliance Management Systems could also be implemented within an educational institution to support the same goals and by that safeguard the responsibility and integrity, compliance, image and trust in the educational sector. An adequate Integrity and Compliance Management Systems aims to secure the proper conduct of operational activities, which in this specific sector would be research and education. It facilitates processes and structures, opens new possibilities, strengthens the transparency and creates safe surroundings for educational activities. Proper Integrity and Compliance Management is therefore indispensable when considering a new approach of responsible management education in the digitalized world.

In Chap. 10, Luciana Cezarino, Lara Liboni, Flavio Martins and Alessandro Goulart subsequently provide us with their insights into business education, which has been—in their perspective—endeavouring to keep up with an evolving real-world business environment. Despite signs of progress and advances, there is still a long way to go: the civilizational challenges from today figure themselves as a daunting task that future proves the career being developed within business schools today. Complex sustainable development challenges such as climate change, biodiversity loss and inequalities have been addressed through educational technologies for a long time. They come into hand to create academic semantics out of complexity. Soft skills and digitalization find common ground in the COVID-19 context since the systemic crisis changes the shape of interaction and e-learning. In this scenario, high education institutions act as living labs for educational innovations alongside crisis management. Here, we aim to scope how business schools are managing the crisis scenario. We describe how a Brazilian institution promoted the digitalization of its teaching activities and how students felt during this process through a case study. The results indicate that students did not face issues related to digital literacy or readiness. Most challenges are linked to resource constraint setups, such as internet access and a proper place to study. Students also related their need for peer interaction, counselling and tutoring activities. Resilience and social and emotional skills have been shown to be essential features of distance education's learning challenges.

Adding further insights, Florencia Librizzi, Carole Parkes and Ana Simaens take on business and management-related education from their point of view in Chap. 11, as well as higher education more broadly, in their chapter and based on their vies. They emphasize the very important role of integrating responsibility and sustainability across their teaching and learning. As we have now entered the Decade of Action for the 2030 Agenda and the Sustainable Development Goals (SDGs), this need becomes even more critical. While the COVID-19 pandemic has shaken up traditional ways of teaching and learning, the role that online content and tools, particularly open educational resources (OERs), can have (in advancing responsible management education (RME) and sustainable development) in remote teaching and learning has also been made more evident. This chapter aims to provide a better understanding of how online resources and specifically content and tools, including massive open online courses (MOOCs) and open educational resources (OERs), can be utilized to enhance RME and discuss some of the challenges, including the role of the COVID-19 pandemic. The chapter will feature the case of the SDG Academy—the flagship education initiative of the Sustainable Development Solutions Network (SDSN), a global initiative for the United Nations—with the mandate of creating and curating the best available educational content on sustainable development and making it available as a global public good (https://sdgacademy.org/). With a large catalogue of MOOCs, videos and podcasts, this initiative aims to support the current and next generation of educators, practitioners and citizens to advance sustainable development everywhere. Finally, the chapter will discuss the opportunities and challenges and provide recommendations for faculty and practitioners on how to make the most of online content and tools to teach and learn responsibility and sustainable development.

In Chap. 12, Abiola Makinwa argues that as the continuing news of financial and corruption scandals show, there is often a gap between the 'theoretical' knowledge acquired in professional ethics training and the 'actions' of professionals in the work field. Can digital tools help train future professionals to bridge the 'gap' between 'intention' and 'action'? Can EdTech be used to increase the likelihood of graduates who positively contribute towards a more sustainable and morally responsible society'? This chapter focuses on the 'Integrity Digital Learning Module', a digital educational tool that helps students to develop 'moral awareness' and 'moral assertiveness'. A review of reflections submitted after using the tool suggests that students are helped to (1) develop more awareness of personal integrity frameworks; (2) create 'moral reference points' and 'moral commitments'; and (3) learn in advance, a 'values-based response mechanism', which can be applied when confronted with ethical challenges. These competences and skills may increase moral resilience and positively influence the ability to act as a responsible professional in the work field.

In Chap. 13, Daniela Ludin, Wanja Wellbrock, Erika Mueller and Andrea Herterich Suzana address changes in corporate behaviour that are considered as eminent for meeting the complex challenges of today's world. Humanity has to face challenges arising from climate change, scarcity of natural resources, increasing poverty, globalization and digitization. In recent years, there has been a shift in many business areas from profit-oriented management to the integration of the triple bottom line of economic, social and environmental performance as outlined in the approach for sustainable development schemes. Moreover, digital key competences have become a crosscutting need in business, civil society, politics, science and education. The COVID-19 pandemic has stressed this necessity. International frameworks such as the UN Sustainable Development Goals (SDGs), which have been developed under the 2030 Agenda, try to highlight what is needed for a shift towards sustainability (United Nations, 2015). In addition, the Digital Economy and Society Index (DESI) shows that four out of ten adults in Europe lack basic digital skills. In this context, companies are seen as important drivers for sustainable development and digitization. Therefore, companies need change makers in business that bring along the adequate skills, knowledge and mindset for creating sustainable digital business model innovation. Universities have a key role in preparing young people for the future and educating them in sustainability and digitization issues regardless of their study topic. In this chapter, a best practice example of matching sustainability and digitization in training and teaching shall be given. Since November 2019, the Heilbronn University of Applied Sciences (Hochschule Heilbronn, Germany, HHN) has adopted the UN Principles of Responsible Management Education. As an institution of higher education, the Heilbronn University is involved in the development of current and future managers. Following the above-mentioned trend, the Faculty of Management & Sales of the University of Applied Sciences Heilbronn has adapted its educational training for students. A bachelor's program has been developed in 2019, which integrates sustainability and digitization aspects with management. Lessons learned are presented and discussed.

In Chap. 14, Lauren Traczykowski and Paul Dale clarify that 'business people' do not make decisions about the future of their companies without first checking with their lawyers (or, at least they shouldn't). Lawyers are there to advise on the regulatory, ethical and, sometimes the governance implications of any new product or process the business is introducing. The concepts required for responsible management education may also be found in disciplines which advise businesses. Teaching law students about the regulation, ethics and governance of AI and tech is, therefore, imperative. We have developed a new module for first year Law students which considers 'the future of law' and the impact that tech, AI, robots, bots and so on will have on their practice. Technological enhancements are rapidly changing the nature of the legal industry. This module has been developed with the understanding that ethics leads the development of law. But lawyers must first understand the tech being developed before we can begin to apply ethics and make laws to govern the tech or AI. Drawing upon the lessons being learnt from the development of this new module, the chapter will assess the impact that technological advancements are having on legal education and how they inform the students' role as future lawyers and lawmakers.

In his subsequent Chap. 15, Walter Baets clarifies that PRME knew, from the very beginning 15 years ago, that while principles one and two (what to teach and what to research) are evident and straightforward to implement, principle three, the method (how to do that) is a tricky but impactful one. Against the reality of disruptive forces—technological, environmental, demographic, socioeconomic—that challenge our societies like never before, we need people who can think, act and lead differently to address these challenges. It is no longer sufficient to 'teach' more relevant content. (Innovation) Ecosystems that harness disruption for the benefit of people and organizations are needed. Transformative learning as part of an innovation eco-system is able to transform mindsets to empower people and organizations to embrace radical but meaningful change and create a more sustainable world and more humane societies. While technologies available today can be marvellous tools, they should be deployed to serve the purpose: create a value adding, impactful and inclusive society; support people in how to learn to continuously learn; develop the competencies of the future, so that people can reinvent themselves at any time and are not limited to a no longer existing profession they were trained for. Therefore, principle three was important, although less obvious than the first two. In this contribution, an approach is suggested, inspired by science but rooted in experience. The aim of principle three is to ensure that we deliver responsible, learning and caring individuals who not only know what should be done but are able to achieve it.

Then, in Chap. 16, Sreerupa Sengupta and Divya Singhal review how the COVID-19 pandemic, a 'Black Swan Event' (Taleb, 2011), has disrupted the entire global community. The pandemic began as an unprecedented global health challenge but quickly transformed into a development crisis. Governments across the world implemented a range of measures to contain the spread of the virus (ILO 2020). The mitigation measures had a severe impact on every aspect of our lives and education was no exception. The continuity of higher education became the biggest challenge. Although higher education institutions (HEIs) made concerted efforts to maintain continuity of learning and were quick to replace face-to-face lectures with online learning, challenges remained (OECD 2020). The biggest question was how we make higher education available for all, across classes in the society. It was this burning question which pushed HEIs towards greater openness and digital transformation. Pandemic also made a strong case for discussions on sustainability, inclusivity and equity in education and advocated for the expansion of responsible management education. In last few years, Massive Open Online Courses (MOOCs) have gained pre-eminence as a means to enhance accessibility to higher education, reduce the inadequacies ingrained in our education systems and achieve greater democratization of higher education. MOOCS have also become the preferred tool for creating sustainability mindset and sharing knowledge on social responsibility, inclusion, empathy and responsible management education. Their chapter will focus on the role MOOCs and Open Education Resources (OERs) can play in the transition to sustainability and promotion of an inclusive approach in higher education. The chapter will explore the various MOOC courses and OERS developed on SDGs for Responsive Management Education. Further, the chapter will suggest a new framework for MOOCs and OERs—highlighting how they can address the issue of perceived privileges inherent in business schools which throttle the capability of their graduates to contribute to and solve grand challenges of our societies.

Chapter 17 by David Steingard and Simon Linacre details how artificial intelligence (AI) can be used—and is very much needed—to reinvent academic research evaluation in terms of quality and impact. First, we review the current literature on academic research assessment examining two overarching questions: What normative standards are employed to determine the quality of academic research? What explicit methodological rationales, unstated assumptions and academic cultural dynamics determine the definition of quality? Second, we offer a literature review and alternative model for assessing the quality of academic research in

terms of impact—that is, does academic research make a positive differ-ence in the material conditions of humanity and sustain the natural envi-ronment, and how does academic research praxis transform 'words into worlds'? Third, we examine how impact is being adopted by the publish-ing industry in a paradigm shift from limited notions of 'quality' to the broader consequences of societal and sustainable 'impact'. We critique how the Journal Impact Factor, as a gold standard of academic publica-tion value, has eclipsed other possibilities for assessing real-world impacts of academic outputs: quantification without qualification. Fourth, we present a case study applying an AI rating system to ascertain the degree of impact of SDG impact intensity on academic journals. The AI system utilizes the United Nations 17 Sustainable Development Goals (SDGs) criteria as normative standards to rate the impact of academic journals. We discuss the implications of such a system and SDG-focused research on business schools and scholarly outputs for academia. We critically consider the challenges of employing our algorithmic technique as a digi-tal transformation technology for responsible management education and ultimately to serve the common good and environmental sustainability.

Then, Chap. 18 by Adriana Krasniansky and Mary C. Gentile provides an overview of the famous Giving Voice to Values (GVV) approach for values-driven leadership development and practice, with particular atten-tion to some of the ways it addresses ethical challenges raised by techno-logical developments in processes and products. Then as an illustration, the authors include a case on programming a fairer system without biases. It tells the story of Timothy Brennan, founder and CEO of Northpointe, Inc., who has created COMPAS, an artificially intelligent (AI) software tool for US court systems that predicts a defendant's likelihood to reoff-end and informs sentencing decisions. Brennan originally created COMPAS to standardize decision-making within the criminal justice system and to reduce the likelihood of human error or bias impacting court rulings. However, several years after COMPAS's widespread adop-tion within US court systems, an investigative report claims that COMPAS is more likely to mislabel Black defendants as higher risk and White defendants as lower risk of recidivism. At first, Brennan's challenge is to organize a response to investigate bias within the COMPAS software, while still protecting the complexity and intellectual property of the product. The chapter continues with Brennan's actual response and review its implications for Northpointe and the US criminal justice system, and they are encouraged to consider how Brennan could have responded more creatively and constructively.

In Chap. 19, Arindam Das and Ishwar Haritas raise the much-needed question of effectiveness. How effective are digital platforms? As the global focus on sustainability increases, a growing number of individuals, organizations and institutions are working on social and environmental challenges in their communities. It is therefore important for future managers to understand, engage with and eventually incorporate into their lived experience the various contexts (and actors) within which sustainability-related imperatives are most acutely felt, for instance equity within value chains, waste management and circularity of products and processes; the means to address the specific sustainability-related issues and finally test and scale solutions to optimize impact. This chapter presents a case of experiential sustainability education for postgraduate management students at a premier business school in India. With the COVID-19 pandemic affecting India since early 2020, the course, which originally involved a significant level of face-to-face interactions at project locations and with different stakeholders, had to be restructured to move almost all interactions to digital platforms. We highlight how the shift to digital platforms has impacted students' learning and project outcomes and identify key takeaways for the adoption of digital platforms in delivering experiential courses in sustainability in both purely virtual and hybrid formats.

A final conclusions chapter then brings our joint learning journey to an end. We summarize emerging insights, suggest overcoming rather binary thinking of digital transformation as either opportunity or threat, and emphasize just how important the so-called addendum principle of PRME is.

References

Amann, W., Pirson, M., Spitzeck, H., Dierksmeier, C., Kimakowitz, V., & E. (Eds.). (2011). *Business schools under fire—humanistic management education as the way forward*. Palgrave.

Borton, T. (1970). *Reach, teach and touch*. Graw Hill.

Chamorro-Premuzic, T. (2021). The essential components of digital transformation. *HBR*. https://hbr.org/2021/11/the-essential-components-of-digital-transformation

Christian, Br. (2020). The Alignment Problem: Machine Learning and Human Values. Norton.

Forth, P., Reichert, T., de Laubier, R., & Chakraborty, S. (2020). Flipping the odds of digital transformation success. https://www.bcg.com/publications/2020/increasing-odds-of-success-in-digital-transformation.

Ghoshal, S. (2005). Bad management theories destroy good management practices. *Academy of Management Learning & Education, 4*(1), 75–91.

Mintzberg, H. (2004). *Managers, not MBAs: A hard look at the soft practice of managing and management development*. Berrett-Koehler Publishers.

Shooter, K. (2021). McKinsey: Unlocking success in digital transformations. https://www.technologymagazine.com/data-and-data-analytics/mckinsey-unlocking-success-digital-transformations.

Spender, J., & Locke, R. (2011). *Confronting managerialism: How the business elite and their schools threw our lives out of balance*. Zed Books.

Swanson, D., & Frederick, W. (2011). Are business schools silent partners in corporate crime? *The Journal of Corporate Citizenship, 9*(1), 24–27.

Taleb, N. (2011). The future has thicker tails than the past: Model error as branching counterfactuals. NYU-Poly Institute https://arxiv.org/ftp/arxiv/papers/1209/1209.2298.pdf

2

Creativity and Disruptive Technology

Gary Evans and Xiao Chen

2.1 Introduction: Forward Technology and Creativity

We live in a world of massive change, and each decade appears to move faster and faster. It is not just the inventions that are picking up speed, but the adoption of technologies is increasing by businesses and consumers. The early adaptors switch to general consumption at an increasing pace. Part of the increase in adoption is attributed to challenges such as a pandemic. Nevertheless, in general, the concepts of a VUCA (volatile, uncertain, complex, and ambiguous) are becoming a standard year-on-year driven by the exponential growth of knowledge and, therefore, technology (Jari & Lauraeus, 2019). As this chapter will explain, this exponential growth in technology would not be possible without the creative surge upon us. Organizations are promoting out-of-the-box thinking and creativity. Historically, creativity was only necessary for the arts

G. Evans (✉) • X. Chen
University of Prince Edward Island, Charlottetown, PE, Canada
e-mail: gevans@upei.ca

and philosophical thinkers. Creativity has moved to its rightful place as part of our problem solving. No discussion of disruption is complete without addressing the work of Harvard professor Dr. Christensen, who for over 20 years has looked in detail at the phenomenon of disruption at the technology and business model levels. Christensen was not just aware of some new technologies' disruptive nature and provided guidelines on how organizations should view different disruptive technologies (Christensen, 1997; Christensen, 2015; Christensen et al., 2018). Academic institutions and business schools need to embrace creativity and technology as part of the core skill sets required for successful organizations.

2.2 Exponential Thinking Versus Linear

For 150,000 years, we have been watching the benefits of linear development, but that world is behind us, and to grow and prosper, we need to see the future from a different perspective. As a futurist and inventor, Kurzweil explains, people are driven to think linearly based on experience. We like to think in steps. If you take 30 linear steps, you will likely be approximately 30 m from your starting point. If you take 30 exponential steps, you will be a billion meters away or approximately 26 times around the planet (Diamandis & Kotler 2016). Our brains are hardwired to think linear, but we now live in a world based on Moore's law (Funk, 2013). In 2020/2021, the world saw a massive adaptation to technology due to the COVID-19 pandemic. The technology was not new but has existed for years. Nevertheless, suddenly, we had a need to adapt, and while many organizations struggled to survive, those with creative and exponential thinking had double- and triple-digit growth.

Knowledge doubles each year, and we break new barriers when we are willing to remove the constraints of linear thinking. Companies and organizations that fail to adopt exponential thinking need to consider the ramifications that could put their very existence in jeopardy. Kodak, whose scientists developed the first digital images, did not see digital technology as an opportunity and led to their bankruptcy in 2012 (Diamandis & Kotler, 2016; Lund & Safouhi, 2019).

Those critical of exponential thinking will quickly point out Moore's law is based on the doubling of circuits on the microchip, which has reached the maximum possible and that continued expansion is not feasible. This is a typical restriction based on existing technology. Why do we think that circuits of the future need to be based on silicon? Google is exploring crystals, and others who are trying to break the quantum computing challenge where quantum processing melts the same chip that is being asked to do the computation are looking at upsetting the traditional concepts of computing by using organic processors. If you can remove the process of on or off 1 or 0 and instead look at the human neurological system, new options become available. A new concept of how to approach binary technology opens new possibilities for what can be accomplished with AI technology. Gartner Group, August 2021, on their recently published hype curve, identified quantum computing on the hype curve with a 10-plus year development. A production-capable quantum computing platform would make all computers today look like the old manual adding machines and, at best, the vacuum tube computers of the past. In the past, new entries on the Gartner Hype Curve could become obsolete before they could even come to market because the technology took another leap forward. A leapfrog of quantum computers would change every industry and everything we currently know in science.

One of the big questions that both academics and practitioners strive to answer is the speed of technology adoption and the facts that move some advances forward and hold others back. Why are we so bad at predicting the future state? Part of the problem is trying to break out linear thinking. Using history as a predictor uses long time frames for change, but these have been getting shorter and shorter. Historically, we have measured technology adoption in years, but it is now estimated in months (Drejer, 2018; Evans, 2017; Funk, 2013; ICD, 2019; NACD, 2018). Using 25% of the US population as an adoption rate, Electricity (1873) took 46 years to be adopted, Telephone (1876) took 35 years, Radio (1897) took 31 years, PC (1975) 16 years, Internet (1991) 7 years, Facebook Social Media (2005) 2 years, and Tiktok (2019) 1 year (Auxier & Anderson, 2021). Even though these statistics are misleading, when you expand to the global community, you now have 2.7 billion Facebook users and over one billion Tiktok users. Some statistics are changing so fast it is difficult even to track as the numbers change within days of release. The Future Today, Institute forecasts that every industry should prepare to be disrupted within 10 years (Webb, 2020). Technology changes the fabric of our business world, and academics will need to revisit the role of institutions as we train the next generation of managers, leaders and executives. Industries will be disrupted by complicated technologies, including automatous cars and other sectors, such as social media, by new media ideas or those in the service industry by AI technologies. The speed of adoption may vary depending on a range of variables and situations. Software that can use existing technologies will have potential adoption rates in days vs. months or years. Technologies that require more complex integration may take longer until 5G or 6G networks become available. Zooms were founded in 2011 in the United States and had over 300% growth during the COVID-19 pandemic. Some of the technology growth will capture significant market share, and a company such as Zoom changed in 9 years from an idea by the founder Eric Yuan to communicate with his girlfriend to a 35-billion-dollar empire.

This type of overnight success may become increasingly common, and at the same time, the desire to find new ways to doing things will only speed up. The traditional ways to market are changing exponentially, and it will be easy to be left behind. No industry or service will be spared the new exponential wave of change. Several authors and organizations have indicated that organizations need to move from linear to exponential mindsets to engage with the latest technologies more effectively (Drejer, 2018; Evans 2017, 2020; ICD, 2019, IOD 2019, NACD 2016, NACD 2018).

The difficulty is that when we open our minds to what is possible, anything we can perceive could be available in decades. Nevertheless, it is unlikely that humans will adopt all that is possible for a range of reasons. Existing infrastructure could be a block for some technologies and human resistance to change another. The pandemic has taught us that change can speed up when it becomes necessary. It may facilitate new industries and crush those who struggle to adapt. A lesson to be learned from the indigenous people of North America is to think in multiple generations instead of years. The indigenous concept is seven generations, which represent approximately 130 years. If you think of what could be in 130 years, it is most likely, in reality, only a couple of decades away. As put forward in the Harvard Review, linear thinking is about improving on what exists and exponentially creates something new (Bonchek, 2016). Padayachee et al. (2017) conclude in their research that technologies enable better planning, new directions and opportunities. The constraints to technologies are the mindset that embraces old methodologies and an unwillingness to change.

Much of our thinking around strategic planning is based on linear processes and thinking. We intuitively look for an incremental step that we can take to improve our organizations (Botha & Pretorius, 2017, Evans, 2020). Past tools still provide value but can mislead us into a false sense of security, and the dominant use of existing marketplace data may fog our view of the future. Organizations with strong leadership are more likely to develop new philosophies and ways of thinking to better predict technology disruption. Business schools teach in silos using models of the past to predict the future. New tools and methodologies need to be developed to help predict industry growth and structure (Evans, 2020; Farmer and Lafond 2016; Jari & Lauraeus, 2019; Olson et al., 2016).

2.3 New Strategic Models

Most of the strategic tools that exist today are based on linear thinking and step change. Academics need to explore new tools that embrace the concepts of creativity and exponential thinking. Many of our existing tools can still add value but must be adapted to work within the new world of change. Strategic tools need to consider technology and the forces of adaptation and reduction in the life cycles of products and services provided by traditional models (Kaplan, 2017; Lund & Safouhi, 2019). The concept of step change is locked into the fiber of many organizations blinding them from what should be predictable changes in marketplaces. Organizations continue to use the same tools and methods as if the world had not and will not change (Evans, 2020; Lund & Safouhi, 2019; Raymond, 2014). Researchers need to develop a better understanding of disruptive and radical innovation. The research is in, and it is time to think differently to gain the benefits of new technologies (Hopp et al., 2018). It is well documented that disruptive technologies are changing the fabric of companies' business models. Strategic thinking needs to embrace new business models and develop tools that can help evaluate these new models and the role of these futuristic models in shaping future industries (Cozzolino et al., 2018, Schiavi & Behr, 2018). Examples of companies that created new business models to dominate a new industry sector are growing, as demonstrated by Amazon, who used the strength of cloud technology to create new revenue streams for their company (DaSilva et al., 2013).

To foresee technological disruption, it is critical to study the technologies at the forefront and follow the fringe technologies that are still in development. The exponential accumulation of knowledge and research technologies can quickly jump the gap from fringe to mainstream. To add to the confusion, organizations struggle whether to take a defensive or offensive approach to strategy. The lack of clarity between legacy and new business models can result in missing the opportunity and creating a new level of competition (Bughin & Zeebroeck, 2017). More tools are being developed and proposed to address the need for better assessment by a combination of academics and private practitioners. Jaris and Lauraeus outlined in 2019 a model that used six dimensions of learning, anticipate, challenge, interpret, decide, and align to aid executives in understanding the impact of disruptive technologies. The Gartner Group, a well-respected consulting and marketing company, has published their "hype cycle" to assist organizations in understanding better developing and emerging technologies. The hype cycle comes in various forms, from specific technology sectors to broader views of new or fringe technologies to those that have gone to market. The Future Today Institute (FTI) publishes an annual review of all technologies and monthly newsletters on specific developments ranging from medical science to blockchain technologies (Evans, 2020; Gartner, 2021; Webb, 2019; FTI, 2021).

In conjunction with many professional firms, several governance organizations have made a range of evaluation tools available to their clients and members. The Institute of Corporate Directors in Canada (ICD), the National Association of Corporate Directors (NACD) in the United States, and the Institute of Directors (IOD) in the UK all offer training and tool kits to their members to help evaluate the impact of disruptive technologies. Consulting firms, including the Big Four accounting firms and strategic consulting companies, offer a range of strategic tools to aid in market analysis and evaluation of innovative technologies. One of the tools put forward by the FTI helps determine which technologies need to be included in the strategic plan now, shortly, or table for later consideration (Webb et al., 2019). The 2021 FTI report on technologies lists over 300 technologies and industries and potential industry disruptions due to specific technologies (FTI, 2021).

A range of methodologies is used to predict technology trends, from big data to analysis of research spending of the major technology companies (Segev et al., 2013). Reviewing the spending habits of the top nine global technology giants can provide insights into which technologies are moving from fringe to mainstream market entry. The nine companies described by Webb as the G-MAFIA: Google, Microsoft, Amazon, Facebook, IBM, and Apple and the big three China companies of BAT: Baidu, Alibaba, and Tencent (Galloway, 2018; Webb, 2019).

The next change in disruptive technologies is more likely to come from the synchronization of technologies rather than one specific technology (Petzold et al., 2019). The combination of AI, data lakes, blockchain, 5G, and Internet of Things (IoT) will only be available when breakthrough technologies come together to solve a multitude of problems simultaneously (Hopp et al., 2018; Metallo et al., 2018; Petzold et al., 2019). The convergence of technologies will lead to breakthroughs, and the creation of new market opportunities has yet to be defined (Kaplan, 2017; Prokhorenkov & Panifov, 2018; Lund & Safouhi, 2019). The challenge is not if a change will occur but rather when (Webb, 2021; Leatherberry et al., 2019).

2.4   Developing Improvisational Creativity: Actor-Centered Versus Context-Centered Approaches

Creativity is a crucial driver of innovation, growth, and societal development (Zhou & Hoever, 2014). In the age of disruptive change, creativity is an even more vital means for organizations to respond to unprecedented challenges, proactively develop dynamic capabilities, and ultimately thrive in uncertain and complex environments. Historically, creativity research in organizational psychology and management has predominantly utilized an *actor-centered* approach to creativity (e.g., Barron & Harrington, 1981). This approach focuses on the roles of individual differences (e.g., creative ability and personality) and the interplay of multiple actor-level variables on creativity. Applied to the context of management education, the actor-centered perspective suggests that creative learners are born rather than nurtured.

Increasingly, however, research on contextual factors of creativity has burgeoned to complement the conventional actor-centered approach. Departing from the actor-centered method that exclusively determines creativity as individual dispositions, the context-centered approach began to study the influence of task nature and environment (e.g., physical, social, organizational) on individual creativity. Accordingly, management education that takes the context-centered approach may shape the teaching-learning environment to influence learner creativity (yet not necessarily attend to individual differences and needs).

Integrating these distinctive perspectives, Zhou and Hoever (2014) advance an actor-context interactionist approach to creativity. This approach provides many managerial and pedagogical implications. Research on workplace creativity has shown that if the organizational context is unsupportive (even), creative individuals cannot realize their creative potential (e.g., George & Zhou, 2001; Liao et al., 2010). In contrast, when supervisors create an environment that supports creativity, even individuals who are not predisposed or inclined to be creative (low in creative personality) may become creative (e.g., Zhou, 2003; Zhou et al., 2009). Applied to the classroom setting, these perspectives suggest that educators should exhibit supervisory behavior that facilitates rather than inhibit creative processes and learning.

To develop learners' creative potential, educators should attend to actor-context interactions and should also facilitate creative processes. Wallas' (1926) seminal work *The Art of Thought* delineates four distinctive stages of creativity: (a) *preparation* (i.e., detect the problem to be solved and identify relevant data), (b) *incubation* (i.e., the problem is "left alone" for the unconscious mind to process it), (c) *illumination* (i.e., the idea or solution suddenly emerges), and (d) *verification* (e.g., idea or solution being tested against known criteria). Wallas seems to have adequately captured much of the essence of creativity in that the creation of new products usually involves carefully executed and planned processes. Nevertheless, such staged processes have yet to account for the exponential growth of processes, operations, and models.

The notion of "improvisational creativity" addresses yet another form of the creative process, which is not marked by distinct stages of development across time. Fisher and Amabile (2009) define creative improvisation as "actions responsive to temporally proximate stimuli, where the actions contain both a high degree of novelty and a low temporal separation of problem presentation, idea generation and idea execution" (p. 44). When such actions occur in an organizational setting, *organizational improvisational creativity* is realized. Unlike the conventional creativity model, Fisher and Amabile point out two unique features of improvisational creativity: (a) preparation occurs prior to improvisation, and (b) problem presentation, response generation, and response execution occur simultaneously in "fluid" stages. To improvise, "actors must simultaneously identify new challenges and generate responses, with little or no time to prepare" (Fisher & Amabile, 2009, p. 41). In the age of rapid digital transformation of work, actors experience substantially higher levels of challenges. Management educators are thus responsible for creating, maintaining, and developing such "fluid" stages for learners to perform and improvise.

2.5   The Pedagogical Mindset: Interplay of Forces of Change

In an area of technological transformation and radical changes across industries, to create "fluid" stages for improvisational creativity, management education needs to train and develop learners to think exponentially (Evans, 2020). Unlike incremental thinking, which "delivers immediate and steady results," exponential thinking "generates results that accelerate over time" (Bonchek, 2016, p. 2). Exponential thinking is likely to generate improvisational creativity. We propose that management educators' pedagogical mindsets and recognition of forces of change jointly shape learners' propensity for incremental vs. exponential thinking. Accordingly, we develop a typology describing the interplay of pedagogical mindsets (inhibitive vs. facilitative) and forces of change (incremental vs. disruptive) on exponential mindsets (see Fig. 2.1).

Pedagogical Mindsets Pedagogical mindsets can be either inhibitive or facilitative. Inhibitive pedagogies form an unsupportive learning environment that prevents learners from active learning, whereas facilitative pedagogies create a supportive learning environment that promotes active learning. Applied to management education, these empirical findings suggest that educators exhibit supervisory behaviors that facilitate rather than inhibit creative processes and behavior (cf. Zhou & Hoever, 2014).

Forces of Change Change is an environmental constant for modern organizations. Educators may construe forces of change along an incremental-disruptive continuum. Whereas incremental change refers to improvements within existing processes, operations, and models, disruptive change occurs when the existing models are fundamentally challenged. The interplay of pedagogical mindset (inhibitive vs. facilitative) and forces of change (incremental vs. disruptive) yield four distinctive types of learners of incremental vs. exponential mindsets: *stucker* (inhibitive-incremental), *conformer* (facilitative-incremental), *stuckformer* (inhibitive-disruptive), and *transformer* (facilitative-disruptive).

		"Conformer"	"Transformer"
Pedagogical Mindset	Facilitative	**Characteristics** Facilitated learners, (but) recognizing change as incremental. **Example** "I like AI, but I am not ready for it"	**Characteristics** Facilitated learners, (and) recognizing change as disruptive **Example** "I like AI, and I am ready…"
vs.	Inhibitive	"Stucker" **Characteristics** Inhibited learners, (and) recognizing change as incremental. **Example** "I dislike AI, and I am not ready for it."	"Stuck-former" **Characteristics** Inhibited learners, (but) recognizing change as disruptive. **Example** "I dislike AI and I know what's coming, but I am not ready…"

Forces of Change

Incremental   vs.   Disruptive

Fig. 2.1 A typology of the "Pedagogical Mindset—Forces of Change" interaction effects on learner mindset

Stuckers are the most inhibited learners who typically recognize forces of change as merely incremental. They are made to depreciate the value of radical change. Accordingly, their motto is, "I dislike AI, and I am not ready for it." As such, stuckers are most likely to employ incremental thinking. However, when the learning environment becomes supportive, stuckers may become *conformers* who readily embrace the change. Nevertheless, they are still inclined to passively accept what is being introduced to them, staying in their pre-existing comfort zones of learning. In other words, conformers share the sentiment "I like AI, but I am not ready for it."

Stuckers, however, under certain conditions, can be guided to embrace forces of change as disruptive. Although their thinking styles may still be shaped by an inhibitive learning environment, they readily recognize forces of change as disruptive. Hence, stuckers become stuck-formers who typically claim, "I dislike AI and I know what's coming, but I am not ready…."

Finally, stuck-formers may ultimately become *transformers* provided that the teaching-learning environments become facilitative. Transformers can make true exponential thinkers in that they are empowered to embrace forces of change as disruptive. Transformers readily voice, "I like AI, and I am ready."

2.6   Conclusion

The speed of change will continue to accelerate, and business schools will need to be prepared for disruption within their own structure. Skill sets will change, and a greater focus will be on problem solving and creativity. Educational institutions and academics will need to work closely with practitioners to develop new evaluation techniques of potential disruption. Agile will be expected, and business models will need to change. The greatest challenge is not the technology but the ability to adjust the mindset to cope with the change. The model put forward by the authors offers a starting point to measure the readiness of individuals to change and the mindset they find themselves in. Courses will need to be developed to help students realize their creative potential in the high technology disruptive world. Business schools will need to foster and support the changing landscape of business. Just as business will need to develop new skills to stay agile, academic institutions will need to lead the way in agile thinking and fostering the creative spirit of innovation and problem solving.

References

Auxier, B., & Anderson, M. (2021). Social media use in 2021.

Barron, F., & Harrington, D. M. (1981). Creativity, intelligence, and personality. *Annual Review of Psychology, 32*, 439–476.

Bonchek, M. (2016). How to create an exponential mindset? *Harvard Business Review*.

Botha, A. P., & Pretorius, M. W. (2017). Future thinking: The scarce management skill. Technology management for interconnected world. *Proceedings of PICMET, 2017*, 1–10.

Bughin, J., & Zeebroeck, N. (2017). 6 digital strategies, and why some work better than others. *Harvard Business Review*, 1–5.

Christensen, C. M. (1997). *The innovator's dilemma: When new technologies cause great firms to fail*. Harvard Business School Press.

Christensen, C. M. (2015). Disruptive innovation is a strategy, not just technology. *Business Today*, 4 Jan. 2015, Interview. http://link.galegroup.com/apps/doc/A394465959/ITOF?u=otta0998&sid=ITOF&xid=b86b4559. Accessed 4 June 2019.

Christensen, C. M., McDonald, R., Altman, E. J., & Palmer, J. E. (2018). Disruptive innovation: An intellectual history and directions for future research. *Journal of Management Studies, 55*(7), 1043–1078.

Cozzolino, A., Verona, G., & Rothaermel, F. (2018). Unpacking the disruption process: New technology business models, and incumbent adaptation. *Journal of Management Studies, 55*(7), 1166–1292.

DaSilva, C. M., Trkman, P., Desouza, K., & Lindic, J. (2013). Disruptive technologies: A business model perspective on cloud computing. *Technology Analysis & Strategic Management, 25*(10), 1161–1173.

Diamandis, P., & Kotler, S. (2016). *Goodbye linear thinking: Hello exponential! Rotman magazine* (pp. 39–43). Rotman School of Management, University of Toronto.

Drejer, A. (2018). Disruption and strategic management: What are the theoretical implications of disruption on strategy? *Journal on Business Review, 5*(3), 1–10. https://doi.org/10.6176/2010-4804_5.3_111

Evans, G. (2017). Disruptive technology and the board: The tip of the iceberg. *Economic and Business Review, 3*(17), 205–223.

Evans, G. L. (2020). Technology and the corporate board 2020 and beyond. In R. LeBlanc (Ed.), *The handbook of board governance, (second edition) a comprehensive guide for public private and not-for-profit board members* (pp. 469–488). Wiley.

Farmer, J. D., & Lafond, F. (2016). How predictable is technology progress? *Research Policy, 45*, 647–665.

Fisher, C. M., & Amabile, T. M. (2009). Creativity, improvisation and organizations. *Rotman Magazine, 2009*, 41–45.

Funk, J. L. (2013). What drives exponential improvements. *California Management Review, 55*(3), 134–152. University of California Berkeley.

Future Today, Institute. (2021). The Future Today, Institute (FTI) helps leaders and their organizations prepare for deep uncertainty and complex futures. Retrieved from: https://futuretodayinstitute.com/.

Galloway, S. (2018). *The four: The hidden DNA of Amazon, Apple, Facebook and Google.* Portfolio/Penguin.

Gartner. (2021). Gartner top strategic technology trends for 2021. https://www.gartner.com/smarterwithgartner/gartner-top-strategic-technology-trends-for-2021/.

George, J. M., & Zhou, J. (2001). When openness to experience and conscientiousness are related to creative behavior: An interactional approach. *Journal of Applied Psychology, 86*, 513–521.

Hopp, C., Antona, D., Kaminski, J., & Salge, T. O. (2018). What 40 years of research reveals about the difference between disruptive and radical innovation. *Harvard Business Review*, 2–5.

ICD. (2019). Emerging technologies understanding the disruption ahead: An introduction for corporate directors. *Institute of Corporate Directors Quebec Chapter, 2019*, 1–11.

IoD. (2019). Cyber security for your business. Institute of Directors (UK). https://www.iod.com/news-campaigns/cyber-security-for-your-business#tab-Blogs.

Jari, K., & Lauraeus, T. (2019). Analysis of Gartner's three megatrends in 2017 to thrive the disruptive business, technology trends 2008-2016, dynamic capabilities of VUCA and foresight leadership tools. *Advances in Technology Innovation, 4*(2), 105–115.

Kaplan, J. (2017). Viewpoint artificial intelligence: Think again. *Communications of the ACM, 60*(1), 36–38.

Leatherberry, T., McCormack, D., Kark, K., & Lamm, R. (2019). The tech-savvy board engages with CIOs and manages strategy, risk, and performance. *Deloitte Insights*, http://www2.deloitte.com/insights/us/en/topics/leadership/cio-board, 1–13.

Liao, H., Liu, D., & Loi, R. (2010). Looking at both sides of the social exchange coin: A social cognitive perspective on the joint effects of relationship quality and differentiation on creativity. *Academy of Management Journal, 53*, 1090–1109.

Lund, T., & Safouhi, H. (2019). Exponential life an analysis of exponential technologies. *University of Alberta Libraries.* https://doi.org/10.7939/R36H4D67F,1-29

Metallo, C., Agrifoglio, R., Schiavone, F., & Mueller, J. (2018). Understanding business model in the internet of things industry. *Technological Forecasting and Social Change, 136,* 298–306.

NACD. (2016). *Cyber-risk oversight: Director's handbook series.* National Association of Corporate Directors. Retrieved from: https://www.nacdonline.org/cyber

NACD. (2018). *The report of the NACD blue ribbon commission on adaptive governance: Board oversight of disruptive risks.* National Association of Corporate Directors. Retrieved from: https://www.nacdonline.org/insights/publications.cfm?ItemNumber=61319

Olson, N., Remick, T., & Tapia, A. (2016). As global business transforms, boards must keep pace. The Corporate Board, November/December, 17–22.

Padayachee, R., Matthee, M., & der Merwe, A. V. (2017). Disruptive technologies and IT decision making in an agile business environment. *IEEE Africon 2017 Proceedings,* 843–848.

Petzold, N., Landinez, L., & Baaken, T. (2019). Disruptive innovation from a process view: A systematic literature review. *Creative Innovation Management, 28,* 157–174. Wiley.

Prokhorenkov, D., & Panifov, P. (2018). *Discovery of technology trends from patent data on the basis of predictive analytics, IEEE 20th conference on business informatics* (pp. 148–152).

Raymond, C. (2014). *The exponential mind, renowned futurist ray Kurzweil models a better way of thinking* (pp. 62–66). Success.

Schiavi, G. S., & Behr, A. (2018). Emerging technologies and new business models: A review on disruptive business models. *Innovation and Management Review, 15*(4), 338–355.

Segev, A., Jung, C., & Jung, S. (2013). Analysis of technology trends based on big data. *IEEE International Congress on Big Data, 65,* 419–420.

Wallas, G. (1926). *The art of thought.* J. Cape.

Webb, A., Giralt, E., Palatucci, M., & Perez, K. (2019). Tech trends report: Emerging science and technology trends that will influence business, government, education, media and society in the coming year. *Future Today, Institute,* 12 annual edition, www.futuretodayinstitute.com.

Webb, A. (2019). *The big nine: How the tech titans and their thinking machines could warp humanity.* Public Affairs.

Webb, A. (2020). Amy Webb: Quantitative futurist and professor of strategic foresight at the NYU Stern School of Business.

Webb, A. (2021). Tech Trends Report: Strategic Trends That Will Influence Business, Government, Education, Media and Society in the Coming Year. Future Today Institute, 14 Annual Edition, www.futuretodayinstitute.com

Zhou, J. (2003). When the presence of creative coworkers is related to creativity: Role of supervisor close monitoring, developmental feedback, and creative personality. *Journal of Applied Psychology, 88*, 413–422.

Zhou, J., & Hoever, I. J. (2014). Research on workplace creativity: A review and redirection. *Annual Review of Organizational Psychology and Organizational Behavior, 1*, 333–359.

Zhou, J., Shin, S. J., Brass, D. J., & Choi, J. (2009). Social networks, personal values, and creativity: Evidence for curvilinear and interaction effects. *Journal of Applied Psychology, 94*, 1544–1552.

3

Challenges for Responsible Management Education During Digital Transformation

Dušan Kučera

3.1 Introduction

A crucial practical teaching experience with digitization was given by the COVID-19 pandemic when the schools were forced in 2020 to switch to online teaching immediately. Most teachers were not prepared for this change in education, and we are still struggling with it today (Cook & Grant-Davis, 2017). On the one hand, we were aware of the technological offerings and possibilities of working online, but on the other hand, teacher mindsets and pedagogical approaches needed to be adjusted. The same challenges awaited students. They were not part of a traditional classroom. We lost face-to-face contact and direct communication. Selective screen transmissions replaced face-to-face conversations. The teacher could not see the student in the school, and students were reluctant to intervene in the discussion directly. Much-needed conversations linger. We have replaced oral exams with tests and term papers. More

D. Kučera (✉)
University of Economics Prague, Praha, Czech Republic
e-mail: dusan.kucera@vse.cz

adventurous teachers have required face-to-face meetings with students—albeit via TEAMS, SKYPE, or ZOOM. When we asked for face-to-face interviews, we teachers got slightly more insight into the students, who they were, where they came from, what they thought, what they had read, and how they felt and understood the subject. Therefore, digital transformation in education helped to overcome the pandemic, but it could not completely replace the necessary encounters and dialog between teachers and students and between students. The social and pedagogical dimension of education has suffered, even though we have cutting-edge technology that we never had before. The question is what the consequences will be. Technology has shown its advantages, which we read about everywhere, and its limits and dangers, which are less talked about. The primary lesson from the school environment is also true for companies and society as a whole. However, our experience of the consequences of the pandemic is only a tiny part of the implications of the optimism of technological development and digital transformation. There are many challenges for responsible management education during digital transformation.

The chapter aims to capture the critical challenges for responsible management in the era of digital transformation. We understand digitalization as an effort to automate and digitize processes that were previously handled manually or mechanically. Digitalization wants to master tasks that can perform with the help of computer technology and the "networking" of various processes without much physical human involvement, thus freeing up space and the necessary workforce for more practical purposes (Wolff & Göbel, 2018). Naturally, each consideration of this topic points out the double impact of digital transformation: positive (blessings) and critical (curses) in different areas. We will try to open them up in the following three selected levels and formulate concrete challenges for responsible management education:

The first level concerns the importance of the human discovery of technology and the long-term consequences of giving technical discovery-free rein in society.

The second level describes the prevailing optimism of rational thought and the focus on the natural sciences that found application in technology development. However, enthusiasm for technological development and its benefits to business and society have several severe challenges for management education.

The third level concerns misunderstandings in the field of anthropology and the resulting social consequences. Digital technology wanted to serve people. However, after the first experiences of digital transformation, we know that it strongly affects the very notion of the human being and changes the idea of human life, freedom, democracy, and the development of civil society. Let us ask how digitalization is changing the concept of humanism. We will have to ask how digitalization is changing. The idea of the human being as an original personality in the corporate environment. How does digitalization change human freedom, security, moral values, and decision-making? All this is important for education.

The last level builds on the first three parts and summarizes the challenges for management education in the era of digital transformation in specific sectors.

We attempt to describe the first three parts equally, as the implications of digital transformation relate to philosophical challenges, challenges of anthropology and sociology, and pedagogical challenges for business schools. The purpose of the chapter is based on the conviction that the difficulties for responsible management education in the age of digital transformation are not merely a fashion or a short order of a global trend. Any education must be based on the more profound and broader context of the chosen subject. This challenge also applies to business schools, even if it seems that management education primarily pursues pragmatic goals and financial outcomes for companies. The Principles for Responsible Management Education (PRME) clearly defines and deepens this with chapters that articulate a range of responsibilities and the pursuit of sustainable capitalism through digital transportation. Contemporary management, with the help of global organizations and universities, subscribes to the so-called "Sustainable Development Goals" (Sustainabledevelopment, 2015) and sees the given challenges as inherently multidisciplinary challenges (Verhoef et al., 2021).

The fact that digital transformation is not a single discipline, a short-term or fashionable trend in technological development, is recognized by many experts. Digital transformation involves a multidisciplinary dimension of science and management education that must not neglect the psychological, pedagogical, environmental, social, and political contexts in addition to its economic and financial focus. All these areas strongly influence us and change our situation. Naturally, we cannot reduce the digital transformation to a technical problem (e.g., cloud computing, IT in disaster management). Information technology has implications for personal life (e.g., wireless services). Of course, digital transformation affects social transformation (IT control of society) and finally organizational transformation (change of strategy in companies, cities, and military), as described in the works mentioned above (Daim, 2020). A university student should be familiar with all the contexts discussed above, be able to navigate them, and be able to apply their knowledge in practice responsibly.

3.2 The Discovery of the Human Ability to Control Technology

To answer what Responsible Management Education means in digital transformation, we should recall a few key moments of modern philosophy that still influence us today. Indeed, technology has historically occupied a new position in companies and society and now its digital form. Philosophically, however, it goes back to old and outdated assumptions.

The development of technology in Western society was influenced by Greek philosophy, which wrote about "*techne*" (art, or craft-knowledge). However, Aristotle (384–322 BC) strictly distinguished between the domains of "*physis*" (the domain of natural things) and "*poiesis*" (the domain of nonnatural things). If we have shared Aristotle's philosophy of science, theory of cause and effect, and principles of argumentation, then we must not ignore his critique of the atomic mechanism, which ignores living beings in the natural laws under investigation. From the very beginning, we are faced with a complex conception of science, which means that any imbalance between the development of technology and the development of society will be risky. Today, we are indeed witnessing a solid admiration, and interest in technology or digitalization is becoming independent. Thus, in modern IT and digitalization, we must not only follow the "clusters of atoms" while neglecting the social and environmental consequences of the ongoing transformation (Anzenbacher, 2002).

Aristotle's philosophy was revived in many areas for centuries by Thomas Aquinas (1225–1274). He influenced modern science by teaching the causes and consequences of all motion. Although we know Aquinas as a strict Catholic thinker who believed in God as the essential mover of all things, it was nevertheless the first time that a respected teacher of the Church, in the spirit of Aristotle's teachings, admitted a specific division between supernatural (divine) and natural (human) faculties of knowledge. In understanding natural laws, he opened the way for developing the human potential of reason and sensory expertise. In the development of modern thought, however, we can observe the disappearance of universal sense and the action of a separate line of natural sciences using natural, rational methods that will richly use in the development of technology (Pasnau & Shields, 2019). This means that the development of technology is at the risk of being at the expense of the social and humanities domains of life.

After the disintegration of the medieval belief in the universal church and the existing concept of universal knowledge, Renaissance thought focused on astronomy, mathematics, geometry, physics, and energy sources (M. Copernicus, G. Galilei, G. Bruno). The universal challenges of the Middle Ages split into individual (fragmented) subjects. The vertical (value) dimension of science is displaced by a horizontal (pragmatic) and individualistic approach. According to many philosophers of history, the disintegration of the medieval church has created the need to seek new certainties. Galileo began to look for them in trying to measure everything. Critical rational thinking and measurement awakened the first great technological discoveries and the subsequent growth of industry and, of course, the economy. *The Encyclopedia of Philosophy* directly introduced the "*Philosophy of Technology*" (Olsen et al., 2009).

An important Renaissance figure in the development of science and technology was Francis Bacon (1561–1626). Bacon initially *did not distinguish between science and technology, as we do today, but saw technology as an integral part of natural philosophy*" (Internet Encyclopedia of Philosophy, 1995). In practice, however, Bacon came to privilege technology over other areas of science as an essential part of society. He regarded natural causes as "*power*" with the vision that a kind of "*perpetual mobile*" could be created. Again, we trace another source of industrial and technological development. Bacon used the term "*pure investigation*" of nature.

What is the relevance of these philosophical roots for the present? This means that after Bacon, we will still have to deal with the unequal status of science and technology. Schools are faced with beginning to revive social, humanities, environmental or ethical subjects that interest in technology has suppressed.

3.3   Modern Optimism of Technological Progress

To understand the challenges of digital transformation for responsible management education today, we need to be aware of other essential philosophical roots of contemporary optimism about technological progress in general. Many students of business schools think they do not even need such philosophical consideration because they want to learn how to be successful using technology and financial tools in the business world. However, herein lie the current challenges for responsible management education.

Optimism of Critical Rationalism

Rationalism first formulated the laws of mechanics, physics, and other laws of nature, which we still use today in digitalization. The philosophical and scientific changes of the sixteenth and seventeenth centuries were formulated primarily by Rene Descartes (1596–1650). He believed that human reason is capable of such critical thinking that it can rule out errors and uncertainties. As a mathematician, Descartes assumed that through systematic, rational thought, we would regain the certainties lost due to the disintegration of the medieval conception of the world and the loss of the church's monopoly. Although he has remained a religious man, he has formulated the optimistic idea that human reasoning can think "*clearly and distinctly*" (Descartes, 2007). He devoted himself to the study of the laws of nature. Today, we would say he wanted to understand how it all "*works.*" Under his influence, modern scientific thinking begins to emerge with an emphasis on mechanics.

Descartes' rationalism follows Bacon's "*pure investigation*" of natural laws. This deliberate concentration on specific facts began to celebrate its first successes: discoveries of technology, engineering development, and the flowering of industrial production. In connection with Descartes, however, we must recall the "*Cartesian dualism*" that separated critical rational thought from natural and social consequences (*res cogitans* vs. *res extensa*). The power of rationalism was evidently confirmed in the fact that technological inventions found rich pragmatic, military, and economic fields. The British thinker Thomas Hobbes (1588–1679) echoed what his teacher Bacon had written before him: Scientia potentia est (Hobbes, 1996, p. 63). Many other thinkers have used the view that knowledge is the power to this day. Historically, the first industrial revolution was followed by a second, a third—and we are already talking about Industry 4.0, typical of the digital takeover of businesses and society. It is appropriate to reiterate the responsible handling of knowledge.

The Optimism of Uncritical Faith in Progress

We consider the current digital form of industrial transformation to be the pinnacle. With a certain amount of optimism, we are not even afraid to refer to the further technological possibilities of development and the almost infinite frontiers of artificial intelligence that have become part of futuristic ideas. This enthusiastic vision has also been embraced by artists, science fiction literature, and films. Of course, world political events have not been left out. We see the pinnacle of digitalization for management because through its rational deductions and biological applications with the use of other disciplines, we can increase the efficiency of our work, production, transport, sales, and financial flows use natural resources more efficiently.

The industrial and technological revolution architects believed that with the help of technology and the current digital transformation, the world would be a better and more progressive place. That is why digitalization is appearing in national and transnational agendas (Madelin, 2015).

The author's optimism shines through in the very opening sentence, *"I believe that the internet and digital technologies are set of revolutionary tools that can advance humankind."* The European Committee document then lists several planned steps, including creating a *"Grand coalition for skills."* Various Consulting Groups (Boston, Mc Kinsey) and other international documents, such as the Australian Government's *"Digital Economy Strategy 2030"* (Commonwealth of Australia, 2021), have taken an active approach to digitalization.

Naturally, we started to measure the benefits of digitalization and therefore created *"key metrics"* for it (Kotarba, 2017). We believed that life would be even better with the investment in digitalization and the digitalization of work processes than before. Published research on the benefits of digitalization for society has tracked various factories telling us about the increase in *"quality of life"* (Kryzhanovskij et al., 2021). The World Happiness Report and the Human Development Index (HDI) were chosen as auxiliary sources for quality of life. The world digital competitiveness ranking (WDCR) was used as a measure for digitalization. The authors concluded that their research *"could show the greater potential of statistical instruments in managing the processes of digitalization in the context of quality of life"* (Sect. 4.2).

In communist countries, the population has heard for decades the application of Marx's thinking that *"science and technology"* will solve all existing problems and usher in a kind of new age. As we know, this did not happen. Further issues of the modern era have emerged. The Czech philosopher Božena Komárková, in her lectures, analyzed the general phenomenon of progress, which she defined as *"the spontaneous movement toward perfection"* (Komárková, 1991, p. 10). The belief in progress (*progressus*) was already present in the Stoics, who believed in a divine destiny in the gradual renewal and improvement. Today, digitalization will play an essential role in this renewal process because it multiplies the limited human capabilities. The passage of time itself has become a factor in the improvement of life. In biology, we know this from Darwinism. In sociology, we also know it from Robert Spencer's Social Darwinism, which has found great resonance in the Western world (Degler, 1993). The past is still undeveloped, whereas today and the future promise entirely new dimensions for society-wide transformation through technology and digitalization. Even human thought itself seems to need digital assistance to move the world forward.

We are witnessing a specific reduction of technological progress to a few selected features, and we can ask: is this naivety or such a strong optimism in the power of cyberization and digitalization? The timelessness of the implications of digitalization transcends even historical legacies. Business and management become downright impersonal with digitalization, not worrying too much about the present's social, moral, and ethical implications, believing in a kind of "golden age" of the future determined by the digital economy (Bondarenko, 2019). The optimistic belief in the benefits of digitalization and AI is also evident in the EU's 2021 investment plans for AI, as shown in the Fig. 3.1 below: The United States plans to invest 12.1–18.6 trillion of EUR, ASIA 6.5–9.7 trillion, and EUROPE 2.4–3.2 trillion of EUR:

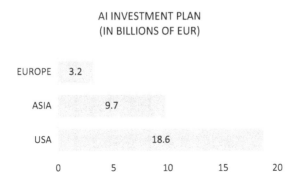

Fig. 3.1 AI investment plan (Source: European parlament, 2021)

Limits of Technological Optimism

Of course, technological optimism and the emphasis on digital transformation also have weaknesses and limits. If we talk about responsible management education, let us recall the well-known technological disasters (Chernobyl, Fukushima), the negative impacts of big cities, the misuse of technology in biology, military, state security, technical manipulation of data abuse for political purposes, and population control.

We cannot accept rationalistic optimism without reservation for the philosophical reasons opened by Immanuel Kant (1724–1804) in his Critique of pure reason (Kant, 1998a). Our thinking is always based on specific concepts, experienced categories, uses transcendence, and needs understanding, not only information applied in a digital function. The rational way of reasoning, analyzing, and deducing is a beautiful tool in technology, but we have to use it judiciously in all relevant contexts. The challenge for responsible management education during digital transformation always remains the need for broader understanding and reflection ability.

Kant's Critique of Practical Reason drew attention to the dangerous separation of the natural sciences and rational self-consciousness from universal values and contexts. The last decade has seen the domination of physical laws by automata, robots, and digital transformation at the expense of pursuing an overall conception of scientific responsibility. The vertical dimension of science has been reduced to the horizontal—the natural and pragmatic uses of science. Scientific thinking has been fragmented into monolithic scientific disciplines and specializations in modern times. In our context, there has been a separation of the natural sciences from the social sciences.

Furthermore, there has been a specific separation of economics (financial interests) and management from social sciences and environmental responsibility (Anzenbacher, 2002). Fragmented disciplines have been reduced to pragmatic functions, mainly in industry and commerce, without regard for future generations (Kučera, 2020). This means that increasingly more limits of the positivist belief in technological progress are being shown to us, which we need to draw attention to in management education. In addition to technological one-sidedness in science, the literature focuses on many other convergences: the spread of poverty, issues of global citizenship, social solidarity, media violence, and legal order (Mirabelli et al., 2020).

It follows from the above paragraphs; therefore, management education needs not only technical education and its applications but also a return to a balanced perspective of complex scientific thinking (see the Fig. 3.2 below).

In terms of time, the industry has limited itself mainly to the current challenges without considering the long-term implications for the future development of society. Unique risks include so-called *digital discrimination* (Criado & Such, 2019), environmental discrimination, and discrimination against future generations. An overall concept of sustainable responsibility is presented, for example, by Schüz (2012) in his study: *Sustainable Corporate Responsibility—The Foundation of Successful Business in the New Millennium*. In this sense, digital transformation cannot be an exception to managerial responsibility.

For further study of the social impacts of Industry 4.0, we can recommend detailed descriptions of the changes that digital transformation will cause in work processes and human ways of working (Hermeier et al., 2018). In addition to the term *"Industry 4.0,"* it introduces the word *"Arbeit 4.0"* because it analyzes the many changes and potential risks digital transformation will cause in almost all fields of human activity.

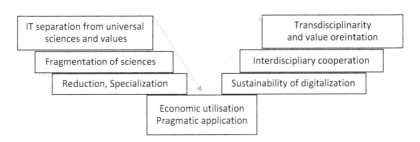

Fig. 3.2 Reflection in changing scientific thinking (Source. Own adaptation)

3.4   Challenge for the Position of Human Being

Digitalization is based on rationalism, which contains a specific unsafe philosophical basis, which we find in Descartes and his pupil La Mettrie. Both of them opened up a pretty simplistic idea of man. What kind of anthropology did the rationalists have in mind? How did they influence the understanding of human beings during the contemporary notion of digital transformation?

Basic Anthropology of Rationalism

The French rationalists thought that the human body could be rationally described as a kind of "*animae rationalis.*" Descartes is far from useful to us today with his reflections on the human body, which he conceived as a kind of aerodynamic machine composed of a skeleton, nerves as conduits for life energy, and so on. Very naturalistically, he understood the animal system as a functioning mechanical system without emotion. La Mettrie (1709–1751) formulated the title of his writings directly as "*L'homme Machine*" (de La Mettrie, 1994). He was an atheist and materialist of French enlightenment. He believed in one material essence of everything, and instead of God, the Creator introduced all the principles of motion into matter itself. Any philosophical concepts that help us today, he considered as an obstacle to natural science.

All this is good to be aware of, because today, during the digital transformation, we are faced with similar mechanistic concepts when describing artificial intelligence that is supposed to imitate humans. Many technological productions of robotization, automation, and autonomous systems are based on precise technology, but their anthropology is naive. I still meet students in my lectures who believe in mechanisms:

- The mechanism of the market.
- The mechanism of economic laws.
- The functioning of society.
- The mechanism of marketing.
- Ultimately, the natural ability to influence and control humans.

Digital transformation is offered in natural functions, including mechanical (chemical, biological, neurological) human organisms, way of thinking, and natural reactions. La Mettrie was the first mechanical materialist who observed significant similarities in functions of the human body with animals. The value of workers he would see primarily in their physical processes, which are capable of learning and developing the ability to work in companies.

A final crucial philosophical pillar that plays into today's understanding of digital transformation is the evolutionary theory of Charles Darwin from the nineteenth century. The belief in spontaneous Bing Bang, the confidence in the more or less random development of cells and organisms, has seeped into technological evolution and digitalization philosophy. Even if we wanted to avoid other disciplines such as biology, we could not prevent a similar philosophy from being applied to the development of the corporate organism or human society. The challenge for responsible management education is to compare the assumptions of natural and social Darwinism (Rennie, 2009) with the evolutionary philosophy of dynamic mechanisms used by the application of artificial intelligence (Radanliev et al., 2020).

Limits of Anthropological Imitation of Artificial Intelligence

The very notion of "*intelligence*" reminds us that we will need a deeper dimension of nontechnical education to understand all the connections. The basic definition is that human intelligence—a mental quality "*consists of the abilities to learn from experience, adapt to new situations, understand and handle abstract concepts, and use knowledge to manipulate one's environment*" (Encyclopedia Britannica, 2022).

By definition, AI learns from the human it wants to imitate. We can only hope that it will not be the other way around one day, namely, that humans learn from AI. Indeed, today, we are concerned with four kinds of human intelligence (Nazemoff, 2014): logical thinking (IQ), social intelligence (SI), emotional intelligence (EI), and spiritual intelligence (SpI). If we engage neuroscientists in the debate, we soon recognize that AI significantly reduces such complex human abilities and the number of brain cells that we cannot accurately count (Kok, 2020). As neuroscientific knowledge of the brain's capabilities continues to expand, it alerts us to the uncritical expectation of technological imitation of human intelligence. Business schools are aware of several benefits and capabilities of artificial intelligence. However, it also has many limitations and socioeconomic implications that depend on the extent to which human responsibility is applied in the design, production, and application—management of technological processes (Ajoudani et al., 2018).

Management students should know the differences of the level we would like to embed in robots or other autonomous systems that we want to control digitally. This is of course of interest to many scholars today (Korteling et al., 2021). The authors respond to attempts to view AI as a "*team member*" using different metaphors like "*mate,*" "*partner,*" "*alter ego,*" "*intelligent collaborator,*" "*buddy,*" or "*hybrid teams.*" IT and management students face the task of navigating the many similarities of AI with human capabilities but also with fundamental differences (see the Table 3.1 below):

Table 3.1 The difference between AI prerequisites and human prerequisites for responsible management education

Artificial conditions	Human assumptions
Logic algorithm	Logic thinking, context understanding Self-awareness
Computational complexity	Complex learning, critical thinking
Highly objectivity	Personal responsibility, social relations, love, feelings, empathy, partnership, friendship
Speed of data processing	Natural and social conditions, patience, long-term value orientation
Machine with no human characteristics	Beliefs, hopes, patience, joy, kindness, goodness, faithfulness, self-control
Machine with no moral and ethical responsibility	Moral and ethical responsibility, ethical dilemma solutions on many different levels, future value—orientation

Source: Own adaptation

We do not pursue all the differences between AI and human intelligence, but we focus on the fundamental challenges for future management education, stressing the responsibility of digital transformation. Fast technologies promise to solve many human problems, manage and control many processes and systematically even replace a man. However, the fundamental question remains whether AI supports or undermines humanity (Collins, 2018). Stephen Hawking told the BBC: "*The development of full artificial intelligence could spell the end of the human race.*" *(Cellan-Jones,* 2014*)*.

Ethical Challenges of Digital Transformation

In a situation of technological development, the ethical dimension of managerial responsibility acquires a critical size. Responsible ethics education for managers and entrepreneurs shows that quantitative indicators of matrix management models are inadequate to evaluate individuals with their complex capabilities and fragility (Jódar & De la Poza, 2020). Management responsibility courses (including machine ethics) are qualitative, very different from a technological set of various mechanically (electronically) conceived functions (Tonkens, 2009; Tzafestas, 2016). Responsible management education will repeatedly try to deal with the optimistic expressions of evolutionary psychologists, with Pinker, for example, calling humans a "*wet computer*" (Pinker, 1997), opening up space for artificial imitations of them.

As already indicated above, the management of ethics opens up economic, social, environmental challenges but also challenges of the future. It is typical of pure rationalism that it fails to appreciate the implications of technological development for future generations. Perhaps the first to articulate the principles of responsibility in the age of growing technological power and influence back in the 1980s was Hans Jonas (1985). Empirical and scientific thinking alone does not contain a vision for the future. We do not even have a clear idea of what consequences uncritical admiration for the technology of robots can bring if we entrust their decisions for future situations. Jonas started to draw attention to the dangerous implications of what is still proving a form of "*science fiction*" and create a new morality and social sense. This topic engages many scholars from many perspectives and a complex way that can undoubtedly better prepare young managers for their future responsible professions in an environment that adores "*big data*" and the digital control of technological devices (Boobier, 2018).

A practical attractive example of technological optimism was probably the idea of a marketer who, a few years ago, was successful in presenting the so-called *Sophie* (a humanoid robot like a young woman). Artificial creation has already acquired her first citizenship (Fitzsimmons, 2017). The audience, through digital technology, admired the human form of the robot, the changes of clothes, the language, and the learned responses. During the public presentations, the audience was full of technological enthusiasm. It was as if we were reanimating a very limited LaMetrrie concept reduced to the idea of humans as "*machines*." These examples lead us to many concrete ethical challenges for responsible management education. Examples include the concept of "digital humanism" (Nida-Rümelin & Weidenfeld, 2018) or the concept of values and ethics for the twenty-first century, which a group of authors has endorsed from different disciplines (BBVA, 2012).

3.5 Challenges for Management Education

Responsible management education refers to the personal education of future managers. The described challenges to responsibility are possible if we think about personal managerial responsibility. This is tempted by various trends in the age of digitalization. In academia, we can encounter views that technology is value-objective and "*value-free*." Indeed, we can find many publications showing us that modern science wants to be objective, positivistic, value-free, and independent of moral values. Business school, in particular, struggles with the theory that morality is good in society, but business follows its laws. Some economists (Schwarz et al., 2016) believe that Adam Smith's concept of "invisible hand" applies only to the market, free competition, private business, not to the value framework of the whole society. All dangerous neoliberal positions in economics have historical and philosophical reasons in the fractional orientation we have described above. In reaction to these trends, we suggest a holistic value perspective (Gonzalez, 2013) and ethical challenges relating to a new search for technological applications between metaphysical responsibility and science (Boucher, 2019).

Challenges for Technology Departments

IT and IS with digital transformation represents the powerful influence of practical experience, which has become a defining aspect in our decades.

IT faculties have specific professional programs for companies and institutions. However, some schools have introduced social courses that place IT skills in a broader context. It is clear that the more advanced technologies we develop and use, the more pressing the issues we face. For example, the subject of economic demographics helps in applying demographic data and considering all the implications in practice. Taking IT students should understand the broader societal developments that IT is meant to serve, not the other way around. Students should learn to anticipate future demographic results in economic, statistical, and social terms. They will need this in businesses with a shortage of workers or as analysts in banks, insurance companies, or the government. However, the current challenge is also posed by study programs that prepare interdisciplinary IT professionals. Some schools are thus responding to the globalizing information society. The study covers the areas of long-term strategy, information theory, cognitive informatics, logic and semantics, neuroscience and its ethical limits, self-organization theory, modeling, simulation, intelligent and complex systems, ontological engineering, knowledge, project management, science methodology, philosophy of language, philosophy of mind, management informatics, business process engineering, environment, and so on. Graduates of the program will find a wide range of applications, especially in large companies, in strategic design and management of company development, or public administration.

The expert discussion also focuses on philosophical issues of IT and digitalization. The typical use of empirical methods in technology leads us back to John Locke's philosophy, which did not need to look at the past or the potential implications for the future because it was based only on present experience. The perspective of total responsibility has also been eroded over several centuries, thanks to the writers of Romanticism's emphasis on subjective feelings, emotions, personal desires, and dreams. The focus on feelings and emotions has never been formally adopted into AI's natural and engineering sciences. However, the risk of using AI to mimic and interpret human emotions is currently high. Reducing complex social-psychological situations contains many potential misunderstandings (Purdy et al., 2019). The authors point out that IT has long been active in stores to influence and manipulate customers.

The boom of automation and robotics supported by digitalization is related to the onset of psychology and the discovery of the subconscious' power. A major influence on business psychology was social Darwinism a aplikovaná biologie resulting in the formulation of "selfish gen" (Dowkins, 2016). In the environment of Darwinistic understanding of "natural selection," nemá personal responsibility much space. Modern technology's positive development has gradually rebounded at the peak of progress—supermachines that will be smarter than humans (Bostrom, 2014; Grace et al., 2017). The pinnacle of ethical concerns is that the dream of the Second Machine Age (Brynjolfsson and McAfee, 2014) has occurred, that we can trust AI and have no need to haunt fire alarm which would create a cutting-edge for scientific projects (Yudkowsky, 2018). Even the technological vision for Industry 4.0 was initially stronger than thinking about its ethical implications for society and future generations (Solomon, 2016). However, Peter W. Singer's publications are concerned that with digitalisation a more dramatic period has opened up than the industrial revolution (Singer, 2018). Many publications are concerned with the dangers of the internet, which lie in the kind of people who run it (Nakamura & Chow-White, 2011). Finally, even the recent experience with COVID-19 showed that we could not just rely on a purely biomedical and technological approach but involve active personal moral responsibility and health prevention (Bashir & Samavia, 2020).

Challenges for General Management

Gunnar Myrdal has dealt at length with the question of whether we will be able to retain all the implications of economics as a social science that is not "*objective*" but has certain subjective elements and biases, which we will have to constantly re-explain, reinterpret and ultimately evaluate (Myrdal, 1969).

Against personal attitudes pursuing managerial accountability, technology offers a particular anonymous progress function without human moral involvement. However, it can resist similar risks and dangers associated with digital transformation. For schools, this means, above all, developing a philosophy of responsible value orientation (Rachinger et al., 2018).

Experts describe Industry 4.0 with an awareness of additional contexts beyond the technological functions themselves (Lasi et al., 2014). The social risks of digitalization are not discussed much in the technical fields. Today, we are beginning to realize that, for example, through digitalization and artificial intelligence, we can control social structures and personal life, which will fundamentally undermine the principles of democracy. Therefore, we will have to think about what management students learn about the context and consequences of digitalization not only for production, supply chain, business, financial flows, marketing, and customer behavior. A new area of challenges opens up for us, including the legal implications of digitalization, organizational changes, psychological changes among employees, and the effects on personal and social life. Digitalisierung: German researchers (Wolff & Göbel, 2018) realize that we are standing at crossroads that steer digitalization in two directions. However, they are not equally valuable. One they described as a "*blessing,*" the other as a "*curse.*" Therefore, there are at least two opposing approaches that change our world, lives, and work. Industry 4.0 über is necessarily linked to IT-Security 4.0, Business education 4.0, Heals 4.0, Smart Home 4.0, Marketing and Sales 4.0. Let us also say Humanity 4.0.

Challenges for International Management

In addition to your personal, corporate, local responsibility, there is the world. We are part of it and participate in its development or contribute to its imbalance and instability. We must not forget that technology and digitalization are also involved in wars, revolutions, and dirty tricks. Technology is attractive for many reasons, including the acquisition of more power. A seminal contribution on this topic is the book "*The Origin of Strategic Stability*" (Elbridge & Michael, 2013). Technology is described as a deterrent. Paradoxicality is the combination of the words "*nuclear balance.*" Technology in weapons both protects and threatens. International analyses of global developments have many critical issues (O´Neil, 2017). These include anticipating the social and political implications of digital networks: "*Who owns the future?*" (Lanier, 2014).

Henry Kissinger, in his analyses, worries about the consequences of digital transformation that no one knows where they are dragging us all (Kissinger, 2015, chapter IX). He points out several points, which provoke a new and renewed discussion:

(a) We are turning human activities into "data." (Mayer-Schönberger & Cukier, 2014). The variety, diversity, and creativity of our lives are gradually changing in a situation where we are exposed to the daily reception of different information, static data, advertisements, and campaigns for anything. Don Clark calls this the "internet of things" (Clark, 2014). Digital space is changing the forms of human communication and cultural rules and needs some regulation.

(b) The cyber and digital era has no internal limits or restraints, thus tempting various unstable personalities and regimes to be aggressive in communication between people and world powers. Since the cyber proctor has become strategically indispensable, it is naturally the target of many cyber-attacks and manipulation. Practically, this means a considerable vulnerability of state institutions, companies, and society as a whole. With the growth of data, we must also think about protecting it from hostile theft or destruction (Musik & Bogner, 2019). Reducing cyberspace to a momentary effect (business, political). Focusing on today displaces interest and time for learning from the past (history).

(c) Threats to the human personality in general and the personality of the manager in particular. Modern economics began to build on human selfishness (Hobbes, Locke, Hume, Smith). Later psychology embraced the dark corners of the human subconscious, emotions, fear, self-preservation, and aggression. The internet counts on all this in its influence far more than its plan to promote wisdom and inner search. Ale právě lepší budoucnost poučená chybami z minulosti je náš úkol (Krugman, 2020).

3.6   Conclusion

The first thing we realized is the huge context that digital transformation holds. All scientific, technological, legal, social, and ethical challenges affect the future. The managerial challenges of digital transformation have recently been very clearly summarized concerning sustainability management by Steffen Lange and Tilman Santarius (Lange & Santarius, 2020).

In the presentation of this chapter, we can summarize the individual points and challenges for responsible management education in a clear way:

(a) Understand the historical and philosophical development of modern science that has created unheralded emphases in management education.

(b) Recognize the immense optimism in technological advancement and digitalization that tends to weaken managers' critical and value-based thinking on ethical issues.

(c) To understand the basics of personal responsibility within an anthropological understanding of the uniqueness of the human being that technology seeks to imitate.

(d) To reflect on the specific challenges of management education and apply them to the educational practice of managers of the future.

The author of the chapter certainly does not claim to be exhaustive of all possible connections. However, he presents the points made with the hope that they will inspire readers, teachers, students, and managers to engage in personal and corporate activism, the creation of new human, social, and environmental values or quality culture, even though we are so strongly influenced by digital transformation (Weber, 2020).

References

Ajoudani, A., Zanchettin, A. M., Ivaldi, S., et al. (2018). Progress and prospects of the human–robot collaboration. *Autonomous Robot, 42*, 957–975. https://doi.org/10.1007/s10514-017-9677-2

Anzenbacher, A. (2002). *Einführung in die Philosophie*. Herder.

Bashir, C. F., & Samavia, R. (2020). COVID 19: Frontline experience at a tertiary care hospital in UK. *Journal of Global Health, 10*, 1. https://doi.org/10.7189/jogh.10.01035

BBVA. (2012). Values and ethics for the 21st century. TF Artes Gráficas.

Bondarenko, V. (2019). Digital economy: A vision from the future. *Journal of Economic Science Research*. https://doi.org/10.30564/jesr.v3i1.1402

Boobier, T. (2018). *Advanced analytics and AI: Impact, implementation, and the future of work*. Wiley. Incorporated.

Bostrom, N. (2014). *Superintelligence. Paths, dangers, strategies*. Oxford University Press.

Boucher, S. C. (2019). An empiricist conception of the relation between metaphysics and science. *Philosophia, 47*, 1355–1378. https://doi.org/10.1007/s11406-018-0040-4

Brynjolfsson, E. & McAfee, A. (2016). *The Second Machine Age: Work, Progress, and Prosperity in a Time of Brilliant Technologies*. W. W. Norton & Company; Reprint edition.

Cellan-Jones, R. (2014). Stephen Hawking warns artificial intelligence could end mankind. *BBC News*, 2 December 2014. https://www.bbc.com/news/technology-30290540.

Clark, D. (2014). "Internet of Things" in reach. *The Wall Street Journal, 5*, 2014. https://www.wsj.com/articles/SB10001424052702303640604579296580892973264

Collins, H. M. (2018). *Artifictional intelligence: Against Humanity's surrender to computers*. Polity.

Cook, K. C., & Grant-Davis, K. (2017). *Online education: Global questions, local answers (Baywood's technical communications)*. Routledge.

Criado, N., & Such, J. (2019). Digital discrimination. In K. Yeung & M. Lodge (Eds.), *Algorithmic regulation*. Oxford Scholarship Online. https://doi.org/10.1093/oso/9780198838494.003.0004

Daim, T. U. (2020). Digital transformation. Evaluating emerging technologies world. *Scientific Series in R & D Management, 6*. https://doi.org/10.1142/11675. https://www.worldscientific.com/worldscibooks/10.1142/11675

Degler, C. (1993). In *Search of human nature: The decline and revival of Darwinism in American social thought*. Oxfort University Press.

Descartes, R. (2007). *Discourse on method*. Focus Publishing.

Digital Economy Strategy 2030. (2021). Commonwealth of Australia.

Dowkins, R. (2016). *The selfish gene*. Oxford Landmark Science.

Elbridge, A. C., & Michael, S. G. (Eds.). (2013). *Strategic stability: Contending interpretations*. Paperback by Strategic Studies Institute, Military Bookshop.

European Parlament. (2021). https://www.europarl.europa.eu/news/cs/headlines/priorities/umela-inteligence-v-eu/20201015STO89417/pravidla-pro-umelou-inteligenci-co-navrhuji-poslanci.

Fitzsimmons, C. (2017). Why Sophia the robot is not what it seems. *Sunday Morning Herald*. 31 October 2017. [Online]. Available at https://www.smh.com.au/opinion/whysophia-the-robot-is-not-what-it-seems-20171031-gzbi3p.html.

Gonzalez, W. J. (2013). Value ladenness and the value-free ideal in scientific research. In C. Luetge (Ed.), *Handbook of the philosophical foundations of business ethics*. Springer. https://doi.org/10.1007/978-94-007-1494-6_78

Grace, K., Salvatier, J., Dafoe, A., et al. (2017). When will AI exceed human performance? Evidence from AI experts. ArXiv:1705.08807.

Hermeier, B., Heupel, T., & Fichtner-Rosada, S. (2018). *Arbeitswelten der Zukunft: Wie die Digitalisierung unsere Arbeitsplätze und Arbeitsweisen verändert*. Springer Gabler.

Hobbes, T. (1996). *Leviathan, Cambridge texts in the history of political thought*. Cambridge University Press.

Internet Encyclopedia of Philosophy. (1995). Philosophy of technology. https://iep.utm.edu/home/about.

Jonas, H. (1985). The imperative of responsibility: In search of an ethics for the technological age. University of Chicago Press.

Kant, I. (1998a). *Critique of pure reason*. Cambridge University Press.

Kant, I. (1998b). *Kant's metaphysics of morals*. University of Memphis, Department of Philosophy.

Kissinger, H. (2015). *World order*. Penguin Books.

Kok, A. (2020). *Functions of the brain: A conceptual approach to cognitive neuroscience*. Routledge.

Krugman, P. (2020). *Arguing with zombies: Economics, politics, and the fight for a better future*. W. W. Norton & Company.

Komárková, B. (1991). Božena Komárková a její hosté. Eseje a rozhovory. Eman.

Korteling, J. E., van de Boer-Visschedijk, G. C., Blankendaal, R. A. M., Boonekamp, R. C., & Eikelboom, A. R. (2021). Human versus artificial intelligence. *Frontiers in Artifitial Intelligence*. https://doi.org/10.3389/frai.2021.622364

Kotarba, M. (2017). Measuring digitalization—key metrics. *Foundations of Management, 9*(1), 123–138. https://doi.org/10.1515/fman-2017-0010

Kryzhanovskij, O. A., Baburina, N. A., & Ljovkina, A. O. (2021). How to make digitalization better serve an increasing quality of life? *Sustainability, 13*(2), 611. https://doi.org/10.3390/su13020611

Kučera, D. (2020). Philosophical challenges of business ethics. Book chapter in...Palgrave Macmillan.

Lange, S., & Santarius, T. (2020). *Smart green world? Making digitalization work for sustainability*. Routledge.

de La Mettrie, J. O. (1994). *Man a machine and man a plant*. Hackett Publishing..

Lanier, J. (2014). *Who owns the future?* Simon & Schuster.

Lasi, H., Fettke, P., Kemper, H., Feld, T., & Hoffmann, M. (2014). *Business & information systems engineering*. Berkeley. https://doi.org/10.1007/s12599-014-0334-4.

Lucas Jódar & Elena De la Poza, 2020. "*How and Why the Metric Management Model Is Unsustainable: The Case of Spanish Universities from 2005 to 2020,*" Sustainability, MDPI, vol. 12(15), pages 1–19, July.

Madelin, R. (2015). *Digital economy, digital society: The European vision*. Eyes on Europe #21—the Juncker Commission: A wind of Change. (pp. 16–17). https://issuu.com/eyesoneurope/docs/10739066_10204567267476209_92983627/17.

Mayer-Schönberger, V., & Cukier, K. (2014). *Big data: A revolution that will transform how we live, work and think*. Mariner Books.

Mirabelli, M., Dib, N. B., & Mih, S. (2020). *Digitalization, economic development and social equality. Turbulent convergence*. Cambridge Scholars Publishing.

Musik, Ch. & Bogner, A. (2019). *Digitalization and society. A sociology of technology perspective on current trends in data, digital security and the internet.* VS Verlag für Sozialwissenschaften.

Myrdal, G. (1969). Objectivity in social research. Random House Trade Paperbacks.

Nakamura, L. & Chow-White, P. (2011). Race after the internet. Routledge.

Nazemoff, V. (2014). The four intelligences of the business mind: How to rewire your brain and your business for success. Apress.

Nida-Rümelin, J., & Weidenfeld, N. (2018). *Digitaler Humanismus: Eine Ethik für das Zeitalter der Künstlichen Intelligenz.* Piper Verlag.

Olsen, J. K. B., Selinger, E., & Riis, S. (Eds.). (2009). *New waves in philosophy of technology.* Palgrave Macmillan.

O'Neil, C. (2017). Weapons of math destruction: How big data increases inequality and threatens democracy. Crown.

Pasnau, R. Shields, C. (2019). *The philosophy of Aquinas.* Routledge.

Pinker, S. (1997). *How the mind works.* Norton.

Purdy, M., Zealley, J. & Maseli, O. (2019). The Risks of Using AI to Interpret Human Emotions. *Harvard Business Review.* https://hbr.org/2019/11/the-risks-of-using-aito-interpret-human-emotions.

Radanliev, P., De Roure, D., Walton, R., et al. (2020). Artificial intelligence and machine learning in dynamic cyber risk analytics at the edge. *SN Applied Sciences, 2*, 1773. https://doi.org/10.1007/s42452-020-03559-4

Rachinger, M., Rauter, R., Müller, C., Vorraber, W., & Schirgi, E. (2018). Digitalization and its influence on BMI. *Journal of Manufacturing Technology Management.* https://doi.org/10.1108/JMTM-01-2018-0020

Rennie, J. (2009). Dynamic Darwinism: Evolution theory thrives today. The naturalist would approve of how evolutionary science continues to improve. *Scientific American.* Jan 1. 2009.

Schüz, M (2012): *"Sustainable Corporate Responsibility—The Foundation of Successful Business in the New Millennium"*, in: Central European Business Review, 2, p. 7–15, Prague: VSE.

Schwarz, J., Kočenda, E. & Šíma, J. (2016). *Předmluva* in Smith, A. (2017) *Bohatství národů*, Liberální institute.

Singer, P. W. (2018). LikeWar: The weaponization of social media. Eamon Dolan/Houghton Mifflin Harcourt.

Smolan, R., & Erwitt, J. (2012). *The human face of big data.* Against All Odds Productions.

Solomon, M. (2016). The 4 big ethical questions of the fourth industrial revolution. *World Economic Forum.* https://www.weforum.org/agenda/2016/10/how-can-we-enjoy-the-benefits-of-the-fourth-industrial-revolution-while-minimizing-its-risks

Sustainable development transforming our world: The 2030 agenda for sustainable development. (2015). https://www.sustainabledevelopment.org.

Sternberg, Robert J. (2022). "human intelligence". Encyclopedia Britannica, Invalid Date, https://www.britannica.com/science/human-intelligence-psychology.

Tonkens, R. (2009). A challenge for machine ethics. *Minds and Machines 19* (3): 421–438.

Tzafestas, S., G. (2016). *An Introduction to Robophilosophy.* River Publishers.

Verhoef, P. C., Broekhuizen, P. C., Bart, Y., Bhattacharya, A., Dong, J. Q., Fabian, N., & Haenlein, M. (2021). Digital transformation: A multidisciplinary reflection and research agenda. *Journal of Business Research, 122,* 889–890. https://doi.org/10.1016/j.jbusres.2019.09.022

Weber, A. (2020). *Digitalization for value creation: Corporate culture for a digital world.* Springer.

Wolff, D. & Göbel, R: (2018). *Digitalisierung: Segen oder Fluch: Wie die Digitalisierung unsere Lebens- und Arbeitwelt verändert.* Springer.

Yudkowsky, E. (2018). *How to Actually Change Your Mind (Rationality: From AI to Zombies).* Machine Intelligence Research Institute.

4

PRME Principles: A Framework for Addressing Digital Transformation Challenges

Consuelo García de La Torre and Osmar Arandia

4.1 Introduction

Although digital transformation is currently a much-mentioned term in the business context, this construct is still an emerging topic for academia. At the same time, organizations are already experiencing extraordinary challenges, not only because of the COVID-19 pandemic but also because of rapid environmental changes and the quick adoption of digital processes. These two features stress the organizations and the people within them.

From Fortune 500 firms to SMEs around the world, firms are facing different dilemmas when they consider entering the digital transformation world. Some of these dilemmas are related to the ethical implications of using personal data, specifically from customers and collaborators.

C. G. de La Torre (Deceased)
EGADE Business School Monterrey, San Pedro Garza García, NL, Mexico

O. Arandia (✉)
Universidad de Monterrey, San Pedro Garza García, Mexico
e-mail: osmar.arandia@udem.edu

© The Author(s), under exclusive license to Springer Nature Switzerland AG 2023
C. Hauser, W. Amann (eds.), *The Future of Responsible Management Education*,
Humanism in Business Series, https://doi.org/10.1007/978-3-031-15632-8_4

Another kind of implication is related to respect for the human dignity of the individuals within the firm and the potential repercussions for the labor force when a firm adopts a digital transformation strategy.

Under this idea, PRME principles may help business schools address the abovementioned implications by providing a general framework for a theoretical and empirical analysis of the conflicts that may occur in organizations when adopting a digital transformation strategy. Considering the aforementioned, a question emerges: How are digitalization and disruptive innovations linked to responsible management education?

Therefore, the objective of this chapter is to present a theoretical model of PRME's six principles and how each of them may shed business schools light on how executives and firms may address the ethical implications of adopting a digital transformation strategy.

4.2 The Six PRME Principles and Their Implications for Business Education

The Sustainable Development Goals are humanity's guiding star for addressing the different challenges in an ever-changing context such the one we are living in. Responsible management education is a response from business schools to those challenges and has the mission of helping society through education to generate positive impacts regarding the actions derived from firms.

After the approval of the 17 Sustainable Development Goals in 2015, 193 of the state's members of the United Nations adopted a plan to achieve a better future for all. They are laying a path over the next 15 years to end extreme poverty, fight inequality and injustice, and protect our planet. At the heart of "Agenda 2030" are the SDGs that clearly define the world we want for our descendants.

Under this idea, business and management schools have a unique opportunity to advance the SDGs and help to create a more sustainable future for all. They can influence students with responsible business practices while driving research on the business case for sustainability and leadership. Fulfilling the sustainable development goals through responsible management education is the vision of PRME. This is at the core of everything we do, and we believe it to be the most important work of our lifetime.

Academic institutions that transform their teaching, research, and thought leadership to serve societal needs while developing the responsible leaders of tomorrow will become pioneers in the growing field of responsible management education.

The six Principles of PRME offer a framework for transforming business and management education. The six principles defined by PRME consider that purpose should be driven by a profound ethical reflection of the possible impact on society caused by the firm's activities. That purpose needs to be embedded in core values that will also guide the firm executive's decision making. To achieve this, business schools must develop educational processes and methodologies that help their students understand and realize how an ethical framework can guide the firm's operations.

Additionally, constant and valuable research will feed the necessary knowledge to create new sustainable business models and at the same time will give BS students understandable answers to all queries regarding the relation between ethics, responsibility and business practices. Higher education institutions understood that such a challenge cannot be addressed by a single institution; in contrast, the emerging problems associated with better business practices need to be addressed in cooperation with society and its different institutions, such as governments, firms, and universities. Because of the need to include a broad spectrum of participants, a profound reflexive dialog is needed among all the participants in the creation of a better world (Table 4.1).

PRME is the largest organized relationship between the United Nations and business- and management-related higher education institutions, working to raise the profile of sustainability in schools around the world and to equip today's business students with the ability to deliver change tomorrow.

Table 4.1 PRME principles definitions and meanings

Principle	Definition	Meaning
1. Purpose	We will develop the capabilities of students to be the future generators of sustainable value for business and society at large, and to work for inclusive and sustainable global economy	Future business leaders must be able to create sustainable and inclusive business models
2. Values	We will incorporate into our academic activities, curricula, and organizational practices the values of global social responsibility as portrayer in international initiatives such as the United Nations Global Compact	Sustainability and ethical reflection will be part of the core values in any school engaged with PRME principles. This will help future executives to align their own initiatives to the sustained development goals
3. Method	We will create educational frameworks, materials, processes, and environments that enable effective learning experiences for responsible leaderships	Build up the business case for sustainability requires a broad and profound method of teaching
4. Research	We will engage in conceptual and empirical research that advance our understanding about the role, dynamics, and impact of corporations in the creation of sustainable social, environmental, and economic value	To have a better understanding of sustainability and its relationship with the business world, institutions must engage in research activities
5. Partnership	We will interact whit managers of business corporations to extend our knowledge of their challenges in meeting social and environment responsibilities and to jointly explore effective approaches to meeting those challenges	It will be necessary the participation of the different institutions to strength the develop of more sustainable practices

(continued)

Table 4.1 (continued)

Principle	Definition	Meaning
6. Dialog	We will facilitate and support dialog and debate among educators, students, business, government, consumers, media, civil society organizations and other interested groups and stakeholders on critical issues related to global social responsibilities and sustainability	Constant dialog is a must when a higher education institution wants to engage its different stakeholders in sustainable practices

Source: Authors' creation based on PRME's principles, 2021

4.3   The Digital Transformation Era and Its Challenges for Humans

Digital transformation has become a well-accepted idea in the business context, at least in the last five to ten years. Many firms worldwide have adopted specific strategies to develop their own digital transformation pathway from different perspectives. According to Matt et al. (2015), "firms in almost all industries have conducted a number of initiatives to explore new digital technologies and to exploit their benefits. This frequently involves transformations of key business operations and affects products and processes, as well as organizational structures and management concepts."

In this sense, digital transformation refers to the strategy adopted by the firm in which the organization reorganizes and redefines its business model and its processes to better assess what stakeholders need, always considering technology and digitalization as tools for achieving the mentioned goals (Tang, 2021; Schallmo & Williams, 2018). Under this idea, the business environment has suffered a profound impact regarding the way firms conceive technology and the relationship between people and technology (Kane, 2019). From this perspective, technology is considered only a tool, while people are the real actors in a digital transformation process within the firm.

A common idea regarding DT is to consider technology and digitalization as a tool for broader purposes, such as a better fit of customer needs, best usage of resources, reconfiguration of purposes to enhance productivity within the organization, and fostering innovation in the business model of the firm (Gong & Ribiere, 2021). This conception of digital transformation necessarily implies a profound redefinition of the firm's business model, where technology as a tool for dialog between the company and its stakeholders acquires an important role in the performance of the company, and where—precisely given that leading role of technology—there is a risk that it will gradually replace people, with the respective deterioration in the well-being of the company's employees (Akaev et al., 2021).

Under this idea, DT presents different challenges for the people within the firms that are considering implementing DT strategies in their operation. One of the main concerns regarding the evolution of digital transformation worldwide is the growing inequality between the groups that have access to digital tools and those whose socioeconomic conditions prevent them from accessing the tools and benefits of digital transformation (DiMaggio et al., 2004). Another concern is the ethical implications of more use of digital tools such as artificial intelligence in our business process, with the possibility of negative impacts for the firm's workforce and its consequent damage to the dignity of the firm's workers (Kirchschlaeger, 2021).

4.4   How to Reduce the Gap Between Those Who Have Access to Digital Tools and Those Who Do Not Have Access to Digital Tools and Digital Education

Inequality is a phenomenon originating from unequal access to similar conditions for all people. Unequal access to digital abilities, digital tools or digital opportunities may be a crucial factor to extend the development gap between those who can access these factors and those who cannot.

In this vein, Cooper in 2002 emphasizes that the difference in digital capabilities among society may diminish the possibility for a great part of the population to access development opportunities for that population segment. Cooper (2002) also mentions that the virtuous circle in the economy originating from the development of digital capabilities may become a vicious circle for those who have no access to new technologies. Inequality has increased between firms and between workers (Qureshi, 2020), and the pandemic caused by COVID-19 deepened that inequity. In this sense, Qureshi (2020) mentions that firms that have access to technological advance have gained a significant advantage compared to firms that do not have the mentioned access to technology.

Another problem that arose originated from the increasing automation of low- to middle-skill tasks, which has shifted labor demand toward higher-level skills, hurting wages and jobs at the lower end of the skills spectrum (Qureshi, 2020). Under these conditions, two levels of analysis emerge to understand the abovementioned phenomena: the first refers to the unequal access for firms to technological resources that may derive in unequal business opportunities, and the second refers to the impact for employees with lower technological skills.

When analyzing the result of the combination of both levels of analysis, we found a comprehensive development problem, which impacts not only the companies involved but also the employees of those companies. This phenomenon becomes a vicious circle, since companies without technological capabilities lose market opportunities and therefore cannot develop the technological capabilities of their collaborators, condemning themselves to stay away from development opportunities. Meanwhile, at the same time, employees without technological capabilities receive less income or are not hired, which condemns them to not have sufficient personal income to invest in the development of their technological capabilities. In this sense, this lack of digital skills condemns both companies and individuals to remain oblivious to the economic development caused by digital transformation (Fig. 4.1).

PRME's principles may be a response to breaking this type of vicious circle. *Principle 5: Partnership* is defined as the desirable interaction between schools and firms to explore jointly effective approaches to meet challenges such the one exposed in this chapter.

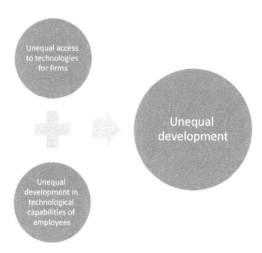

Fig. 4.1 Two levels of analysis in technological inequality. (Source: Authors' creation, 2022)

Under this idea, business schools may offer an answer to the unequal opportunities for firms and people by fostering cooperation between academia, developed firms and, of course, undeveloped firms and their employees. Higher education institutions such as business schools must be promoters of innovation and dissemination of knowledge and technological capabilities. The participation of business schools as key actors in the dissemination of knowledge and the creation of new capabilities in firms' collaborators is essential to reduce the gap between firms or tech skilled people and nontech skilled people and nondeveloped firms.

In this sense, partnership plays a significant role in business schools in an effort to reduce the technological gap. Digital literacy should be a goal for societies, and academic institutions are called to lead this effort. For example, Universidad de Monterrey (UDEM) and Tecnológico de Monterrey (ITESM), two Mexican institutions participating in PRME, are leading a regional initiative called industry 4.0 in which in a triple helix model, universities and governments cooperate to reduce the technological gap existing in small firms that want to participate in the value chain of national and international big corporations.

Both institutions serve as mentors and promoters for SMEs that may not have the necessary technological skills to participate in global markets but are willing to develop them with the help of these universities. Both companies and their employees have benefited from different continuous training programs, where they have been allowed to develop the necessary technological skills to be part of the value chain of large international and national companies. The program has already accelerated many regional SMEs in coordination with the municipal and state government and some anchor corporations. The result of such initiative is the development of tech capabilities not only in the participating SMEs but also in their employees. The initiative has also considered a specific roadmap for spreading this help for the vast majority of SMEs in the region (Fig. 4.2).

As seen in the model, the participation of higher education institutions helps both society and government achieve their goals in the development of digital capabilities and knowledge for the less-favored levels of society. Thus, partnership may be an adequate strategy in the pursuit of a broader participation of SMEs in the digital economy. Another example on how ***Principle 5. Partnership*** may help to develop the digital capabilities for the majority within a society is the one presented by the

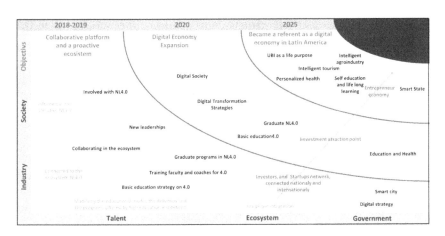

Fig. 4.2 NL 4.0 roadmap. Source: Authors based on NL government strategic plan, 2021. (Source: Authors' creation, 2022)

Gordon Institute of Business Science, an institution based in Johannesburg South Africa. In its 2019 report, GIBS presents how, in cooperation with Harvard Business School, they were able to develop the necessary managerial, innovative, and digital skills of the executives of different sub-Saharan countries, enabling them to enhance their productivity and benefits for their employees.

"GIBS has partnered with Harvard Business School (HBS) for the last five years to deliver the Senior Executive Programme Africa. Commencing in 2016 in Cape Town, the programme was run in Rwanda, Ghana and Mauritius. In 2020.21, the programme thus far has been run online, with a module planned at the HBS campus in Boston, Massachusetts, for the first time later in 2021. The programme is taught by faculty from HBS and from GIBS. The programme comprises senior executive participants from companies and organizations across Sub-Saharan Africa (SSA). With up to 60 executives attending the programme annually, GIBS, together with HBS, have built a strong executive development brand in SSA, attracting participants from South Africa, Nigeria, Zimbabwe, Zambia, Malawi, Ghana, Mozambique, Mauritius and other countries. The programme focuses on equipping executives with strategy skills, deep leadership competencies and innovative mindsets to help their organizations thrive on the continent" (GIBS, 2021).

Both examples demonstrate how a strong collaboration between higher education institutions, governments, and firms may help to diminish the digital gap and transform societies by the inclusion of less-educated sectors in the technological economy. Thus, if we need to see the importance of partnership in developing digital capabilities within society, we can see it as presented in the next Fig. 4.3:

4.5   How Can Human Dignity Be Promoted in the Context of Digital Transformation?

The second problem that may arise from the increasing development of the digital economy is the potential negative impact for people when a firm decides to engage in the digital transformation boom.

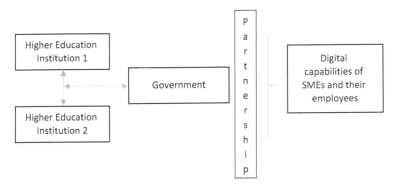

Fig. 4.3 Principle 5 partnership as a means for developing digital capabilities. (Source: Authors' creation, 2022)

In this sense, the increase in the use of technology in companies could lead to a growing wave of layoffs caused by the replacement of people by technological tools or systems. This situation could exacerbate the development gap between individuals and societies because it condemns less technologically skilled workers to unemployment or not to well-paid jobs. We must consider that, according to Dengler and Matthes (2018), most of the current jobs are susceptible to automation in the next 10 years. However, according to the authors, since the range of automation does not include specific tasks, they consider that only 15% of the German working population may be affected by this phenomenon. In a similar idea, Mönnig et al. (2019) state that *"the increasing demand of high-skilled employees is reflected in an increase in wage inequality. However, the relatively low impact of digitalization on low-skilled employees prevents a stronger increase in wage inequality."* Despite this optimistic analysis, we need to consider that these studies were conducted in some highly developed countries, which may affect the final conclusions.

For instance, Hanna (2018) considers that the state plays a fundamental role in the digital economy because it is the main actor that can contribute to reducing digital illiteracy among society. However, considering this, and if educating the population in technological skills may require a considerable amount of time, what can firms do when they face the dilemma of substituting the labor force for automation processes?

Under this idea, firms may develop inclusion strategies for collaborators lacking tech skills, and at the same time, firms may consider possible employee externalities and their solutions in the design of their digital business models (Kirchschlaeger, 2019). Moreover, preparing the unskilled population in digital capabilities is a mandatory request for firms if we want to reduce the inequality gap around the globe (Zhang & Hon, 2020). In addition to the inequality problem, other ethical inquires arise from the analysis of the individual and social implications due to the usage of individual data in different business processes. For example, according to Zhang and Hon (2020), a large survey across the world demonstrates people's concerns about the usage of their own personal and private data by firms such as Microsoft and other technological giants.

Under the same idea, North (2002) suggested that legal institutions must be developed at the same time as technological advances to protect individuals and their private information from possible abuses of large corporations. Data security and access to private data have become profound ethical problems for the marketing field since companies find the valuable usage of customer information for designing products and advertising campaigns (Işıkay, 2021).

Under these ideas, *Principle 1: Purpose* may help in the task of building a strong sense of ethical reflection and responsible spirit in today's and future executives. Developing an ethical sense in company managers would facilitate the establishment of protocols for the reflection and prevention of negative impacts on stakeholders when they decide to deepen their digital transformation strategies. Clerx (2020), in his doctoral dissertation, proposes four tools that may help firms and their executives make ethical decisions while assuming a digital strategy:

1. Being guided by a mission or ethical code.
2. Openness in talking ethical concerns.
3. Training.
4. Transparency in all decisions.

These four simple actions give ethical direction to the firm's executives when the firm engages in a digital transformation process. Under the same idea, developing an ethical framework for firms will help them

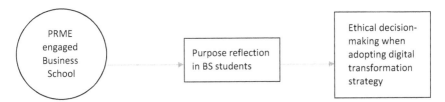

Fig. 4.4 Principle 1 purpose as a driven for solving the ethical implications of digital transformation. (Source: Authors' creation, 2022)

avoid externalities and damage to their stakeholders regarding the firm's digital strategy (Guryanova et al., 2020). Moreover, Waddock et al. (2010) consider that when schools teach their students about their purpose, these later executives become more reflexive in their decision-making process because they are able to understand the misuse of their skills and how they can harm the people.

Abdelgaffar (2021) says that business schools engaged with PRME principles are developing abilities in their students to address the different challenges from VUCA contexts and digital transformation booms. Thus, evidence suggests that executives with a strong sense of purpose may react more ethically when implementing digital transforming initiatives in their companies (Fig. 4.4).

4.6 Some Lessons from PRME to Business Schools That Are Becoming Involved in the Digital Transformation Wave

There are some learned lessons from what business schools are doing regarding the inclusion of sustainable practices while a firm adopts a digital transformation strategy. We have already mentioned the examples of UDEM and Tec de Monterrey and their participation in the government's initiative called Nuevo León 4.0. We also commented how these two universities, well recognized in their region, helped some SMEs develop digital skills to allow them to be a part of the digital transformation boom in different industries. We also commented how, in partnership with Harvard Business School, The Gordon Institutes of Business

Science has developed the necessary skills in sub-Saharan executives to address the challenges of digital transformation in their companies.

Considering the importance of *Principle 1. Purpose*, Xi'an Jiaotong-Liverpool University states that now more than ever, individuals emerge that are able to bridge global divides and work together across borders to solve issues that threaten mankind as a whole (University, 2019). There are other schools, such as the Universidad de Los Andes in Colombia, which is very well known in Latin America for its extensive collaborative network with different organizations. In this strategy, Los Andes is capable of positively impacting firms and organizations seeking to enlarge digital inclusion for those with no digital capabilities. In another example, CETYS, a regional but prestigious school in Northwestern Mexico, has developed a strong collaboration with the many international industrial firms settled in Baja California.

This collaborative perspective has led CETYS to develop different digital literacy programs designed to reduce the technological gaps among the workers who want to get a job in the different firms located in the region. They have also developed some research paths to understand how digital illiteracy may negatively impact the wellbeing of the people in the region. It is observable in both cases, how *Principle 5; Partnership* has been a guidance for the school when they want to engage the community in the pursue of a common goal such as digital literacy.

4.7   Conclusions

PRME principles may be a helpful tool in the arduous task of diminishing the negative impacts of digital transformation in our society. For example, as mentioned in this chapter, *Principle 1, Purpose* and *Principle 5, and Partnership* may be powerful tools for higher education institutions to become enhancers of digital inclusion and guards of people's dignity. The next graphical model shows us in which way, these two principles may help in the pursuit of a more inclusive digital society (Fig. 4.5).

Purpose enhances the capacity of the alumnae of doing a profound reflection on the potential impacts of whatever strategy they are

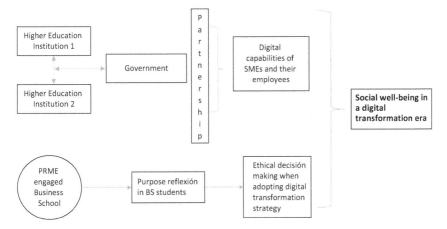

Fig. 4.5 Partnership and purpose as well-being generation in a digital transformation era. (Source: Authors' creation, 2022)

proposing to the company and its stakeholders. The six Principles of PRME offer a framework for transforming business and management education. The SDGs are an opportunity to go beyond. To achieve the goals by 2030, PRME is calling on all business- and management-related higher education institutions to fully embrace the SDGs in teaching, research, and thought leadership. This also includes the ability to consider the new digital economy and its implications on the SDGs, for example, as mentioned before, the impacts on people's dignity and inclusion as a driver for equitable opportunities in the digital era.

References

Abdelgaffar, H. A. (2021). A critical investigation of PRME integration practices of the third cycle champion group. *The International Journal of Management Education, 19*(1), 100457.

Akaev, A. A., Rudskoy, A. I., & Devezas, T. (2021). Technological substitution of jobs in the digital economy and shift in labor demand toward advanced qualifications. In *The economics of digital transformation* (pp. 85–103). Springer.

Clerx, A. (2020). The role of ethics in digital transformation. Doctoral dissertation, University of Groningen. Faculty of Economics and Business.

Cooper, M. N. (2002). Inequality in the digital society: Why the digital divide deserves all the attention it gets. *Cardozo Arts & Ent. LJ, 20*, 73.

Dengler, K., & Matthes, B. (2018). The impacts of digital transformation on the labor market: Substitution potentials of occupations in Germany. *Technological Forecasting and Social Change, 137*, 304–316.

DiMaggio, P., Hargittai, E., Celeste, C., & Shafer, S. (2004). From unequal access to differentiated use: A literature review and agenda for research on digital inequality. *Social Inequality, 1*, 355–400.

GIBS. (2021). *UN principles for responsible management education*. UN PRME.

Gong, C., & Ribiere, V. (2021). Developing a unified definition of digital transformation. *Technovation, 102*, 102217.

Guryanova, A. V., Smotrova, I. V., Makhovikov, A. E., & Koychubaev, A. S. (2020). Socioethical problems of the digital economy: Challenges and risks. In *Digital transformation of the economy: Challenges, trends and new opportunities* (pp. 96–102). Springer.

Hanna, N. (2018). A role for the state in the digital age. *Journal of Innovation and Entrepreneurship, 7*(1), 1–16.

Işıkay, T. (2021). *Marketing ethics: Digital transformation and privacy ethics. In multidisciplinary approaches to ethics in the digital era* (pp. 129–146). IGI Global.

Kane, G. (2019). The technology fallacy: People are the real key to digital transformation. *Research-Technology Management, 62*(6), 44–49.

Kirchschlaeger, P. G. (2019). Digital transformation of society and economy-ethical considerations from a human rights perspective. *International Journal of Human Rights and Constitutional Studies, 6*(4), 301–321.

Kirchschlaeger, P. G. (2021). Digital transformation and ethics.

Matt, C., Hess, T., & Benlian, A. (2015). Digital transformation strategies. *Business & Information Systems Engineering, 57*(5), 339–343.

Mönnig, A., Maier, T., & Zika, G. (2019). Economy 4.0–digitalisation and its effect on wage inequality. *Jahrbücher Für Nationalökonomie Und Statistik, 239*(3), 363–398.

North, D. C. (2002). Institutions and economic growth: A historical introduction. In *International political economy* (pp. 57–69). Routledge.

Qureshi, Z. (2020). Tackling the inequality pandemic: Is there a cure? Reimagining the global economy: Building back better in, 71.

Schallmo, D. R., & Williams, C. A. (2018). History of digital transformation. In *Digital transformation now!* (pp. 3–8). Springer.

Tang, D. (2021). What is digital transformation? *EDPACS, 64*(1), 9–13.

University, X. J.-L. (2019). *PRME sharing information process*. PRME.

Waddock, S., Rasche, A., Werhane, P. H., & Unruh, G. (2010). *The principles for responsible management education. Toward assessing business ethics education* (pp. 13–28).

Zhang, J., & Hon, H. W. (2020). Towards responsible digital transformation. *California Management Review, 62*(3).

5

Responsible Management Education in the Digital Age: An Experiment with Liberal Art and Science Education in China

Liang Yu

5.1 Introduction

The phrase *Fourth Industrial Revolution* was introduced by Professor Klaus Schwab, Founder and Executive Chairman of the World Economic Forum in 2015. Building on the Third Industrial Revolution, Schwab argues that the boundaries between physical, digital, and biological domains will be blurred by combining technologies in the Fourth Industrial Revolution (Schwab, 2016). Furthermore, the nonlinear nature of technologies (such as artificial intelligence, the Internet of Things, robotics, blockchain, and quantum computing) will create exponential changes in our society during this revolution. In addition to

L. Yu (✉)
Duke Kunshan University, Kunshan, China
e-mail: liang.yu@duke.edu

© The Author(s), under exclusive license to Springer Nature Switzerland AG 2023
C. Hauser, W. Amann (eds.), *The Future of Responsible Management Education*,
Humanism in Business Series, https://doi.org/10.1007/978-3-031-15632-8_5

technology development, COVID-19 has also accelerated the worldwide process of digital transformation and "pushed companies over the technologies tipping point – and transformed business forever" (McKinsey 2020b). Thus, the forthcoming digital transformation will revolutionize how business and government work and radically change the way people consume, live, and work. Thus, the impact of such transformation on our society will not just be the extension of the previous industrial revolutions; it will be more volatile, much more significant in scope, and much faster in speed (Schwab, 2016).

5.2   The Alignment Problem

While there are apparent reasons how digital technologies such as AI will benefit the business, government, and consumers, the exponential transformation has created new challenges for future leaders in making responsible decisions. One of the critical challenges is "the alignment problem," which describes the disconnection between human intention and results generated by digital technologies. As the mathematician Norbert Wiener highlighted in 1960, "We had better be quite sure that the purpose put into the machine is the purpose which we truly desire" (Wiener, 1960). A biased training dataset can cause "the alignment problem." A classic example would be the case of a web developer Jacky Alciné, an African American, who was labeled in 2015 as "gorilla" by a "racist" Google Photo together with one of his friends, also an African American (BBC, 2015). The biased training dataset causes such a failure: some demographic groups are not well represented in the training database, and conditions such as lighting, resolution, and other essential factors affect the face recognition result (Labeled Faces in the Wild, 2019). The second reason for the alignment problem can come from the biased algorithm. One flagship example is COMPAS (which stands for Correctional Offender Management Profiling for Alternative Sanctions), a tool that judges and parole officers are increasingly using to assess a criminal defendant's likelihood of becoming a recidivist. After using COMPAS for many years by some US courts, researchers eventually found the tool severely biased toward African American defendants, who are more likely to be incorrectly judged to be at a higher risk of recidivism (Jeff Larson, 2016). There is a complicated analysis involved in assessing situations such as this. However, Brian Christian, the author of the *Alignment Program*, concluded that it is impossible to consider a set of equally desirable criteria for any given model (Christian, 2020). Hence, the seemingly "neutral and objective" algorithm cannot give humans a fair result.

The "racist Google Photo" and flawed COMPAS tool are just one of the millions of alignment problems that digital technologies have created. However, it would be unfair for a human to attribute such problems to the digital transformation revolution. Some problems, such as human bias and prejudice, have already existed without any correlation to digital technologies. For example, more articles are written about professional haircuts using pictures of white men. Hence, the Google Picture search with "professional haircut" will rarely show examples from females or people of color (Satell & Abdel-Magied, 2020). At the same time, other problems exist because of the limitations of the technology. For example, even if a driverless car can be reliable in millions of miles tests in Phoenix, it does not mean it will continue to function well during a monsoon in Bombay (Marcus & Davis, 2019). Thus, although, in a sense, some might see an epic shift for ethical challenges in the age of digital transformation, we might also see the same old human ethical challenges branded in the name of new digital technologies. The question then left for us to answer, even if digital technologies might not have created these alignment problems, what are the unique challenges for responsible decision-making during the fourth industrial revolution? According to Schwab, the impact of responsible decisions during the Fourth Industrial Revolution will be much larger in scale and much more severe in consequences (Schwab, 2016). Cathy O'Neil, a mathematician and the author of *Weapons of Math Destruction*, also echoes this viewpoint that the digital revolution could reinforce racism and amplify inequality (O'Neil, 2017).

5.3   Implications for Future Leaders and Their Learning: Three Essential Capabilities

If digital transformation during the Fourth Industrial Revolution can affect responsible decision-making in scale and velocity, what skills or capability do future leaders need to address alignment problems? Based on our observation and empirical experiences from leadership consulting and executive education perspectives in many industries and business institutions, the ability to align digital and business transformation with values and purposes will matter even more in the digital future. There are three essential capabilities future leaders and organizations need to have to drive successful digital transformation (see Fig. 5.1) with this alignment.

First, organizations will need to be experts with various types of digital technology and their applications in the company or industry context. At the same time, organizations also need to understand the limitations of these technologies to enhance human–machine collaboration (see Fig. 5.2) to "create circles to continuously improve process performance"

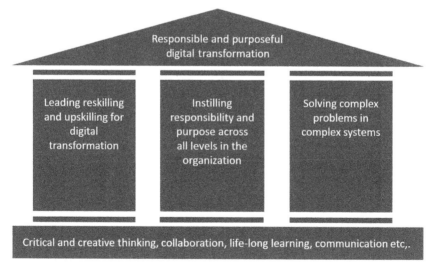

Fig. 5.1 Key leadership capabilities for responsible leadership for digital transformation. *Note*: The figure demonstrates the capabilities that effective leaders need to have to drive responsible digital transformation

Human and machine hybrid activities					
Humans complement machines			AI gives humans superpowers		
TRAIN	EXPLAIN	SUSTAIN	AMPLIFY	INTERACT	EMBODY
Re-humanizing time			Intelligent interrogation		
Responsible normalizing			Bot-based empowerment		
Judgement integration			Holistic melding		
Reciprocal apprenticing					
Relentless reimagining					

Fig. 5.2 Fusion skills for the missing middle in digital age. *Note*: These eight fusion skills demonstrate the skills that humans need to have to effectively collaborate with machines to create new values (Dougherty & Wilson, 2018)

(Dougherty & Wilson, 2018). With that in mind, leaders in various industries need to understand their skill gaps and strategically think about closing those gaps (McKinsey, 2020a). In addition to providing up-to-date skills to their employees, leaders also need to behave differently and create a psychologically safe environment where employees will be emotionally supported and productively challenged (McKinsey Quarterly, 2019). The workforce with the right level of skillset will be able to address the alignment problems. They can conduct great engineering practice of various technologies but can also understand the limitations of these technologies and view the output with critical perspectives. They can automate tedious and repetitive work but are smart enough to sense where how, and when to bring human judgment back into the decision loop. Over time, they can develop a reciprocal apprenticing relationship with technology where humans and machines work together to enhance their capability to create entirely new processes and business models (Dougherty & Wilson, 2018).

Second, effective leaders will instill a sense of purpose and responsibility across and even beyond organizations. These leaders understand that a purposeful and value-based vision has become a determinant of how organizations perform in the digital age (Palsule & Chavez, 2020). It would help organizations retain their best talent, improve their employee engagement, navigate uncertainties and create a sense of stability amidst digital disruptions as a north star (McKinsey Agile Tribe, 2018). In addition to defining the purpose of an organization, leaders need to build systems, incentives, and corporate culture to support that purpose and value-based vision, which will guide teams and employees at every level to develop digital solutions and make decisions amidst all uncertainties. With the organization's purpose in mind, engineers can imbed legal and ethical requirements into their digital solutions, adopt adequate measures to manage and mitigate the risks, ensure robust engineering practice, and promote trustworthy digital products and services.

Third, effective leaders need to understand complex systems and solve complex problems to drive responsible digital transformation. Even though digital technologies can create exponential changes in our society, the Fourth Industrial Revolution would not be successful if we could not solve the perplexing problems, ranging from pandemics, global warming, poverty, to name a few. Most of these problems could not be explained by superficial cause-and-effect relationships and require a deep understanding of different domains of disciplinary areas. Consider the example of making autonomous vehicles: multidisciplinary expertise, such as vehicle power systems, global positioning systems, and communications systems, computer vision and visualization, future mobility policy, human–machine interaction, data security, and privacy, will all be required to develop the solution. Autonomous vehicles are a highly complicated problem. However, future leaders will need to understand the complex domain of knowledge, draw knowledge from different fields and create a solution by thinking across boundaries. During the process, it will be inevitable for leaders to inspire and collaborate with experts with different expertise and to anticipate the fundamental tension between various requirements and principles.

5.4   Complementary Skills

Of course, other fundamental "human" skills, such as critical and creative thinking, collaboration, lifelong learning, emotional and cultural intelligence, persuasion, and so on, are critically important and will likely increase their values as our world keeps digitizing (World Economic Forum, 2018). In addition, some personal qualities or noncognitive skills, such as grit, persistence, resilience, and growth mindset, are also essential for success in the digital age. These fundamental skills and

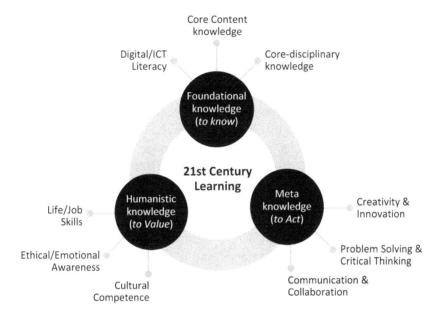

Fig. 5.3 Synthesis of 15 different twenty-first-century leaning frameworks into one visual image. *Note:* This is a study done by scholars at Michigan State University, where the researchers have synthetized 15 mainstream frameworks on twenty-first-century learning to identify common recommendations and elements into one (Kereluik et al., 2013)

personal qualities are also referred to in a comprehensive study on "the most worth knowledge in 21st Century" (Kereluik et al., 2013) conducted by scholars at Michigan State University (see Fig. 5.3). The only way humans can compete with machines is not to become better than what machines can do but to become better at what machines cannot do and responsibly guide the machine to a responsible and sustainable future. In summary, being a responsible human and leader will matter even more under the Fourth Industrial Revolution than in previous decades.

The old world of jobs has been automated at a cutting-neck speed. At the same time, new jobs are created but are challenging to fill because of a lack of skills. According to research conducted by Toyota Motor, more than 2.4 million STEM (Science, Technology, Engineering, and Math) jobs were left vacant in the United States in 2018. However, only 568,000 students in STEM disciplines graduated 2 years before. The lack of

STEM talent may seem to create a massive crisis for the labor force (Kumar, 2019), and universities around the world have adjusted their curriculum to ensure that their students can "survive" the digital workplace.

It seems natural that higher education institutions should help to resolve the skill or knowledge gap in the digital age. However, we need to be careful in truly understanding the skills and knowledge gap. People may narrowly assume that only STEM knowledge is the "gap" needed to perform STEM work. It is not. As mentioned in the above paragraphs, unique "human" skills and leadership skills are all needed to solve particular problems. Some scholars call these knowledge and skills the "most worthwhile knowledge," and Herbert Spencer, an English philosopher, argued over 100 years ago that the mission of education is to provide the most worth knowledge—knowledge, and skills that are most valuable for success in life (Spencer, 1911).

5.5   The Duke Kunshan University as a Case in Point

Duke Kunshan University is trying to answer the unique responsible management challenges in the digital age by reinventing liberal arts & science education in China. The university is a joint-venture partnership university between Duke University in the United States and Wuhan University in China. The partnership is built on Duke University's tradition of "willing repeatedly and fundamentally to reinvent itself" (Brodhead, 2018) and strategy to "Strengthen Duke's capacity to address global challenges" (Duke University, 2017). The partnership is also built on China's desire to enhance higher education by integrating the best higher education models into its current system (Brodhead, 2018). Because of the collaborative motivation on both sides, the partnership has created excellent conditions for innovation in liberal arts & science education. There could be numerous debates around the definition and connotation of "liberal arts & sciences education." However, we could generally agree that liberal arts & sciences education is a traditional concept that originated from the US higher education context. Many of its attributes are deeply rooted in Chinese literary and philosophical traditions dates back to Confucian times (Pickus & Godwin, Liberal Arts & Sciences Innovation in China: Six Recommendations to Shape the Future, 2017). After over half a century of development since the founding of the People's Republic of China in 1949, Chinese universities have made tremendous strides in developing their higher education institutions. However, significant focus is placed on specialization and STEM-related disciplines due to the 3rd Industrial Revolution's dependence on the specialization of labor and China's pursuit to catch up in science and technology.

As China is transforming to an innovation-based economy after entering the new millennium, China will need to "encourage leading universities to set up campuses in China jointly with domestic universities and impart modern governance standard, teaching method, and research" (World Bank, 2013). Duke Kunshan University was founded in 2013 during this crucial historical context. In 2013, China and the United States were already the world's two most significant economics that hold the "most important bilateral relationship of the 21st century," as Obama put it; the two countries are also the most advanced in the world in terms of digital technology. Without the strong collaboration between the United States and China, any of the world's most significant challenges, such as digital transformation, climate change, and pandemics, would not be possible to solve. Duke Kunshan is uniquely positioned at the right time to bring the best of the educational traditions and innovations both in the United States and China to bring a renaissance to liberal arts & science education for the digital future.

At Duke Kunshan University, the curriculum does not rely on traditional majors housed in departments, such as what Duke University is doing with its undergraduate program (Duke Kunshan University, 2021). However, it is built by enabling students to understand and solve the most crucial issues that human beings face. The faculty structured the curriculum to reflect critical areas of development during the students' learning journey at Duke Kunshan University (see Fig. 5.4). There are four critical areas to ensure that higher education institutions such as Duke Kunshan can prepare students to solve complex problems in the future. First, students need to understand the complex nature of future challenges through disciplinary and interdisciplinary lenses. Disciplinary knowledge is still needed to help solve some of the critical issues. However,

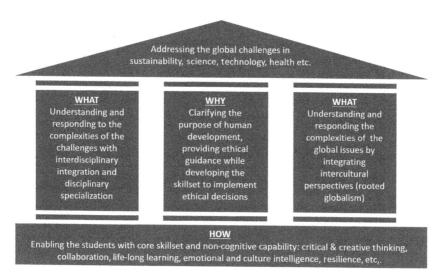

Fig. 5.4 Problem-based curriculum from Duke Kunshan University and critical areas for development for undergraduate students

some of the grand challenges human beings face, such as climate change, artificial intelligence adoption, or COVID-19 pandemic, truly require an understanding of the perspectives from different disciplines, which are closely interconnected. A particular perspective or method from one disciplinary area might be perfectly correct when standing alone within disciplinary boundaries. However, it will create conflict when mingling with another perspective for a different disciplinary area. Another lens students need to learn is the intercultural lens. In a profoundly global and connected world, cultural differences in technological, commercial, historical, political, and other areas could create major global misunderstandings and misalignment challenges. Understanding the "what" and these cultural differences in various areas would be a prerequisite to addressing intercultural challenges. Students also need to know "how" to conduct effective intercultural communication, and this component is also included in the curriculum design. The third lens answers the fundamental ethical question: why do we want to solve this problem? Unlike the previous two critical areas, this area develops the student's capability of ethical reasoning and decision-making. As mentioned in the previous paragraphs, value and purpose provide the orientation and stability at a time of dramatic changes and are perhaps one of the most critical determinants for organizational success—the last critical area addresses "how" students can solve future challenges. Critical skillsets or noncognitive capability include but are not limited to critical and creative thinking, collaboration, lifelong learning, emotional and cultural intelligence, and resilience, and these components are deeply embedded in the curriculum design.

With an understanding of what to teach with the undergraduate curriculum, Duke Kunshan structures the curriculum on those critical areas to develop. Essentially, the curriculum is built on interdisciplinary and disciplinary components in and across three thematic areas: (1) natural and applied sciences, (2) social sciences, and (3) arts and humanities (Duke Kunshan University, 2021). The core components of the curriculum involve common core courses, language courses, majors, electives, and experiential learning opportunities (see Fig. 5.5) and their requirements for completion (see Figs. 5.6 and 5.7). In addition, the university has adopted seven animating principles (see Fig. 5.8) that guide the design and implementation of the undergraduate curriculum. Table 5.1 reflects how teaching in different areas is fully embedded in the Duke Kunshan undergraduate curriculum.

The founding partners of the university started the university with the courage to fundamentally recreate liberal arts & science education. Duke University in the United States and Wuhan University in China are among the top 10 universities in their respective countries. Duke University has enjoyed a worldwide reputation in liberal arts and science education for undergraduates, and Wuhan University is one of the most prestigious and selective universities in China. However, these two universities have decided to fundamentally reinvent themselves (Brodhead, 2018) with the Duke Kunshan partnership and hope to achieve what Duke University could not succeed in the United States and what Wuhan University could not achieve in China. There are three significant ways that Duke Kunshan has experimented with creating the innovation, and these innovations carry distinct features from a digital-ready organization such as Google and Amazon.

- **Common Core courses** required of all students focus on big questions and critical challenges. Students take one per year for three years.
- **Language courses** required in English, Chinese or potentially a thrid language.
- **Majors that have interdisciplinary and disciplinary components**, with the former serving as the entry point and primary definition of a students' academic community and the latter providing specialized training, as well as **divisional foundation courses** that prepare students for advanced study and **signature work** that focuses on a question, problem or issue and includes independent research, a senior thesis or creative production.
- **Electives** that broaden students' educational experience via simple distributional requirements and additionally enable them either to develop greater specialized knowledge or to further increase the breadth of their study.
- **Experiential learning opportunities** that align the formal curriculum with practica, internships and other hands-on offerings are required.

Fig. 5.5 The key components of Duke Kunshan University's undergraduate curriculum

- **General Education:** 3 common core courses (12 credits), 2-4 language courses (8-16 credits) depending on proficiency, 3 electives (12 credits) as distributional requirements, and one Quantitative Reasoning course (4 credits)

- **Major:** 16-19 courses (64 to 76 credits) (foundation, interdisciplinary, disciplinary, and capstone

- **Electives:** 8-13 courses (32 to 52 credits) depending on division and language proficiency, which include the three electives as distributional requirements and one Quantitative Reasoning course in General Education

- **Other requirements:** 1 non-credit mini-term course and 1 Signature Work project that includes a practice-oriented Experiential Learning component (internships, civic engagement, etc.)

Fig. 5.6 Specific requirement for the core components within the Duke Kunshan undergraduate curriculum

5.6 Lessons Learnt

First, Duke Kunshan University, like many other innovative organizations such as Apple and Tesla, abandoned yesterday and created a new model of higher education from scratch. As a newly established higher education institution, Duke Kunshan University took advantage of the unique opportunity to completely redesign the curriculum and reconfigure the traditional structure. The curriculum is designed with the purpose of innovation in interdisciplinary integration, problem-based and

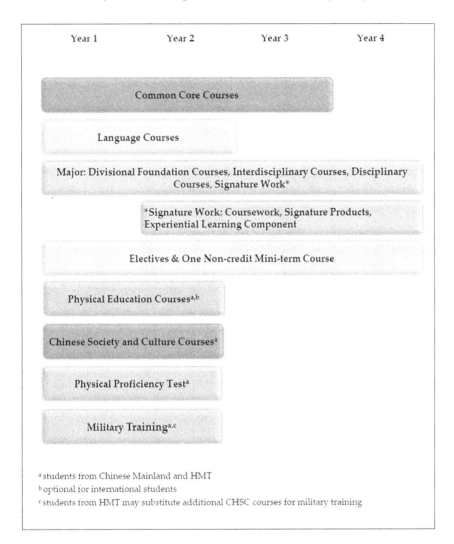

Fig. 5.7 Duke Kunshan undergraduate curriculum course distribution and graduation requirements

team-based learning, engagement with research inquiry, and local-global perspectives that will enable students worldwide to lead purposeful and productive lives (Duke Kunshan University, 2021). Without any past to depend upon, the founding members of Duke Kunshan University are

- **Rooted Globalism:** *To cultivate informed and engaged citizens who are knowledgeable about each other's histories, traditions of thought and affiliations; and skilled in navigating among local, national and global identities and commitments.*

- **Collaborative Problem-Solving:** *To instill the habits of collaboration and the ability to synthesize disparate insights in solving complex challenges.*

- **Research and Practice:** *To enhance the ability to forge links between theory and practice in the many-sided and rapidly changing world of human need.*

- **Lucid Communication:** *To develop the ability to communicate effectively, both orally and in writing, and to listen attentively to different viewpoints in coming to mature judgments.*

- **Independence and Creativity:** *To nurture free inquiry, deep reflection and a drive to ask interesting questions and find compelling answers.*

- **Wise Leadership:** *To shape thinkers and doers who possess the moral compass to guide communities and institutions toward a common good and who have the wisdom and technical competence to deal effectively with complexity.*

- **A Purposeful Life:** *To form reflective scholars who their test core beliefs, connect their course of study to big questions of meaning, and who build the capacity for lifelong learning and exploration.*

Fig. 5.8 Seven Animating principles for Duke Kunshan University's undergraduate curriculum. *Note*: These are the guiding principles for the undergraduate curriculum at Duke Kunshan University. These principles aim to "help students develop a sense of social responsibility and global citizenship as well as strong and transferrable intellectual and practical skills" (Duke Kunshan University, 2021)

able to reconfigure the traditional university structure to align with its purpose. In the areas of natural science, social science, and arts and humanities, three divisions were established to organize the faculty and the curriculum. It helps the university move away from traditional rigid structures of majors or departments, gives faculty the freedom to recreate completely new courses from multidisciplinary perspectives, and provides the students the flexibility to craft their pathways according to their intellectual interests (Pickus & Godwin, Liberal Arts & Sciences Innovation in China: Six Recommendations to Shape the Future, 2017). The structural change also dictates all the other university activities along the higher education value chain, ranging from faculty hiring, incentives and development, and cocurricular activities to academic advising and tutoring. Similar to successful case studies of the most successful digital transformation, structuring the organization and the teams to fit the purpose is critical.

Table 5.1 How teaching in different development areas is fully integrated to develop students' capability in solving complex problems

Key components	Sub-key components	WHAT Development of interdisciplinary integration and disciplinary specialization	WHY Develop ethical and purposeful leaders	WHAT Develop intercultural perspectives (rooted globalism)
General education	Interdisciplinary common core course	Global challenges in science, technology and health (year 2)	Ethics, citizenship and examined life (year 3) Giving voice to values[a] pedagogy is used in the course to improve students' capability for ethical implementation	China in the world (year 1)
Language courses	Practice the communication of interdisciplinary or disciplinary issues in English	Practice the communication of ethical issues in English	Language courses are required for English, Chinese, and potentially a third language. Faculty teach culture with language courses and constantly compare the cultural differences	Major
	Divisional foundation courses	• Prepare students for advanced study to understand fundamental challenges in the chosen divisional area • Interdisciplinary courses define student's entry point and provide students with multiple perspectives toward the same problem	• Key ethical challenges are highlighted throughout the different courses in all the majors • Specific courses, for example, "Environmental Justice," could be an interdisciplinary course for environmental science major students but could also be an elective course for computation and design major students	• Intercultural components are highlighted in the course, especially in arts & humanities and social science related courses • Faculty members encourage students to view and discuss a single idea from multiple cultural perspectives

(continued)

Divisional interdisciplinary courses	Divisional disciplinary courses	Experiential learning	Signature work	
	Philosophy, incentive, and structures **HOW**: Develop the core skillset and noncognitive capabilities 7 Animating principles, team-based learning, divisional areas of knowledge (rather than traditional majors or departments), flexible curriculum, practical experiences on each Friday, faculty hiring and development, small class teaching, academic advising, and so on			Signature work is a problem-based experiential learning opportunity that combines "the what," , "the why," and "the how" aspect of solving complex problems

[a] Giving Voice to Values (GVV) is an innovative approach to values-driven leadership development that has shifted the focus of teaching ethics from ethical reasoning to ethical implementation

Second, like many successful digital players, Duke Kunshan put the "customer experience" at the center of university operations and worked with different stakeholders in the community to cocreate the experience. The resounding strength of the Duke Kunshan undergraduate program comes from the close collaboration among multiple parties around students' experience and results. A hallmark of such collaboration is the partnership between faculty members from different disciplinary backgrounds to cocreate interdisciplinary courses. Most of the faculty members join Duke Kunshan from other universities, some with many years of teaching experience, and others may graduate from a PhD program. With the unique feature of the undergraduate curriculum, the faculty could not take the courses they teach in other universities directly to Duke Kunshan and would need to collaborate with others from different disciplinary perspectives and completely recreate the course (Rascoff & Pickus, 2018). The Duke Kunshan requirement is rarely seen in other universities, including Duke University in the United States, where interdisciplinary education is "achieved only through the narrow paths laid out for them that conveniently reinforce existing departmental architecture" (Community Editorial Board, 2021). Like many successful digital-based companies, Duke Kunshan also involves their "customers," university students, to cocreate their learning experiences on campus. Ranging from a flexible curriculum that students can customize their learning journey according to their intellectual interest in small classroom teaching and personalized academic advising, the university is creating enough spaces to personalize the students' experience at Duke Kunshan University. As Prof. Noah Pickus, the founding Dean of Curricular Affairs and Faculty Development, explained in his email about students' involvement in the whole Duke Kunshan community in fall 2018, "remember that the heart of a liberal arts education is the mind-on-mind experience, the magical moment in which faculty and students think anew about the universe. No curriculum and no course can substitute for the intensity of that experience. Invite your students into the world that you love, and they will love it too."

Third, like many innovative companies in Silicon Valley, Duke Kunshan promotes a culture of startup and continuous learning. While traditional companies may struggle with putting the right culture in place for transformation, the university was born as a startup. The culture dictates what kind of talent we attract (in this case, the type of faculty we attract, as not every faculty member is passionate about collaborating with other faculty members from a different disciplinary area), how we involve our customers (in this case, our students), and how we develop our products (in this case, our curriculum) with an iterative agile approach.

In a sense, Duke Kunshan University is a profound higher education collaboration between the United States and China. It may be too early to call such an experiment a success, but it would provide an opportunity for people to see what can be achieved in higher education to prepare students for the digital future.

References

BBC. (2015, July 1). *Google apologises for photos app's racist blunder*. Retrieved from BBC: https://www.bbc.com/news/technology-33347866.

Brodhead, R. (2018, August 15th). *Brodhead: Where Duke Kunshan University came from and why it matters*. Retrieved from Duke Today: https://today.duke.edu/2018/08/brodhead-where-duke-kunshan-university-came-and-why-it-matters.

Christian, B. (2020). *The alignment problem, machine leaning and human values*. W. W. Norton & Company.

Community Editorial Board. (2021, March 2nd). *Prioritizing the liberal arts*. Retrieved from The chronicle. https://www.dukechronicle.com/article/2021/03/prioritizing-the-liberal-arts.

Dougherty, P. R., & Wilson, H. (2018). *Human + machine: Reimagine work in the age of AI*. Harvard Business Review Press.

Duke Kunshan University. (2021, August). *Undergraduate bullet (2021–2022)*. Retrieved from Duke Kunshan University. https://undergrad.dukekunshan.edu.cn/en/undergraduate-bulletin.

Duke University. (2017, September). *Together Duke: Advancing excellence through community*. Retrieved from Duke Academic Strategic Plan. https://strategicplan.duke.edu/about/together-duke/.

Jeff Larson, S. M. (2016, May 23). *How we analyzed the COMPAS recidivism algorithm*. Retrieved from Propublic: https://www.propublica.org/article/how-we-analyzed-the-compas-recidivism-algorithm.

Kereluik, K., Misra, P., Fahnoe, C., & Terry, L. (2013). What knowledge is of most worth: Teacher knowledge for 21st century learning. *Journal of Digital Learning in Teacher Education*, 127–140.

Kumar, R. (2019, August 27th). *The liberal arts degree is alive and well—and critically important to the future of tech*. Retrieved from CNBC: https://www.cnbc.com/2019/08/27/the-critical-skill-liberal-arts-grads-provide-to-the-stem-industry.html.

Labeled Faces in the Wild. (2019). *Labeled faces in the wild*. Retrieved from Labeled Faces in the wild. http://vis-www.cs.umass.edu/lfw/index.html.

Marcus, G., & Davis, E. (2019). *Rebooting AI: Building artificial intelligence we can trust*. Vintage.

McKinsey. (2020a, February 12). *Beyond hiring: How companies are reskilling to address the talent gaps*. Retrieved from McKinsey & Company: https://www.mckinsey.com/business-functions/organization/our-insights/beyond-hiring-how-companies-are-reskilling-to-address-talent-gaps.

McKinsey. (2020b, October 5). *How COVID-19 has pushed companies over the technology tipping point—and transformed business forever*. Retrieved from McKinsey & Company. https://www.mckinsey.com/business-functions/strategy-and-corporate-finance/our-insights/how-covid-19-has-pushed-companies-over-the-technology-tipping-point-and-transformed-business-forever.

McKinsey Agile Tribe. (2018, January 22). *The 5 trademarks of agile organizations*. Retrieved from McKinsey & Company: https://www.mckinsey.com/business-functions/organization/our-insights/the-five-trademarks-of-agile-organizations.

McKinsey Quarterly. (2019, December 5). *Redefining the role of the leader in the reskilling era*. Retrieved from McKinsey: https://www.mckinsey.com/business-functions/organization/our-insights/redefining-the-role-of-the-leader-in-the-reskilling-era.

O'Neil, C. (2017). *Weapons of math destruction: How big data increases inequality and threatens democracy*. Crown Publishing Group.

Palsule, S., & Chavez, M. (2020). *Rehumanizing leadership: Putting purpose back into business*. LID Publishing.

Pickus, N., & Godwin, K. A. (2017, November). *Liberal arts & sciences innovation in China: Six recommendations to shape the future*. Retrieved from The

Boston College Center for International Higher Education. https://www.bc.edu/content/dam/files/research_sites/cihe/pubs/CIHE%20Perspective/CIHE%20Perspectives%208_10NOV2017.pdf.

Rascoff, M., & Pickus, N. (2018, October 31st). *Open source as a model for global education*. Retrieved from Inside Higher Ed: https://www.insidehighered.com/digital-learning/views/2018/10/31/spirit-open-source-educators-should-collaborate-even-rivals.

Satell, G., & Abdel-Magied, Y. (2020, October 20). *AI fairness isn't just an ethical issue*. Retrieved from Harvard Business Review: https://hbr.org/2020/10/ai-fairness-isnt-just-an-ethical-issue.

Schwab, K. (2016, January 14). *The fourth industrial revolution: What it means, how to respond*. Retrieved from World Economic Forum: https://www.weforum.org/agenda/2016/01/the-fourth-industrial-revolution-what-it-means-and-how-to-respond/.

Spencer, H. (1911). What knowledge is of most worth. In *Essays on education and kindred subjects*. Dent/Aldine Press.

Wiener, N. (1960). Some moral and technical consequences of automation. *Science*, 1355–1358.

World Bank. (2013). *China 2030: building a modern, harmonious, and creative society.* : World Bank Group.

World Economic Forum. (2018, September 17). *The future of jobs report 2018*. Retrieved from World Economic Forum: https://www.weforum.org/reports/the-future-of-jobs-report-2018.

6

Responsible Management Through Responsible Education: The Central Role of Higher-Education Lecturers

Jorge Gomes and Tania Marques

6.1 Introduction

The ambition underlying the Principles for Responsible Management Education (PRME) is not trivial. Stating that "PRME engages business and management schools to ensure they provide future leaders with the skills needed to balance economic and sustainability goals" (https://www. unprme.org/about) is an exceptional objective for several reasons. First, it will be a colossal task to persuade the existing 16,000 business and management programs all over the world to adhere to the PRME. Second, business and management schools are historically designed to perpetuate a particular economic model, in which words such as profit, growth, and

J. Gomes (✉)
ADVANCE/Lisbon School of Economics and Management, University of Lisbon, Lisbon, Portugal
e-mail: jorgegomes@iseg.ulisboa.pt

T. Marques
CARME – Centre of Applied Research in Management and Economics, School of Technology and Management, Polytechnic of Leiria, Leiria, Portugal

© The Author(s), under exclusive license to Springer Nature Switzerland AG 2023
C. Hauser, W. Amann (eds.), *The Future of Responsible Management Education*,
Humanism in Business Series, https://doi.org/10.1007/978-3-031-15632-8_6

competition are far more culturally entrenched than sustainability, responsibility, and cooperation. Third, even if change starts at an institutional level, the challenge of cascading down change to the individual level will be extraordinary. Fourth, the rapid and recent evolution of digital and remote learning has brought new issues into play, such as the roles of trust and influence in a virtual education environment.

This chapter addresses the pivotal role of educators and university lecturers in PRME's ambition. The text contends that educators and university lecturers are the key linchpins in a process that requires institutional, structural, cultural, and individual change. In fact, instructors at other educational levels are equally vital, but the specific duties and activities of HE scholars, as well as their boundary spanning position—right between academic and professional life—endow them with a central role in the change movement toward a more responsible economy, culture, and society.

This chapter first elaborates on the traditional roles and responsibilities of HE academics, after which learning and teaching are considered, including traditional and modern education approaches. Performance in teaching is the subject for the third section, and section four addresses responsible management and responsible leadership, which are key theoretical pillars for implementing PRME and other emerging education movements. The last section addresses the new roles of HE lecturers in teaching responsible management and developing responsible leaders.

6.2   Roles and Responsibilities of HE Lecturers

The terms "lecturer," "professor," "instructor," and "teacher" are often used interchangeably in English; however, they refer to different subjects. "Teacher" describes teaching in schools, whereas lecturers, instructors, and professors work in universities. Lecturers deliver lessons, and instructors assist skill development; both terms apply to those teaching at the university level that do not hold a PhD degree. Professor describes both a position and a range of roles, from teaching to researching. Other terms such as "tutor," "trainer," "faculty member," "scholar," "academic," and "university professor" add complexity and variety to the topic. In other languages and countries, such terms might refer to different things. For example, in Portugal, "teacher" and "professor" have one single translation: "professor." Thus, a professor is someone who is teaching either at primary or secondary school or at universities. In all cases, the lecturer is someone who is the fundamental production asset in education institutions, as he or she is in close contact with the main stakeholder: the student. Without educators, education does not exist. The current chapter targets teaching and performing other activities at the university level, and the term HE lecturer is used to include most of the aforementioned concepts.

Here is what a British job-seeking website defines as being an HE lecturer (https://www.prospects.ac.uk/job-profiles/higher-education-lecturer): "Higher education (HE) lecturers teach academic or vocational subjects to undergraduate and postgraduate students aged 18 and over." This position requires the following tasks: teaching (using various methods, from lectures to tutorials and e-learning), researching (that contributes to department or institution and that can be published), administrative (such as student admissions and planning induction programs), and coordinating and managing (such as taking on the role of head of department). Among the many responsibilities, HE lecturers can supervise undergraduate projects, masters or PhD dissertations, prepare bids to attract funding, participate in conferences and seminars, establish collaborations with other institutions, and participate in staff training activities.

Although variations exist across countries and, within the same country, across HE institutions, the above describes the four main roles and responsibilities of educators at the university level: teaching, researching, managing, and administering. A fifth set of activities often develops in business schools: that of consultant, which requires preparing and delivering projects aimed at improving or changing individuals or organizations external to the HR institution. This role is relevant to developing a practical mindset in academic staff (see, e.g., Gomes et al., 2005).

The combination of these components varies according to various individual and organizational factors (e.g., seniority, scientific area), but in general, they will be part of a career as an educator in HE institutions.

The variety of tasks and activities involved in each means that an HE lecturer is performing four/five jobs in one. Teaching, for instance, requires distinct skills and training than researching and publishing. The literature provides a few guidelines regarding the competencies of HE lecturers, with considerably more information found, for example, on university websites.

Concerning the first type of source, Blašková et al. (2014) collected questionnaire data from nearly 700 students in Slovakia, which led the authors to define seven competencies for university teachers (their term): professional, educational, motivational, communicational, personal, science & research, and publication.

Moving on now to examples from websites, Walden University (based in Washington) defines faculty development based on eight competencies: engagement, pedagogy, feedback, assessment, ethics & values, international, scholarship & service, and social change.

In the specific case of business schools, accreditation standards provide a framework for both organizational and individual work. AACSB Accreditation, for instance, recommends that accredited schools work out behaviors, values, attitudes, and decisions, along the following principles and expectations (AACSB Accredited, 2020): ethics and integrity, societal impact, mission-driven focus, peer review, continuous improvement, collegiality, agility, global mindset, and diversity and inclusion. Nevertheless, according to the same document, several standards depend directly or indirectly on individual educators: teaching effectiveness and impact, impact of scholarship, and engagement and societal impact.

In sum, an HE lecturer in business schools is someone who is expected to liaise with multiple internal and external stakeholders (e.g., from students to other researchers, from HE peers to other professional groups, from societal to private agents), pursues multiple and often opposite goals (e.g., from class delivery to long-term publication aims, from student development to student assessment), and is required to deliver various outcomes (e.g., publications, students' learning and development, funding). At the same time, due to the fast-evolving nature of science, HE lecturers ought to be constantly updating their knowledge and expertise.

In recent years, HE lecturers have experienced additional tasks and obligations, which are the result of important global changes, such as internationalization (e.g., running international master programs), digitalization (e.g., teaching via online platforms), accreditation and rankings (e.g., engaging in certification processes), and the UN SDGs (e.g., setting up projects with external communities or entities in relation to specific SDGs).

Despite this great variety of traditional and new tasks, HE professionals' main activity is still to teach and develop students. For this, they use several methods and techniques, which are addressed in the following section. The focus is again on HE lecturers in business schools.

6.3 Teaching: Delivery Methods and Techniques

The usage of methods and techniques to deliver content depends on the scientific field and, within the same field, on the subject being taught. In management sciences, subjects range from purely technical to soft-skill development and training, but variety—and performance—is compounded by other factors, such as the size of student groups, lecturer style and experience, and university history and culture, among others.

There is no shortage of sources describing the characteristics, advantages, and drawbacks of a plethora of delivery methods and techniques at the HE level in business and management. Readers interested in learning more about teaching methods in business and management can use the following keywords in search engines: handbook, business, management, teaching, education, and guide. Should a specific search be sought, then the interested reader can add keywords such as marketing, strategic management, or people management, for example. The publisher editing the current book has several texts that focus on methods and techniques in teaching various management areas. See, for example, Gonzalez-Perez et al. (2019) and Iñiguez and Lorange (2021).

Among the many examples from practice, the one presented here is based on the information shown on the University of Manchester's website. The information outlines the main methods and materials used in teaching undergraduates, and it targets prospective students. However, it was chosen because it exemplifies typical information shown in many other cases that address HE methods and techniques at other education levels, including MBA and executive courses. When appropriate, the authors add their comments or examples from their own experience. The first method on the University of Manchester's website is regular lectures. These are normally used to deliver technical content, theories and factual data to large groups of students. A lecture is a presentation or demonstration of a topic, usually centered on the speaker, with limited participation from students.

Next in the university's site are seminars and tutorials, which target smaller groups of students, are less informal, allow closer contacts between lecturers and students, address open discussions around specific topics and are much more centered on students. Active learning is likely to be an important output of using seminars and tutorials. The third item is independent study, taken as autonomous work performed by students to accomplish diverse course work and activities, as well as time allocated to studying. Independent work is in many cases what allows the student to prepare individual or group assignments.

Learning by doing is an important method in many courses, especially those involving technical competence, but is also relevant in training and developing soft skills. Learning by doing happens in laboratories or through practical learning, such as case studies and internship periods in companies. Another method exposed on the website is fieldwork or field trips. These are increasingly used by many universities as a way of putting theoretical knowledge into practice. One of the authors of the current chapter was recently asked to organize a field trip to MBA students for a Finish university interested in learning how conventional industries are making the transition to the digital economy. The outcome was a three-day visit to Portuguese wine and olive oil producers, who introduced the latest digital technologies into two highly mature and traditional markets.

The sixth method is problem-based/enquiry-based learning, and it requires groups of students to work on real-life problems or scenarios (problem-based, PBL) or on new lines of enquiry (enquiry-based, EBL). As part of their experience as the MBA Director, one of the authors of this text introduced PBL projects rooted in real challenges provided by several companies. In the first year of this new practice, MBA students worked on projects for three banks, one large credit institution, and the Portuguese postage company.

The three last methods displayed by the University of Manchester are e-learning, projects, and learning through research. The first one is dealt with in the next section. Projects and learning through research are discussed together, as they are often alternative or complementary methods used in the final part of many courses, such as those taught by the authors of this chapter.

Company projects and research projects are usually final individual works that involve field work and that lead to a public presentation and discussion. Projects in companies are intervention plans that require data collection and a report with proposed changes to the organization. It is a way of bringing students into real organizations and giving them a first account of working settings. Research projects are investigation work aimed at training and developing skills related to data collection and analysis in a scientific field of interest to the student, in marketing, organizational behavior, or accounting, among others. Both company and research projects are frequently done at the end of a course under direct supervision of an HE lecturer. As the previous examples show, the HE lecturer is a key part of students' learning and development. The performance of HE lecturers is, therefore, an important component of any university's success and public image.

6.4 Performance in Teaching and Performance in the Digital Era

As shown in Sect. 6.1, teaching effectiveness and impact are critical elements of AACSB standards, as well as of other international accreditation systems (e.g., the Association of MBAs (2016) follows 10 principles, of which #3 is entirely dedicated to lecturers: "faculty quality & sufficiency"). The AACSB criterion is not limited to a lecturer's performance on a classroom stage; it is also related to the relevance and quality of the course curriculum, to the fit between the lecturer teaching and the school's mission and goals, to diversity and inclusiveness in teaching, and to the impact of teaching (AACSB Accredited, 2020).

This multidimensional view of HE lecturers' performance will be expanded later; for now, the focus is on the more traditional role of lecturers, that is, that of teaching and the professor-student relationship.

Teaching performance is usually measured via students. Modern ways of requiring students' evaluations invariably include questionnaires completed at the end of the course. Questionnaires assess the student's opinion on a number of criteria, such as perceived teaching quality and perceived teacher knowledge of the subject. The study by Blašková et al. (2014) shows other examples of evaluation items, such as capacity to motivate students. Performance as the variation in knowledge acquired by the student is assessed by course exams and tests to students, as well as other individual and group assignments.

HE lecturers' teaching performance seems to depend on various dimensions, as shown by Su and Wood (2012). Based on a qualitative study of 100 students' essays, the authors found that teaching excellence from a student's perspective is a combination of the lecturer's knowledge of the subject, eagerness to help, and usage of inspirational teaching methods. Other relevant factors include humor and feedback delivery.

The Finnish education system is frequently considered to be one of the best in the world (see, for example, https://ncee.org/top-performing-countries/), and the ideas summarized in the conceptual paper by Uusiautti and Määttä (2012) help explain why lecturers play a key role in such a system. The authors put forward various aspects that should be taken into consideration to achieve teaching excellence: mastery over course subjects, focus on students' learning, support for learning, enthusiasm and inspirational, love for pedagogy, and constant upgrading and continuing education. Some of these aspects are similar to those found in Su and Wood's (2012) study, but one particular factor stands out: the focus on the student.

Student-centered learning is at the core of several university movements around the world, such as the European University Association. A report published by this association in 2019 (Gover et al., 2019) defined student-centered learning as "that takes into account the student as a person with a unique background while also ensuring the student's active involvement in shaping his or her own learning path" (p. 6). This is, according to the report, a paradigm shift that requires not only the use of active-learning methods and tools but also a new mindset from universities and HE lecturers.

From the above discussion and from Sect. 6.2, two questions arise: (1) How do teaching methods and techniques relate to modern teaching performance? (2) How does digital teaching affect HE lecturers' performance? The remainder of this section comments on these questions.

Concerning the first issue—teaching methods and techniques, and performance—the case method has always been a popular technique in executive and MBA courses (Garvin, 2007) due to its analysis of past real situations and cases. The method developed mainly by the Harvard Business School is used by other top schools in the world; however, traditional lecture-based teaching is also very popular. A report of Bloomberg BusinessWeek in 2012 (in Byrne, 2012) showed that lecture-based teaching accounts for 40% in some of the US top business schools (e.g., Oxford Said, Vanderbilt, and UCCLA), reaching 50% at Carnegie Mellon; team projects are also highly used (e.g., 25% at Pennsylvania Wharton and Kellogg); and experiential learning accounts for as much as 20% at MIT and 30% at Vanderbilt.

Bloomberg's report might be outdated, but as Garvin predicted in his 2007 article, teaching at the executive and MBA levels is increasingly carried out with action-learning approaches, although old-fashioned lecture-based teaching is still very much in use. Action-centered approaches to teaching are just another way of describing student-centered learning, that is, teaching that is focused on the learner, not on the teacher.

To conclude, it seems reasonable to say that as long as the teaching method and technique is appropriate to the subject and content being taught, then performance—measured as impact on students' learning—is likely to depend more on the focus—on the teacher versus on the student—than on any other factor. Thus, a traditional lecture to 200 students focused on apprentices can be more effective than a case method class to 20 people in which the lecturer is essentially interested in imposing his or her way of thinking and acting upon the specific challenge. Some methods may be more prone to student-centered teaching (e.g., PBL or EBL), but that is not guaranteed to be successful if the method is poorly handled by the HE lecturer.

The final question in this section is how does digital teaching affect HE lecturers' performance? This is a rather fascinating question, as the pandemic caused by COVID-19 will most likely change the face of HE teaching for the years to come. Before the COVID-19 crisis, many studies had been published comparing traditional and internet-based teaching. Mintu-Wimsatt et al. (2006), for example, used five evaluative criteria (teaching skills, rapport with students, grading policies, knowledge of material, and presentation skills) to compare lecturer performance with three pedagogy methods (traditional class, two-way interactive television, and internet-based class). They collected data from MBA students, and their results show that the best evaluations are for instructors using the traditional method and the worst for instructors performing via internet-based or television-based classes. A more recent study, conducted by Hurbult (2018), compared students' progress enrolled in a traditional class versus students in an online class taught by the same instructor. The results show slightly higher grades for the first group of students, and in both cases, instructor feedback was one of the most important aspects of a class.

Studies such as the above are rapidly becoming obsolete in the face of the tremendous changes faced by HE education in 2020 and 2021. If before 2020 researchers were comparing online and traditional teaching, the pandemic forced millions to go straight into remote teaching, with little or no time to adapt. In 2020 and 2021, technology used in remote teaching registered a huge leap forward. The intense and compressed experience lived by students, lecturers, organizations, and HE institutions in the same period is also noteworthy. Remote learning technology and massive individual experience with online teaching and learning means that what was known up to 2020 will need to be rewritten almost from scratch. As if this did not suffice, the emergence of new critical content in HE is pushing the role of educators into new areas. Among such topics, responsible management and leadership are addressed in the next section.

6.5   Responsible Management and Responsible Leadership

Although the concepts of management and leadership differ in terms of depth, range, and impact (Kotter, 1990), it is more reasonable to think that the distinction between the two is more of an academic nature (Mintzberg, 2009). In fact, in a real setting, every leader needs to manage, and every manager needs to lead individuals and tasks; individuals and tasks are part of a complex social network built and in constant evolution toward achieving multiple goals and success (Marques & Gomes, 2020).

Two related and mutually interdependent yet distinct concepts have appeared recently in management and social sciences: responsible management and responsible leadership. These concepts emerged largely due to the 2008 economic meltdown and credit crisis, as well as due to the various corporate and political scandals that have reached public media in the first two decades of the century (Doherty et al., 2015).

The call for a more responsible way of doing business starts with a simple question: "What is responsible management?". In a text written by some of the most prominent authors in the area (Carroll et al., 2020), several definitions are offered. According to Carroll, "responsible management addresses the specific strategies, tactics or actions managers ought to pursue to address business's accountability, obligations and duties to society and stakeholders" (p.57); Mintzberg sees responsible management as "responsible to employees, responsible to customers, responsible to the stakeholders in general, responsible to the society and responsible for being honest" (p. 58); and Freeman's view is "responsible management...the first thing... is being responsible to those people who you can affect and who can affect you. Your own stakeholders... those relationships that you're enmeshed in your life" (p. 63).

As far as the concept of responsible leadership is concerned, existing definitions emphasize the more humane dimensions of social dynamics: "[responsible leadership is] the art of building and sustaining relationships to all relevant stakeholders" (Maak & Pless, 2006, pp. 41); or "a values-based leadership approach that through stakeholder and systems orientation caters for the needs of constituencies directly and indirectly impacted by organizations" (Marques & Miska, 2021, p. 1).

The above definitions emphasize the idea that responsible management and leadership no longer target businesses and shareholders only. Instead, a responsible way of managing and leading should be concerned with people, profits, and the broader society and environment. It moves the frontiers of management out of the borders of the organization to its economic and social environment, the society in which it operates, and the ecological environment, within and across national borders.

This surge of a new paradigm of managing is influencing the way management and leadership are being taught in HR institutions. Responsible management learning (RML) and responsible management education (RME) are two terms that capture this new movement in education (Fougère et al., 2020).

More prosaically, the recently established United Nations program known as PRME aims to become "A global movement transforming business and management education through research and leadership" (PRME, 2021). This initiative pretends to engage "business and management schools to ensure they provide future leaders with the skills needed to balance economic and sustainability goals, while drawing attention to the SDGs and aligning academic institutions with the work of the UN Global Compact" (PRME, 2021). The aim is to stimulate the notion of sustainability in business and management schools around the world so that current and future business leaders will acquire the necessary skills and knowledge to implement the SDGs. Business and management schools have implemented and reported changes that show commitment to the PRME. However, such changes rarely show how HE lecturers can act as a fundamental change agent in the process.

6.6   Concluding Thoughts: Expanding the Role of Educators

From the discussion above, it can be concluded that HE lecturers are one of the most important change engines in education due to their boundary-spanning role and to their proximity to students. HE lecturers are not only delivering knowledge; they are also role models, and in that regard, they are change agents in students' ethical, moral, and human development (Asif et al., 2020).

The implementation of the various movements described along the previous sections—the PRME framework, the 17 SDGs, ethics and morale in business and management, responsible management, and responsible leadership—is therefore highly dependent not only on business schools but also especially on HE lecturers.

The role of business schools is undoubtedly crucial, as attested by several authors. For example, Parkes et al. (2017, p. 61) state that "as educators of the next as well as current generation of business leaders, business schools are in a unique position to influence the mindsets and actions of some of the largest and most powerful organizations on the planet." However, without the adherence of HE academic staff to the same movements, the whole exercise of changing the current state of things can fail.

Recent research suggests that HE lecturers are ready to embrace PRME and other positive changes in businesses (see, e.g., Mousa et al., 2020), but readiness does not necessarily mean that HE lecturers have the knowledge, training, personal attributes, or even the technology required to stimulate a mindset shift in students. Principles 1 (Purpose) and 2 (Values) of the PRME declare, "We will develop the capabilities of students to be future generators of sustainable value for business and society at large and to work for an inclusive and sustainable global economy," and "We will incorporate into our academic activities, curricula, and organizational practices the values of global social responsibility as portrayed in international initiatives such as the United Nations Global Compact." These are noble principles, but they are merely statements of intentions and politically driven thoughts. How such principles translate into practice obviously requires a monumental effort from institutions in terms of new procedures, new instruments, and new theories. The White Paper recently published by the World Economic Forum (2020), in partnership with the Big 4 accounting and consultancy firms (Deloitte, EY, KPMG, and PwC), reveals the commitment of several powerful global institutions to change the current unsustainable business paradigm.

However, the most important change element in the whole equation is likely to be HE academics. It is them who liaise with students, as well as with other relevant stakeholders; it is them who are required to use old and new technologies, to bring not only knowledge but also new ways of thinking, to the future managers and leaders; it is them who trigger change at the most fundamental level: the person.

Are HR educators ready for this challenge? Do they have the competencies and the personal attributes needed to do it? Do they believe that the PRME, the SDGs, and the ideas of responsible and leadership management can make any difference? Are they helped and supported by their affiliating institutions?

These are questions that have seldom been addressed by researchers, decision-makers, practitioners, and society. Ironically, these are likely to be the only questions that matter for a paradigm shift toward a more sustainable society.

References

https://www.unprme.org/about.
https://www.prospects.ac.uk/job-profiles/higher-education-lecturer.
https://ncee.org/top-performing-countries/.
AACSB Accredited (2020). *2020 Guiding principles and standards for business accreditation* AACSB Business Education. Accessed in https://www.aacsb.edu/-/media/aacsb/docs/accreditation/business/standards-and-tables/proposed%202020%20aacsb%20business%20accreditation%20standards%20-%20final%20draft%20-%20april%206%202020.ashx?la=en & hash=B40646D6F0057FBAF289B3B04888A33BB2741A3D.
Asif, T., Guangming, O., Haider, M. A., Colomer, J., Kayani, S., & ul Amin, N. (2020). Moral education for sustainable development: Comparison of university teachers' perceptions in China and Pakistan. *Sustainability, 12*, 1–20.

Association of MBAs (2016). MBA accreditation criteria. London, UK. Accessed in https://associationofmbas.com/wp-content/uploads/2019/09/MBA-criteria-for-accreditation.pdf.

Blašková, M., Blaško, R., & Kucharþíková, A. (2014). Competences and competence model of university teachers. *Procedia, Social and Behavioral Sciences, 159*, 457–467.

Byrne, J. A. (2012). How the world's top business schools teach their MBAs. Accessed in https://poetsandquants.com/2012/11/18/how-the-worlds-top-business-schools-teach-their-mbas/2/.

Carroll, A. B., Adler, N. J., Mintzberg, H., Cooren, F., Suddaby, R., Freeman, R. E., & Laasch, O. (2020). What "are" responsible management? A conceptual potluck. In O. Laasch, D. Jamali, E. Freeman, & R. Suddaby (Eds.), *Research handbook of responsible management* (pp. 56–71). Edward Elgar Publishing Ltd.

Doherty, B., Meehan, J., & Richards, A. (2015). The business case and barriers for responsible management education in business schools. *Journal of Management Development, 34*(1), 34–60.

Fougère, M., Solitander, N., & Maheshwari, S. (2020). Achieving responsible management learning through enriched reciprocal learning: Service-learning projects and the role of boundary spanners. *Journal of Business Ethics, 162*(4), 795–812.

Garvin, D. A. (2007). Teaching executives and teaching MBAs: Reflections on the case method. *Academy of Management Learning & Education, 6*(3), 364–374.

Gomes, J. F. S., Hurmelinna, P., Amaral, V., & Blomqvist, K. (2005). Managing relationships of the republic of science and the kingdom of industry. *Journal of Workplace Learning, 17*(1), 88–98.

Gonzalez-Perez, M. A., Lynden, K., & Taras, V. (Eds.). (2019). *The Palgrave handbook of learning and teaching international business and management.* Palgrave Macmillan.

Gover, A., Loukkola, T., & Peterbauer, H. (2019). *Student-centered learning: Approaches to learning assurance.* Report by the European University Association.

Hurbult, A. R. (2018). Online vs. traditional learning in teacher education: A comparison of student progress. *American Journal of Distance Education, 32*(4), 248–266.

Iñiguez, S., & Lorange, P. (Eds.). (2021). *Executive education after the pandemic: A vision for the future.* Palgrave Macmillan.

Kotter, J. P. (1990). What leaders truly do. *Harvard Business Review*, 3–11.

Maak, T., & Pless, N. (2006). *Responsible leadership*. Routledge.

Marques, T. M. G., & Gomes, J. F. S. (2020). Responsible leadership and/versus responsible management. In O. Laasch, D. Jamali, E. Freeman, & R. Suddaby (Eds.), *Research handbook of responsible management* (pp. 138–154). Edward Elgar Publishing Ltd.

Marques, T. M. G., & Miska, C. (2021). Responsible leadership. In A. Farazmand (Ed.), *Global encyclopaedia of public administration, public policy, and governance*. Springer.

Mintu-Wimsatt, A., Ingram, K., Milward, M. A., & Russ, C. (2006). On different teaching delivery methods: What happens to instructor course evaluations? *Marketing Education Review, 16*(3), 49–57.

Mintzberg, H. (2009). Rebuilding companies as communities. *Harvard Business Review*, 140–143.

Mousa, M., Massoud, H. K., Ayoubi, R. M., & Abdelgaffar, H. A. (2020). Should responsible management education become a priority? A qualitative study of academics in Egyptian public business schools. *The International Journal of Management Education, 18*(1), 1–12.

Parkes, C., Buono, A. F., & Howaidy, G. (2017). The principles for responsible management education (PRME): The first decade, what has been achieved? The next decade, responsible management education's challenge for the sustainable development goals (SDGs). *The International Journal of Management Education, 15*(2), 61–65.

Principles of Responsible Management Education (2021). Accessed in https://www.unprme.org/.

Su, F., & Wood, M. (2012). What makes a good university lecturer? Students' perceptions of teaching excellence. *Journal of Applied Research in Higher Education, 4*(2), 142–155.

Uusiautti, S., & Määttä, K. (2012). How to train good teachers in Finnish universities? Student teachers' study process and teacher educators' role in it. *European Journal of Educational Research, 1*(4), 339–352.

World Economic Forum. (2020). Measuring stakeholder capitalism: Toward common metrics and consistent reporting of sustainable value creation. *World Economic Forum*.

7

Marketing and Artificial Intelligence: Responsible Management (and Marketing) Education at the Nexus of Today and Tomorrow

Al Rosenboom

7.1 Introduction

Digital transformation is inexorably changing the way companies do business. Spurred by the ongoing ability to digitize analog/physical objects, digitalization alone does not explain the digital transformation revolution sweeping through society. Digital transformation needs an ecosystem of technologies that includes the rise of low-cost computing, the continued development of high-speed computer transmission networks, the ability to store exabytes of data in the cloud, and the increasing global market penetration of mobile and smartphones for businesses, if higher education institutions and society are to reap its benefits (Matt et al., 2015). Digital transformation is thus occurring "at a pace and magnitude that disrupt established ways of creating value within and across markets, social interactions, and more generally, our understanding and thinking" (Reimer et al., 2015, p. 4).

A. Rosenboom (✉)
Dominican University, River Forest, IL, USA
e-mail: arosenbloom@dom.edu

© The Author(s), under exclusive license to Springer Nature Switzerland AG 2023
C. Hauser, W. Amann (eds.), *The Future of Responsible Management Education*,
Humanism in Business Series, https://doi.org/10.1007/978-3-031-15632-8_7

Marketing is a leading-edge business disciplines that is fundamentally disrupted by digital transformation. The ubiquity of digital connectivity across the entire lifespan of consumers is, however, a double-edged sword. On the one hand, digital transformation creates opportunities for marketers to communicate with and to deliver value to customers through new channels, such as through digital and social media platforms, as well as through new digital products that communicate with each other to form the Internet of Things (IoT). On the other hand, despite leaving extensive digital footprints of their search, purchase and postpurchase behaviors, the sheer volume of consumer data coupled with the multiple, often fragmented channels through which consumers interact with brands and firms has now created data sets so large, complex, and dynamic that they exceed conventional database architecture for handling them (Weiss & Indurkhya, 1998). In fact, the magnitude of the digital universe is breathtaking. Gantz and Reinsel (2012) estimate that the digital universe will grow by a factor of 300 from generating 130 exabytes in 2005 to 40,000 exabytes (or 40 trillion gigabytes) by 2020. They also claim that by 2020, as much as one-third of the digital universe will contain information of value but will be left unanalyzed. As they note, "Herein is the promise of 'Big Data' technology—the extraction of value from the large untapped pools of data in the digital universe" (Gantz & Reinsel, 2012, p. 3).

In the overall context of digital transformation, big data is often considered "the oil" of the digital economy (Wedel & Kannan, 2016), and artificial intelligence (AI) needs big data to function. Increasingly, AI helps marketers in "areas like segmentation and analytics (related to marketing strategy)…messaging, personalization and predictive behaviors (linked to customer behaviors)…[resulting in increased revenues] through improved marketing decisions (e.g., pricing, promotions, product recommendations, enhanced customer engagement)…[and decreased costs] due to the automation of simple marketing tasks, customer service, and (structured) market transactions (Davenport et al., 2020, p. 25, 27).

Every technology is value neutral (Miller, 2021). However, ethical issues cohere with any technology because human agency decides what, where, why, how, and for whom to use the technology. AI's use in marketing is no exception (Hermann, 2021). Marketing managers therefore have moral obligations to be responsible consumers of AI applications because AI will increasingly be tightly bound to organizational and marketing success. This, in turn, leads to provocative questions about what kind of marketing education students should receive to become wise, reflective users of AI in marketing practice.

Achenreiner (2001) asked the timeless question central to all marketing (and management) education: "Are we teaching students what they need to know?" Marketing educators continually wrestle with this issue, as technology greatly affects fundamental frameworks that guide student learning about marketing (such as in SWOT, PESTLE, and marketing mix analyses). Technology also opens up new domains of marketing practice. Marketing educators have described new courses that bring digital marketing (Wymbs, 2011), social media marketing (Brocato et al., 2015), and data analytics (Liu & Burns, 2018) into the marketing curriculum. AI is just now receiving similar discussion (Elhajjar et al., 2021). However, marketing educators thus far have focused on the technical aspects of AI (Dingus & Black, 2020; Thontirawong & Chinchanachokchai, 2021). Missing from this emerging discussion about AI in marketing, as well as from larger discussions about the purposes and content of marketing education, is a more holistic approach to integrate knowledge domains. Responsible management education (RME) provides an antidote to both.

RME specifically asks educators to integrate ethics, sustainability and responsibility (Laasch, 2018) throughout the curriculum and to embed these three elements into the courses faculty members teach. To date, RME has been discussed within general management. Missing from this discussion has been the adoption of the RME framework specifically within marketing education. Using AI as an example, the chapter's focus is on the application of RME to AI in marketing education.

The chapter begins with a brief discussion of AI, after which current applications of AI in marketing practice and the importance of AI in marketing education are presented. An overview of RME follows, followed by sections on AI and marketing ethics, the need to use stakeholder theory when making AI marketing decisions, and the growing integration of AI within marketing and sustainable development. The chapter concludes with a look at the future of AI and RME.

7.2   What Is Artificial Intelligence?

Artificial intelligence is a branch of computer science that aims to develop computational machines that mimic human capabilities, such as thinking, doing mechanical or physical tasks, and feeling (Huang & Rust, 2021). Extending the comparison to human behavior, Russell and Norvig (2016) classify AI systems according to whether AI systems think like humans, act like humans, think rationally, and act rationally. Although simple in statement, this classification can be used to illustrate the definitional diversity of AI (see Fig. 7.1).

Although AI traces its origins to a 1956 conference at Dartmouth University, the field's growth accelerated greatly only when big data, economic access to computer power, and advances in machine learning converged. Inherent in both the discipline's name and its many definitions is the thorny issue of "intelligence." As used here, intelligence can be thought of as "the ability to act under new circumstances" (Wodecki, 2020, p. 3). AI research has focused on several components of

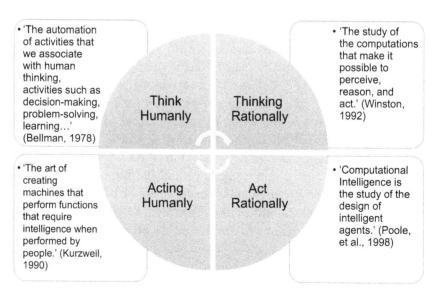

Fig. 7.1 Definitions of artificial intelligence

intelligence: problem recognition, learning, reasoning, perception, and using language.

There are two types of AI: data-driven AI and knowledge-based AI (Pedro et al., 2019). To date, most of the success and advances in AI, which is also true in marketing, have been data-driven. At the heart of data-driven AI is machine learning, that is, "the science (and art) of programming computers so that they can learn from data" (Géron, 2019, p. 2). This definition of machine learning mirrors how social scientists think of learning in individuals (i.e., as a change in behavior based on experience). In the case of machines, "experience" = data. In passing, it is worth noting that one can achieve AI without machine learning, but that would involve millions of lines of code along with complex rules and decision trees. Thus:

> AI thrives on data. AI application outcomes become more accurate with more data. AI needs data to build its intelligence (e.g., using machine learning). Given that big data enables AI to reach its full potential, it would be fair to say that there is no data-driven AI without big data (Pedro et al., 2019, p. 9).

Knowledge-based AI aims to develop expert systems, which "aim to capture the knowledge of human experts to support decision making" (Moore, 2018, para. 1). Expert systems are domain specific (e.g., health care) and attempt to create computer programs that capture the knowledge of experts for use by less experienced or novice users (Tripathi, 2011). As Engelmore (1987) states, "Expertise is always a scarce resource, and costly problems can arise when novices are left to solve problems on their own" p. 8). Expert systems therefore reduce costs and/or improve decision making.

A common misconception is that AI and robotics are synonyms. They are not. AI is a branch of computer science, while robotics is a branch of engineering. Robots are machines that can be programmed, and robotics deals with their construction, operation, and application. AI is software, algorithms, and machine learning. Robots increase work productivity and simply lifestyle. AI makes technology more human. Only when a robot is powered by AI do the two domains come together. This is the "artificially intelligent robot."

7.3 AI in Marketing

The rise of e-commerce and the explosion of digital marketing across industry boundaries have made marketing the business function most to gain from AI (Chui et al., 2018). Consumer packaged goods, retailing, travel, and banking/financial services are those sectors currently best able to benefit from AI because they "involve frequent contact with large numbers of customers, and produce vast amounts of customer transaction data and customer attribute data" (Davenport et al., 2020, p. 25). That "transaction data" can include login information, text, search history, data on purchases or purchase abandonment, digital pictures, geographic location, and natural language text queries, among other digital details (Shrestha et al., 2021).

Marketers are already incorporating AI applications across the entire customer experience (Forrester, 2017). For example, AI can determine what stage of the buying process a consumer is in (from preliminary search to active consideration) and send specifically targeted ads to that individual to motivate purchase (Davenport et al., 2021). AI can also encourage incremental sales through recommendations based on previous purchase history (Paschen et al., 2020). Any website that uses chatbots (themselves an AI application) can use sentiment analysis (the use of AI to determine emotions and feelings in natural language conversations) to enhance responsiveness and customer satisfaction by automatically transferring the customer to a human support specialist when the individual's chatbot responses indicate frustration, anger, or disappointment. Sentiment analysis is also used to monitor comments posted on social media, which are both out of the firm's direct control and which, if left without a prompt response, can damage brand as well as firm integrity and reputation (Laroche et al., 2013). Sentiment analysis improves marketing decision making (Kauffmann et al., 2019).

Retailing is one part of marketing in which the powerful effects of digital transformation are readily seen (Brynjolfsson et al., 2013). Retailing's traditional business model (brick-and-mortar stores with inefficient supply chains) is being disrupted significantly by digital technologies that require omnichannel retailing and for the retailer's themselves to be leaner, more agile, and have more efficient supply chains (Lee et al., 2018). AI solutions will further transform the entire retail value chain through more intelligent "knowledge and insight management, inventory management, operations optimization, and customer engagement" (Oosthuizen et al., 2021). The application of AI across the diverse domains of marketing is vast and is expected to grow exponentially (Drift, 2021).

Two frameworks help summarize AI's value in marketing. From a strategic marketing perspective, Huang and Rust (2021) propose a three-stage marketing planning cycle that includes multiple AI benefits. Figure 7.2 integrates their strategic marketing framework with Russell & Norvig's (2016) classification of AI systems as thinking like humans, acting like humans, thinking rationally, and acting rationally.

Marketing Research

- Data collection → Think rationally
- Market analysis → Think rationally
- Customer understanding → Act rationally

Marketing Strategy

- Segmentation → Act like humans
- Targeting → Think like humans
- Positioning → Act like humans

Marketing Action

- Standardization → Think rationally
- Personalization → Think like humans
- Relationalization → Act like humans

Fig. 7.2 Integration of marketing strategy process (Rust & Huang, 2021) with Russell and Norvig's (2016) AI classification framework

The Drift Report (2021), a collaborative research project between the Drift Consultancy and the Marketing AI Institute, provides a second framework. The Drift Report (2021) categorizes AI contributions to marketing as related to planning (building intelligent strategies), production (creating intelligent content), personalization (powering intelligent consumer experiences), promotion (managing intelligent cross-channel promotions) and performance (turning data into intelligence). The table below lists the top three currently used AI marketing applications as evaluated by more than 400 marketing professionals surveyed for the report (Table 7.1).

7.4   AI and Marketing Education

In a recent review of the effects new technologies (such as AI, robotics, blockchain, big data, and drones) are having on marketing education, Ferrell and Ferrell (2020) observe, from a historical perspective, "Marketing has always been changed and advanced through new technology" (p. 4). Because "[d]igitalization is like a fast-moving tsunami" (Crittenden et al., 2019, p. 5), marketing educators "[need] to be ahead of this technological storm instead of behind it" (Crittenden & Crittenden, 2015, p. 131).

The discussion of how best to incorporate emerging technologies into marketing education is part of the larger debate among marketing educators to first define the skills, abilities and conceptual knowledge needed for successful career entry and advancement (Schlee & Harich, 2010) and then to design marketing curricula and pedagogies that develop those skills, abilities and that requisite conceptual knowledge (LeClair, 2018). To date, only three scholarly articles have discussed AI in the marketing curriculum, and their foci have been very different. Elhajjar et al. (2021) make the case for *why* AI should be included in the curriculum, while Dingus and Black (2020) along with Thontirawong and Chinchanachokchai (2021) discuss *how* to do that (through the use of Watson Tone Analyzer to carry out sentiment analysis on emails and the use of AzureML Studio to create machine learning models for customer churn prediction, respectively).

Table 7.1 Selected AI marketing applications in use (Drift Report, 2021)

AI benefit	Explanation	Top three examples currently used
Planning	Building intelligent strategies	• Choose keywords and topic clusters for content optimization • Analyze existing online content for gaps and opportunities • Score leads based on conversion probabilities
Production	Creating intelligent content	• Create data-driven content • Optimize website content for search engines • Predict content performance before deployment
Personalization	Powering intelligent consumer experiences	• Recommend highly targeted content to users in real-time • Determine offers that will motivate individuals to action • Present individualized experiences on the web and/or in-app
Promotion	Managing intelligent cross-channel promotions	• Adapt audience targeting based on behavior and lookalike analysis • Predict winning creative (e.g., digital ads, landing pages, call to action (CTA) messages) before launch without A/B testing • Deliver individualized content experiences across channels
Performance	Turning data into intelligence	• Measure return on investment (ROI) by channel, campaign and overall • Discover insights into top-performing content and campaigns • Forecast campaign results based on predictive analysis

Source: Adapted from Drift Report (2021)

As AI is still in its infancy in relation to marketing curricula, it is likely that marketing educator discussions will follow patterns previously evidenced around why, where and how to integrate previous emerging technologies into student learning opportunities (Crittenden & Crittenden, 2015; Ferrell & Ferrell, 2020). For example, should AI be integrated into existing courses or should AI receive standalone treatment? What is the right balance between technical skills, general knowledge and soft skills needed by students to understand and be knowledgeable professionals around AI applications? Is some antecedent, foundational knowledge needed (such as statistics, analytics, some basic computer science courses) or not? Where else in the curriculum does AI have application, so that student learning is not just a one-off? Counterbalancing these discussions are pertinent faculty issues (Elhajjar et al., 2021): Who will teach AI? What level of expertise is need? Must the instructor have teaching experience? Is the school's infrastructure able to support AI activities? To date, it is unclear what the answer to these questions will be.

All of the above issues are important and valid. However, it seems that by having these discussions solely from a traditional, disciplinary perspective, marketing educators are missing a significant opportunity to consider how AI relates to responsible management education (RME). RME provides a more holistic, integrated perspective on knowledge, and AI can provide marketing educators opportunities to apply RME perspectives to marketing—something that has not been done thus far.

7.5   Responsible Management (and Marketing) Education

Responsible management (RM) is an integrated approach to managing organizations that places ethics, responsibility, and sustainability at the center of all organizational decision making (Laasch, 2018). RM emerged as the touchstone for managerial action as a direct response to (1) the many high-profile scandals at the beginning of the twenty-first century (e.g., WorldCom, Enron, VW, Parmalat, etc.), (2) the global financial crisis of 2008 and its consequences, and (3) the acknowledgment that many corporate business practices were causing significant, sustained and sometimes irreversible environmental and societal damage (Moratis & Melissen, 2021). RM captures the zeitgeist of the times, which is for an active, critical re-examination of the complex relationship between firms and society. Firms are increasingly being called "beyond the boundaries of their spreadsheets" (Mason & Rosenbloom, 2020, p. 143) to be more reflective and just corporate citizens. This corporate "call to action" had an important inflection point when the Business Roundtable, a group of 181 US CEOs, issued a statement redefining the purposes of the corporation as serving all stakeholders and not just shareholders (Business Roundtable, 2019).

The replacement of shareholder primacy with stakeholder primacy has several implications. First, by affirming stakeholder primacy, society and the obligation firms have to work for and promote the common good were brought directly into every manager's decision-making calculus. Second, stakeholder considerations imply that the dominant theory of the firm, which to date has been profit maximization because shareholder interests were the most important consideration for all organizational decisions, must be reconsidered (Harrison et al., 2020). Purpose is increasingly replacing profit as the new theory of the firm (Mayer, 2018, 2020; van Ingen et al., 2021). Third, stakeholder primacy and responsibility complement each other. Stakeholders are defined as "any group or individual who can affect or is affected by the achievement of the activities of an organization" (Freeman, 1984, p. 46), while responsibility is defined as "the duty in caring for the beings affected by one's actions and policies" (Hans Jonas quoted in Zsolnai, 2020, p. 36). If the two concepts were Venn diagrams, they would overlap with each other completely. Thus, responsible management is moving from the fringes of managerial thought into a more central, dominant position within firms.

Implicit within discussions of responsible management is the need for responsible management education (RME). Similar to RM, RME has its roots in the global financial crisis, corporate ethics scandals, and the need for businesses to be more sustainable (Haertle et al., 2017). As these three situations collided with each other, management scholars began to debate whether management education was responsible for, or at least complicit in, these events (Swanson & Frederick, 2003). Ghoshal (2005) noted that "business school faculty need to own up to our own role in creating Enrons. It is our theories and ideas that have done much to strengthen the management practices that we are all now so loudly condemning" (p. 75). From this reckoning, emerged RME.

Following Rasche and Gilbert (2015), RME can be thought of as "a descriptor for efforts aimed at embedding reflections about corporate responsibility (i.e., the social impact of businesses on society); environmental sustainability (i.e., the contribution of firms to a sustainable economy); and ethics (i.e., reflections about right and wrong in the context of business situations) into business schools' educational practice" (p. 240). As such, RME's aim is to normalize discussions of responsibility, ethics and sustainability in courses that have not traditionally considered those topics, thereby moving such discussions out of siloed courses devoted to one aspect of RME (such as ethics, CSR or sustainable marketing) and into core and elective courses across a curriculum. AI applications in marketing provide opportunities for marketing educators to integrate RM into marketing programs and curricula.

7.6   AI as a RME Issue

As marketing is the lead corporate function currently using AI, marketing educators have direct responsibilities for developing students' critical thinking about AI. Marketing professionals are consumers of AI. They are not AI developers. As such, RME provides an essential context for marketing students to become wise AI consumers/users because it steps away from being enmeshed in too much technical minutia and jargon. RME also requires critical thinking and through its integration of ethics, responsibility and sustainability for students to become morally reflexive individuals (Cunliffe, 2016).

AI Marketing Ethics Discussions about AI marketing ethics fit within the larger domain of AI ethics. AI ethics begins with the fundamental premise that AI is not a value neutral technology. As the World Economic Forum stated more generally, "Technologies have a clear moral dimension…. Technologies reflect the interests, behaviors, and desires of their creators and shape how the people using them can realize their potential, identities, relationships, and goals" (Philbeck et al., 2018, p. 7). Additionally, because AI is driven by data, AI shares many of the same ethical issues as other data-driven fields (such as marketing research and data analytics). AI data issues include how the data are collected, recorded and used. AI algorithms raise issues of transparency, since in machine learning, the initial algorithms steadily improve (i.e., they become "better") without direct human control. However, what happens if the dataset used initially to develop the algorithms is inaccurate, incomplete or unconsciously biased in some way? The output will be flawed and can have serious negative consequences. AI data privacy and AI data security are also important. Safeguards for both must be in place. Hermann (2021) summarizes the main issues of AI ethics for marketers as privacy, transparency, beneficence (the moral obligation to do good), nonmaleficence (the counterpoint to beneficence since nonmaleficence is the obligation to do no harm), autonomy (self-determination and freedom from coercion), trust and justice (accountability if something goes wrong). Each of these ethical issues is important in AI marketing because, as often noted, AI systems are so exceptionally complex that "even their developers cannot explain precisely how their creation reached a specific result" (Dahlin, 2021, p. 2). This has led some scholars to think of AI systems as a black box (Castelvecchi, 2016). However, "when AI goes wrong, marketers who use the AI are likely to be held accountable" (Huang & Rust, 2021, p. 46). RME requires marketing students to consider AI ethics.

Responsible AI Marketing Responsible use of AI in marketing requires students to think beyond ethical considerations and to consider the effect that AI in marketing has on stakeholders. Human agency stands behind all marketing strategy. Therefore, to particularize Dignum's (2021) statement to marketing, AI's use in marketing "requires more responsibility and accountability from [marketers] and organizations involved: for the decisions and actions of the AI applications [in marketing] and for their own decision to use AI in a given application context [e.g., better digital ad placement, targeted product recommendations, sales support, etc.]" (p. 3). Stakeholder engagement is needed for all AI marketing models because they use human data, affect human beings, and outcomes can have moral consequences. However, as Laczniak and Murphy (2012) have observed, marketing is a latecomer to the discussion of and implementation of stakeholder theory. Marketing educators have opportunities to explore the tradeoffs that occur when AI-enabled marketing strategy is considered from a broader stakeholder perspective rather than the narrower customer perspective that has been marketing's traditional focus.

General Data Protection Regulation (GDPR) provides an easy-to-understand example of a marketing stakeholder analysis and the future application of AI. Although GDPR is a data governance law and not a data privacy or security law (Demodia, n.d.), the implementation of the GDPR has digital privacy and security rights implications. "GDPR requires companies to be transparent about what data they collect, take responsibility for what they do with that data and know what their partners do with it" (Demodia, n.d.). Thus, GDPR affects marketers not only across an entire supply chain but also through the interconnections that bind B2B marketing to B2C marketing and sometimes B2G. Marketing databases, sales lists, customer relationship management software (CRM), website design, and email marketing are all affected by GDPR (Demodia, n.d.). Kuzeimski and Pałka (2019) propose three opportunities for policy makers to use AI effectively vis-à-vis GDPR: (1) compliance-centered innovation; (2) empowering civil society advocacy by encouraging citizen engagement and preventing market dominance; and (3) creating permanent groups that facilitate dialog between different regulatory agencies and policy-making bodies. A marketing AI stakeholder analysis would thus include government, businesses themselves, civil society organizations, suppliers, advocacy and watchdog groups. The value of such marketing stakeholder analysis within RME is that students and faculty together raise "questions concerning the responsibilities and liabilities of people and organization in charge of [AI marketing] data processes, strategies and policies" (Floridi & Taddeo, 2016, p. 3).

AI Marketing and Sustainability Marketing scholars are advancing both the discipline's conceptual understanding of sustainable marketing (Lunde, 2018; Tollin & Christensen, 2019) and the application of market research findings to prosocial/sustainable/green consumers, who are engaging in "voluntary simplicity," "sufficient consumption," "frugality," "downshifting," "mindful," "slow," and "ethical and responsible consumption" (Gossen et al., 2019). Similar to the incorporation of stakeholder analysis into marketing, the incorporation of sustainability into marketing pedagogy has been slow (Morales et al., 2020). Rosenbloom

(2021), however, provides an integrated model specifically developed for classroom teaching about sustainability marketing that integrates the triple bottom line (TBL), stakeholder analysis, and the Sustainable Development Goals (SDGs)—all of which support marketing in service of creating a better world. Sustainability marketing is gradually being incorporated in marketing education. Rosenbloom's (2021) teaching framework supports Belz and Peattie's (2009) firm assertions that sustainability marketing supports sustainable development, the most recent expression of which are the SDGs. AI is also being applied to achieving SDGs (Gupta et al., 2021; Mercier-Laurent, 2021; Truby, 2020; Vinuesa et al., 2020). However, often overlooked in SDG business discussions is that an entire ecosystem of organizations, including businesses of various organizational designs, sizes and missions, presently operates within the arena defined by each SDG. Hoek (2018) identifies SDG-related business opportunities as "the trillion-dollar shift," and the *Better Business, Better World* report (Business & Sustainable Development Commission, 2019) states that 389 million new jobs in four sectors (i.e., food and agriculture, ($2.3 trillion), cities ($3.7 trillion), energy and materials ($4.3 trillion), and health and well-being ($1.8 trillion)) would total just over $12 trillion in market opportunities. Marketing educators have significant opportunities here to reframe all student learning about marketing (in introductory marketing classes, in marketing strategy courses, in marketing electives—at undergraduate and MBA levels) from a sustainable development/SDG perspective. Having established the relationship and importance of marketing to sustainable development, AI applications can be layered into this discussion.

7.7   Conclusion: What's Ahead?

As the use of AI continues to diffuse throughout society, the market value of AI applications will increase. In 2020, the estimated market value of all AI applications was slightly over USD 62 billion and was expected to increase to an estimated total market value of USD 998 billion by 2028

(Marketview Research, 2021). The McKinsey Institute (Chui et al., 2018) also estimates that there will be up to a $5.9 trillion annual impact of AI and other analytics on marketing and sales, while IDC (Gantz et al., 2017) projects AI's use with customer relationship management systems could generate over a trillion dollars in additional revenue in 2021. However, 70% of marketing professionals said a barrier to using AI was their lack of education and training on AI (Drift Report, 2021). Herein lies opportunities for marketing education.

In tandem with AI's greatly expanded commercial use is the proliferation of projects that leverage AI for the common good. This is the emerging area of "AI for Social Good" (AI4SG). "AI4SG facilitates the attainment of socially good outcomes that were previously unfeasible, unaffordable or simply less achievable in terms of efficiency and effectiveness" (Cowls et al., 2021, p. 111). Because many of the world's most pressing problems (e.g., poverty eradication, slowing or stopping climate change, eliminating food insecurity, control of pandemics, etc.) are global, complex and interconnected, AI4SG holds the same promise as its commercial applications: To provide innovative solutions that otherwise would be beyond reach through other methods.

RME's overall aims are to develop ethically grounded, reflexive business professionals who are comfortable with tension and paradox that are inevitably embedded in organizational strategies that take into account ethics, responsibility and sustainability. To adapt Philbeck et al.'s observation about technologies in general, AI has the ability to

> interpret, transform and make meaning in the world around us. Rather than being simple objects or processes that are distinct from human beings, [AI applications are] deeply socially constructed, culturally situated and reflective of societal values. They are how we [will increasingly] engage with the world around us. [AI applications] affect how people order their lives, interact with one another and see themselves (p. 5).

AI, marketing, and RME seem especially well suited to take on this challenge. Beginning with introductory marketing principles courses (where AI can be introduced), through a marketing strategy/marketing management course (where AI can be discussed in more detail), and certainly in digital marketing/social media and data analytics courses (where various AI applications can actually be used), the marketing curriculum has many opportunities to engage future marketing professionals with AI. When a responsible management (and marketing) perspective is used, marketing educators not only help develop technically skilled marketing graduates but also help develop morally mature, socially aware marketing professionals who are able "to pursue purposes greater than their own, to incorporate within the management process multiple forms of value creation, measurement and distribution, and to make decisions and achieve results that are not only efficient and effective, but are socially, environmentally and morally favorable" (Mika et al., 2020, p. 262). This is the promise and opportunity of artificial intelligence and responsible management and marketing education.

References

Achenreiner, G. (2001). Market Research in the "Real" World: Are We Teaching Students What They Need to Know? *Marketing Education Review, 11*(1), 15–25.

Belz, F. M., & Peattie, K. (2009). *Sustainability marketing*. Wiley.

Brocato, E. D., White, N. J., Bartkus, K., & Brocato, A. A. (2015). Social media and marketing education: A review of current practices in curriculum development. *Journal of Marketing Education, 37*(2), 76–87.

Brynjolfsson, E., Hu, Y., & Rahman, M. S. (2013). Competing in the age of omnichannel retailing. *MIT Sloan Management Review, 54*(4), 23–29.

Business & Sustainable Development Commission. (2019). Better business, better world. Retrievable from: http://report.businesscommission.org/uploads/BetterBizBetterWorld_170215_012417.pdf.

Business Roundtable. (2019). *Statement on the purpose of a corporation.* Retrieved from https://s3.amazonaws.com/brt.org/BRT-statementonthePurposeofaCorporationJuly2021.pdf.

Castelvecchi, D. (2016). Can we open the black box of AI? *Nature News, 538*(7623), 20.

Chui, M., Manyika, J., Miremadi, M., Henke, N., Chung, R., Nel, P., & Malhotra, S. (2018). Notes from the AI frontier: Applications and value of deep learning. McKinsey global institute discussion paper, April 2018.

Retrieved August 22, 2021 from https://www.mckinsey.com/featured-insights/artificial-intelligence/notes-from-the-aifrontier-applications-and-value-of-deep-learning.

Cowls, J., Tsamados, A., Taddeo, M., & Floridi, L. (2021). A definition, benchmark and database of AI for social good initiatives. *Nature Machine Intelligence, 3*(2), 111–115.

Crittenden, W. F., Biel, I. K., & Lovely, W. A., III. (2019). Embracing digitalization: Student learning and new technologies. *Journal of Marketing Education, 41*(1), 5–14.

Crittenden, V., & Crittenden, W. (2015). Digital and social media marketing in business education: Implications for student engagement. *Journal of Marketing Education, 37*(3), 131–132.

Cunliffe, A. L. (2016). "On becoming a critically reflexive practitioner" redux: What does it mean to be reflexive? *Journal of Management Education, 40*(6), 740–746.

Dahlin, E. (2021). Mind the gap! On the future of AI research. *Humanities and Social Sciences Communications, 8*(1), 1–4. https://doi.org/10.1057/s41599-021-00750-9

Davenport, T., Guha, A., & Grewal, D. (2021). How to design an AI marketing strategy what the technology can do today—and what's next. *Harvard Business Review, 99*(1), 142–147.

Davenport, T., Guha, A., Grewal, D., & Bressgott, T. (2020). How artificial intelligence will change the future of marketing. *Journal of the Academy of Marketing Science, 48*(1), 24–42.

Demodia. (n.d.). How will GDPR affect marketing—everything marketers need to know about GDPR. Retrieved from https://www.demodia.com/discovering-demand/everything-marketers-need-know-about-gdpr.

Dignum, V. (2021). The role and challenges of education for responsible AI'. *London Review of Education, 19*(1), 1–11. https://doi.org/10.14324/LRE.19.1.01

Dingus, R., & Black, H. G. (2020). Choose your words carefully: An exercise to introduce artificial intelligence to the marketing classroom using tone analysis. *Marketing Education Review*, 1–6.

Drift. (2021). 2021 State of Marketing AI Report. Accessible from https://ittechreports.com/whitepapers/2021%20State%20of%20Marketing%20AI.pdf

Elhajjar, S., Karam, S., & Borna, S. (2021). Artificial intelligence in marketing education programs. *Marketing Education Review, 31*(1), 2–13.

Engelmore, R. S. (1987). Artificial intelligence and knowledge. -based systems: Origins, methods and opportunities for NDE. In D. O. Thompson & D. E. Chimenti (Eds.), *Review of progress in quantitative nondestructive evaluation* (pp. 1–20). Springer.

Ferrell, O. C., & Ferrell, L. (2020). Technology challenges and opportunities facing marketing education. *Marketing Education Review, 30*(1), 3–14.

Floridi, L., & Taddeo, M. (2016). What is data ethics? *Philosophical Transactions of the Royal Society A: Mathematical, Physical and Engineering Sciences, 374*(2083), 20160360.

Forrester. (2017). Forrester study reveals benefits of artificial intelligence with the human touch. Genesys. Available at https://www.genesys.com/collateral/forrester-studyreveals-benefits-of-artificial-intelligence-with-the-humantouch.

Freeman, R. E. (1984). *Strategic management: A stakeholder approach*. Pittman.

Gantz, J., & Reinsel, D. (2012). The digital universe in 2020: Big data, bigger digital shadows, and biggest growth in the far east. *IDC iView: IDC Analyze the Future, 2007*(2012), 1–16.

Gantz, J., Murray, G., Schubmehl, D., Vesset, D., & Wardley, M. (2017). A trillion-dollar boost: The economic impact of AI on customer relationship management. Retrievable from https://www.salesforce.com/content/dam/web/en_us/www/documents/white-papers/the-economic-impact-of-ai.pdf.

Géron, A. (2019). Hands-on machine learning with Scikit-Learn, Keras, and TensorFlow: Concepts, tools, and techniques to build intelligent systems. O'Reilly Media.

Ghoshal, S. (2005). Bad management theories are destroying good management practices. *Academy of Management Learning & Education, 4*(1), 75.

Gossen, M., Ziesemer, F., & Schrader, U. (2019). Why and how commercial marketing should promote sufficient consumption: A systematic literature review. *Journal of Macromarketing, 39*(3), 252–269.

Gupta, S., Langhans, S. D., Domisch, S., Fuso-Nerini, F., Felländer, A., Battaglini, M., et al. (2021). Assessing whether artificial intelligence is an enabler or an inhibitor of sustainability at the indicator level. *Transportation Engineering, 4*, 100064.

Haertle, J., Parkes, C., Murray, A., & Hayes, R. (2017). PRME: Building a global movement on responsible management education. *The International Journal of Management Education, 15*(2), 66–72.

Harrison, J. S., Phillips, R. A., & Freeman, R. E. (2020). On the 2019 business roundtable "statement on the purpose of a corporation". *Journal of Management, 46*(7), 1223–1237.

Hermann, E. (2021). Leveraging artificial intelligence in marketing for social good—an ethical perspective. *Journal of Business Ethics*, 1–19.

Hoek, M. (2018). *The Trillion Dollar Shift*. London: Routledge.

Huang, M. H., & Rust, R. T. (2021). A strategic framework for artificial intelligence in marketing. *Journal of the Academy of Marketing Science, 49*(1), 30–50.

Kauffmann, E., Peral, J., Gil, D., Ferrández, A., Sellers, R., & Mora, H. (2019). Managing marketing decision-making with sentiment analysis: An evaluation of the main product features using text data mining. *Sustainability, 11*(15), 4235.

Kuzeimski, M., & Palka, P. (2019). AI governance post-GDPR: lessons learned and the road ahead. *European University Institute Policy Brief*, Issue 2019/07 September 2019. Retrievable from https://cadmus.eui.eu/bitstream/handle/1814/64146/STG_PB_2019_07-EN.pdf?sequence=1&isAllowed=y

Laasch, O. (2018). Just old wine in new bottles? Conceptual shifts in the emerging field of responsible management. *Centre for Responsible Management Education Working Papers, 4*(1).

Laczniak, G. R., & Murphy, P. E. (2012). Stakeholder theory and marketing: Moving from a firm-centric to a societal perspective. *Journal of Public Policy & Marketing, 31*(2), 284–292.

Laroche, M., Habibi, M. R., & Richard, M. O. (2013). To be or not to be in social media: How brand loyalty is affected by social media? *International Journal of Information Management, 33*(1), 76–82.

Lee, H., Mendelson, H., Rammoham, S., et al. (2018). *Value chain innovation: The promise of AI*. Stanford Business. Value chain innovation Ini- retrievable from https://www.gsb.stanford.edu/faculty-research/publications/value-chain-innovation-promise-ai

LeClair, D. (2018). Integrating business analytics in the marketing curriculum: Eight recommendations. *Marketing Education Review, 28*(1), 6–13.

Liu, X., & Burns, A. C. (2018). Designing a marketing analytics course for the digital age. *Marketing Education Review, 28*(1), 28–40.

Lunde, M. B. (2018). Sustainability in marketing: A systematic review unifying 20 years of theoretical and substantive contributions (1997–2016). *AMS Review, 8*(3), 85–110.

Marketview Research. (2021). Artificial intelligence market size worth $997.77 Billion By 2028. Retrievable from https://www.grandviewresearch.com/press-release/global-artificial-intelligence-ai-market.

Matt, C., Hess, T., & Benlian, A. (2015). Digital transformation strategies. *Business & Information Systems Engineering, 57*(5), 339–343.

Mason, G., & Rosenbloom, A. (2020). Poverty and management education. In D. Moosmayer, O. Laasch, C. Parkes, & K. Brown (Eds.), *The SAGE handbook of responsible management learning and education* (pp. 141–164). Sage Publishing.

Mayer, C. (2018). *Prosperity: Better business makes the greater good.* Oxford University Press.

Mayer, C. (2020). The future of the corporation and the economics of purpose. Finance working paper 710/2020. Retrievable from https://ecgi.global/sites/default/files/working_papers/documents/mayerfinal_0.pdf.

Mercier-Laurent, E. (2021). Can AI efficiently support sustainable development? IJCAI-8thAI4KM. Retrievable from: https://hal.archives-ouvertes.fr/hal-03117248.

Mika, J. P., Colbourne, R., & Almeida, S. (2020). Responsible management: An indigenous perspective. In O. Laasch, R. Suddaby, R. E. Freeman, & D. Jamali (Eds.), *Research handbook of responsible management* (pp. 260–275). Edward Elgar Publishing Ltd..

Miller, B. (2021). Is technology value-neutral? *Science, Technology, & Human Values, 46*(1), 53–80.

Moore, J. (2018). Knowledge-based systems (KBS). Retrieved from https://searchcio.techtarget.com/definition/knowledge-based-systems-KBS.

Morales, P. A., True, S., & Tudor, R. K. (2020). Insights, challenges and recommendations for research on sustainability in marketing. *Journal of Global Scholars of Marketing Science, 30*(4), 394–406.

Moratis, L., & Melissen, F. (2021). Bolstering responsible management education through the sustainable development goals: Three perspectives. *Management Learning*, 1350507621990993.

Oosthuizen, K., Botha, E., Robertson, J., & Montecchi, M. (2021). Artificial intelligence in retail: The AI-enabled value chain. *Australasian Marketing Journal.* https://doi.org/10.1016/j.ausmj.2020.07.007

Paschen, J., Wilson, M., & Ferreira, J. J. (2020). Collaborative intelligence: How human and artificial intelligence create value along the B2B sales funnel. *Business Horizons, 63*(3), 403–414.

Pedro, F., Subosa, M., Rivas, A., & Valverde, P. (2019). Artificial intelligence in education: Challenges and opportunities for sustainable development. UNESCO France.

Philbeck, T., Davis, N., & Larsen, A. M. E. (2018, August). Values, ethics and innovation: Rethinking technological development in the fourth industrial revolution. World Economic Forum. Retrievable from http://www3.weforum.org/docs/WEF_WP_Values_Ethics_Innovation_2018.pdf.

Rasche, A., & Gilbert, D. U. (2015). Decoupling responsible management education: Why business schools may not walk their talk. *Journal of Management Inquiry, 24*(3), 239–252.

Reimer, K., Gla, U., Hamann, J., Gilchriest, B., & Teixeira, M. (2015). *Digital disruptive intermediaries: Finding new digital opportunities by disrupting established business models.* The Australian Digital Transformation Lab: The University of Sydney Business School and Capgemini Australia.

Rosenbloom, A. (2021). The sustainability marketing framework: A tool for teaching and learning about sustainability marketing. In J. Bhattacharyya, M. K. Dash, C. Hewege, M. S. Balaji, & W. M. Lim (Eds.), *Social and sustainability marketing* (pp. 13–52). Productivity Press.

Russell, S. J., & Norvig, P. (2016). *Artificial Intelligence: A modern approach* (3rd ed.). Pearson.

Schlee, R. P., & Harich, K. R. (2010). Knowledge and skill requirements for marketing jobs in the 21st century. *Journal of Marketing Education, 32*, 341–352.

Shrestha, Y. R., Krishna, V., & von Krogh, G. (2021). Augmenting organizational decision-making with deep learning algorithms: Principles, promises, and challenges. *Journal of Business Research, 123*, 588–603.

Swanson, D. L., & Frederick, W. C. (2003). Are business schools silent partners in corporate crime? *Journal of Corporate Citizenship, 9*, 24–27.

Thontirawong, P., & Chinchanachokchai, S. (2021). Teaching artificial intelligence and machine learning in marketing. *Marketing Education Review*, 1–6.

Tollin, K., & Christensen, L. B. (2019). Sustainability marketing commitment: Empirical insights about its drivers at the corporate and functional level of marketing. *Journal of Business Ethics, 156*(4), 1165–1185.

Tripathi, K. P. (2011). A review on knowledge-based expert system: Concept and architecture. *IJCA Special Issue on Artificial Intelligence Techniques-Novel Approaches & Practical Applications, 4*, 19–23.

Truby, J. (2020). Governing artificial intelligence to benefit the UN sustainable development goals. *Sustainable Development, 28*(4), 946–959.

van Ingen, R., Peters, P., De Ruiter, M., & Robben, H. (2021). *Exploring the meaning of organizational purpose at a new dawn: The development of a conceptual model through expert interviews* (p. 12). Frontiers in Psychology.

Vinuesa, R., Azizpour, H., Leite, I., Balaam, M., Dignum, V., Domisch, S., et al. (2020). The role of artificial intelligence in achieving the sustainable development goals. *Nature Communications, 11*(1), 1–10.

Wedel, M., & Kannan, P. K. (2016). Marketing analytics for data-rich environments. *Journal of Marketing, 80*(6), 97–121.

Weiss, S. M., & Indurkhya, N. (1998). *Predictive data mining: A practical guide.* Morgan Kaufmann.

Wodecki, A. (2020). *Artificial intelligence in management: Self-learning and autonomous systems as key drivers of value creation.* Edward Elgar Publishing.

Wymbs, C. (2011). Digital marketing: The time for a new "academic major" has arrived. *Journal of Marketing Education, 33*(1), 93–106.

Zsolnai, L. (2020). Identifying and solving the right problem by using multidimensional systems thinking. In L. Zsolnai & M. Thompson (Eds.), *Responsible research for better business: Creating useful and credible knowledge for business and society* (pp. 35–46). Palgrave Macmillan.

8

Compliance and ICT as a Tool to Generate Certainty in Countries with High Corruption Levels: The Case of Blockchain

Jose Godinez

8.1 Introduction

One of the most important tenets of the United Nations Principles for Responsible Management Education (PRME) is to provide students with tools to fight corruption (PRME, 2012). The emphasis on anticorruption education stems from the reality that business students are highly likely to encounter corrupt behavior in their careers (Becker et al., 2013). For that reason, research related to corruption has proliferated in several disciplines, such as history, law, psychology, political science, economics, and business administration. Concurrently, scholars and practitioners have recently developed tools to help future business leaders combat corruption. One of the most promising tools to combat corruption is blockchain (Van Niekerk, 2021). However, blockchain alone is not adequate to create a robust anticorruption program (Davis et al., 2021). For this reason, in this chapter, I outline how business schools should approach

J. Godinez (✉)
University of Massachusetts Lowell, Lowell, MA, USA
e-mail: jose_godinez@uml.edu

the teaching of blockchain technologies to increase their effectiveness in combating corruption in the private sector.

Corruption has increasingly become a serious problem for businesses since an increasing number of stakeholders are demanding firms to abstain from participating in it (Cuervo-Cazurra, 2016). To respond to such pressures, businesses are resorting to finding effective tools to combat them. One of the most promising tools to help firms combat corruption is blockchain. Blockchain is a technology that allows transactions to be recorded in a cyber-ledger and made visible to all stakeholders. Additionally, once transactions are written on the ledger, they cannot be altered and are replicated in all nodes in a network (Aarvik, 2020). Nevertheless, because corruption is a complex issue, a single technology cannot solve this problem. Instead, educators should provide students with a holistic educational approach to understand blockchain technology, including ethics, and collaboration with external stakeholders.

Therefore, in this chapter, I present an initial analysis of how educators should approach teaching the usage of blockchain technologies in business schools to help in the fight against corruption. I begin by describing the issue of corruption, what causes it and its consequences. I then present an analysis of how the fight against corruption has been studied in the extant literature. Subsequently, I present a review of blockchain technology and how it has been proposed to help in the fight against corruption. I finish the chapter by proposing how to effectively create a business education curriculum to combat corruption from the private sector with the aid of blockchain. Here, I argue that business schools should focus not only on blockchain technology to tackle corruption but also on helping students obtain business ethics education and knowledge on how to collaborate with external stakeholders.

8.2   Background

Corruption, the abuse of public power for personal gain (Cuervo-Cazurra, 2006), is considered one of the most important factors in a location (Peng et al., 2008) since it reflects its political, legal, economic, and cultural arrangements (Svensson, 2005). Scholarships analyzing the causes of corruption have discussed various country-level characteristics that could cause it. These characteristics include the culture of arms-length relationships (Tanzi, 1994), cultural dimensions (Zheng et al., 2013), ethnicity (Shleifer & Vishny, 1993), and ethnolinguistic diversity (Mauro, 1995). At the individual level, corruption is the result of the incentives of government officials to request a bribe and for businesses to offer one while not facing serious consequences if caught (Godinez & Liu, 2018).

A country where corruption is rampant and has become an accepted and normal practice shows a disregard for the norms, rules, and regulations that preside economic interactions within a society (Rodriguez et al., 2005). Thus, in locations where corruption is rampant, there are negative effects. Countries with high corruption levels are generally less developed (Mauro, 1998), attract low levels of investment (Habib & Zurawicki, 2002), have a lower average of exports (Lee & Weng, 2013), have nonperforming bank loans (Park, 2012), and have higher environmental degradation (Haseeb & Azam, 2021).

At the firm level, organizations operating in highly corrupt locations face increased costs associated with corrupt payments, which can be seen as a tax on operations (Wei, 2000). Additionally, firms face potential costs, including penalties, fines, and lawsuits (Rabbiosi & Santangelo, 2019), and reputational costs that stem from a negative corporate image if a firm is implicated in corrupt activities (Luo, 2005). Despite the high costs that firms face when operating in highly corrupt locations, scholars argue that the most detrimental effect of corruption on firms is the uncertainty it creates (Rodriguez et al., 2005). This uncertainty makes it difficult for firms to estimate operating costs and whether services, permits, and the allocation of public contracts will be guaranteed after paying bribes (Uhlenbruck et al., 2006).

8.3   Combatting Corruption

Traditionally, anticorruption measures have focused on attempts to improve official public behavior. This approach consists of strengthening governance mechanisms that include rule of law enforcement and property rights. There is evidence that governance variables such as the rule of law enforcement decrease corruption levels (Ades & Di Tella, 1996; Rauch & Evans, 2000). Additionally, conventional approaches include microeconomic agent-principal models that propose that asymmetry of information can allow public officials to pursue their own interest by extracting rents from private-sector organizations (Rose-Ackerman, 1978; Spector, 2005). Thus, the majority of conventional anticorruption actions focus on a combination of measures to improve the enforcement of formal rules along with policies aimed at changing the cost–benefit calculations of public officials in the context of asymmetric information (Khan et al., 2019). Nevertheless, these measures have not delivered positive results because (a) they assume that countries on which corruption is rampant are rule-following and (b) because they have not included the supply side of the equation—the private sector. While improving the institutional environment of a location is necessary to effectively combat corruption, below, I focus on what private firms can do to combat this problem.

To reduce corruption from the supply side, private firms should take concrete steps to stop participation in corrupt deals. To this end, firms should specify what corruption is, what actions are acceptable, create a code of conduct, and implement it (Doh et al., 2003). Additionally, firms should ensure that all members of the organization are familiar with the company's policies and provide them with training to avoid potentially ambiguous situations (Cuervo-Cazurra, 2016). Additionally, firms can create and implement controls to limit employees' ability to engage in corrupt activities, such as paying bribes, by requiring supervisors to approve payments above certain levels, giving donations to political parties or government officials, or to provide payments to individuals or organizations that could create conflicts of interest (Godinez et al., 2021). Companies can also use certifications to signal adherence to anticorruption measures (Montiel et al., 2012).

Recently, scholars and practitioners have argued that the emergence of new technologies can help the fight against corruption from the private sector. Indeed, technological advancement has helped firms create new methods, tools, and mechanisms to combat corruption since they can enhance transparency and trust. One such technology is Blockchain, the technology behind Bitcoin, which is said to help create robust anticorruption systems (Wellisz, 2018). Nevertheless, as with any new technology, it needs to be well understood and applied for it to be effective. Below, I present the pros and cons of teaching students to rely on Blockchain to create anticorruption systems in the private sector.

8.4   Blockchain: Background Information

The history of blockchain can be traced back to Haber and Stornetta's (1991) paper analyzing how to timestamp digital documents. This paper described how cryptographers could tackle the issue of certifying the authenticity of digital content such as audio, video, or text since this could be easily modified or duplicated. Additionally, the certification of the date that digital content could be created or altered was difficult. The solution proposed was to timestamp documents digitally and to link these "certificates" in a chain with the help of cryptography and digital signatures. Hence, the aim of time-stamping digital documents was to make it impossible to back-date or forward-date digital content, which would provide authenticity proof. The concept of timestamping was then further developed, arranging several documents in groups or blocks. This gave rise to the term blockchain (Aarvik, 2020).

Following the emergence of the new technology, electronic cash started arising. At first, electronic cash was used for micropayments, and this technology was embraced by European banks such as Deutsche Bank and Credit Suisse but later abandoned (Baddeley, 2004). Simultaneously, Bit Gold, the predecessor or Bitcoin, was developed but never reached markets. However, in 2008, a famous white paper written by the pseudonym Satoshi Nakamoto described an entirely digital currency from a radical libertarian point of view. In this paper, the author(s) argued that the currency would not be under the governance of any institution but instead would be managed by a network of volunteer stakeholders bypassing central banks.

One of the most important features of the blockchain is that all transactions are made visible to all stakeholders. This means that all transactions are written on the ledger, clustered in blocks, and linked to each other in an unbreakable chain by using cryptographic hashes (Aarvik, 2020). Then, the whole ledger is replicated in all full nodes in the network, which are the computers running the software behind the blockchain. The entire ledger is replicated in all full nodes in the network. Additionally, an algorithm is in place to prevent double spending of coins, to ensure that only valid transactions take place, and to protect the blockchain from attacks. This process is called the "consensus mechanism," which is paramount to generate trust in the blockchain.

Since blockchain is a distributed technology, it has lauded to provide transparency and traceability to complex transactions outside cryptocurrencies. One place where blockchain technologies have attracted attention is transactions in business transactions where peer-to-peer communications ensure that business requirements such as product information (e.g., origin, modifications, production, and custody) are ensured (Sarker et al., 2021). Thus, blockchain allows businesses to establish trust and create traceability by securing and authenticating information in transactions. Moreover, blockchain technology provides transparency and data integrity in a similar manner to centralized, secured e-government systems do in public decision-making processes, which can reduce illegal practices such as corruption.

8.5   Blockchain to Combat Corruption

Blockchain technologies have been touted as effective anticorruption measures since they offer tamper-proof records that corrupt public officials cannot modify. For this reason, the World Economic Forum featured an article stating that blockchain has "emerged as the most promising disruptive technology in the fight against corruption… it possesses important features that can help anchor integrity in bureaucracies, by securing identity, tracking funds, registering assets, and procuring contracts" (Santiso, 2019). The rationale behind utilizing blockchain technologies to combat corruption is that this technology can generate trust in transactions among the public and private sectors.

Looking back at the early online commerce arena, it is safe to say that trust played a pivotal role in its surge since it involved transactions among strangers. Additionally, the sharing economy has benefited from the trust provided by online platforms that serve as intermediaries between the supplier and the receiver of a given service. Hence, proponents of blockchain technologies as an anticorruption tool argue that trust can be gained depending on the quality of the code written for this purpose, adequate testing, and the implementation of security controls (Sarker et al., 2021).

Nevertheless, equally important but less discussed is the role of the "human element" in generating trust in blockchain technology to create anticorruption measures for firms. However, the human element is crucial in this endeavor since humans are in charge of entering records into the blockchain. This is because the records written in the blockchain represent objects or values that do not live in cyberspace but in the physical world. This means that the person (or persons) in charge of entering data for the blockchain must be trusted to ensure that the system works and that the data recorded are reliable and truthful. Hence, educators who decide to promote blockchain technologies in the classroom with the purpose of creating anticorruption strategies need to provide nuances to students regarding the effective use of such technologies, as outlined below.

8.6 Educators' Approach to Using Blockchain Technologies in the Classroom

There is consensus regarding the crucial role of education in enhancing anticorruption efforts (Becker et al., 2013). When discussing private-sector programs aimed at combatting corruption, scholars and practitioners agree on the central role that today's students have in tomorrow's business ethical climate (Birtch & Chiang, 2014). For that reason, business schools are adapting their curricula to create specific courses aimed at enhancing ethical business practices (Manning, 2014), which includes taking advantage of blockchain technologies to combat corruption.

It is important to note that due to the complexities surrounding corruption, there is no "silver bullet" to end this problem. However, blockchain technologies have been regarded as an effective anticorruption tool that can be quickly adapted by businesses (Fanea-Ivanovici et al., 2019). While its potential is real, educators should help students understand that blockchain can be a powerful tool that can help create anticorruption strategies but that more is needed for a comprehensive anticorruption program. Below, I focus on the role of ethics and collaborations with external stakeholders for the effective teaching of the usage of blockchain technologies to combat corruption in the private sector.

Ethics Ethics can be defined as the values that a person utilizes to interpret if a particular behavior or action is considered appropriate and acceptable. To analyze what is appropriate and acceptable, moral values (the principles, character, and the assessment of consequences of actions) must be identified and supported (Stanwick & Stanwick, 2016). While business schools all over the world are creating and implementing business ethics courses in their curricula, it is important to highlight their interdependence with other courses, especially those related to creating anticorruption strategies. Thus, instructors should place special emphasis on *why* it is important to utilize technologies, such as blockchain, to help businesses in their anticorruption endeavors instead of just focusing on *how*.

While there is consensus that ethics should be part of a business education, there is still skepticism regarding whether ethics are being effectively thought in the classroom (Van Liedekerke & Demuijnck, 2011). The criticism geared toward teaching business ethics lays on the argument that by the time that students reach college, their values have already been formed. Others argue that since business is mostly conducted with self-interest, ethics are not of prime importance (Wang & Calvano, 2015). Hence, before venturing to teaching the usage of blockchain to combat corruption, educators must first create a comprehensive business ethics curriculum that addresses possible shortcomings of teaching ethics in the classroom. For this reason, business schools must acknowledge that business ethics and the use of technology to face corruption are not isolated aspects in a curriculum but instead are part of a complex system that will guide future professionals to behave ethically.

Collaborations Educators have to convey students that although block-chain technology has important merits, it is unlikely that it can break institutionalized corruption or eliminate the process of the formation of corrupt systems in a location (Narula, 2019; Davis et al., 2021). Hence, it is important for students to understand that for blockchain technologies to help in the fight against corruption, collaborations with other firms along the supply chain and eventually with governments are needed.

Suppliers and distributors are rarely exclusive to one company. This means that educators must instill in their students the idea that there are steps to be taken with partners before enacting strategies against corruption relying on blockchains. Thus, students should understand that efforts must be made to create collective support for anticorruption strategies, and incentives must be created to reach common goals (to not participate in corrupt deals). Furthermore, constant communication, training, and assessment should be part of the anticorruption strategies as well as the adoption of blockchain technology. If educators stress the importance of these processes accounting for different partners in the supply chain, blockchain technology can mitigate corruption and benefit all parties involved.

A crucial point for blockchain technologies to help in the fight against corruption is their effective usage to deal with public officials. Students should understand that in their careers, they will be likely to encounter illegal requests from government officials (Becker et al., 2013). Thus, it is important for students to understand how to properly utilize technology to minimize their exposure to corrupt government officials. In this case, the nature of blockchain can help since dealings with governments can be recorded in public blockchains, which provide full transparency and immutability. This can help the firm with the transparency needed to operate in locations characterized by high corruption.

8.7   Conclusions

Blockchain technologies have been touted as an effective tool to fight corruption from the private sector. However, for this technology to be effective, business educators need to convey to their students that blockchain technologies alone cannot combat corruption. Instead, educators must tackle the implementation of anticorruption strategies as part of a complex curricula that students must understand. These curricula should rely heavily on the teaching of business ethics and the need to collaborate with external stakeholders in addition to providing knowledge on blockchain technology for blockchain to be utilized in the fight against corruption.

References

Aarvik, P. (2020). Blockchain as anti-corruption tool: Case examples and introduction to the technology. U4 anti-corruption resource centre: Michelsen Institute. https://bit.ly/3f3JjzO.

Ades, A., & Di Tella, R. (1996). The causes and consequences of corruption: A review of recent empirical contributions. *IDS Bulletin, 27*, 6–11.

Baddeley, M. (2004). Using e-cash in the new economy: An economic analysis of micropayment systems. *Journal of Electronic Commerce Research, 5*, 239–253.

Becker, K., Hauser, C., & Kronthaler, F. (2013). Fostering management education to deter corruption: What do students know about corruption and its legal consequences? *Crime Law and Social Change, 60*, 227–240.

Birtch, T., & Chiang, F. (2014). The influence of business schools' ethical climate on students' unethical behavior. *Journal of Business Ethics, 123*, 283–294.

Cuervo-Cazurra, A. (2006). Who cares about corruption? *Journal of International Business Studies, 37*, 803–822.

Cuervo-Cazurra, A. (2016). Corruption in international business. *Journal of World Business, 51*, 35–49.

Davis, M., Lennerfors, T., & Tolstoy, D. (2021). Can blockchain-technology fight corruption in MNEs' operations in emerging markets? *Review of International Business and Strategy.* https://doi.org/10.1108/RIBS-12-2020-0155

Doh, J., Rodriguez, P., Uhlenbruck, K., Collins, J., & Eden, L. (2003). Coping with corruption in foreign markets. *Academy of Management Executive, 3*, 114–127.

Fanea-Ivanovici, M., Musetescu, R. C., Pana, M. C., & Voicu, C. (2019). Fighting corruption and enhancing tax compliance through digitization:

Achieving sustainable development in Romania. *Sustainability*. https://doi.org/10.3390/su11051480

Godinez, J., Bandeira de Mello, R., Sanchez-Barrios, L., & Khalik, M. (2021). Familiarity does not breed contempt: Curbing subsidiary corruption through a legitimacy-enhanced ownership structure. *Latin American Business Review*. https://doi.org/10.1080/10978526.2021.1932518

Godinez, J., & Liu, L. (2018). Corruption and its effects on FDI: Analyzing the interaction between the corruption levels of the home and host countries and its effects at the decision-making level. *Journal of Business Ethics, 147*, 705–719.

Haber, S., & Stornetta, S. (1991). How to time-stamp a digital document. *Journal of Cryptology, 3*, 99–111.

Habib, M., & Zurawicki, L. (2002). Corruption and foreign direct investment. *Journal of International Business Studies, 33*, 291–307.

Haseeb, M., & Azam, M. (2021). Dynamic nexus among tourism, corruption, democracy and environmental degradation: A panel data investigation. *Environment, Development, and Sustainability, 23*, 5557–5575.

Khan, M., Andreoni, A., & Roy, P. (2019). *Anti-corruption in adverse contexts: Strategies for improving implementation.* SOAS-ACE Working Paper No. 13. London: University of London.

Lee, S. H., & Weng, D. H. (2013). Does bribery in the home country promote or dampen firm exports? *Strategic Management Journal, 34*, 1472–1487.

Luo, Y. (2005). An organizational perspective of corruption. *Management and Organization Review, 1*, 119–154.

Manning, P. (2014). Embedding anti-corruption in the MBA curriculum: Reflections on a case history analysis of affinity fraud. *Journal of Global Responsibility, 9*, 111–129.

Mauro, P. (1995). Corruption and growth. *Quarterly Journal of Economics, 110*, 681–712.

Mauro, P. (1998). Corruption: Causes, consequences, and agenda for further research. *Finance and Development, 11*. https://doi.org/10.5089/97814519553220.022

Montiel, I., Husted, B., & Christmann, P. (2012). Using private management standard certification to reduce information asymmetries in corrupt environments. *Strategic Management Journal, 33*, 1103–1113.

Narula, R. (2019). Enforcing higher labor standards within developing country value chains: Consequences for MNEs and informal actors in a dual economy. *Journal of International Business Studies, 50*, 1622–1635.

Park, J. (2012). Corruption, soundness of the banking sector, and economic growth: A cross-country study. *Journal of International Money and Finance, 31*, 907–929.

Peng, M., Wang, D., & Jiang, Y. (2008). An institution-based view of international business strategy: A focus on emerging economies. *Journal of International Business Studies, 39*, 920–936.

PRME. (2012). Anti-corruption guidelines ("Toolkit") for MBA curriculum change. A project by the Anti-Corruption Working Group of the principles for responsible management education (PRME) initiative, United Nations Global Compact.

Rabbiosi, L., & Santangelo, G. (2019). Host country corruption and the organization of HQ-subsidiary relationships. *Journal of International Business Studies, 50*, 111–124.

Rauch, J., & Evans, P. (2000). Bureaucratic structure and bureaucratic performance in less developed countries. *Journal of Public Economics, 75*, 49–71.

Rodriguez, P., Uhlenbruck, K., & Eden, L. (2005). Government corruption and the entry strategies of multinationals. *Academy of Management Review, 30*, 383–396.

Rose-Ackerman, S. (1978). *Corruption: A study in political economy.* Academia Press.

Santiso, C. (2019). Here's how technology is changing the corruption game. *World Economic Forum.* https://weforum.org/agenda/2019/02/here-s-how-technology-is-changing-the-corruption-game/.

Sarker, S., Henningsson, S., Jensen, T., & Hedman, J. (2021). The use of blockchain as a resource for combating corruption in global shipping: An interpretive case study. *Journal of Management Information Systems, 38*, 338–373.

Stanwick, P., & Stanwick, S. (2016). *Understanding business ethics* (3rd ed.). Los Angeles.

Shleifer, A., & Vishny, R. (1993). Corruption. *Quarterly Journal of Economics, 108*, 599–617.

Spector, B. (2005). *Fighting corruption in developing countries: Strategies and analysis.* Kumarian Press.

Svensson, J. (2005). Eight questions about corruption. *Journal of Economic Perspectives, 19*, 19–42.

Tanzi, V. (1994). Corruption, governmental activities, and markets. IMF working paper no. 94/99. http://papers.ssrn.com/sol3/papers.cfm?abstract_id=883840.

Uhlenbruck, K., Rodriguez, P., Doh, J., & Eden, L. (2006). The impact of corruption on entry strategy: Evidence from telecommunication projects in emerging economies. *Organization Science, 17*, 402–414.

Van Liedekerke, L., & Demuijnck, G. (2011). Business ethics as a field of training, teaching and research in Europe. *Journal of Business Ethics, 104*, 29–41.

Van Niekerk, M. (2021). How blockchain can help dismantle corruption in government services. *World Economic Forum.* https://weforum.org/agenda/2121/07/blockchain-for-government-systems-anti-corruption/.

Wang, L., & Calvano, L. (2015). Is business ethics education effective? An analysis of gender, personal ethical perspectives, and moral judgment. *Journal of Business Ethics, 126*, 591–602.

Wei, S. J. (2000). How taxing is corruption in international investors? *Review of Economic and Statistics, 82*, 1–11.

Wellisz, C. (2018). Digital crusaders: Technology offers weapons for the battle against corruption. *Finance and Development, 55*, 40–43.

Zheng, X., Ghoul, S. E., Guedhami, O., & Kwok, C. (2013). Collectivism and corruption in bank lending. *Journal of International Business Studies, 44*, 363–390.

9

Compliance and Integrity as Core Elements of Governance in the Educational Sector in the Digital Age

Bartosz Makowicz

9.1 Introduction

The educational sector builds a substantial and very characteristic part of our society. Scientific inventions followed by science transfer into practice and proper education of young generations offer the foundation for quality of life, economic growth, social progress, and welfare. In recent years, an increasing number of educational and scientific processes have been conducted with the support of digitalized tools. In particular, the pandemic caused an immense acceleration of the digitalization of the educational sector. At the same time, digitalization brings new risks. Educational institutions, however, usually neither have proper tools to address those risks nor have their members a sufficient awareness of it. Digitalization could therefore be compared with a double-edged sword: On the one hand, it creates new chances and possibilities, it supports the

B. Makowicz (✉)
Viadrina Compliance Center at the European University Viadrina,
Frankfurt(Oder), Germany
e-mail: makowicz@europa-uni.de

processes, and it creates an added value; on the other hand, it causes new risks such as breaches of personal data, fake news, unethical manipulation of scientific results, or cyber-attacks, just to mention a few of them. It is a real challenge for academic institutions to bring those two edges into proper action at the same time. On the one hand, they are reliant on using modern IT tools by now, not only to catch up with the latest trends but also to provide continuity in education—if considering lockdowns and e-learning in times like these. On the other hand, they have to ensure that new risks emerging from the use of innovative tools are being addressed through adequate processes and structures.

An answer to this question could be found in governance and management concepts originating from the private sector. Building and strengthening digital ethics and awareness should start at the governance level. It should be supported at the management level, where companies have developed the concepts of compliance and integrity management systems that aim to safeguard responsibility and to support fairness, conformity with rules and regulation, good image and strengthen the trust of their stakeholders. In this contribution, I will analyze whether and to what extent a robust concept of modern governance, compliance management and integrity (GCI) could also be implemented within an educational sector to face the new risks of the digital age. To maintain a practical character of mentioned solutions the analysis will focus on the governance and management perspective. The described concepts may be implemented regardless the national legal regulations. To present the most recent developments in this area and in lack of internationally bounding laws, the following text is partially based on the respective globally acknowledged standards of the International Organization for Standardization (ISO).

9.2   Goals and Advantages of GCI

In sectors other than academia, organizations several years ago have developed robust systematic approaches to address a huge range of risks (including those arising from digitalization). Those systems also aim to strengthen and support awareness and—by implementing adequate procedures and processes—to create a sustainable compliance culture as a core element of organizational governance. In the following years, the focus has been turned on humans and their behaviors, and increasing integrity and ethical aspects have been considered within compliance management systems (CMSs). Currently, an adequate CMS aims to secure the proper conduct of operational activities. It facilitates processes and structures, introduces new possibilities, strengthens transparency and creates safe surroundings for operational business. Notably, one of the main targets is protecting the good image of organizations. Meanwhile, there is no doubt that effective CMS and integrity contribute significantly to the success of companies and sustainably increase their value. The presence of such a system can lead to considerable mitigation of sanctions in cases of liability, as legal systems, such as the highest jurisdiction in Germany shows.[1] However, is it even possible to transfer these approaches to the educational sector, and if so—will applying them be just as promising and successful in this area?

9.3   Justification for Implementation of GCI in the Educational Sector

As stated thus far, the concept of compliance management and integrity forms a part of the governance systems in most organizations from the private sector. This means that the solutions are adjusted to be effective within the hierarchical structure where the purpose of the organization is to make a monetary profit. Before going deeper into those concepts, it therefore must be cleared if it is rational to adopt them within educational institutions. There are some approaches that state a clear justification for it. Only one of them derives from the legal point of view, the others are multidisciplinary oriented.

---

[1] According to the sentence of the German Federal Highest Court the existence of an effective Compliance Management should be considered positive when assessing the number of sanctions against a company.

Terminological Approach

The terminological approach shall be the first one here, so for that reason let us start with some basic definitions. Compliance means fulfilling all organizational obligations—those obligatory and those voluntarily adopted by an organization. Compliance management is a set of inter-relating or interacting elements of an organization to establish policies and objectives, as well as processes to achieve compliance.[2] Integrity in the sense of "organizational integrity" means that all members of the particular organization know and incorporate the organizational values and behave in accordance with them. It is evident that, in this regard, one can only speak of conduct with integrity if the person's inner conviction and values are identical to their behavior. However, it must be mentioned that values and rules defined within an organization are not necessarily always those represented by the individual personally. Therefore, when speaking of organizational integrity or short "Integrity" in this contribution, so-called corporate integrity is meant. Since we are dealing with the educational sector here, the term "educational integrity" seems to be the proper one. Hence, the aim of integrity management will be that the members of the organization incorporate the rules and values that previously have been defined by the organization and behave in accordance with them. In this way, it will be harder for the individual to justify potential breaches to themselves. This leads us to the first interface between compliance and integrity: In both cases, it is about following rules, regulations, and values when acting in or for organizations, and therefore, it is all about human behavior.

However, which conclusions can be drawn from this? First, both systems can and should be combined. Second, the center of attention is the human individual itself in both systems, either as a member of a company or as teaching staff a member of an educational institution. It is therefore irrelevant if we are dealing with corporations, enterprises, churches, or educational institutions: In all those cases, we have to do with human beings, their behaviors, rules and regulations. This is why

---

[2] Definitions after ISO 37301:2021 Compliance Management Systems.

the terminological approach justifies the adoption of compliance and integrity concepts in the educational sector.

Organizational and Moral Approach

The second justification approach is the organizational one. Both companies and educational institutions are included in the category "organization." It may sound controversial and radical at this point, but most of us would agree on this, that humans are gregarious animals. The image of the herd is based on our society's comprehension. We feel stronger and safer when appearing in a herd. Sticking together and working in a group turned out to be more effective because of the assignment of responsibilities and tasks to particular group members. In this way, a better and faster track for achieving various purposes is provided. Over time, organizations emerged out of loose and informal groups. Those groups are conceived on a sustainable basis, pursue certain targets and, as such, are part of a larger picture. Thus, from the societal perspective, organizations provide our shared public asset. Once having stated that, it is obvious that no matter with what kind of organization—private company or educational institution—we have to deal with it, it should be a moral obligation of their members to behave in accordance with rules and regulations and to act in line with values. Only this responsible conduct will ensure that organizations will prosper correctly and contribute in the desired way to our societies.

Risk Approach

However, groups and especially organizations are creating risks that would not appear if acting individually. It is not unusual that the organization itself creates an environment where it seems easier to take actions against the values one has or predetermined values or even to violate regulations. Through groups, new dynamics and possibilities come into existence. Therefore, it does not matter which organization, in particular, it is about and irrespective of whether there is a legal obligation for it (in most cases there is none), all types of organizations should take responsibility for the risks they create by detecting them and by addressing them adequately. This moral obligation grows with the function organizations play for society. Considering the importance of the educational sector for social and economic progress, it becomes obvious that this kind of organization should also identify and address their risks with the help of a systematic approach. Reflecting on that ground the thoughts from the beginning of this chapter (groups and organizations form the core of our society), it is clear that ensuring the integrity of all kinds of organizations should be in the interest of both the state and society.

The third approach for justification is therefore a risk-based approach. Research institutions are also organizations composed of several individuals who pursue certain goals and that have structures and processes in place. As such, they are exposed to numerous risks, such as misconduct of educational staff, breach of data protection laws, and others, that can lead to clear consequences—legal, financial, and reputational ones. It is therefore the inherent obligation of any organization, including educational institutions, to assess their compliance risks and appropriately address them as well as to clearly promote organizational integrity.

Interim Conclusion

Summarizing this chapter, it can be concluded that all mentioned approaches—terminological, organizational, and risk approaches—justify the adoption of the concepts of compliance management, and integrity to the educational sector.

9.4   The Concept of Compliance and Integrity Management

After having elaborated that it does make sense to think about implementing the concept of governance, compliance management, and integrity, in this chapter, some consideration will follow on the core of this article, namely, the overview of these concepts and how they could be adopted in the educational sector. To present the "state of the art" in those areas, the following thoughts will be based mainly on two international standards. The first one is the ISO 37301 Compliance Management Systems that was revised (former ISO 196000) and published in 2021 by the International Organization for Standardization and is applicable in any kind of organization.[3] The second is the brand-new standard ISO 37000 Governance of Organizations, which is also applicable to all kinds of organizations and was published in September 2021. Although the ISO standards may be in general a subject of discussion in scientific circles, they are widely spread and globally acknowledged not only by the enterprises but also by organizations in other sectors, including public administration and NGOs.

General Remarks

However, before starting the short analysis, the general character of ISO standards should be explained. The ISO constitutes an umbrella organization for national standardization bodies. This means that it is a private organization that develops industrial and management system standards with worldwide recognition. Over 150 national standardization institutes are members of ISO. What needs to be stressed here is that ISO standards are not legally binding laws. In other words, following ISO standards is voluntary. Each organization decides whether to follow an ISO standard. On the other hand, keeping in mind that those standards represent global know-how in certain areas, they usually become very rapidly the "state of the art" in the relevant fields and therefore can influence the application of the law.[4] In other cases, companies would not deal with their partners if the latter did not provide evidence of having implemented a particular ISO standard, for example, in the area of quality management.

---

[3] ISO 37301:2021 replaced the former standard ISO 19600 Compliance Management Systems after its revision.

[4] In this way certain things are introduced by German case law, so ISO standards can apply as so-called anticipated expert examination.

By developing a new standard for compliance management systems (ISO 19600) approximately 10 years ago, ISO started with standardization in the fields of governance and compliance management. Subsequently, in 2016, the standard in the area of antibribery management systems (ISO 37001) followed.[5] In 2021, another standard concerning whistleblowing management systems (ISO 37002) was published. Nevertheless, another standard was published in September 2021: ISO 37000 Governance of Organizations. This standard is supposed to overarch the standards for management systems. It lies within the usual relation between governance and management from the perspective of an organization. While governance is about the principles, views and goals with overarching importance ("doing the *right things*"), management is about how those approaches can be achieved correctly in the operating business ("*doing* the things right").

A similar relationship between governance and management can also be drawn when thinking about educational institutions, even if they are marked by the characteristics of academia (more on that later). Furthermore, educational institutions have their goals regarding strategic development, but they do also have their administrative structures, policies, and processes to reach them, and by that, they come close to the business sector. Therefore, the distinction between the governance and the management level can easily also be drawn regarding educational institutions, so these two standards (governance and compliance) can also be implemented in an educational institution.

Finally, there is another ISO-specific distinction criterion when dealing with ISO standards that should be mentioned. Whether there is a certain need for this kind of standard from the organizational perspective and depending on which management area is supposed to be standardized, there are standards of type A and B in the ISO nomenclature. Type B standards are so-called guidance with recommendations, while type A standards are those with requirements. The most substantial difference is the certifiability, which only comes with type A standards (requirements).

---

[5] Since bribery risks are covered by the brother term of compliance risk and can effectively be addressed within a Compliance Management System it will not be a subject of this article. If an organization has already a robust Compliance Management System in place, addressing also bribery risks with it, it does not need an additional stand-alone Anti-Bribery Management Systems.

Only a standard of this type can be subject to an audit once it has been implemented in an organization. At the end of a successful certification process, a certificate stating conformity with the requirements of the standard is to be issued. This possibility is not given in regard to type B standards. When applying this to the previously mentioned relevant standards, ISO 37000 is a type B standard, while ISO 37301 is a type A standard. Both of them, however, are still flexible enough to be adjusted to the size, structure, type, and complexity of a particular organization and thus to an educational institution.

Governance

Since the concept of governance stands as a roof over several management systems, the following short analysis of its adoption to the educational sector will first focus on this part.

First, ISO 37000 applies to all types of organizations, regardless of type, size, location, structure, or purpose. Although mainly developed to be implemented in the private sector, its guidelines and principles regarding good governance are therefore universal and can be adopted easily in educational institutions as well.

ISO 37000 provides a flexible set of rules (so called "principle driven standard") that offers organizations excellent orientation when thinking about modern approaches in governance. It defines key principles and recommendations on how the governing body can meet its responsibilities and enable the organization to fulfill its purpose.[6] Bevor having a closer look at its adoption to the educational sector, let us focus on some of the core principles and its relationship with compliance management.

The standard is systematically divided into three levels. First, it starts with foundational governance principles such as purpose, value generation, strategy, oversight and accountability. The second level focuses on operational governance and tries to answer the question of how foundational governance principles can be achieved. It contains some thoughts on stakeholder engagement, underlines the role of leadership, data and

---

[6] No. 4.1 ISO 37000:2021 Governance of Organizations.

decisions, risk governance, social responsibility, and finishes with sustainability. The last, third level contains governance outcomes, achievable with good governance, which are responsible stewardship, effective performance and last but not least ethical behavior.[7] The standard itself interestingly also specifies some goals of governance, which are to perform as required, to realize value for stakeholders and to remain in compliance with regulations.[8] Regarding this aspect, we can see a direct relationship with compliance management. The further link to compliance is created by "responsible stewardship," which means that organizations make responsible use of resources, effectively balance negative and positive impacts, consider its global context, and ensure sustainability.[9] Finally, there is ethical behavior that includes but is not limited to integrity and transparency, fairness, and accountability.[10] Thus far, it is obvious that the concepts of governance and compliance, on which ISO standards are based, are very close to each other.

Regarding ISO 37000, it is not only the mentioned basic principles and goals that can easily be adopted within an educational institution but also the methodology suggested by the standard to reach those goals and implement those principles. Some examples will be now provided.

Let us start with performance as one of the mentioned governance principles. There is no doubt that one of the main goals of educational institutions is to deliver excellent performance in research and education. This is precisely where the first challenges are about to begin. Most educational institutions, for example universities, have a wide spectrum of diverse stakeholders whose concerns need to be addressed. In regard to teaching, it is certainly students but also representatives of private and public sectors (future employers) who expect certain study programs to be offered in a way that allows graduates to perform their jobs properly in the future. In terms of research, the whole society is interested in scientific progress, covering the development of all aspects of life, whether it is medicine, industry, or new technologies, so that research should be

---

[7] Fig. 1 ISO 37000:2021 Governance of Organizations.
[8] No. 6 ISO 37000:2021 Governance of Organizations.
[9] No. 6 ISO 37000:2021 Governance of Organizations.
[10] No. 6 ISO 37000:2021 Governance of Organizations.

conducted in close relationship to practice. Only by doing so can the transfer of knowledge and technology be ensured.

The second main principle makes it even more interesting: responsible stewardship. A responsible and responsive administration is the basic requirement for effective and efficient education. Often, educational institutions have to deal with overwhelming administrative structures that are not up to date at all. Even in regard to very simple research projects that could result in valuable educational programs, the application procedure can be highly complex and long lasting. To this end, destructive administration can be deterring and therefore prevent starting new and interesting scientific projects. Let us elaborate a little deeper on that point regarding the educational area. Our rapidly changing world, strong globalization and digitalization demand dynamic processes. As a result, interdisciplinary and innovative study programs must come into existence. The lack of deep interdisciplinary cooperations between faculty members and the time-consuming procedures of certification of new study programs are the main obstacles that can negatively impact the creation of new innovative education programs. Speaking of administration leads us automatically to digitalization. If one considers an educational institution as an operating unit in which processes and structures exist that are supposed to lead to certain goals (research and teaching), it becomes obvious that by a robust systematic governance approach, many of the just-mentioned structures and processes can be significantly accelerated and simplified.

This brings us to the third principle: ethical behavior. As a goal of good governance, it has great relevance for the operation of educational institutions, not only on one but also on several levels at the same time. If beginning with the area of research, implementing a robust Code of Ethics for Researchers that are already in place at most educational institutions is not enough. Further processes and structures should be implemented to ensure that the fundamental values of each educational institution and thus the educational sector form the basis for the daily behavior of its teaching staff (integrity). The same applies to the research area too. Ethical conduct should be demanded not only from students but also and especially from academic teachers. They usually fill the position as a role model for the students. At this point, the so-called "tone from the top" can play a significant role. It can be practiced in the daily interaction between students and teachers in regard to values such as equal treatment, respect, fairness and others.

What can be stated thus far is that the new standard ISO 37000 will be useful for those who govern organizations as well as for managers, consultants and other stakeholders. It addresses both environmental and social aspects and fits best into the modern concept of ESG (environmental, social and governance). Furthermore, due to the high-level structure, it can be implemented jointly with management system standards, mainly the abovementioned new ISO 37301 (compliance management systems) and the ISO 37002 (whistleblowing management systems). Governance and management are complimentary within organizations and should interact and influence each other. The abovementioned examples easily demonstrate that the fundamental governance principles included in ISO 37000 and at the same time the core of good governance can be perfectly applied in the educational sector and, indeed, should be applied. It would go beyond the scope of this contribution if we took a look at all the measures recommended by the standard, which help with pursuing and achieving those principles. Instead, it will be continued with a different section dealing more specifically with ensuring compliance and integrity within an educational institution.

Compliance and Integrity

After focusing on the level of governance, it is time to move forward to the operational level of management and to see how the approach of compliance management in line with ISO 37301 and integrity can be adopted in educational institutions. The main goal of any compliance management system should be to create and support a sustainable compliance culture and integrity. It means it should create an environment in which every single member of the organization not only knows, understands, and follows her or his obligations and duties (compliance) but also knows and understands the organizations´ ethical values and behaves in accordance with them (integrity). In that sense, a compliance management system is defined by the standard as the values, ethics and beliefs (again the terminology of integrity) that exist throughout an organization and interact with the organization's structures and control systems to produce behavioral norms that are conducive to compliance outcomes (which is to fulfill all obligations).[11]

Compliance as a Management System

Before going into detail, it should be stressed that the abovementioned goals will only be achieved when implementing compliance and integrity as a management system. It is a continuous and systematic quality process in which not only the outcome counts but also the continuous improvement of the system itself. The CMS as recommended by ISO 37301 therefore follows the so-called PDCA cycle. In the sense of this cycle deriving from the quality management discipline, any management system should start with planning (P), followed by doing (D), checking (C), and acting (A). In terms of a management system, it means that the system or its element should first be carefully planned, then implemented within the organization and subsequently checked and improved. PDCA is one of the possible approaches ensuring that the goals of compliance and integrity would be pursued systematically and sustainably.

Coming now back to educational institutions, there seems to be no doubts this kind of systematic management approach could also be implemented within this kind of structure. Educational institutions also have their particular structures, processes and policies, creating risks that should be adequately addressed based on a systematic and reliable approach.

Adopting a CMS in Educational Institutions

Following the structure of this article, after having shortly analyzed the extent of adoption of the concept of governance in educational institutions, the same is to be done but in regard to the concept of compliance management. To ensure that the outcome of this short analysis is reliable,

---

[11] See No. 3.4 ISO 37301:2021 Compliance Management Systems.

the focus will be placed on the core elements of a CMS in line with the ISO 37301 Compliance Management Systems.

Any CMS starts with understanding the context of the organization, mainly with determining the compliance obligations and with the identification and assessment of compliance risks. At this stage, it is obvious that it could also freely be implemented within an educational institution. Those institutions also constantly take part in the economic and particularly in the social aspect of life. Therefore, an educational institution and its members generate several compliance risks that often stay completely undetected and do not talk about adequately addressing them. Referring to the topic of this contribution, in particular, many risks occur in the field of digitalization. For example, the risk of spying out of research results, the violation of data protection regulations and basic legal regulations, for example, concerning employer-employee relationships. One should not underestimate typical compliance risks that organizations are often confronted with, such as orruption or unfair competition—if considering that public institutions usually spend tax money—but also environmental issues.

Once the organization, in our case, an educational institution is aware of its obligations and the risks that may occur, the next step is to create a compliance policy. When doing so, the size, structure, nature, and complexity of the organization should be taken into consideration. The compliance policy as a kind of basic framework for further operational steps should address mainly:

- the fundamental goals of the system,
- its elements that need to be adapted,
- compliance obligations and risks,
- the assignment of roles and responsibilities to all members of the organization,
- the role of the top management, and
- every other aspect of the functioning of the system.

On that basis, transparency will be ensured, one of the fundamental principles required by good governance. The system becomes clearer and more comprehensible for all members of the organization and will be accepted by them even much more likely. Last but not least what is also important is that the compliance policy should be in line with the overall policy, goals, and principles of the educational institution in which it will be implemented. To activate its functions, it can also be considered to include the members of the organizations in the process of developing this kind of policy. What is a small detail but important is that the compliance policy should be formally signed by the governing body to demonstrate the "tone from the top."

Particular roles for compliance and integrity should be assigned to all members of the organization in the next step. Which role will be assigned to which person depends on the level in the hierarchy of the given educational institutions and its risk exposure. First, there is the top management and governing body who play a fundamental role in regard to compliance management. In this area, the "tone from the top" approach has been developed and demands that every single person in a leading position demonstrate the best example in regard to compliance and integrity. Second, there is a large group forming the administration of the educational institution. Additionally, in this relation, assigning roles and responsibilities regarding CMS should not cause any problems, since usually those members of the organizations are employed on a regular contractual basis. However, what can turn out to be a challenge is implementing this procedural step to the research and teaching staff, who usually can refer to the basic rights of freedom of research and teaching. Last but not least, there is one special dedicated member of the organization that plays a crucial role in a CMS, which is the person managing the system, usually called a compliance officer or compliance manager. Once all members of the organization know and understand their duties and obligations, they can act on that basis and fulfill their functions. It is finally obvious that assigning roles on the paper would never be an effective tool, further operational steps within the CMS should follow.

This brings us to the core of any CMS, which is the operational part of it. The scope of activities and elements that can be implemented at this stage varies and depends on the risk portfolio, structure, size, characteristics and other individual aspects of the organization. Just to mention some common operational elements of a CMS: training, clear communication, whistleblowing channels, codes of conduct, investigations and any other activities adequate to the just mentioned aspects of the given educational institution.

What is eventually important is that all steps should be documented and evaluated. It helps when subsequently evaluating the system but can also create evidence of keeping the duty of care in regard to a noncompliance case and its consequences.

Another challenge emerges at this point: When looking from an operational perspective, how can an effective CMS be implemented in an educational institution? Here, some mechanisms can be realized that have proven to be successful in the corporate sector. First in line are an effective code of conduct and other internal compliance guidelines. While basic risks are covered in the code of conduct whose content should depend on the outcome of the risk analysis and which also gives behavioral recommendations, compliance guidelines cover different, more specific risk areas. They also give details about how to deal with those areas in particular. However, of course, it does not end with the code of conduct. An effective concept of compliance communication, including training, discussions, and meetings, should be the basis of the portfolio of every single CMS.

Eventually, the CMS as a system should be evaluated and improved. In this way, the compliance manager can determine if the system is effective, so if the pursuit targets can still be achieved by running the system. Additionally, at this point, several methods to measure organizational culture or, in this case, academic culture could be put in place. What is important is that in any case the evaluation showed some gaps or failures, the system should be immediately improved to maintain its effectiveness.

Interim Conclusion

The above short analysis delivered some reliable evidence that the concept of a compliance management system can also be implemented within an educational institution. Systematically operating a CMS can ensure that these institutions support the compliance culture and integrity of their members. This kind of system should start with the context of the educational institution and risk assessment, followed by defining the policy, assigning the roles and responsibilities, implementing adequate procedures, and evaluating and constantly improving the system.

Finally, it must be underlined that those approaches are only general. In any case, a CMS should be "tailor-made" with respect to the size, complexity, and structure of the particular educational institution.

Whistleblowing System

One of the fundamental elements of an effective CMS is the Whistleblowing System. Due to its importance and specifics, it should, however, be treated separately in this article, whereas it builds an integral element of a CMS in practice. Especially in the EU, this topic has gained importance and affects educational institutions as well. It is related to the directive enacted by the EU,[12] which determines that both private companies of a certain size and public institutions will be obligated to introduce Whistleblowing Systems and to protect Whistleblowers. The directive was suposed to be implemented in the legal system of each member state by the end of 2021. That is why educational institutions already need to think about a way to implement the directive's requirements.

Let us start with the goals of Whistleblowing Systems. With the creation of safe and efficient ways of reporting as well as the corresponding communication of its functions and targets, the so-called "SpeakUp" culture shall be supported in organizations and therefore also in educational institutions. It is a culture in which issues and conflicts will be addressed and solved in a fair dialog, furthermore, a culture in which mischiefs will be pointed out—speaking up is a behavior that will be seen as ethically correct and as the only possible way to do right. Whistleblowing systems entirely constitute an interdisciplinary matter, and they are classified from the ethical perspective differently depending on different cultures. What, however, must be said is that a CMS will not achieve its goals without an effective Whistleblowing System. Therefore, such a system

---

[12] Directive (EU) 2019/1937 of the European Parliament and the Council of 23 October 2019 on the protection of persons who report breaches of Union law.

must be implemented within the CMS properly. It also should not be implemented as a stand-alone system. Thus, it has to be anchored in the compliance policy but also discussed in compliance training and ideally mentioned in the code of conduct or be subject in one of the internal compliance guidance. Furthermore, it needs to be ensured that the reporting channels are established properly, reports get evaluated carefully and if needed other actions follow, for example, internal investigations.

Whistleblowing systems can be implemented in various shapes. Additionally, this kind of system should be tailor-made. Disregarding specific requirements of particular hard laws, the general scope for design may be mentioned here. Whistleblowing systems can be shaped open or anonymously, which means that educational institutions will have to decide if they accept anonymous reports or if they only take those signed by the whistleblower. Both models have advantages and disadvantages, especially in regard to rossing the psychological boundaries concerning the report. Another criterion is the internal or external way of reporting. If an external office outside of the educational institution is responsible for receiving the report, it would be the external approach. Everything being received within the educational institution, for example, if it is received by the compliance officer, would be the internal way. Additionally, this distinction has pros and cons that should be carefully considered before implementation. Last but not least, a whistleblowing system can be offered conventionally as a mailbox or hotline or designed in a more modern way, for example, with the help of an already available digitalization tools.

Whatever model will be implemented, it must fulfill the requirements of the mentioned EU directive, which will be implemented soon into the national legal systems of the member states (some of them have already implemented it). What is, however, also crucial is to have an effective overall concept on how Whistleblowing will fit into the existing or planned CMS, what measures will be undertaken to promote it and—extremely important—how Whistleblower will be protected. Only when considering and implementing this aspect is it possible to fulfill the purpose of a management system and therefore primarily the purpose of good governance.

9.5 Conclusion

The three fundamental approaches of terminology, risk and culture showed that governance, compliance management and integrity are highly flexible concepts. It is, therefore, more than justified to adapt the existing concepts in any kind of organizations, including educational institution. Several clear and proven methods can be undertaken at the institutional level that will foster the culture of compliance and integrity of all members of a particular educational institution, addressing the new risks emerging from digitalization. However, consideration shall be given to the "nature" of the educational institutions and its staff the academics—her or his highly individualized position, which is usually protected by the constitutional freedom of teaching and research. Effective governance and compliance management must not interfere with or restrict these individual freedoms. On the other hand, scholars also represent a part of the organization to which they belong and to which they are obliged; they also play a fundamental role in our societies to whom they should be responsible. It is, therefore, our moral duty to contribute in the best possible way to enable the concept of governance and compliance management, supported by integrity, to effectively ensure a safe, reliable, and trustful research and teaching environment in the digital age.

10

Need for Silence, Craving for Communication: The Dyad Digital Education and Soft Skills in an Emerging Economy Context

Luciana Cezarino, Lara Liboni, Flavio Martins, and Alessandro Goulart

10.1 Introduction

Technology omnipresence has changed all dimensions of our life: the way we work, study, and leisure (Lau et al., 2018). Classrooms evolved from a unidirectional, textbook-supported, lecture-based, and group feedback-dependent learning context to a physically independent, everywhere-everytime learning environment (Heflin et al., 2017) that is not restricted to study-oriented platforms such as Moodles and resources designed

L. Cezarino • F. Martins (✉)
University of São Paulo, São Paulo, Brazil
e-mail: fpmartins@usp.br

L. Liboni
Faculty of Economics, Administration and Accounting of Ribeirão Preto, University of São Paulo, São Paulo, Brazil

A. Goulart
Bandtec Digital School, São Paulo, Brazil

adequately for educational outcomes such as massive open online courses (MOOCs) but also percolates work-oriented platforms such as Google's toolkit and LinkedIn and social media interaction platforms such as Facebook and Instagram (Thomas et al., 2018; Shafer et al., 2018).

Changes are not restricted to a specific educational level, and they can be observed from early childhood to tertiary education. Children as young as 4 years old are exposed to digital learning experiences in kindergartens, and technology assessment is said to be an essential tool for supporting educators in child-oriented pedagogy (Danniels et al., 2020; Donohue & Schomburg, 2017). At the secondary level of mathematics teaching, technology is observed to aid the collaborative development of mathematical knowledge inside the classroom. At higher education and postgraduate learning, changes manifest accordingly to different contexts, students from Spanish (Gil-Fernández et al., 2021) and South African (Mpungose, 2020) universities increased their use of social media and tools such as WhatsApp for educational goals.

The changes were intensified by the crisis: before pandemics, some said that teachers used digital education tools at least once per week and that during pandemics, the usage varied at an individual level but increased overall (Kaarakainen & Saikkonen, 2021). From the organizational perspective of the schools, there was a tsunami of online education. However, technology use in education is not exactly a novelty. Some of the highly popular online platforms today, such as WebCT, Moodle, Docebo, Adobe Captive, Google Classroom, Lectora, Udemy, and Blackboard, have been presented for more than a decade. Some niches were still creating momentum or lagging behind in digital technology usage, and COVID-19 acted as an intensifier for it (Goldschmidt, 2020).

The employability context is shaped by Industry 4.0 Rajnai and Kocsis (2017), and the demands are being tractioned by market requisites for professionals with adequate literacy to operate the new digital paradigm (Flynn et al., 2017), inducing an increase in the offer of online education, specifically for degrees in technical disciplines (Ruthotto et al., 2021). As information and communication technology (ICT) advances in education, the boundaries separating the physical and digital world become blurred. A major call for soft skills in technology-oriented courses appears, which has been the subject of growing research interest in the past few years (Lau et al., 2018; Lavi et al., 2021; Goulart et al. 2021a, b). The student-educator interaction changed dramatically: The group discussions and case-study solving, face-to-face feedback, and tutoring (McDuffie et al., 2009) gave room to the "endless" calls at zoom.

Despite the almost exponential growth, distance education comprises challenges that need to be overcome so that the learning objectives are achieved in a way equal or superior to on-site teaching. The result is a result of the structural order, such as the need for virtualization of learning and teaching technologies and the challenges arising from this.

The experience that students might have in their course is influenced by factors such as demographics and professional background (Ruthotto et al., 2021) and, on the other hand, also has a transformational impact on countries' employment demographics (Flynn et al., 2017).

The digital divide is more evident than ever in the COVID-19 era, which is also reflected in the increase in socioeconomic inequalities linked to access to education. Bhandari (2019) indicates that access to technologies carries a strong component of gender inequality and that although the samples are influenced by the context, in general, women are in a vulnerable situation.

Digital literacy and qualification in emerging economies are a second layer of digital education gaps that are reflected in the personal development and economic advancement of countries (Goulart et al. 2021a, b). Although new technologies can bring a reduction in the cost of learning, their ability to reduce gaps and minimize global inequalities in education is still an uncertain field (Pollack Ichou, 2018). By COVID-19's health crisis, in particular, by promoting "forced digitization" (Karakose, 2021) and accelerating agents who were building momentum for digital technology migration is an open road for research to harness theoretical and practical implications.

10.2   Socioemotional Skills for TI in the COVID-19 Era

The use of information technology alternatives for teaching and learning has grown exponentially in the context of the need for physical isolation caused by COVID-19. Some schools were still on the sidelines of digitization or using the tools incrementally, and as support for teaching practice, COVID-19 had a transforming role, which allows us to look at the recent past in light of the living concept. Labs for education (Siekkinen et al., 2020) and specifically for digital education (Sroufe, 2020). A careful reading of how a sanitary crisis, systemic and global, changed the educational context at a global level in a window of a few months is of paramount importance for continuity in the development of the theoretical framework in digital education.

Nevertheless, many of the efforts were rushed: Teachers and schools saw themselves in a context of mandatory digitization of their pedagogical approach. This movement has two main implications, one that is grounded on technology constraints, mostly related to vulnerable settings (i.e., emerging economies and impoverished communities) and second, the one referred to the losses of educational potential in solutions that are just transposed to the digital world.

Both dimensions are intertwined. Cost related to the acquisition of digital teaching solutions such as games and specific software (Scherer et al., 2019) and dependence on practical activities (Kaarakainen & Saikkonen, 2021) influences how easy the pedagogical approach can be converted in distance learning. Regular e-learning tools can have a wide array of possibilities, from digital textbooks (Lau et al., 2018) to highly interactive activities such as web-based learning (WBL) (Adi et al., 2021) and the uses of machine learning-based platforms (Balica, 2018). Therefore, it is possible to work on a gradient between the complexity of tool resources and interaction demands, and the gradient is empowered from the perspective of the digital readiness of the millennial generation. In an environment without extreme resource constraints, students have either a good digital literacy level or are easily trained with technical competencies to access an educational environment.

To achieve long-lasting and meaningful education, the process must be grounded in discursive, interactive, and reflexivity activities, which is both a call and a shortcoming of digital e-learning solutions (Laurillard, 2002). Studies show that digital education can act in both ways, also being successful in fostering the development of general communication skills and mental readiness (Adi et al., 2021).

Soft skills or socioemotional skills have a crucial role in higher education for IT professionals, and the offering of a degree combining IT education with socioemotional skills requires a higher level of communication between students and educators (Goulart et al. 2021a, b). A similar situation is found in engineering degrees. Valeyeva et al. (2019) concluded that the development of IT skills, information literacy, teamwork skills, flexibility competencies and metacognitive skills are only fully possible with soft skills training.

10.3 Methodological Approach

We split our work into two main steps, first comprising exploratory bibliometrics grounded on keyword mapping and keywords in context analysis. The tool used here is VOSviewer software for building keywording semantics that provides visual aggregated analysis while grounded on validated algorithms (Ding & Yang, 2020). Cluster visualization is a way to obtain an overall picture of the published content interwovenness and to flag research trends and gaps (Fergnani, 2019).

The usage of VOSviewer algorithms for the higher education context is recurrent and spread in a wide array of specific thematics, such as (1) sustainability in gray literature at higher education (de Souza Marins et al., 2021), (2) entrepreneurial skills evaluation (Xiyang, 2020), (3) physical education management (Zhangyin, 2017), (4) augmented reality in physics education (Putri et al., 2021), and (5) interdisciplinarity at education for sustainable development (Martins, 2021). As expected, the tools were also applied to COVID-19-specific topics (Noor et al., 2020). The exploratory review was carried out using keyword strings that combined the constructs related to "information technology" and "soft skills" and their variants. The results are shown in a keyword graph format, where nodes are the terms and the edges are the weighted co-occurrences in the papers.

The second step comprised a questionnaire with 15 structured questions and one open-ended question; it was applied in a school that has a specific purpose within the Brazilian higher education market: they focus on information technology bound with business education internship programs and carry its mission grounded in the development of socio-emotional skills.

10.4   Results and Discussion

Keyword Clustering

An exploratory review carried out with two strings of keywords aimed to scope the constructs in the opposite networks to identify the role and representativity they had in relation to each other. In summary, we scope the place and relevance of "information technology" in the "soft skills" network and the other way around (Table 10.1).

The first conclusion that rises is the size of the research field when narrowed down by the higher education context. Information technology returns 10 times more papers. Soft skills are being widely propagated as pedagogical guidance principles and practices. Nevertheless, it is somehow a novel topic that has yet to be defined as a construct and as a research field (Versuti et al., 2020). The papers retrieved from String 1 were loaded in VOSviewer software, and the keyword graphs (see the Fig. 10.1 below) were formed by the 241 most recurrent keywords (>5 counts).

The figure shows 07 main clusters representing the IT framed under the higher education construct. Clusters allow data visualization at an aggregated level (Van Eck & Waltman, 2017), and inferences using the communities formed by clusters to scope interdisciplinarity connections are being used in areas such as management and sustainable development education (Cezarino & Corrêa, 2015; Martins, 2021). Clusters are divided and interconnected in thematics that are hardly detached from each other; for instance, the keywords "employability," "employment,"

Table 10.1 Keyword string parameters

String 1	
Keywords in title—boolean operator "OR"	"information technology," "IT," "Information and Communication Technology," "ICT"
Keywords in title, abstract or keywords—boolean operator "AND"	"Higher education"
Language	English
Document type	Article
Time frame	N/A
Field area	Open—all fields
Returned amount of papers	1546 articles
String 2	
Keywords in title—boolean operator "OR"	"Soft skills" OR "noncognitive skills" OR "character skills" OR "life skills" OR "21st century skills" OR "socioemotional" OR "socioemotional"
Keywords in title, abstract or keywords—boolean operator "AND"	"Higher education"
Language	English
Document type	Article
Time frame	N/A
Field area	Open—all fields
Returned amount of papers	155 articles

and "career" appear in different clusters, same happens to "gender" and "gender equality." Additionally, the number of clusters formed (07) considering a small network (241) indicates the heterogeneity of thematics widely connected among them. It is not possible to make inferences regarding communities orbiting around specific thematics or field areas.

The meaningful result that can be extracted from this network is that there is mention of "soft skills," "socioemotional skills," or similar terms, in other words, when fetched the most relevant 1546 papers with IT and scoped in higher education institutions, and soft skills were not mentioned five times in papers title, abstract and keywords. Additionally, the concept of sustainable development is in a central position of the network connected to a wide array of clusters.

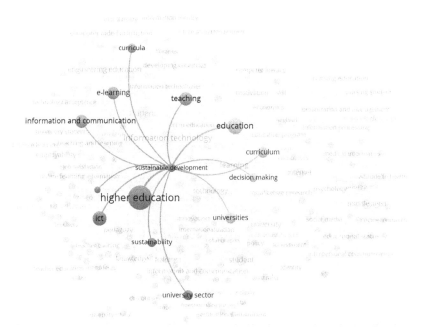

Fig. 10.1 Clusters formed in the IT network

String 2 returned a total count of 155 articles, despite indicating a huge leap in the publication amount after 2016 (Fig. 10.2). The network formed by the 29 most recurrent keywords (>5 counts) showed no direct mention of information technology or ICT constructs. Nevertheless, adjacent constructs such as "e-learning" and "computer-aided instruction" appeared in a modest and peripheral way (see the Fig. 10.3 below).

The suggested rationale underlying the presence of a construct that is closer to IT or ICT in the soft skills can be followed by the spreading of the topics among different knowledge areas: at the soft skill network, "Computer Science" appears as the second most recurrent field for the publications, followed by "Engineering." Therefore, relevance seems to have been given to these connections between the so-called "hard sciences" and the "soft skills," in accordance with studies from

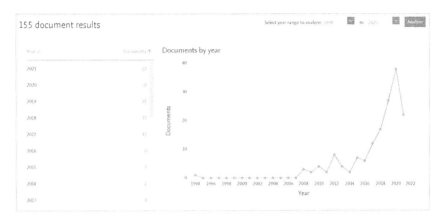

Fig. 10.2   Evolution of publications in soft skills thematic

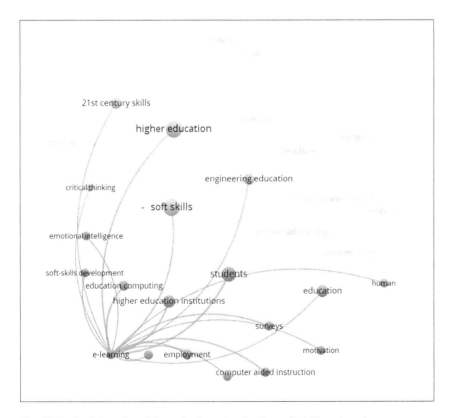

Fig. 10.3   Peripheral position of e-learning in the soft skills network

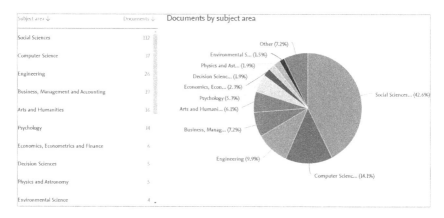

Fig. 10.4 Representation of publications through the fields of knowledge

Goulart et al. (2021a, b) for computer sciences and Fernández-Sanz et al. (2017), Schipper and van der Stappen (2018), and Valeyeva et al. (2019) for engineering teaching and education (Fig. 10.4).

Questionnaire Responses

We obtained 301 answers to our questionnaire. Fifty-six percent of the respondents said to have had no major difficulties accepting the social distance measures, while 41% reported challenging situations. The results are somehow unexpected, considering the pandemic's context. Approximately 85% of the students from 180 countries have fully migrated to digital classes (World Bank, 2020), and COVID-19 is being addressed by recent research as a predominantly stressful event (Lee et al., 2021; Masha'al et al., 2020). The hindering factor for students' motivation and learning outcomes is grounded on a systemic chain of wellbeing factors such as sleep and dietary disturbances (Du et al., 2021).

Fourteen percent of the students said that they did not face any kind of difficulties with online learning, and the remaining 86% of the students categorized their difficulties in three dimensions: technical and operational difficulties (23.3%), emotional difficulties (28.7%), and difficulties related to learning (34.3%). Some of the respondents chose to clarify their points in a qualitative way, as reported in the two tables below.

The majority of the students (186) were also working part-time during the time of the COVID-19 outbreak. Almost 100% of them did not have their salaries reduced or changed in any matter, which indicates another specificity of the sample. In the Indian context, the crisis conundrum greatly impacted the employability of undergraduates (Das, 2021). Despite the regular stability of the student's remuneration, their families faced impoverishing situations: 64% of the respondents reported a reduction in their familiar income, and 28% reported a high degree of financial limitations in their families. Family impoverishment has been identified as one of the factors that was re-energized during pandemics and that is responsible for sustaining or widening educational disparities, especially in emerging economies (Mengistie, 2021) (Table 10.2).

Only one of the respondents mentioned that the university's educational dashboard was a barrier. The sample's digital readiness seems to be unaffected by COVID-19, in accordance with results from Händel et al. (2020) on its evaluation of technology availability, literacy, and skills for digital learning. This finding suggests that to enhance the effectiveness of

Table 10.2 Students' observations regarding technical, operational, and infrastructure challenges

Noisy environment and a few limitations of my PC
I cannot use the platform well and I find the process complicated
My family's frequent gaze makes me uncomfortable and even limits some of my actions
I do not have a suitable environment to study, staying in common and noisy areas of the house
My chair is very bad and my family fights a lot
The only problem I had during two classes was the internet, but apart from these exceptions it was pretty quiet
I end up working more than I should, making leisure time impossible
Internet at home is very unstable
I'm not having difficulty, but my internet sometimes goes down
Sometimes the internet goes down or is very slow
Lots of distractions indoors
The internet fails sometimes
Noisy environment
I do not have space dedicated to it and the family is always around
I have restrictions or limitations for computer use, and my internet is bad or nonexistent.

e-learning, easy-to-use collaborative platforms and tools need to be provided to enable users to work together to evaluate and create from what they have learned in the previous stages (Lau et al., 2018).

Educational and professional platforms are each day more similar to daily leisure spaces; they resemble well-succeeded gamified experiences from social media platforms, allow interaction and development of bonds among colleagues, and allow replication of the content in multiple platforms with different goals. The level of literacy needed to navigate through an MBA dashboard is nowhere different from managing a Facebook friends group. The common syllabus reduces the learning curve while dramatically increasing tool familiarity. In addition to a wide array of educational platform options, many of them are free of charge, making tool interaction the least of the issues. There is a strong perception that educational platforms should consider blending with personal e-learning tools, such as WhatsApp (Mpungose, 2020), and COVID-19 empowered, even more, this movement toward blending between educational/ leisure e-tools (Gil-Fernández et al., 2021).

Abuselidze et al. (2021) note that stressful aspects related to digital learning refer to the lack of universal access to the internet and other demands on physical infrastructure. Our sample biggest challenges portrait refers to issues with internet availability and instability and a proper workspace with silence and fewer stressing factors. This connects our sample with studies from other emerging economies, such as Romania (Roman & Plopeanu, 2021), where the same dyad internet access + space for the study was highlighted. Many respondents from our sample pointed out issues related to "unwanted family interactions" during digital classes that hinder their learning potential. This saying sheds light on how systemic the effects of the pandemic are and how it interconnects education with other dimensions of life, not only students but also the educators and families of both (Karakose, 2021).

Regarding the student's engagement and motivation, 79% of them reported that their study intensity (hours dedicated to study) remained unaltered or even increased during the pandemic, while 19% said to have been experiencing shortcomings in their study outcomes. Approximately 30% of the students reported some degree of difficulties with online education, while 58% of them said that they have no issues with online classes, and it does not change their motivation or engagement, either in a positive way with more engagement (26%) or in a negative way, by hindering the motivation (32%) (Table 10.3).

The learning tool format plays an important role in regard to issues related to interaction in digital learning. While static learning resources (i.e., recorded lectures and textbooks) that are grounded in view and reading activities require low, or zero, maintenance from a teaching point of view (Lau et al., 2018); the more complex and collaborative the tools are, the more communication they will require. Additionally, the field of knowledge and teaching thematics have their own impact: The fewer practical assignments needed, the easier it is for the content to be digitalized without much effort (Kaarakainen & Saikkonen, 2021).

The socioemotional skills approach requires, by default, a more interactive milieu. Social contact changes caused by the crisis are traumatic and have long-lasting effects, remaining one of the shortcomings of digital education (Naidoo & Cartwright, 2020). Since our sample belongs to an information technology college, it is expected that a great amount of learning by doing activities will be present, and this aligns with the major concerns of the students, which does not seem to have any kind of difficulties with technology and demands a "silent study environment" while craving for communication and peer interaction.

10.5 Emerging Insights

COVID-19 pandemics are already the major educational game changer of the decade. Its impacts are perceptible, although there is a long way to go for them to be measured and detailed in such a way as to serve as further guidance for decision-making. Study conclusions are aligned with similar and contextual-based perceptions with case studies recently carried out around the world. The educational trauma of pandemics is not circumscribed in the teaching and learning dimension and is far from having its nexus located at the digital readiness of our generation.

Our sample is composed of students from a technology-based higher education school located in an emerging economy country with a motto for socioemotional skill development. This configuration is specifically

Table 10.3 Students' observations regarding emotional and/or learning challenges

Emotional Difficulties
Ah laziness increased considerably and procrastination consequently
I feel like I do not enjoy 100% of the class because it is online
The longer you spend in isolation, the harder it becomes to maintain 100% in every way
I do not feel good about the isolation, it lets me down, however, knowing that I try to dedicate myself in addition to "planned" to eliminate the feeling of "wasting" time or content
In my view, the difficulties are related to my mental fatigue. Additionally, along with some points specifics of the previous options, I normally learn but I believe that in-person I learn more, isolation is starting to disturb me emotionally
The biggest difficulty is the lack of interaction with other students, as this brings a new learning
The biggest difficulty I have is accessing people. It is slower to ask questions and ask for help. At the face-to-face model, for example, it is much easier to contact colleagues and talk to people and ask some kind of help, even with people from other classes during break time, was simpler to solve problems by being there together even on the same machine. In addition, in the classroom, it was something more dynamic and interactive, almost like a conversation with the teachers. The remote model does not have these things
Difficulties Related to Learning
Sometimes I cannot absorb the entire content of the class, but then I review my notes and review the class
I have no difficulties with online teaching. Of course, I would prefer the situation to be better, with classes in person, without daily deaths by the thousands and without the fear of leaving the house... However, no difficulties as for online teaching! I notice the teachers' effort to teach and I try to show them my effort to learn!!
I have difficulty answering questions
I miss the shifts after classes, as doubts were already taken away more quickly
I have a degree of attention deficit, which hinders me a little in more theoretical classes
Difficulties in solving doubts
The biggest difficulty I have is the distraction sometimes
Pay attention for a long period of time
I do not have much discipline
I have some doubts and sometimes by video it is bad to learn
I lose focus more easily
Difficulties in staying focused
Study routine
My biggest difficulty is procrastination, which has gradually become even less frequent

relevant to address tertiary education in a context that demands both digital readiness and emotional resilience. The major issues related by our sample of students refer to learning difficulties that are connected to the lack of structure (namely, internet access) and emotional instabilities caused by isolation. In alignment with studies such as Mbunge et al. (2020), we highlight the call for the same degree of attention to the provision of psychosocial assistance alongside improved internet bandwidth services. Hybrid solutions applied to counseling services and peer tutoring are valid alternatives for extenuating the social distancing conundrum caused by COVID-19 (Naidoo & Cartwright, 2020).

There is also an alarming call for an "educational tipping point," caused by the extensive challenges faced by undergraduates in emerging economies such as Brazil, India, and South Africa that can result in a lost generation (Mbunge et al., 2020) and widen even more the global educational gaps.

10.6 Theoretical and Practical Implications and Study Limitations

The results achieved here contribute theoretically to the development of the area represented by the overlap between digital education and soft skills. Practical implications lie in the specificity of the case study here: the discussion refers to a critical issue for national development, in a geographically specific context, of an emerging country, temporally unique, considered the COVID-19 crisis, and the characteristics of the sample. Questions with transformational potential are raised, which propose a remodeling of an educational system strongly supported by the hard sciences, which, in the midst of a systemic crisis that demands isolation, turns its eyes to human interaction and formation. The background of uncertainty about the technical skills demanded by the future gains clearer contours amid the challenge posed to educational agents related to the difficulty in dealing with their emotions and social challenges, despite digital readiness.

Limitations of the study reflect the specificity of the case. The generalization of our findings is limited. The context is very specific, and further studies might enforce our conclusions. Our sample is also small, and this does not allow quantitative validation of findings. Further studies might expand the connections between soft skills and ICT education in a feasible framework, with empowered generalization capabilities, for emerging economies.

References

Abuselidze, G., Radzivilova, I., & Mohylevska, O. (2021). Psychological-pedagogical problems and prospects of distance learning of students during the Covid-19 pandemics. In *E3S Web of conferences* (Vol. 258, No. Article No.: 10016). EDP Sciences.

Adi, K. R., Kurniawan, B., & Siddik, S. (2021). Encouraging student's soft-skill by web-based EColloquium learning approach to enhance advance feedbacks. *International Journal of Emerging Technologies in Learning, 16*(7).

Balica, R. (2018). Big data learning analytics and algorithmic decision-making in digital education governance. *Analysis and Metaphysics, 17*, 128–133.

Bhandari, A. (2019). Gender inequality in mobile technology access: The role of economic and social development. *Information, Communication & Society, 22*(5), 678–694.

Cezarino, L. O., & Corrêa, H. L. (2015). Interdisciplinaridade no ensino em Administração: visão de especialistas e coordenadores de cursos de graduação. Administração: ensino e pesquisa, 16(4), 751–784.

Danniels, E., Pyle, A., & DeLuca, C. (2020). The role of technology in supporting classroom assessment in play-based kindergarten. *Teaching and Teacher Education, 88*, 102966.

Das, P. K. (2021). Impact of pandemic Covid-19 on higher education-Indian context. *Universal Journal of Business and Management, 1*(1), 13–21.

de Souza Marins, B. V., de Souza Ferreira, G., & Ramos, H. C. (2021). Sustainability reporting in higher education institutions: A systematic approach using VOSViewer and Iramuteq software. *International Journal of Advanced Engineering Research and Science, 8*, 3.

Ding, X., & Yang, Z. (2020). Knowledge mapping of platform research: A visual analysis using VOSviewer and CiteSpace. *Electronic Commerce Research*, 1–23.

Donohue, C., & Schomburg, R. (2017). Technology and interactive media in early childhood programs: What we've learned from five years of research, policy, and practice. *YC Young Children, 72*(4), 72–78.

Du, C., Zan, M. C. H., Cho, M. J., Fenton, J. I., Hsiao, P. Y., Hsiao, R., & Tucker, R. M. (2021). Health behaviors of higher education students from 7 countries: Poorer sleep quality during the COVID-19 pandemic predicts higher dietary risk. *Clocks & Sleep, 3*(1), 12–30.

Fergnani, A. (2019). Mapping futures studies scholarship from 1968 to present: A bibliometric review of thematic clusters, research trends, and research gaps. *Futures, 105*, 104–123.

Fernández-Sanz, L., Villalba, M. T., Medina, J. A., & Misra, S. (2017). A study on the key soft skills for successful participation of students in multinational engineering education. *International Journal of Engineering Education, 33*(6), 2061–2070.

Flynn, J., Dance, S., & Schaefer, D. (2017). Industry 4.0 and its potential impact on employment demographics in the UK. *Advances in Transdisciplinary Engineering, 6*, 239–244.

Gil-Fernández, R., León-Gómez, A., & Calderón, D. (2021). Influence of COVID on the educational use of social media by students of teaching degrees. *Education in the Knowledge Society, 22*, e23623.

Goulart, V. G., Liboni, L. B., & Cezarino, L. O. (2021a). *Balancing skills in the digital transformation era: The future of jobs and the role of higher education* (p. 09504222211029796). Industry and Higher Education.

Goulart, A. R., Liboni, L. B., & Cezarino, L. O. (2021b). Qualification as a societal challenge and the role of higher education from a system approach. Higher Education, Skills and Work-Based Learning.

Goldschmidt, K. (2020). The COVID-19 pandemic: Technology use to support the wellbeing of children. *Journal of Pediatric Nursing, 53*, 88.

Händel, M., Stephan, M., Gläser-Zikuda, M., Kopp, B., Bedenlier, S., & Ziegler, A. (2020). Digital readiness and its effects on higher education students' socioemotional perceptions in the context of the COVID-19 pandemic. *Journal of Research on Technology in Education*, 1–13.

Heflin, H., Shewmaker, J., & Nguyen, J. (2017). Impact of mobile technology on student attitudes, engagement, and learning. *Computers & Education, 107*, 91–99.

Kaarakainen, M. T., & Saikkonen, L. (2021). Multilevel analysis of the educational use of technology: Quantity and versatility of digital technology usage in Finnish basic education schools. *Journal of Computer Assisted Learning*.

Karakose, T. (2021). Emergency remote teaching due to COVID-19 pandemic and potential risks for socioeconomically disadvantaged students in higher education. *Educational Process: International Journal, 10*(3), 53.

Lau, K. H., Lam, T., Kam, B. H., Nkhoma, M., Richardson, J., & Thomas, S. (2018). The role of textbook learning resources in e-learning: A taxonomic study. *Computers & Education, 118*, 10–24.

Laurillard, D. (2002). *Rethinking university teaching: A conversational framework for the effective use of learning technologies*. Routledge.

Lavi, R., Tal, M., & Dori, Y. J. (2021). Perceptions of STEM alumni and students on developing 21st century skills through methods of teaching and learning. *Studies in Educational Evaluation, 70*, 101002.

Lee, J., Jeong, H. J., & Kim, S. (2021). Stress, anxiety, and depression among undergraduate students during the COVID-19 pandemic and their use of mental health services. *Innovative Higher Education*, 1–20.

Martins, F. P. (2021). Interdisciplinarity in education for sustainable development: Business schools perspectives, University of São Paulo, Ribeirão Preto – SP, Master Thesis.

Masha'al, D., Rababa, M., & Shahrour, G. (2020). Distance learning–related stress among undergraduate nursing students during the COVID-19 pandemic. *Journal of Nursing Education, 59*(12), 666–674.

Mbunge, E., Fashoto, S., Akinnuwesi, B., Gurajena, C., Metfula, A., & Mashwama, P. (2020). COVID-19 pandemic in higher education: Critical role of emerging technologies in Zimbabwe. Available at SSRN 3743246.

McDuffie, K. A., Mastropieri, M. A., & Scruggs, T. E. (2009). Differential effects of peer tutoring in cotaught and nonco-taught classes: Results for content learning and student-teacher interactions. *Exceptional Children, 75*(4), 493–510.

Mengistie, T. A. (2021). Higher education students' learning in COVID-19 pandemic period: The Ethiopian context. *Research in Globalization*, 100059.

Mpungose, C. B. (2020). Is Moodle or WhatsApp the preferred e-learning platform at a South African university? First-year students' experiences. *Education and Information Technologies, 25*(2), 927–941.

Naidoo, P., & Cartwright, D. (2020). Where to from here? Contemplating the impact of COVID-19 on South African students and student counseling services in higher education. *Journal of College Student Psychotherapy*, 1–15. Chicago

Noor, S., Guo, Y., Shah, S. H. H., Fournier-Viger, P., & Nawaz, M. S. (2020). *Analysis of public reactions to the novel coronavirus (COVID-19) outbreak on Twitter*. Kybernetes.

Pollack Ichou, R. (2018). Can MOOCs reduce global inequality in education? *Australasian Marketing Journal, 26*(2), 116–120.

Putri, C. R., Soleh, S. M., Saregar, A., Anugrah, A., & Susilowati, N. E. (2021, February). Bibliometric analysis: Augmented reality-based physics laboratory with VOSviewer software. In *Journal of Physics: conference series* (Vol. 1796, no. 1, p. 012056). IOP Publishing.

Scherer, R., Siddiq, F., & Tondeur, J. (2019). The technology acceptance model (TAM): A meta-analytic structural equation modeling approach to explaining teachers' adoption of digital technology in education. *Computers & Education, 128*, 13–35.

Schipper, M., & van der Stappen, E. (2018, April). Motivation and attitude of computer engineering students toward soft skills. In *2018 IEEE global engineering education conference (EDUCON)* (pp. 217–222). IEEE.

Siekkinen, T., Pekkola, E., & Carvalho, T. (2020). Change and continuity in the academic profession: Finnish universities as living labs. *Higher Education, 79*(3), 533–551.

Sroufe, R. (2020). Business schools as living labs: Advancing sustainability in management education. *Journal of Management Education, 44*(6), 726–765.

Thomas, R. B., Johnson, P. T., & Fishman, E. K. (2018). Social media for global education: Pearls and pitfalls of using Facebook, Twitter, and Instagram. *Journal of the American College of Radiology, 15*(10), 1513–1516.

Rajnai, Z., & Kocsis, I. (2017). Labor market risks of industry 4.0, digitization, robots and AI. In *2017 IEEE 15th international symposium on intelligent systems and informatics (SISY)* (pp. 000343–000346). IEEE.

Roman, M., & Plopeanu, A. P. (2021). The effectiveness of the emergency eLearning during the COVID-19 pandemic. The case of higher education in economics in Romania. International Review of Economics. *Education, 37*, 100218.

Ruthotto, I., Kreth, Q., & Melkers, J. (2021). Entering or advancing in the IT labor market: The role of an online graduate degree in computer science. *The Internet and Higher Education*, 100820.

Shafer, S., Johnson, M. B., Thomas, R. B., Johnson, P. T., & Fishman, E. K. (2018). Instagram as a vehicle for education: What radiology educators need to know. *Academic Radiology, 25*(6), 819–822.

Valeyeva, N. S., Kupriyanov, R. V., Valeeva, E., & Kraysman, N. V. (2019, September). Influence of the fourth industrial revolution (industry 4.0) on the system of engineering education. In *International conference on interactive collaborative learning* (pp. 316–325). Springer.

Van Eck, N. J., & Waltman, L. (2017). Citation-based clustering of publications using CitNetExplorer and VOSviewer. *Scientometrics, 111*(2), 1053–1070.

Versuti, F. M., Dalle Mulle, R. L., Guerreiro, C. A. R., Martins, F. P., & Peralta, D. A. (2020). Habilidades Socioemocionais e Tecnologias Educacionais: Revisão Sistemática de Literatura. *Revista Brasileira de Informática na Educação, 28*, 1086–1104.

World Bank. (2020). The COVID-19 pandemic: Shocks to education and policy responses.

Xiyang, H. (2020). Bibliometric Analysis and Visualization of College Students' Entrepreneurial Psychology Research Based on VOSviewer Software. *International Journal of Research in Engineering and Science, 8*(12), 36–43.

Zhangyin, S. U. N. (2017). Analysis on the hot topics of the physical education Management in China Based on VOSviewer. *Journal of Wuxi Institute of Technology, 3*(4).

11

Advancing Responsible Management Education (RME) and Education for Sustainable Development (ESD) Through Online Resources

Florencia Librizzi, Carole Parkes, and Ana Simaens

11.1 Introduction: Responsible Management Education (RME) and Education for Sustainable Development (ESD) in Times of the COVID-19 Pandemic

The 17 Sustainable Development Goals (SDGs) represent the 2030 Agenda of the United Nations (UN) for the period 2015–2030, as precluded in the document entitled "Transforming our world" (UN General Assembly, 2015). The SDGs were developed to call for the entire planet, contrary to its predecessors the 8 Millennium Development Goals (MDGs) that targeted developing countries (Sachs, 2012). The SDGs

F. Librizzi (✉)
SDG Academy, UN Sustainable Development Solutions Network (SDSN), New York, NY, USA

C. Parkes
University of Winchester, Winchester, UK

expanded the eight MDGs to include a broader set of areas and actors involved, calling for collective action (Leal Filho et al., 2019). They were negotiated over 3 years in a special political process that drove their elaboration and had key differences when compared to the MDGs in terms of the number of goals and targets and their purpose (Fukuda-Parr, 2016). SDGs have been considered a potential help to move the world to a sustainable trajectory (Sachs, 2012) and are not only broader but also more transformative than MDGs (Fukuda-Parr, 2016).

This chapter focuses on how to advance responsible management education (RME) and education for sustainable development (ESD) through online resources focused on the SDGs. To address this topic, the chapter is organized in four sections. In this first section, we discuss some key points of the current scenario of RME for the SDGs and how the COVID-19 pandemic has affected teaching and learning in particular. This includes challenges and opportunities related to these unprecedented times. In the second section, we address the role of open educational resources (OERs), online content and tools to enhance RME and ESD. In the third section, we discuss the case of the SDG Academy—the flagship education initiative of the Sustainable Development Solutions Network (SDSN), a global initiative for the UN—which aims to support the current and next generation of educators, practitioners and citizens to advance sustainable development everywhere by creating and curating the best available educational content on sustainable development and making it available as a global public good. Finally, the chapter discusses key lessons learned and provides recommendations for faculty and practitioners on how to make the most of online content and tools in the delivery of teaching and learning for RME and ESD.

Business- and management-related education, as well as higher education more broadly, are called upon to play a very important role in integrating responsibility as well as sustainability across their teaching and learning, and it is suggested that "advancements we see in the field (of responsible business and management education) could be in part due to

A. Simaens
Instituto Universitario de Lisboa (ISCTE-IUL),
Business Research Unit (BRU-IUL), Lisbon, Portugal

a greater understanding of the nature of the subject with all its complexity and challenges" (Moosmayer et al., 2020, p. 24). It is clear that universities are vital to attaining the SDGs (Leal Filho, 2011) because they can train the next generation to solve sustainability issues and conduct research that advances the agenda (Mori Junior et al., 2019). Despite some barriers that can be faced when trying to implement an interdisciplinary approach to sustainability, including time and knowledge, management education needs to integrate sustainability across disciplines (Annan-Diab & Molinari, 2017).

As we have now entered the Decade of Action for the 2030 Agenda, this need becomes even more critical. Nevertheless, recent research shows that despite increasing innovative approaches to address the SDGs in management education, there is limited engagement of students in the SDGs (Weybrecht, 2021). Cornuel and Hommel (2015) also argued that most business schools are slow adopters and have not fully engaged in RME. However, COVID-19 has been seen as a potential boost for the internalization of RME in business schools (Mousa, 2021).

In the last decade, higher education institutions (HEIs) in general have faced great changes in digital terms. For instance, the literature discusses the main tensions arising from the digital transformation process in terms of the various dimensions of the HEI business model, which includes education and potential solutions (Rof et al., 2020), knowing that higher education online courses require specific qualities from instructors (Martin, 2021). This has only been exacerbated by the event of COVID-19. The COVID-19 pandemic has affected teaching and learning globally, including posing related challenges and opportunities. Higher education institutions in general and business schools in particular moved almost overnight to the online (e.g., Agasisti et al., 2020; Alshamsi et al., 2020; Edelhauser & Lupu-Dima, 2020). The Global Covid Education Recovery Tracker (https://www.covideducationrecovery.global, 2020), an initiative by John Hopkins University, the World Bank Group, and UNICEF (e.g., Agasisti et al., 2020; Alshamsi et al., 2020; Edelhauser & Lupu-Dima, 2020), continues to monitor the situation for all education providers worldwide but mirrors the changes in HEI.

Both students and teachers have been faced with new challenges that required solutions focused on surviving the more extreme periods of lockdown, but that may have introduced practices that will remain beyond the pandemic. Another example related to entrepreneurship education identifies multidisciplinary and innovative educational approaches and techniques, including automated software to boost student business concepts (Mavlutova et al., 2020). The challenges faced by academics and students alike are well documented in a range of sources, including Giselle Weybrechts' "How business schools are responding to COVID-19," providing examples from the Principles for Responsible Management Education (PRME) community (Weybrecht, 2020). These insights include the organization and communication of the organization's response, processes for moving everything online and supporting the transition, curriculum changes and assessment, supporting colleagues and students, health and well-being, wider partnerships and research, and moving forward.

The increased use of online teaching in particular has brought some opportunities. These include access to experts and materials "beyond the classroom" as well as the potential for greater inclusion and diversity with a global reach that in turn supports the scaling up of education and its democratization. For both teaching staff and students alike, the ability to work from home also has advantages, including enhancing work/life balance, reducing travel time and expenses, and reducing carbon emissions. However, this shift is not without its challenges, and these are not just technological (Dhawan, 2020).

At the outset, access and availability of the technology are fundamental together with the ability of the institution to provide the infrastructure and support its use. This may be straightforward for well-funded organizations but limited in some contexts and locations. In addition, there is a need for suitable, safe workspaces.

The different platforms for delivery each have their own particular requirements and idiosyncrasies, which may require training and support. Facilitating the changes also requires ongoing effective communication and feedback loops to respond to problems and concerns as they arise. Some HEIs set up "risk management" or staff and student support groups to oversee the changes, but these need to be agile to respond to different needs and changing circumstances.

It is clear that it is often not simply migrating traditional teaching online, and delivering the curriculum in different forms can require changes to the content and assessment. Thinking through potential changes to meet the required outcomes for programs and courses can be complex, and the opportunity to talk them through with colleagues is important as well as understanding the student perspective on such changes. Simply providing recorded lectures with minimal interaction can lead to a reluctance to engage with the materials, and the provision of such materials does not automatically translate into transformational or impactful learning. Refocusing teacher presence and related learning activities is a critical part of enhancing teaching and learning practice (Rapanta et al., 2020).

The advantages of more "home" working can also bring challenges, especially with the need to have a clear separation of work and home life and the much reported "zoom fatigue" that can be detrimental to health and well-being (Bailenson, 2021). A key part of health and well-being is the social needs of both staff and students. From a learning point of view, social learning not only adds to the efficacy of the learning itself (Bandura, 1985) but also often responds to the human need for interaction (Hurst et al., 2013).

Student satisfaction is a key consideration in designing the structure and delivery of material, but of paramount importance is the effectiveness of the learning itself. Experiential learning (in its many forms) has been shown to provide enhanced learning for the complexities and interdisciplinary requirements of education for sustainable development (Hope et al., 2020). Opportunities to enhance provision with mechanisms for experiential and social learning as well as systems thinking are paramount.

While the COVID-19 pandemic has shaken up traditional ways of teaching and learning, the role that online content and tools, particularly OERs, can have (in advancing RME and ESD) in remote teaching and learning has also become more evident. Huang et al. (2021, p. 1) present the online merge-offline learning approach, which "utilizes a hybrid infrastructure that combines open educational practices and real-time learning spaces, both online and offline." This type of approach, boosted by COVID-19, opens a wide range of opportunities to the use of OERs in general and to advance RMEs and ESDs in particular.

11.2   The Role of Open Educational Resources and Online Content and Tools to Advance RME and ESD

Open Educational Resources, a term coined at UNESCO's (2002) Forum on the Impact of Open Courseware for Higher Education in Developing Countries (UNESCO, 2002), designates

> teaching, learning and research materials in any medium, digital or otherwise, that reside in the public domain or have been released under an open license that permits no-cost access, use, adaptation and redistribution by others with no or limited restrictions. Open licensing is built within the existing framework of intellectual property rights as defined by relevant international conventions and respects the authorship of the work. (UNESCO, 2012, p. 1)

Simply put, OER describes "any educational resources (including curriculum maps, course materials, textbooks, streaming videos, multimedia applications, podcasts, and any other materials that have been designed for use in teaching and learning) that are openly available for use by educators and students, without an accompanying need to pay royalties or license fees." (Butcher, 2015, p. 5). As Butcher (2015, p. 5) continues, "OER is *not* synonymous with online learning or e-learning, although many people make the mistake of using the terms interchangeably" [*italics* in the original].

It is important to explain the related concept of massive open online courses (MOOCs), where Massive "relates both to the student experience as well as the structure of the system"; Open "refers to the opportunity for students to enroll in the course at no monetary cost"; Online "deals with the mode and method of course access and activity"; and Course "is a term used to denote the registration and association with an affiliated instructional group, as well as the course's existence in space and time" (Moe, 2015, pp. 15–16).

Following the Paris Declaration in 2012 (UNESCO, 2012), several initiatives have been put in place to advance the OER, including regional consultations, as that declaration recommended "that governments create enabling environments for OER through appropriate policy, capacity building, research, advocacy, collaboration and above all encouraging the open licensing of educational materials produced with public funds." (Commonwealth of Learning, 2017, p. 1).

Some of the benefits and advantages of OERs identified in those consultations included (Commonwealth of Learning, 2017): improved access to textbooks, improved quality, improved teacher professional practice, increased access to non-English language resources, cost savings for learners, support for lifelong learning, and cultural diversity. Open educational resources have also been seen as a catalyst for innovation in teaching and learning made possible by technology (Orr et al., 2015) and as change agents (Ossiannilsson, 2021). Several studies have highlighted the role of OERs during the pandemic in various areas of study, including sustainable forest management (Zeng et al., 2020), or of MOOCs in building intrapreneurial capabilities (Guerrero et al., 2021). As noted by Ossiannilsson (2021, p. 105), "[n]ever before have so many high-quality, wide-ranging initiatives, software, tools, publications, resources and ideas been shared by individuals, teachers, publishers, companies and organizations around the globe in communities and among networks."

Despite the benefits, HEIs also face challenges regarding the OER. These include, for instance, quality assurance and financial sustainability (Hodgkinson-Williams, 2010). Notwithstanding the efforts to ensure quality, one of the challenges can be quality assurance for OERs (Almendro & Silveira, 2018). This is particularly relevant when considering that OERs are regarded as a potential support for the achievement of SDG4, which is to "ensure inclusive and equitable quality education and promote lifelong learning opportunities for all" (Commonwealth of Learning, 2017, p. 2). Financial sustainability is also a critical issue, considering that OERs require intensive labor and capital at different stages, from development to maintenance. There are various financial sustainability models, including membership, donations, institutional, governmental, to name a few (Hodgkinson-Williams, 2010).

Advancing RME and ESD through OERs and online content and tools requires integrating them in person, remote and hybrid learning environments and in synchronous and asynchronous education. Determining the right learning environment means defining the most suitable way of setting up the classroom environment. In general, these can be divided into three categories: (1) traditional face-to-face, (2) virtual or online, or (3) hybrid. More recently, the term modern learning environment (MLE) has been used to refer to the use of digital technology tools, modernizing the learning and teaching process (Huda et al., 2018). The choice of the right learning environment relies on the identification of the most appropriate pedagogical and technological approach. As noted earlier, OER is not the same as online learning or e-learning, as these resources can be used in traditional face-to-face learning environments. Hence, irrespective of the learning environment, OERs can play an important role in exploring new opportunities to engage with resources developed in a wide variety of sources, democratizing access to knowledge and experts that otherwise would not be reached.

OERs involve a multiplicity of parties—including intergovernmental organizations, governments, educational institutions, quality assurance agencies, private sector, civil society organizations, research agencies and consortia, teachers and librarians, and, of course, learners—and they are all called to action (Commonwealth of Learning, 2017). Recommendations for action regarding OERs for educational institutions, including HEIs, include (Commonwealth of Learning, 2017, p. 7): developing and implementing an institutional OER policy; creating institutional mechanisms for OER quality assurance; recognizing faculty contributions to OERs; instituting an award for the best OER; creating an institutional repository for OERs; regularly organizing capacity-building programs for teachers; conducting and supporting research on OERs; collaborating with other institutions to avoid reinventing the wheel; taking steps to improve the institution's ICT infrastructure; and developing accessible OERs.

11.3   Online Teaching and Learning Resources Available for RME and ESD

While the COVID-19 pandemic has put online teaching and learning on the top of the education agenda, online teaching and learning, including distance learning, has been around for a long time (Simonson & Berg, 2016). Online learning can involve tools and resources such as courses, virtual classes, lectures, podcasts, and microlearning, among others, which can be contrasted with the traditional courses taken in the conventional setting of a school campus. As discussed above, OERs became increasingly relevant during this time, facilitating access to education, educators, and students. Over time, many business schools and HEIs, UN agencies, non-for-profits and other organizations globally have created online teaching and learning resources, some of which are OERs. The same can be said regarding online teaching and learning resources focused on RME, ESD and sustainable development, whose creation has steadily increased in recent years. A few examples of this trend from UN agencies themselves, as well as initiatives launched by the UN, are the launch of UN CC: Learn in 2009 (CCLearn, 2021), the SDG Academy in 2014 (SDSN, 2020a), the UN Global Compact Academy in 2018 (3BLMedia, 2018), SDG:Learn in 2019 (UNITAR, 2019), and the FAO e-learning Academy in 2020 (FAO, 2020). Each with its own characteristics and among other existing platforms in the space, they offer a diversity of online resources with a spectrum of modalities of access, from free access and/or open access such as the SDG Academy (n.d.), SDG Learn (n.d.), FAO e-learning Academy (n.d.) and CCLearn (2021) to access limited only to participants of the initiative such as the UN Global Compact (UN Global Compact, 2021). Other interesting examples of online resources used by business schools globally are the Sulitest (n.d.), Aim2Flourish (n.d.), and platforms that curate resources such as the PRiMETIME Resources to support your COVID-19 response Giselle Weybrecht (2020) and the launch of the UNESCO Global Education Coalition for COVID-19 as "a platform for collaboration and exchange to protect the right to education," bringing together more than 175 members from the UN, civil society, academia and the private sector

(UNESCO, n.d.). A remarkable resource produced by SDSNs is the accelerating education for the SDGs in universities guide, which is a new guide "that aims to help universities, colleges, and tertiary and higher education institutions implement and mainstream this "education for the SDGs" within their institutions" (SDSN, 2020b). The guide was launched together with a case study website with nearly 50 innovative and inspiring examples of universities around the world taking measures to accelerate the implementation of ESD (SDSN, 2020b).

Acknowledging the existence of diverse platforms and resources in this increasing field of online education and with the objective of highlighting a rather comprehensive catalog of OERs and free content focused on sustainable development free to everyone, we discuss below the case of the SDG Academy.

The SDG Academy as a Platform for Content and Community to Advance Education for

Sustainable DevelopmentThe SDG Academy as a flagship educational initiative of SDSN

The SDG Academy is the flagship educational initiative of the Sustainable Development Solutions Network (SDSN), which was established in 2012 under the auspices of the UN Secretary-General "to mobilize global academic and scientific expertise to promote practical solutions for sustainable development, including the implementation of the Sustainable Development Goals (SDGs) and the Paris Climate Agreement" (SDSN, n.d.-a). SDSN brings together a network of 1500+ universities and research centers from around the world to advance the SDGs (SDSN, n.d.-b)

The SDG Academy is hosted by the SDSN Association and was launched in September 2016 with the goal of becoming a premier world's leading creation and curation site for educational content on the SDGs (SDSN, n.d.-c). The SDG Academy vision is "A world in which the SDGs are achieved through the efforts of the current and next generation of educators, practitioners, and citizens," and its mission aims "to create and curate relevant educational content on the SDGs and nurture a global community to prepare this generation and the next to achieve sustainable development" (SDSN, 2021, p. 8). Aligned to that purpose, the SDG Academy creates and curates online educational content covering a spectrum of sustainable development issues, making it available at scale, for free, as a global public good and providing opportunities for peer learning and partnership. The SDG Academy has recently adopted a Creative Commons license (https://creativecommons.org/) to amplify its impact by "sending a clear message that learners and educators can feel confident using and sharing our educational resources to continue our goal of providing everyone access to high-quality educational content on sustainable development" (SDSN, 2021, p. 8). Since inception, this initiative has garnered over 641,070 enrollments across its MOOC platforms from 193 countries (SDSN, 2021, p. 14).

This initiative serves a diverse audience from around the world with self-paced MOOCs and multimedia resources designed into a global online curriculum in the context of the SDGs and the 2030 Agenda. As a core of its work, the SDG Academy nurtures a community of institutions and individual learners committed to advancing ESD globally (SDSN, 2020a). SDG Academy's learners include students and young professionals, educators, researchers, policymakers, and other change agents interested in expanding their knowledge on these issues, as well as getting connected with like-minded individuals and organizations that are committed to addressing the world's most pressing social, economic, and environmental issues (SDSN, 2020a).

In this section, we will discuss the SDG Academy resources, the community opportunities, and then some strategies and examples to leverage the resources and community to teach the SDGs in your own context.

SDG Academy's Resources

The SDG Academy's educational resources are developed and designed to raise awareness and improve understanding of the science and policies behind sustainable development aiming to empower policy-makers, practitioners, and citizens to make informed decisions and be drivers for sustainable development (SDSN, 2020a). By delivering content addressing all the SDGs, including issues such as human rights, health, climate change, biodiversity, agriculture, and sustainable investment, the SDG Academy works with partners and other experts to create and curate educational resources as a public good for a diverse global audience. The SDG Academy leverages its ability to bring together a diverse body of leading experts across geographies and institutions to provide open and free quality educational tools and resources to drive action for the SDGs. In that sense, the SDG Academy's approach aims to merge "substantive expertise with grassroots movements, putting SDG knowledge in the hands of people who need it most [by designing resources that] combine the best scientific knowledge, global and local perspectives, and a pedagogical approach that is thought-provoking and transformative" (SDSN, 2020a, p. 4).

Massive Open Online Courses
The SDG Academy has been producing massive open online courses (MOOCs) for over 8 years since the launch of its first MOOC "The Age of Sustainable Development" with Prof. Jeffrey D. Sachs, President of SDSN and University Professor at Columbia University. The SDG Academy's online courses—of this robust catalog now counting more than 35 online courses—include documentary-quality video lectures from experts in sustainable development issues, complementary materials, readings, assessments, discussion fora, and other activities as well as live webinars with faculty and other experts. Most SDG Academy online courses are hosted on edX (https://www.edx.org/) and are available self-paced so learners can access and complete the course at their own time and schedule (SDSN, 2020a).

As an initiative of the SDSN, the SDG Academy is able to leverage its access to an extensive network of experts from universities, research centers, think tanks, development agencies, and the UN System to create and curate content. The SDG Academy's global faculty includes more than 250 experts who believe in the power of education to build a sustainable, inclusive, and peaceful world. In that sense, Prof. Michael Mann, Distinguished Professor of Atmospheric Science at Penn State University, USA, stated that

As a climate scientist and science communicator, I believe that public understanding of the science behind climate change can facilitate our collective efforts to address the climate crisis. By partnering with the SDG Academy, I have been able to reach more than 15,000 new learners in less than a year. Our efforts have helped citizens worldwide gain the knowledge needed to advocate for climate action. (SDSN, 2020a)

Similarly, Prof. Martin Visbeck and Dr. Avan Anita, Kiel University, Germany, stated the following:

As academics, we had a unique opportunity to engage with global learners and sustainability practitioners. We learned that scientific content was as important as inspiration, context and reflection. Delivery of our MOOC within the SDG Academy was critical in this experience, as we could place the ocean in the context of sustainable development and access thousands of global learners through their network. (SDSN, 2020a)

The beauty of engaging with relevant partners on a wide array of topics allows the SDG Academy to create courses appealing for a large and diverse audience, as noted by Margarita Battle, PhD, Senior Research, Data & Learning Officer Natural Resource Governance Institute (NRGI):

In the context of increasing demand for online learning opportunities, our partnership with CCSI Columbia and the SDG Academy led to an innovative mini-MOOC on contract negotiation that allows learners to understand the challenges governments face in negotiating strong contracts. With the support of the SDG Academy, we were able to design a course that is relevant for multiple stakeholders in different regions of the world, which will be a great complement to our in-person or live online training. (SDSN, 2021, p. 10)

During the pandemic, the SDG Academy experienced a dramatic increase in MOOC enrollment, which coincides with and can be explained by the overnight shift to remote teaching and learning in March 2020. In that sense, this initiative saw a 3.2 times enrollment increase in the period of 17 March to 30 June 2020, counting approximately 90,138 new learners (SDSN, 2020a). Additionally, the initiative saw a 72%

increase in overall learners from Fiscal Year (FY) 2019 to FY 2020, a 105.82% increase in new learners pursuing a course certificate and an 18.83% increase in the ratio of the learner population pursuing a verified course certificate (SDSN, 2020a). Another important trend was an increasing student interest in content related to ethics and other humanistic disciplines that offer a deeper perspective on human existence and purpose. In that sense, the "Ethics in Action" course saw an increase in enrollment from 26,681 to 5211 students in the same lockdown period (SDSN, 2020a).

During FY21, the course Natured-based Solutions for Disaster and Climate Resilience reached 43,239 enrollments, becoming the best performer with the highest rates of enrollments in the history of the SDG Academy (SDSN, 2021).

As stated in the SDG Academy Annual Report 2021 (SDSN, 2021), enrollments in SDG Academy courses have substantially increased in the last 2 years, which seems to indicate a growing interest in this type of content and knowledge. A trend that one can appreciate is that there has been an even greater increase in learners choosing to pursue a verified course certificate. In that sense, "85% of all SDG Academy courses outperformed the edX average of 3.6% of all learners verified-track enrollment" (SDSN, 2021, p. 17), with percentages ranging from 3.9% to 15.3%.

The SDG Academy Video Library

The SDG Academy Library was launched in 2019 to provide a searchable repository of educational videos and lectures on sustainable development curated from SDG Academy courses, SDG Academy and SDSN webinars, and other select content. This video library provides a platform for expanding the reach of high-quality OERs on sustainable development and disseminating essential knowledge as a global public good that can be further shared, integrated and contextualized. This video repository of 1500+ videos continues to grow as a fundamental tool for remote teaching and learning, especially during the pandemic. All of the content in the library can be searched by SDGs, lecturers, subjects, video series and more. Prof. David S. Steingard, Director, SDG Dashboard, Saint Joseph's

University, shared his experience utilizing these resources in class during the COVID-19 pandemic:

> The SDG Academy Library empowers students to transform companies with the SDGs. Saint Joseph's University (USA) utilizes videos from the SDG Academy Library as a foundation for its undergraduate capstone course in their Leadership, Ethics, and Organizational Sustainability (LEO) degree program. Throughout the semester, students reviewed, analyzed, and presented 2 videos per individual SDG for classroom dialog. The videos provide content knowledge necessary for these students to effectively consult with live companies using the SDG Action Manager, an online assessment tool that measures corporate SDG impact. The SDG Academy video library offers an inspiring and invaluable contribution to student learning. As a result, students are directly empowered to accelerate the achievement of the SDGs in their professional careers after graduation. (SDSN, 2021, p. 18)

The Book Club with Jeffrey Sachs: A Platform, Webinars, and Podcasts Series
The Book Club with Jeffrey Sachs (https://www.bookclubwithjef-freysachs.org) is a global forum on the most important issues of humanity launched in January 2021 and offers monthly live conversations with renowned authors, a podcast series, and an interactive platform on edX to access book excerpts, supplementary resources, giveaways, and a discussion forum. The platform has more than 5000 members and more than 10,000 podcast downloads to date. Prof. Jeffrey D. Sachs, host of the Book Club, shared the following:

> When the pandemic started, I started taking a long walk for daily exercise because I wasn't going to the office. In addition, on those walks, I was listening to audio books and have listened to dozens and dozens of audio books on my COVID-19 era walks and the books that are coming out. The ones that I'm listening to are phenomenal books about history, social justice, and the way forward for building a fair world. In addition, I decided whoa, that's a great book. I want to talk to the author because I didn't know many the authors. In addition, so, I called up the authors. I said, could we

do an interview together? And that's how the book club started. (UN SDGLearn, 2021)

The Book Club with Jeffrey Sachs provides very informative and thought-provoking conversations and podcast episodes with experts and authors that inspire reflection and action to address the issues that historically have held us back from achieving a sustainable, equal and just world.

SDG Academy's Community

Throughout the existence of the SDG Academy, it has been evident the importance of building a community around its content not only to help disseminate knowledge globally but also to cocreate and curate content and provide possibilities for peer exchange, sharing good practices and thought leadership.

From the University Partnership Program to the Community of Practice

Since the start, the SDG Academy has promoted the use and integration of its content by faculty and educators to help the teaching and learning of the SDGs. To support that premise, in 2017, the SDG Academy launched the first cohort of its University Partnership Program (UPP), an initiative focused on increasing "universities' capacity to teach about sustainable development by integrating SDG Academy content into new or existing academic programs" (SDSN, 2020a, p. 31). Throughout its 3 years, the UPP supported 33 universities across 20 countries. Landouard Habiyaremye, Associate Director for Academic Support, Kepler, Rwanda participant of the UPP, shared their experience stating that:

> At Kepler, we decided to use SDG Academy courses for our students to benefit from the content and obtain an opportunity to connect the learning with the SDGs. We tried to adapt the content to our teaching model to help students internalize the learning. To date, more than 100 students have taken the content of the Global Public Health and Human Rights and Human Wrongs courses in different cycles. Students witnessed how well the resources provided were beneficial to them. 'We were given materials

that gave us factual and helpful information that we can use for a lifetime,' one student said. (SDSN, 2020a, p. 31)

After running the UPP program for 3 years, the SDG Academy took stock of the important learnings of this program, including the unique needs of every partner; the value of sharing good practices, challenges, and opportunities among and beyond HEIs; the opportunity to leverage the expertise of the participants; and the opportunity scale up the impact of the program. For this reason, in September 2020, the SDG Academy launched the first cohort of the SDG Academy Community of Practice, building on those lessons learned, with the aim of building and nurturing a circular and vibrant community focused on education for sustainable development, "through peer learning and the sharing of best practices, customized resource development, and opportunities for research and thought leadership" (SDSN, 2020a, p. 32). The SDG Academy Community of Practice brings together global higher education institutions, NGOs, for-profit businesses, and relevant government entities that have the opportunity to engage with the SDG-focused resources offered by the SDG Academy; personalize these resources for their own needs and institutional contexts; and develop their own content, communities of learning, networks, and dialogs across the wider community. In its first year, the Community of Practice engaged 52 institutions globally, including 15 partners and 37 members representing 27 countries (SDSN, 2021). While this is a very new program with still much potential to realize, Prof. John Dilyard, St. Francis College, USA, reflects on his experience as a member of the Community of Practice:

As an educator passionate about sustainability and SDGs, I constantly strive to integrate ways to introduce my undergraduate students to the topic of sustainability and to the purpose and objectives of the SDGs. The Community of Practice has been invaluable for that purpose, as it not only provides access to incomparable educational resources through the SDG Academy but also provides the opportunity to share experiences and best practices with other like-minded educators across the globe. Being a member has empowered me to encourage my peers and those within my other networks who want to teach sustainability to use what the community has to offer as excellent complements to their own teaching. (SDSN, 2021, p. 24)

Alumni Network

Created in 2018, the SDG Academy Alumni Network Facebook Group convenes 5500 course alumni to discuss their SDG learnings, their experience taking the course, their stories of impact, and resources and other opportunities. To foster further engagement and growth, in the past year, the SDG Academy piloted an alumni advocates program with three alumni to understand how best to encourage alumni engagement. This pilot will inform the creation of an Alumni Advocates program in the near future.

The Alumni Network is an important source of information regarding the impact of the SDG Academy's content. Through the "Learner's Perspectives" blog series, alumni share their stories showcasing the positive impact that they have driven, affecting their lives and work and their overall increased commitment to sustainable development as a result of engaging with the SDG Academy's content. Currently, 17 alumni blog stories tell readers about real life stories: "each story tells us about a unique human being with dreams, purpose, and possibility to make the world a better place" (SDSN, 2021, p. 28). The first blog story was written by Atula Owade, a young engineer from Kenya who was inspired by the SDG Academy course "Feeding a hungry Planet":

> As a recent graduate, I have very little experience in the real world and hence need guidance as I start practicing. The seven modules cover an array of topics that provide the guidance I was looking for… Although I was already familiar with most of the concepts, the instructors opened my eyes to new approaches in the sustainable intensification of agricultural systems… My experience with the course has been great, and I would encourage anyone seeking an online program in sustainable food and agriculture to consider signing up for the SDG Academy's Feeding a Hungry Planet. I have a feeling that it may help you achieve your professional or hobbyist goals, wherever you are in the world. (SDSN, 2020a, p. 35)

Students have also pointed out how the SDG Academy content has helped them grow in their understanding of the holistic nature of sustainable development. In that sense, for instance Becky Fox, from New Zealand, stated that:

> As a science teacher, when I first started taking SDG Academy courses, I thought I had a good grasp on the concepts of sustainability. However, I never expected to learn so much, or for the courses to lead me on a path where I am now: pursuing a Master's in Sustainable Development through SOAS University of London. I first started looking into sustainability from an environmental point of view. However, it turns out to be much more complicated than I initially thought. As a consequence, the courses have shifted my attention toward the importance of education and poverty eradication. (SDSN, 2020a, p. 18)

Similarly, some students have said that the SDG Academy content has inspired them to take action. For instance, Rosanele Romero, Senior Basin Researcher, IHS Markit, Malaysia, stated that

> The SDG Academy courses empower and enable us to take action. The course on Environmental Security and Sustaining Peace presented with StoryMaps is perfect for private, government and community stakeholders affected by destructive industries who want to change the narrative in pursuit of sustainability. The Natural Resources for Sustainable Development is a great follow-up course that highlights how geology is at the core of so many of our world's challenges. The courses highlight the need for boundary workers and communicators to become involved in resource management and governance by bridging the gaps between technical and nontechnical disciplines. (SDSN, 2020a, p. 31)

11.4 Leveraging Resources and Community to Teach and Learn the SDGs in Your Own Context

As schools and universities globally shifted lessons online due to COVID-19, many educators and learners struggled to adapt to remote teaching and learning and to find innovative ways to keep students engaged in a fully remote learning environment. With this in mind, the SDG Academy has been well positioned to support educators in "creating engaging, multimodal online learning experiences in a variety of disciplines, and took an active role in supporting the global education community from the beginning of the pandemic" (SDSN, 2020a, p. 29). To support the shift globally and as part of its COVID-19 Response (SDG Academy, 2020), the SDG Academy joined the UNESCO Global Education Coalition for COVID-19 (UNESCO, n.d.), which completed and shared resources as well as best practices to help transition to remote learning. The SDG Academy hosted several expert webinars on issues related to COVID-19 as well as more pedagogical webinars to facilitate the access and integration of the SDG Academy content to business schools and universities, including as the pandemic started the "Engaging Online: Teaching and Learning with the SDG Academy" webinar in March 2020 to help faculty navigate the SDG Academy resources.

Throughout the pandemic, the SDG Academy team participated in many webinars and events to help disseminate its content, as well as provide space for reflection and for good practices from its community regarding how best to use these resources during this time of fully remote teaching and learning. An event that is worth mentioning was the 5th UN PRME NE Virtual Conference "Sustainable Development Goals: Transforming Business Education and Practice" (Rutgers, 2020b), where the SDG Academy team presented a workshop called "MNGT 101: Sustainable Development Integration in the Classroom with the SDG Academy" (Rutgers, 2020a). During this workshop, the SDG Academy team presented some ideas of integration of the SDG Academy resources and lessons learned gathered through the UPP and Community of Practice. Based on these experiences and the cocreated workshop, below, we present a few key ideas to use and integrate the SDG Academy content in business and higher education settings:

1. Asynchronous use of resources with synchronous or asynchronous discussion:

    (a) Faculty can request students to watch SDG videos before their class (as they would typically request readings) and discuss them in an in-person or online class (synchronous) or in a discussion board or forum (asynchronous).

(b) Some faculty have requested students to select and watch videos, courses or podcasts based on their interest (asynchronous) and to present their learnings to the class (synchronous).

2. Synchronous use of resources with synchronous discussion:

(a) Some faculty use videos during in-person or online synchronous discussions for learners to watch together and engage in a discussion. This can be used as an introduction to a topic or as a way to present more in-depth information or alternative points of view to the issue.

(b) Videos can be used during class to help illustrate the topic with examples, bring inspiration or with concrete activities such as issue spotting, mapping stakeholders, identifying opportunities and threats, discussing due diligence and risk mitigation strategies, and so on and to debate and consider solutions to specific, real-world problems.

(c) The content can also be used across departments by engaging faculty and students in different disciplines and engaging in interdisciplinary conversations around sustainable development issues.

3. Use resources for faculty development to further advance knowledge or take ideas from:

(a) Some faculty have enrolled in SDG Academy MOOCs to borrow assessments, additional readings, discussion prompts, or ideas or to get inspired and learn more about a subject.

(b) Some faculty have used SDG Academy videos to integrate them in faculty development workshops or to share with colleagues to make them aware of a specific issue.

4. SDG Academy resources used as requisite for admission or credit:

(a) Faculty have requested a regular or customized version of an SDG Academy course as a prerequisite for admission into their program.

(b) Faculty have requested to take a regular or customized version of an SDG Academy course as part of a course, in which the students engage in course discussion or activities and write a final paper or take a final exam.

5. Use content to create new programs for your institution:

(a) Faculty have also used the SDG Academy content to curate lecture series for their students or completely new programs.
(b) Faculty have used the SDG Academy to design courses using "blended learning" strategies. Typically, this might include students taking parts of or the full MOOC at home and then using the in-class synchronous time (in person or online) to discuss the content included in the course, videos or podcasts, engagement in teamwork, project-based activities, advising companies or other stakeholders, and so on.

Apart from these examples and as part of the Community of Practice, higher education, nonprofit, business, and government representatives join together discussions and "Community Conversations" to share challenges, opportunities, good practices, lessons learned on teaching and learning the most pressing issues of our times. By engaging in circular conversations that acknowledge the complexity and deep interrelations among the issues and the importance of thinking global as well as contextualizing the issues, this initiative aims to leverage the expertise that each member brings to the room and to support and nurture a community to help educators around the world advance education for sustainable development.

Moving Forward: Reflections Beyond the Pandemic

The need for the use of different approaches to RME and the incorporation of sustainable development into education has been reinforced during COVID-19. What has become clear is that online education is here to stay. It is untenable to imagine that everything will just be reset and return to pre COVID-19 times, but it is important that lessons be learned to enable future teaching and learning to incorporate the positive benefits and to minimize (where possible) any negative impacts.

Based on the previous sections of the chapter, one can assume that the increased use of online teaching in particular has brought some opportunities. These include but are not limited to (1) the potential for greater inclusion and diversity from increased global expertise and reach; (2) access to experts and materials "beyond the classroom"; (3) the possibility of using online resources to increase life-long learning opportunities; (4) the scaling up of education and its democratization; (5) flexibility in work patterns, enhancing work/life balance; and (6) reduced travel time and expense, together with the associated reduction in carbon emissions.

However, this also presents challenges. Again, these include, but are not limited to: (1) Access and availability of technology and the infrastructure/support is, unfortunately, not a given in all contexts; (2) Provision of suitable, safe work spaces with training and support; (3) Effective communication and feedback systems to respond to issues as they arise; (4) Curriculum in different forms can require changes to the content and assessment to meet the needs of required outcomes for programs and courses. This is particularly important where experiential and/or social learning is a key part of the curriculum; (5) Mechanisms to enable peer learning and dialog to support the changes; (6) Student perspectives and feedback opportunities are also important, particularly on aspects of the structure and delivery; (7) The shift to more "home" working can also bring challenges including the need to separate work and home life; the problems of "zoom fatigue" and the importance of maintaining social interaction.

Finally, maintaining the innovation and creativity of teaching and learning is critical, and opportunities to share methods and resources are vital to the collective response of education to the challenges we all face.

Ensuring educational opportunities that cultivate sustainable mindsets, skills and behavior requires a very intentional focus to provide opportunities for human interaction that are often more challenging to create in an online format. For that reason, providing one-one-one coaching, advice sessions, counseling, mentoring and "buddy" support, small team networking and community building opportunities (whether in person or remote) are key to creating an educational experience that contemplates a whole-person learning (WPL) approach (GRLI, n.d.) to RMEs and ESDs. Even within remote learning settings, a purposeful use of synchronous sessions for this kind of endeavor is highly recommended. In that sense, a hybrid model that combines the best use of synchronous and asynchronous and, when possible, in-person and online education seems to be an appropriate way to combine the efficiency and other advantages of the online model while making it possible to enhance human connection and social interaction.

More than ever, RME and ESD must be integrated into business and management education and higher education more broadly. This critical and ambitious endeavor will require an ongoing reflection on purpose and impact; a focus beyond knowledge to enable sustainable mindsets, skills, and behaviors through human connection and empathy; and the critical thinking and flexibility to make the best use of the resources available to provide a meaningful and transformative educational experience.

References

3BLMedia. (2018). *The UN Global Compact launches the Academy—A new digital learning platform to help companies become more sustainable.* 3BLMedia.com. https://www.3blmedia.com/News/UN-Global-Compact-launches-Academy-new-digital-learning-platform-help-companies-become-more

Agasisti, T., Frattini, F., & Soncin, M. (2020). Digital innovation in times of emergency: Reactions from a school of management in Italy. *Sustainability (Switzerland), 12*(24), 1–17. https://www.scopus.com/inward/record.uri?eid=2-s2.0-85098493222&doi=10.3390%2Fsu122410312&partnerID=40&md5=3e7d07fd77ed8e5989dd3135aee8b338

AIM2Flourish. (n.d.). Retrieved September 12, 2021, from https://aim2flourish.com/

Almendro, D., & Silveira, I. F. (2018). Quality assurance for open educational resources: The OER trust framework. *International Journal of Learning, Teaching and Educational Research, 17*(3), 1–14. https://www.researchgate.

net/profile/Douglas-Almendro/publication/323882739_Quality_ Assurance_for_Open_Educational_Resources_The_OERTrust_Framework/ links/5d03dd1f458515b055d27599/Quality-Assurance-for-Open-Educational-Resources-The-OERTrust-Framework.pdf

Alshamsi, A., Mohaidat, J., Hinai, N. A., & Samy, A. (2020). Instructional and business continuity amid and beyond covid-19 outbreak: A case study from the higher colleges of technology. *International Journal of Sustainability in Higher Education, 9*(6), 118–135. https://www.scopus.com/inward/record. uri?eid=2-s2.0-85091174485&doi=10.5430%2Fijhe.v9n6p118&partnerI D=40&md5=9ca132da72c36c6ab1e087e1a48ae46c

Annan-Diab, F., & Molinari, C. (2017). Interdisciplinarity: Practical approach to advancing education for sustainability and for the Sustainable Development Goals. *International Journal of Management Education.* https://doi. org/10.1016/j.ijme.2017.03.006

Bailenson, J. N. (2021). Nonverbal overload: A theoretical argument for the causes of Zoom fatigue. *Technology, Mind, and Behavior, 2*(1). https://doi. org/10.1037/tmb0000030

Bandura, A. (1985). Model of causality in social learning theory. In M. J. Mahoney & A. Freeman (Eds.), *Cognition and psychotherapy* (pp. 81–99). Springer. https://doi.org/10.1007/978-1-4684-7562-3_3

Butcher, N. (2015). *A basic guide to Open Educational Resources (OER).* Commonwealth of Learning (COL). http://oasis.col.org/handle/11599/36

CCLearn. (2021). *CC learn who we are.* https://www.uncclearn.org/about/ who-we-are/

Commonwealth of Learning. (2017). *Open educational resources: From commitment to action.* Commonwealth of Learning. http://hdl.handle. net/11599/2789

Cornuel, E., & Hommel, U. (2015). Moving beyond the rhetoric of responsible management education. *Journal of Management Development, 34*(1), 2–15. https://doi.org/10.1108/jmd-06-2014-0059

Dhawan, S. (2020). Online learning: A panacea in the time of COVID-19 crisis. *Journal of Educational Technology Systems, 49*(1), 5–22. https://doi. org/10.1177/0047239520934018

Edelhauser, E., & Lupu-Dima, L. (2020). Is Romania prepared for elearning during the COVID-19 pandemic? *Sustainability (Switzerland), 12*(13). https://www.scopus.com/inward/record.uri?eid=2-s2.0-850878988 76&doi=10.3390%2Fsu12135438&partnerID=40&md5=33bcc498301e9 a6e20c2113fa999f262

FAO. (2020). *Launch of the FAO elearning Academy: Strengthening capacity to face global challenges.* http://newsletters.fao.org/q/13XCxX76b8 GmtGzd1pQt1/wv

FAO. (n.d.). Retrieved September 12, 2021, from https://elearning.fao.org/

Fukuda-Parr, S. (2016). From the millennium development goals to the sustainable development goals: Shifts in purpose, concept, and politics of global goal setting for development. *Gender & Development, 24*(1), 43–52. https://doi.org/10.1080/13552074.2016.1145895

GRLI. (n.d.). *Whole Person Learning (WPL).* GRLI. Retrieved September 14, 2021, from https://grli.org/initiatives/whole-person-learning-wpl/

Guerrero, M., Heaton, S., & Urbano, D. (2021). Building universities' intrapreneurial capabilities in the digital era: The role and impacts of Massive Open Online Courses (MOOCs). *Technovation, 99*, 102139. https://doi.org/10.1016/j.technovation.2020.102139

Hodgkinson-Williams, C. (2010). *Benefits and challenges of OER for higher education institutions.* http://oasis.col.org/handle/11599/3042

Hope, A., Croney, P., & Myers, J. (2020). Experiential learning for responsible management education. In D. C. Moosmayer, O. Laasch, C. Parkes, & K. G. Brown (Eds.), *The SAGE handbook of responsible management learning and education.* SAGE. https://doi.org/10.4135/9781526477187

Huang, R., Tlili, A., Wang, H., Shi, Y., Bonk, C. J., Yang, J., & Burgos, D. (2021). Emergence of the online-merge-offline (OMO) learning wave in the post-COVID-19 era: A pilot study. *Sustainability (Switzerland), 13*(6) https://www.scopus.com/inward/record.uri?eid=2-s2.0-851031226 53&doi=10.3390%2Fsu13063512&partnerID=40&md5=0bba701c0ffea6 544a93eff107a7eb1f

Huda, M., Maseleno, A., Mat Teh, K. S., Don, A. G., Basiron, B., Jasmi, K. A., Mustari, M. I., Nasir, B. M., & Ahmad, R. (2018). Understanding modern learning environment (MLE) in big data era. *International Journal of Emerging Technologies in Learning (iJET), 13*(05) https://onlinejour.journals.publicknowledgeproject.org/index.php/i-jet/article/view/8042

Hurst, B., Wallace, R. R., & Nixon, S. B. (2013). The impact of social interaction on student learning. *Reading Horizons.* https://scholarworks.wmich.edu/cgi/viewcontent.cgi?article=3105&context=reading_horizons

Leal Filho, W. (2011). About the role of universities and their contribution to sustainable development. *Higher Education Policy, 24*(4), 427–438. https://doi.org/10.1057/hep.2011.16

Leal Filho, W., Shiel, C., Paço, A., Mifsud, M., Ávila, L. V., Brandli, L. L., Molthan-Hill, P., Pace, P., Azeiteiro, U. M., Vargas, V. R., & Caeiro, S. (2019). Sustainable development goals and sustainability teaching at universities: Falling behind or getting ahead of the pack? *Journal of Cleaner Production, 232*, 285–294. https://doi.org/10.1016/J.JCLEPRO.2019.05.309

Martin, A. M. (2021). Instructor qualities and student success in higher education online courses. *Journal of Digital Learning in Teacher Education, 37*(1), 65–80. https://doi.org/10.1080/21532974.2020.1815106

Mavlutova, I., Lesinskis, K., Liogys, M., & Hermanis, J. (2020). Innovative teaching techniques for entrepreneurship education in the era of digitalisation. *WSEAS Transactions on Environment and Development, 16*, 725–733. https://www.scopus.com/inward/record.uri?eid=2-s2.0-850954490 66&doi=10.37394%2F232015.2020.16.75&partnerID=40&md5=0621b2 0cd751ffe366ce923b6a7dd618

Moe, R. (2015). The brief & expansive history (and future) of the MOOC: Why two divergent models share the same name. *Current Issues in Emerging eLearning, 2*(1), 2. https://scholarworks.umb.edu/ciee/vol2/iss1/2/

Moosmayer, D. C., Laasch, O., Parkes, C., & Brown, K. G. (2020). *The SAGE handbook of responsible management learning and education.* SAGE. https://play.google.com/store/books/details?id=31jGDwAAQBAJ

Mori Junior, R., Fien, J., & Horne, R. (2019). Implementing the UN SDGs in universities: Challenges, opportunities, and lessons learned. *Sustainability (United States), 12*(2), 129–133. https://doi.org/10.1089/sus.2019.0004

Mousa, M. (2021). Responsible management education (RME) post COVID-19: What must change in public business schools? *International Journal of Management & Enterprise Development, 40*(2), 105–120. https://www.scopus.com/inward/record.uri?eid=2-s2.0-85099933237&doi=10.110 8%2FJMD-10-2020-0316&partnerID=40&md5=f58712bc7ca202b9ee9 b38bc9c685d59

Orr, D., Rimini, M., & van Damme, D. (2015). *Open educational resources.* OECD. https://doi.org/10.1787/9789264247543-en

Ossiannilsson, E. (2021). Some challenges for universities, in a post crisis, as Covid-19. In D. Burgos, A. Tlili, & A. Tabacco (Eds.), *Radical solutions for education in a crisis context: COVID-19 as an opportunity for global learning* (pp. 99–112). Springer. https://doi.org/10.1007/978-981-15-7869-4_7

Rapanta, C., Botturi, L., Goodyear, P., Guàrdia, L., & Koole, M. (2020). Online university teaching during and after the Covid-19 crisis: Refocusing teacher presence and learning activity. *Postdigital Science and Education, 2*(3), 923–945. https://doi.org/10.1007/s42438-020-00155-y

Rof, A., Bikfalvi, A., & Marquès, P. (2020). Digital transformation for business model innovation in higher education: Overcoming the tensions. *Sustainability, 12*(12). https://doi.org/10.3390/su12124980

Rutgers. (2020a). *5th UN PRME NE virtual conference MNGT 101: Sustainable development integration in the classroom with the SDG academy.* Rutgers Institute for Corporate Social Innovation. https://www.youtube.com/watch?v=_U7L2JT6bFY

Rutgers. (2020b). *Fifth PRME Northeast virtual conference "sustainable development goals: Transforming business education and practice."* https://www.business.rutgers.edu/ricsi/prme-northeast-conference

Sachs, J. D. (2012). From millennium development goals to sustainable development goals. *The Lancet, 379*, 2206–2211. https://doi.org/10.1016/S0140-6736(12)60685-0

SDG Academy. (2020). *Teaching and learning during COVID-19.* https://sdgacademy.org/teaching-and-learning-during-covid-19/

SDG Academy. (n.d.). Retrieved 2021, from http://sdgacademy.org

SDG Learn. (n.d.). Retrieved September 14, 2021, from https://www.unsdglearn.org/

SDSN. (2020a). *SDG academy 2020 annual report.* SDSN. https://resources.unsdsn.org/sdg-academy-2020-annual-report

SDSN. (2020b, September 21). *Accelerating education for the SDGs in universities a guide for universities colleges and tertiary and higher education institutions.* https://resources.unsdsn.org/accelerating-education-for-the-sdgs-in-universities-a-guide-for-universities-colleges-and-tertiary-and-higher-education-institutions

SDSN. (2021). *SDG academy 2021 annual report.* https://resources.unsdsn.org/sdg-academy-2021-annual-report

SDSN. (n.d.-a). *About us.* Retrieved August 30, 2021, from https://www.unsdsn.org/about-us

SDSN. (n.d.-b). *Members.* Retrieved August 30, 2021, from https://www.unsdsn.org/sdsn-members

SDSN. (n.d.-c). *SDG Academy.* Retrieved August 30, 2021, from https://www.unsdsn.org/sdg-academy

Simonson, M., & Berg, G. A. (2016). Distance learning. In *Encyclopedia Britannica.* https://www.britannica.com/topic/distance-learning

Sulitest. (n.d.). Retrieved September 12, 2021, from https://www.sulitest.org/en/index.html

UNESCO. (2002). *Forum on the impact of open courseware for higher education in developing countries* (No. CI-2002/CONF.803/CLD.1). UNESCO.

UNESCO. (2012). *2012 Paris OER Declaration.* World Open Educational Resources (OER) Congress. http://www.unesco.org/new/fileadmin/MULTIMEDIA/HQ/CI/CI/pdf/Events/English_Paris_OER_Declaration.pdf

UNESCO. (n.d.). *Global education coalition.* Retrieved September 14, 2021, from https://en.unesco.org/covid19/educationresponse/globalcoalition

UN General Assembly. (2015). *Transforming our world: The 2030 agenda for sustainable development (No. A/RES/70/1).* https://www.refworld.org/docid/57b6e3e44.html. Accessed 8 Sept 2021.

UN Global Compact. (2021). *Academy.* https://www.unglobalcompact.org/academy

UNITAR. (2019). *Launch of the UN SDG learn at the HLPF.* https://unitar.org/about/news-stories/featuredarticles/launch-un-sdglearn-2019-hlpf

UN SDGLearn. (2021, August 24). Goal-based development: Do they actually work?—Revisiting the UN goal-setting as a policy tool with Professor Jeffrey Sachs of SDSN. In *SDG Learncast.* SDNS. https://www.unsdglearn.org/podcast/goal-based-development-do-they-actually-work-revisiting-the-un-goal-setting-as-a-policy-tool/

Weybrecht, G. (2020, March). *How business schools are responding to COVID-19.* https://primetime.unprme.org/2020/03/26/how-business-schools-are-responding-to-covid-19-examples-from-the-prme-community-updated-regularly/#Organising-response.

Weybrecht, G. (2021). How management education is engaging students in the sustainable development goals. *International Journal of Sustainability in Higher Education, 22*(6), 1302–1315. https://doi.org/10.1108/IJSHE-10-2020-0419

Zeng, M. Q. M., Chen, H., Shrestha, A., Crowley, C., Ng, E., & Wang, G. (2020). International collaboration on a sustainable forestry management OER online program—A case study. *Journal of Higher Education Theory and Practice, 20*(8), 120–128. https://www.scopus.com/inward/record.uri?eid=2-s2.0-85102256434&doi=10.33423%2Fjhetp.v20i8.3235&partnerID=40&md5=5b2fdcfdae98a7becfcbb17d41736bf3

12

Developing 'Moral Awareness' and 'Moral Assertiveness' in Future Professionals Using a Digital Learning Module

Abiola Makinwa

12.1 Introduction

As the continuing news of financial and corruption scandals shows, some professionals who have been trained in what is 'right' and 'wrong' are not *acting* on that knowledge. There is a gap between the 'head knowledge' acquired in training and the actual actions in the workplace. This is not due to a lack of knowledge about what the 'good' or 'right' course of action is. In contrast, most trained professionals already *know* what the right thing to do is but may lack the courage to act in alignment with that knowledge. This gap between 'intention' and 'action' undermines the best corporate governance and anti-white-collar crime efforts.[1]

---

[1] This is referred to as the so-called 'integrity gap'. Ernst and Young, for example, propose 'The Integrity Agenda', that focuses on 'bridging the gap between management's intentions and the actual behaviors of employees and third parties on the ground.' See Gordan (2018).

A. Makinwa (✉)
The Hague University of Applied Sciences, The Hague, The Netherlands
e-mail: a.o.makinwa@hhs.nl

The decision-making processes of professionals should therefore be a key aspect of professional education. As the World Economic Forum Agenda for Business Integrity notes, '[r]ules and processes cannot be developed for every eventuality, and it is more important—and effective—to equip employees with tools to help them optimize their own decision-making and build ethical awareness (World Economic Forum, 2020). In a somewhat similar vein, Hu Chen[2] commenting on US Department of Justice criteria in assessing a company's compliance training notes that prosecutors want to see that …'[a] company that has taken a thoughtful approach … with a focus on behavior and processes (Interview by Broad Cat, n.d.).

Can we train future professionals to *act* with the moral courage to do what they already know is the right thing to do? If yes, what will this training encompass, and how will this training be delivered? This proposition raises obvious challenges. If the training objective is to guide students along what is by its very nature a personal inward-looking journey of self-discovery and personal growth, how can this be realized in a manner that is externally assessed, achievable and sustainable? What would the learning objectives be and how would they be assessed?

This chapter describes the Integrity Digital Learning Module (IntegrityDLM) (Makinwa, 2020a), a training tool developed and funded under the auspices of a Netherlands Initiative for Education Research Senior Comenius Fellow Grant, 2018–2020 (Makinwa, 2018) that addresses these particular concerns. The essential focus of the IntegrityDLM is to help students develop the moral courage to *act* in accordance with what they already know is the right and to become more resilient in the face of situational pressures by developing the competencies of *integrity awareness* and *integrity assertiveness.* These competences culminate in a *'values-based response mechanism'* that reflects the students' own intrinsic motivations, emotions, attitudes and inner principles learned in advance of a real-world ethical challenge. The digital format of the IntegrityDLM encourages self-honesty by providing a private, safe

---

[2] Hui Chen wrote the Department of Justice's original *Evaluation of Corporate Compliance Programs* in 2017. See U.S. Department of Justice Criminal Division (2017)

place for students to start on a very personal journey of self-reflection and moral skills development.

IntegrityDLM has been incorporated into the Compliance Minor curriculum for undergraduate Law students at the Hague University of Applied Sciences since the 2020–2021 academic session. After completing the IntegrityDLM, students submitted an *Integrity Self Reflection* on their experiences with the digital module. While merely illustrative, the analysis of the reflections of 21 students provides a window into the 'real experiences' of students and important feedback regarding the use of this educational tool (Makinwa, 2020b).

Section 12.2 briefly summarizes the theory that underpins the design and content of the IntegrityDLM. Section 12.3 describes the pedagogy adopted and how this has been used to design the IntegrityDLM *competences of 'Integrity Awareness'* and *'Integrity Assertiveness'*.[3] Section 12.4 explains the choice for, and development of, a digital learning platform for the module. Section 12.5 describes the key themes and insights that emerge from the illustrative analysis of students' reflections. Section 12.6 concludes the chapter with conclusions and recommendations on integrity education for future professionals using a digital platform.

12.2 Theoretical Underpinning

Rather than an extrinsic external-looking process, the IntegrityDLM is an intrinsic inward-focused journey of self-reflection, self-awareness, and self-actualization. The design and content of the IntegrityDLM is informed by more theories that see ethical decision-making as a dual cognitive-emotional process rather than on prescriptive notions of right and wrong.

Tenbrunsel and Smith-Crowe (2008a), in their overview of ethical decision-making models, note that most well-established models assume that ethical decision-making is a *reason-based process*, ignoring the roles of

---

[3] These competences were designed with a view to the future professional path of the students in Corporate Governance, Compliance, Finance, Data Privacy, Data Protection and Legal Tech. However, these competences are also generally relevant in any professional field.

emotions, the *subconscious*, and. The authors reference research which challenges some of the basic assumptions underlying these models. For example, the assumption that moral awareness is a precursor to ethical decision-making is challenged by authors who assert that individuals faced with ethical dilemmas often make unethical decisions that may be inconsistent with the decision-maker's true intentions (Banaji, & Bhaskar, 2000; Banaji et al., 2003). Additionally, referenced is the work that suggests decision-making is riddled with biases (Messick & Bazerman, 1996), as well as the work that argues that 'moral judgments are the result of a very quick, intuitive, emotion-based process, rather than a reason-based process' (Haidt, 2001).

All this aligns with Blasi's earlier conclusion that while moral reasoning is indisputably important, the link between moral reasoning capacities and moral action is seen as weak (Blasi, 1980). In a similar vein, Narvaez and Bock remarked that the centrality of deliberative reasoning in behavior is a fading paradigm across psychology (Narvaez & Bock, 2014).

This train of research leads to approaches that focus less on 'investigating simple correlations between independent variables and ethical decision making' and instead 'focus on investigating the *processes* that underlie ethical decision making' (Tenbrunsel & Smith-Crowe, 2008b). A focus on *processes* that underlie ethical decision-making is also a central finding of the OECD report on *Behavioral Insights for Public Integrity* to the effect that an individual's moral choices can be affected 'by emphasizing or raising their moral reference points' (OECD, 2018). The OECD report discusses evidence that a small message, a 'moral reminder', can be sufficient to induce ethical reflection and notes that moral choices can be invoked by creating commitments and by mentally preparing individuals for ethical temptations (OECD, 2018).

Building on this theoretical underpinning, the central objective of the IntegrityDLM is to help students create their own *process* of ethical decision-making. By learning and practicing responses based on the self-knowledge generated by their experiences in the module and by developing moral reminders, moral commitments and moral reference points, students develop a moral vocabulary, a personal moral code, and a method for tackling ethical challenges.

12.3   The IntegrityDLM: Competences and Learning Objectives

The IntegrityDLM makes use of existing pedagogies that it has adopted and adapted to realize the learning objective of helping students create a process of ethical decision-making.

With a view to decision-making as a cognitive-emotional process and with a target audience of young undergraduates with little life experience, this author considered it important to ground the notion of moral reminders, moral commitments and moral reference points, not in more abstract universally applicable hypernorms but in the *real experience* of the students. The IntegrityDLM Integrity Awareness competence was therefore designed using the experiential ethical training exercise anchored on *personal core values* developed by Sheehan and Schmidt as a scaffold (Sheehan & Schmidt, 2015). This is a values clarification exercise that helps the student to define what their core values are and to engage with the importance of these values by creating a hierarchy of these values in the form of a *pyramid of values*.

The IntegrityDLM also adopts Mary Gentile's 'Giving Voice to Values (GVV)' moral teaching pedagogy (Gentile, 2010). Her GVV pedagogy is based on research that shows that rehearsal at the cognitive and intellectual level as well as at a personal behavioral or experiential level influences the ability to act with moral conviction. Students practice *how* to respond to ethical situations to build 'moral muscle memory' by asking Gentile's key question, *'Once you know what is right, how do you get it done?'* (Gentile, 2010). Students learn that there are choices that can be made between doing nothing and blowing the whistle. The IntegrityDLM has adopted the term *Integrity Assertiveness* for this competence, where users learn to give voice to and to assert their values.

Throughout their engagement with the IntegrityDLM, students are guided through a self-reflection process. All their outputs, as well as these reflections, are recorded by the student for future reference in their IntegrityDLM Toolkit. Each competence is taught in a separate module. These competences are described further below.

Integrity Awareness

Learning Objective: 'At the end of this module, students can identify, articulate and engage with their intrinsic core values. They are more aware of WHO they are, WHAT they STAND FOR, and the IMPACT they would like to have in their personal and professional life'.

In the *Integrity Awareness* module, students answer the questions, who am I? what are my core values? What are my moral reference points? What are my moral reminders? What are my moral commitments to myself?

There are four steps in integrity awareness training: (1) identifying core values: students identify ten personal core values using the IntegrityDLM *Values Game* (Makinwa, 2020c),[4] (2) creating a hierarchy of core values: students engage further with their identified personal core values and gain insight into how these values interrelate in forming their moral identity by creating a hierarchy of personal core values in a pyramid of values. (3) *Comparing different Frames of Values*: Students also engage in group exercises to create a group pyramid with randomly selected students, as well as an organizational pyramid for a particular sector. Students then compare their personal pyramids with these group and organizational pyramids and reflect on what they observe as commonalities or differences. (4) *Creating a Personal Code of Conduct*: Students motivate and explain to themselves why it is important that they live in alignment with each of their identified core values by giving advice to their future professional self with respect to each of these values. Each piece of advice is a promise to themselves or moral commitment for their personal code of conduct.

Integrity Assertiveness

Learning Objective: 'At the end of this Module, students have developed and learned to apply a values-based response mechanism that equips them to counter rationalizations and empowers them to DO what they already KNOW is the right thing to do when faced with ethical challenges'.

---

[4] Adapted from Sheehan & Schmidt. The Values Game is a deck of cards that can be played with a real deck of cards or digitally at https://integritydlm.net/values-game/.

In the Integrity Assertiveness Module, students ask and develop a process to answer the questions, how do I assert my values? How do I deal with rationalizations? How can I use my knowledge of my personal core values and my values-based personal code of conduct to respond to ethical challenges?

There are ten steps in this *process*. These steps are based on Gentile's world-famous 'Giving Voice to Values' (GVV) pedagogy, which teaches the students how to ACT on their Values, by breaking the process down into its component parts, and, by encouraging students to prescript, rehearse and practice GVV in a safe space (Gentile, 2010). The 'Seven Pillars' of the GVV pedagogy are incorporated into a *values-based response mechanism* that is developed by the student and that the student can use as a moral reminder and moral reference point for future ethical decision-making.

The ten steps of the *values-based response mechanism* are as follows: (1) *Affirmation*: Students create an affirmation that calms the fight or flight response and reminds them to begin to apply the *values-based response mechanism* they have developed; (2) *Goal setting*: Students articulate their GOAL regarding the ethical challenge. (3) *Count the Cost*: Students identify the risks and consequences of what they may stand to lose if they do what they know is the right thing to do;[5] (4) *Countering Rationalizations*: Students identify the excuses not to do what they know is right that they may give to themselves when confronted with an ethical challenge. Students use their 'core values', their 'personal code of conduct' rules and their growing self-knowledge to develop persuasive *counterarguments* to the most common rationalizations.[6] This is done in advance of a 'real life' ethical challenge. (5) *Countering False Ethical Dilemmas*: Students learn to recognize rationalizations disguised as ethical dilemmas using the most

---

[5] Because of the preceding exercises in Integrity Awareness, this counting of the cost, is contextualized within the framework of the new self-knowledge about their core values and moral commitments to themselves.

[6] Adapted from Mary Gentiles work, the typical rationalization that the students develop counterarguments to are (1) 'It is not my responsibility'; (2) 'It is just standard practice'; (3) 'It is not hurting anyone' and (4) 'I know it is not fair, but I do not want to get X into trouble by raising this issue'.

common ethical dilemmas as scaffolds.[7] (6) *Reframe:* Students learn to reframe the ethical challenge as an *opportunity* rather than a negative 'fear-inducing' situation. (7) *Identify Enablers*: Students learn to identify information (levers) and/or people (allies) that they can use to help them achieve their goal of giving voice to their values. (8) *Plan!* Students develop a plan of action and write a script of what they will say or do to realize their goal to live according to their values. By learning to develop alternative scenarios, students are helped in the realization that between doing nothing and blowing the whistle, there are other avenues that can be explored and that may have a less traumatic effect on their careers. (9) Rehearse! Students practice asserting their values by seeking out peers to rehearse their script with. (10) Review: This takes place after students have acted on their values. Students are advised to look back and review how asserting their values played out and what they can do better in the future.

12.4 The Choice for a Digital Learning Platform

This training in the IntegrityDLM calls for a process of self-discovery, self-honesty and personal development that is very difficult to accomplish in a 'one size fits all' classroom. The classroom cannot provide the appropriate learning environment to encourage honesty regarding emotions, feelings, beliefs, knowledge and perspectives that the student needs to explore to create a value-based response mechanism to apply to future ethical challenges. A digital learning environment was therefore chosen as the best platform for instruction. This provides privacy and autonomy for what is ultimately a personal journey of self-reflection and the development of a new self-story.

A big advantage of the digital platform is the flexibilities it gives to use all the different learning networks, that is, the affective, cognitive, and

---

[7] Adapted from Mary Gentiles work, most common ethical dilemmas explored are, (1) Truth v. Loyalty; (2) Individual v. Community, (3) Short term v. Long term; (4) Justice v. Mercy.

psychomotor domains. The digital platform recruits students' interest by facilitating storytelling and visual aids. For example, the primary teaching tool for the Integrity Assertiveness modules is the *IntegrityDLM Teaching Scenario*. This *scenario* draws the student into the life of a protagonist, a young graduate called Soraya. Students get to know her story, her values, her hopes, her fears and then watch as she encounters an ethical challenge at her place of work. The students watch and learn to apply the *values-based response mechanism* as the protagonist goes through the ten steps of *integrity assertiveness*. At the same time, they are developing their *own* personal responses to the different rationalizations and ethical dilemmas and creating their own *values-based response mechanism* as they progress through the story.

The digital format allows the students to experience emotions and fears along with Soraya, as well as the temptation to rationalize, in a very personal way and at a level that merely reading a case story is unlikely to provoke. This digital visualization of the protagonist encourages the students to step into her shoes and *to participate in* her ethical challenge. When they join her in looking for solutions or options to achieve her goal of giving voice to her values, students experience this almost as if they are advising a '*real person*' that they have come to know rather than engaging in abstract ethical dilemmas.

The parameters for the design of the IntegrityDLM were arrived at in discussion with students about how to reach a young undergraduate audience and how to motivate engagement. The character of the protagonist, her style, her language, her stage in life, her background, and her name were carefully discussed to arrive at 'a girl next door' character that the students could easily relate to and identify with. The following points summarize the website design principles: (1) No 'One size fits all'; (2) Privacy guaranteed; (3) Easy, Accessible, Fun; (4) Certificate to encourage completion; (5) Platform to Learn and Share; (6) Directed at undergraduates but useful to anyone.

The IntegrityDLM also encourages group learning by providing exercises for students to share compare experiences. Students interact in a formative process to develop a group pyramid and an organizational pyramid and to share their experience, reflection, and insights. This can take place physically or digitally. The IntegrityDLM was built by this author using easily accessible platforms of WordPress, Elementor, and LearnDash.

12.5   Insights from Student Experiences with IntegrityDLM

The IntegrityDLM was completed in 2020 and used as a complete module in the 2020–2021 Academic year.[8] After completing the IntegrityDLM, students submitted an *Integrity Self Reflection*. A thematic strategy of data analysis based on systematically coding the students' reflections and organizing the data generated into themes was adopted (Makinwa, 2020c).[9]

The student reflections provide some interesting insights that are grouped under the following theme headings. Students (1) experienced the moral learning experience of the IntegrityDLM as interesting; (2) they felt that this journey of self-discovery was a gap in their prior education; (3) students discovered new aspects of their personal identity and (4) expressed a desire to live in alignment with the personal values they had identified. Students expressed a (5) growing understanding of 'why they value what they value' and (6) becoming more active 'observers' of their own personal decision-making processes. This (7) engendered a desire to plan for, and practice ahead, future ethical dilemmas. Student (8) showed empathy for the values of the 'other' and for the diversity of value frameworks in society. Finally, (9) students expressed more confidence in dealing with future ethical challenges. These themes and the excerpts from the students' reflections are presented below.

---

[8] With 3rd Year undergraduate students of the Compliance Minor LAW Program at the Hague University of applied Sciences in the Netherlands.

[9] Student consent was sought and obtained. Students were informed that excepts from their Integrity Self-Reflections would be reproduced in this chapter and that their privacy would be protected. The students are referred to anonymously as Students 1–21. A short summary is made under each theme and a selection of quotes is included to illustrate the particular theme. As much as possible these quotes are left intact, so the reader is able to reference the insights described directly from the students responses. Please note that this data analysis is merely illustrative.

Experiencing IntegrityDLM as an Interesting Learning Journey

Students seem to have experienced the Integrity DLM as interesting and fun. They use words such as 'grateful', true revelation', 'excited', 'great tool', and 'interesting task' to describe their experiences of the module.

- Student 2: I am very grateful for the Integrity Digital Learning Module
- Student 10: The process of creating my pyramid of values was a true revelation.
- Student 7: I am very excited to have a completed integrity toolkit
- Student 10: The integrity awareness module has been a great tool for self-discovery.
- Student 17: The exercise of creating my personal pyramid of values was an interesting task.

Noticing 'Self-Discovery' Gap in Prior Education

The students' reflections indicate that many had not considered their personal values prior to the IntegrityDLM. Some students noted the lack of opportunity to examine questions about personal values in their prior education.

- Student 2: Before the Integrity Awareness Module, I was not able to clearly state what my core values were and how to argue why they were my values.
- Student 3: Before the Integrity Awareness module, I did not have a profound comprehension of my core values. I have never put serious thoughts on what I value and what my core values are.
- Student 5: During the first integrity awareness class discussion, I realized that people do not get the chance to talk openly and directly about their values as often.
- Student 14: Some of us promptly identified their core values; however, some of us required more time and effort to put our values on a piece of paper.
- Student 16: I was kind of forced to truly think about who I am as a person and what I want in life.
- Student 16: I am not truly used to critically assess myself, so this was an eye-opening but challenging process.

Discovering New Insights into Personal Identity

Some students were surprised to determine what they considered important, what they valued most, and what they prioritized. Some students' reflections seem to show an 'expansion' of their self-story or of their understanding of their personal identity.

- Student 1: I was very surprised to see my pyramid of values come together, as I never thought that loving would be on the top spot on my pyramid.
- Student 3: I never realized the difficulties and the importance of self-acceptance.
- Student 5: What I realized during the class discussions is that knowledge is what I value the most because knowledge translates to power, and power translates to well-being.
- Student 7: The module is an eye-opener on your perspective to the world and what kind of person you are and want to become.
- Source 9: [T]hrough the exercises where we had to put down and elaborate on what is most important to us. I started to realize that personal values are not rigid but rather fluid.
- Student 10: I tried to be honest and realized that for me, the perfect life would be a combination of family life and career life that would go hand in hand. Balance is the solution after all.
- Student 16: [C]oncretely narrow down who I want to be and what I want to achieve in my future personal and professional relationships.
- Student 19: It helped me realize that my most important values relate back to feeling good about myself rather than being successful in my future carrier.

Expressing the Importance of Living in 'Alignment' with Personal Values

Completing the IntegrityDLM seems to encourage students to develop new visions, a desire to engage in life in a new way, to not compromise on their values. Students use expressions such as 'not compromise', 'living in line', 'remind myself', 'stick to', 'beneficial to me', 'stand my ground', and 'strength to speak up', indicating a greater commitment to live in alignment with their values by acting consistently with what they value. At the same time, students seem to recognize the challenges that this new awareness and desire to live in alignment may evoke.

- Student 1: Through this, I will be able to articulate my goal in solving those kinds of situations in a way that will not compromise my values and will allow me to stay true to myself.
- Student 3 With the completion of the Integrity Awareness module, I am convinced that living in line with my core values is the key to unlocking the door of happiness, balance, professionalism, and productivity.
- Student 7: I can return to this code of conduct and remind myself why and how I should live by and respect my values.
- Student 16: It also made me aware how important it is to stick to my values and not let me get swept away by comparing myself to others,
- Student 17: [I]t is my responsibility to make sure I uphold the values I consider to be important to me. In addition to ensuring that I act and react in a manner that will be beneficial to me but always in line with my values.
- Student 19: [T]o make sure I stand my ground in times of threat.
- Student 14: [G]ave strength to speak up and tell my part of the story and how I see it, what I value the most and how I see myself in the future.
- Student 10: I have realized that one of the risks or consequences that may encounter if I choose to act according to my values is the possibility of losing my financial stability.
- Student 17: It became clear that ethical adversities can easily be rationalized... a possible effect of rationalizing your professional life rather than maintaining personal or group core values is the loss of everything you have worked hard for.
- Student 19: It was also eye opening to see how hard it actually is to adhere to its own Values in a situation like Soraya's.

Expressing a Growing Understanding of Why 'They Value What They Value'

Students used words such as 'explain', 'comprehend', 'understandable', 'opportunity', and 'questioning' to describe how their new self-knowledge sheds light on their behavior and choices. By observing themselves, exploring their beliefs, listening to themselves, identifying emotions, and identifying personal value systems, students seem to become more aware of why they value what they value.

- Student 2: I was able to explain the motivation behind my choices in my values.
- Student 3: A good comprehension of my own core values will help me to understand more about myself.
- Student 5: It is perfectly understandable to assert that all these values will be reflected in the way one behaves.
- Student 6: Integrity awareness represented a good opportunity for myself to discover the personal core values that I have.
- Student 10: Self-awareness and self-discovery should be a priority for everyone because you can only know the world around you if you know yourself first.
- Student 17: [I] think it would be important for everyone to sometimes take a step back and view things in this kind of a way, questioning why we value what we value.
- Student 19: Integrity awareness helped me reflect on me and my values at a deeper level.

More Active 'Observing' of the Personal Decision-Making Process

Students seem to become more aware of their personal *process* of decision-making and their underlying motivations. Students use phrases such as 'helping significantly', 'how to weigh', 'how they influence'; 'what action is the best one', 'think about what I have not taken into consideration', and 'principles I can apply' to describe this process of observation. Of particular note were references to their personal codes of conduct. They expressed the belief that this will help with their decision-making.

- Student 1: As the integrity awareness module taught me about cost analysis, it showed me how to weigh my decisions and carry out a risk evaluation in situations of ethical ambiguity.
- Student 2: At the end, I understood that if you are clearly aware of your personal core values and can articulate them, they will help you significantly in your personal and professional life.
- Student 6: This discovery offered me the possibility to understand what the aim of each of these values is, how they influence my decision-making process and what influence my perspectives and positions that I adopt regarding various topics.
- Student 7: Step by step, I saw how to implement the rules laid down in the code of conduct to decide what action is the best one to take in which situation.
- Student 10: Luckily, the module helped me in the decision-making process
- Student 15: Integrity Assertiveness has shown me that it is often better to not only act based on what I think is correct but also review why I think so and if there are things I haven't taken into consideration.
- Student 19: The value-based approach helped me to breakdown my arguments
- Student 10: The circumstances I will have to face in the future cannot be predicted. However, now that I have a personal Code of Conduct, I can predict my reaction and the way I will deal with certain problems.
- Student 17: Being more aware of our own moral compass can be a huge asset, especially in the times where I may often hyperfocus and lose sight of the larger picture.
- Student 19: It also gave me a set of principles that I can use in situations that require me to make a risky decision.

Experiencing Need to Plan for and Practice Ahead

Students showed a desire to manage this new self-knowledge. This found expression in seeking to come up with a 'plan', to 'articulate specific goals', to 'put into writing' desired responses to future ethical challenges.

Additionally, interesting is the fact that students seem to see the need to 'practice' their responses in advance of 'real' ethical challenges.

- Student 3: It is important to develop an affirmative plan with specific goals in response to ethical challenges.
- Student 16: I learned how important it is for me to set my goals into writing, because that enables me to have a clear view of what I want to achieve.
- Student 6: From a personal perspective, Integrity Assertiveness represented another good opportunity for me to create an overview of a specific plan that I would like to adopt to analyze and implement a specific decision in my decision-making process.
- Student 19: My most important take away are that I need to remain calm and have a structured plan, how I want to tackle the situation and practice what I am going to say.
- Student 5: That is why people need to see the enforcement of values as a personal exercise that leads to personal well-being, such as going to the gym or keeping oneself informed.
- Source 17: Ideally, I would say that I should practice maintaining my core values in my everyday life, both private and professional.
- Student 19: The course gave me many things to think about for my future path... My goal is to keep practicing from time to time ... Just like a good compliance department needs regular training to stay up to date to detect potential risk, I need to do the same to stay compliant with my own Values

Showing More Empathy for the 'Other' and for the Diversity of Value Frameworks in Society

Students seem to become more sensitized to the diversity of 'values frameworks' in their daily lives. Their experience with the IntegrityDLM also seems to engender more empathy for the 'other' and more awareness of the complex societies in which we live.

- Student 3: Each person has a different set of core values and different perspectives. It is important to be respectful toward such diversity.
- Student 3: After the module, I was able to grasp the understanding of the diversity of cultures and values of society.
- Student 16: We all have a different approach to life, and it's important to learn from those who don't share the same point of view as I do.
- Student 17: The integrity awareness component of the IntegrityDLM. Helped me to acknowledge the fact that although I may be a part of a group, my personal core values may not matter at all. Based on the fact that the majority prevails.
- Student 19: I realized that the group values are like layers that are added to my personal values.
- Student 19: One of the biggest discoveries I made was that Values are very subjective, which is why the first step to understand others is knowing my values first to respect the values of others.

More Confidence to Deal with Future Ethical Challenges

Students seem more confident of their ability to confront future ethical challenges. Interestingly, students see the IntegrityDLM as a useful tool that they can use postgraduation and their Pyramid of Values, Personal Code of Conduct, Values-Based Response Checklist as important reference materials to refer back to and reflect upon into the future.

- Student 1: it is also an excellent tool for future use, and I will be sure to make use of it if I am ever put in a position that is morally ambiguous and against my values ...: I will be able to confidently navigate my life and career in a way that I know is right and true to who I am and my values
- Student 2: This module has significant importance for my future professional life.
- Student 6: Furthermore, from a professional perspective, the discovery of the personal core values answered my question of whether I am suitable for being a legal practitioner for the rest of my life.
- Student 17: Moreover, continuously reflecting on how the values that I have identified has my core values plays a part in my personal and professional life and development.
- Student 3: In daily life and professional life, it is common to encounter certain situations on ethical challenges. In these situations, strong ethical consideration is required. The module provided a detailed overview of guidelines on tackling this issue.

12.6   Conclusions and Recommendations

The temptation to rationalize a choice not to do the right thing or to keep silent instead of speaking up is exacerbated when we caught are unaware or unprepared. Helping students to become more *morally aware* and *morally assertive* by developing an explicit *process* of ethical decision-making that they can plan and practice in advance of real-world challenges should arguably contribute to shaping future professionals with the *moral courage* to act as *change agents* to the benefit or their places of work and to society at large. The IntegrityDLM is not prescriptive. There are no right or wrong answers. By going through the steps to develop the IntegrityDLM competences of *Integrity Awareness* and *Integrity Assertiveness*, students develop a *process* and a *moral vocabulary* to guide their ethical decision-making and to help them build up the courage to do what they already know is the right thing to do. This is a life-long learning process. Ultimately, maintaining integrity with the 'self' will encourage maintaining integrity in the 'real world'.

The flexibility of education in a digital age opens new doors to developing moral learning experiences that can take the student on an empowering journey of self-discovery. Using a digital learning platform is essential because it gives students the privacy and autonomy to explore and become more aware of their intrinsic emotions, feelings and personal worldviews. The feedback from students suggests that the IntegrityDLM was experienced as a fun, accessible, and practical tool that recruited students' interest, encouraged student autonomy, helped students internalize the new self-knowledge they gained about their personal integrity frameworks, and promoted confidence to face ethical challenges in the future.

Recommendations

1. **Addressing the 'human factor' in white collar crime in professional training:** Responsible management education ought to address the primary driver of corrupt behavior by professionals; that is, their own personal ethical decision-making processes should therefore focus

on developing practical *training tools* to help professionals become more resilient and show moral courage.

2. **Professional education should address the 'moral skills' gap:** There should be less emphasis on the theory of what is ethical and more focus on HOW to behave ethically. This means providing students with a *process* that they can learn and apply when confronted with ethical challenges. This preparation and rehearsal should reduce the likelihood of being 'overwhelmed' by situational pressures when they enter into their eventual places of work, but a longitudinal study would be required to establish this hypothesis. Practical tools to help students become aware of their core values and motivations as well as the ability to act and 'give voice' to their values should be an important component of professional education.

3. **Develop moral skills *competences* and *learning objectives* for curricula**: Practical moral skills *competences*, *learning objectives,* and *assessment methods* should be cocreated, developed, and shared by relevant stakeholders across courses and institutions. The focus should be on learning from the 'inside out', that is, to provide the student with opportunities to garner new self-knowledge and self-understanding that encourages new motivations and new ethical decision-making skills. The competences of *Integrity Awareness* and *Integrity Assertiveness* developed for the IntegrityDLM provide an example.

4. **Digital platforms greatly enhance the moral skills learning experience: T**he private, personalized, safe, journey of self-reflection and growth necessary for moral skills development is not realizable in one-size-fits-all classrooms. The development of moral skills digital learning platforms, such as the IntegrityDLM, should be encouraged and optimized.

5. **Digital platforms create synergies to learn and share across institutions and cultures:** opportunities for students to engage in guided cross-cultural experiences and to gain an intuitive understanding of the complexity of value frameworks in our diverse societies are made possible by digital platforms such as the IntegrityDLM and should be leveraged and optimized.

References

Banaji, M. R., Bazerman, M. H., & Chugh, D. (2003). How unethical are you? *Harvard Business Review, 81*(12), 56–64.

Banaji, M. R., & Bhaskar, R. (2000). Implicit stereotypes and memory: The bounded rationality of social beliefs. In D. L. Schacter & E. Scarry (Eds.), *Memory, brain, and belief* (pp. 139–175). Harvard University Press.

Blasi, A. (1980). Bridging moral cognition and moral action: A critical review of the literature. *Psychological Bulletin, 88*(1), 1–45. https://doi.org/10.1037/0033-2909.88.1.1

Chen, H. (2017). The department of justice's original evaluation of corporate compliance programs.

Gentile, M. C. (2010). *Giving voice to values: How to speak your mind when you know what's right.* Yale University Press.

Gordan, A. (2018, July 23). How the integrity agenda bridges intentions, actions and measurement. EY US—Building a better working world. https://www.ey.com/en_gl/assurance/how-the-integrity-agenda-bridges-intentions-actions-and-measurement

Haidt, J. (2001). The emotional dog and its rational tail: A social intuitionist approach to moral judgment. *Psychological Review, 108*(4), 814–834. https://doi.org/10.1037/0033-295X.108.4.814

Interview by Broad Cat. (n.d.). *What does the government look for in compliance training?* Broad Cat. https://www.thebroadcat.com/hui-chen-doj-compliance-training-interview

Makinwa, A. O. (2018). Integrity education using an anti-corruption compliance digital learning module. NRO Projectendatabase Onderwijsonderzoek. https://www.nro.nl/onderzoeksprojecten-vinden/?projectid=405-18865-478-integrity-education-using-an-anti-corruption-compliance-digital-learning-module;

Makinwa, A. O. (2020a). The Integrity digital learning module IntegrityDLM. https://integritydlm.net/

Makinwa, A. O. (2020b). [Unpublished raw data of Integrity Self-Reflections]. The Hague University of Applied Science.

Makinwa, A. O. (2020c). The Values Game. IntegrityDLM. https://integrity-dlm.net/values-game/

Messick, D. M., & Bazerman, M. H. (1996). Ethical leadership and the psychology of decision making. *MIT Sloan Management Review, 37*(2), 9–22.

Narvaez, D., & Bock, T. (2014). Developing ethical expertise and moral personalities. In L. Nucci, D. Narvaez, & T. Krettenauer (Eds.), *Handbook of moral and character education* (2nd ed., pp. 141–158). Routledge.

OECD. (2018). *Behavioral insights for public integrity: Harnessing the human factor to counter corruption*. See Chapter 2.

Sheehan, N. T., & Schmidt, J. A. (2015). Preparing accounting students for ethical decision making: Developing individual codes of conduct based on personal values. *Journal of Accounting Education, 33*(3), 183–197. https://doi.org/10.1016/j.jaccedu.2015.06.001

Tenbrunsel, A. E., & Smith-Crowe, K. (2008a). Ethical decision making: Where we've been and where we're going. *Academy of Management Annals, 2*(1), 545–607, at p. 547. https://doi.org/10.5465/19416520802211677

Tenbrunsel, A. E., & Smith-Crowe, K. (2008b). Ethical decision making: Where we've been and where we're going. *Academy of Management Annals, 2*(1), 545–607, at p. 583. https://doi.org/10.5465/19416520802211677

U.S. Department of Justice Criminal Division. (2017) Evaluation of Corporate Compliance Programs (Updated June 2020). https://www.justice.gov/criminal-fraud/page/file/937501/download

World Economic Forum. (2020). *Good intentions, bad outcomes? How organizations can make the leap from box-ticking compliance to building a culture of integrity: Agenda for business integrity*. http://www3.weforum.org/docs/WEF_GFC_on_Transparency_and_AC_pillar2_good_intentions_bad_outcomes.pdf at p.5.

13

Responsible Management Education and Digital Transformation Beyond SDG 12: B.A. Sustainable Procurement Management at Heilbronn University's Bachelor's Program as an Example for Integrating SDGs and Future Digital Skills Requirements

Daniela Ludin, Wanja Wellbrock, Erika Mueller, and Andrea Herterich Suzana

13.1 Challenges of Responsible Management Education and Digital Transformation

Changes in corporate behavior are considered eminent for meeting the complex challenges of today's world. Humanity has to face challenges arising from climate change, scarcity of natural resources, increasing poverty, globalization and digitization. In recent years, there has been a shift

D. Ludin (✉) • W. Wellbrock • E. Mueller • A. Herterich Suzana
Department of Business Administration, Heilbronn University,
Heilbronn, Germany
e-mail: daniela.ludin@hs-heilbronn.de

© The Author(s), under exclusive license to Springer Nature Switzerland AG 2023
C. Hauser, W. Amann (eds.), *The Future of Responsible Management Education*,
Humanism in Business Series, https://doi.org/10.1007/978-3-031-15632-8_13

in many business areas from profit-oriented management to the integration of the triple bottom line of economic, social and environmental performance, as outlined in the approach for sustainable development schemes (Longoni & Cagliano, 2018; Yuan et al., 2018). Moreover, digital key competences have become a crosscutting need in business, civil society, politics, science and education (García-Pérez et al., 2021; Stifterverband für die Deutsche Wissenschaft e.V., 2018). The COVID-19 pandemic has stressed this necessity (Stifterverband für die Deutsche Wissenschaft e.V., 2021).

In this chapter, a best practice example of matching sustainability and digitization in training and teaching is given. The chapter presents the study program in detail and shows its connection to other programs of Heilbronn University; for example, the master program "M.A. Digital Business Psychology" (diBsy). Furthermore, it shows other supporting activities in sustainability and digitization of Heilbronn University.

13.2　The Sustainable Procurement Management Degree Program as a Key to Responsible Management Education and Digital Transformation

With approximately 8300 students, Heilbronn University (HHN) is the largest academic educational institution in the Heilbronn-Franken region and one of the largest universities of applied sciences in Baden-Württemberg. Founded in 1961 as an engineering school, in 2021, the university offers more than 50 practice-oriented bachelor's and master's degree programs in the fields of business, computer science and technology, divided among seven faculties and four locations (Hochschule Heilbronn, 2020a, p. 6 f.). Since November 2019, Heilbronn University has adopted the UN Principles of Responsible Management Education. As an institution of higher education, Heilbronn University is involved in the development of current and future managers (Hochschule Heilbronn, 2020a, p. 41, 2020b).

The Bachelor's Program "Sustainable Procurement Management, SPM"

Following the abovementioned trend, the Faculty of Management and Sales of Heilbronn University has adapted its educational training for students. A bachelor's program was developed in 2019 and is located at the campus in Schwäbisch Hall (Hochschule Heilbronn, 2021b). The program started in the winter semester 2011/12 under the name "Management and Procurement, MBW" (MAP) and was then profiled and further developed, especially with regard to future-oriented study contents of sustainability and digitization. This development resulted in new study and examination regulations, which have been valid for the study program "Sustainable Procurement Management, SPM" since the winter semester 2019/2020 (Hochschule Heilbronn, 2018).

The study program "Sustainable Procurement Management, SPM" aims at highly qualified management training of academic management trainees for the procurement sector, which is designed against the background of sustainability and digitization requirements in the company. The study program is tailor-made for qualified career entry in the field of procurement and purchasing, logistics, supply chain management, materials management, and sustainability management in companies of all industries and sizes. Upon successful completion of the program, graduates will have broad knowledge of business administration and will be familiar with the decision-making fields of corporate procurement management, particularly with ecological and social concerns and against the backdrop of digital requirements.

In addition to the professional qualification, the study program "Sustainable Procurement Management, SPM" aims at the special promotion of the personal development of the students with regard to the social and personal competences relevant for future specialists and managers.

The Advisory Board of the Bachelor's Program "Sustainable Procurement Management, SPM"

The concept of the study program was developed in close cooperation with companies in the region, which support and promote the development of the Schwäbisch Hall campus of Heilbronn University in general and the study program in particular. The aim was to jointly ensure the practical relevance of the courses offered and to refer to the specific requirements of the current and foreseeable future labor market. A specially established advisory board, appointed by the University Foundation Schwäbisch Hall, accompanies the further development of the program. Regular exchanges take place with representatives from the business world to improve the topicality of the course and to further sharpen its profile. The advisory board consists of five members: three full-time professors and two external members. On the one hand, the external members contribute their practical expertise to discussions on the further development of the content of the study program. On the other hand, they provide valuable assessments of the importance and acceptance of study programs from a practical perspective. The Advisory Board has the following objectives:

- Participate in public relations activities for the degree program.
- Platform for the exchange of professors from the study program with business and society, connection of the study program with the environment of the university.
- Support of the transfer between university and economy and society through projects.
- Idealistic and material support of the study program.

Due to the very strong professional field orientation of the study program and the close contact with the economy, high labor market relevance is guaranteed. The orientation of the study program to the needs of the economy, with simultaneous independence in research and teaching, is the basis for preparing students for specialist and management tasks in procurement management in a practice-oriented manner with broad knowledge in the areas of sustainability management and digitization.

The Practical Relevance of the Bachelor's Program Sustainable Procurement Management, SPM

In addition to the exchange within the framework of the advisory board and an integrated practical study semester, there are regular lectures and project works with companies and excursions during the semester. These factors create direct practical insights and a relationship between companies and students. To further anchor the practical relevance, exemplary negotiation trainings are held as one-day events with companies. In addition, the "campus meets company" event series and the "Kompass" company contact fairly promote contact between students and business representatives. In addition, an interdisciplinary symposium is organized every 2 years, which aims to familiarize students and experts from different disciplines as well as the interested public with topics through presentations from various practical and scientific fields. In 2017, the Sustainable Procurement Symposium took place. It was organized jointly with the Forest Stewardship Council e.V. (FSC) and the German Association for Materials Management, Purchasing and Logistics e.V. (BME), under the patronage of Franz Untersteller MdL, State Minister for the Environment, Climate and Energy Management, Baden-Württemberg, and Hermann-Josef Pelgrim, Mayor, City of Schwäbisch Hall (Wellbrock & Ludin, 2019). In 2019, the Symposium on Sustainable Consumption took place. It was organized jointly with the NGO Brot für die Welt e. V. and the German Association for Materials Management, Purchasing and Logistics e.V. (BME), under the patronage of Peter Hauk MdL, State Minister for Rural Areas and Consumer Protection, Baden-Württemberg, and Harry Mergel, Mayor of the City of Heilbronn (Wellbrock & Ludin, 2021).

In addition, university teaching is supplemented by the management and leadership knowledge of motivated and qualified lecturers with practical experience from the areas of purchasing, procurement, logistics, sustainability, and digitization. Thanks to their many years of work in well-known companies, these lecturers have extensive practical and theoretical knowledge and are therefore ideally suited for practice-oriented teaching.

Student research projects within the framework of seminars also increase the exchange with practice. In their bachelor theses, which are usually carried out in cooperation with companies, the students also work closely on issues that are relevant in corporate practice and for which solutions are sought. In addition, an exchange and transfer of knowledge between science, teaching and practice takes place through research projects.

Furthermore, the BME Heilbronn University Group (BME = German Association of Materials Management, Purchasing and Logistics) was founded at the beginning of 2017. Since then, students of the NBW program have been involved in the group and organize their own events with excursions, company tours and lectures. Furthermore, they also ensure networking among students as well as with representatives from the professional world (BME Hochschulgruppe HHN, 2021).

The International Reference of the Bachelor's Program Sustainable Procurement Management, SPM

To further promote the practical relevance and internationalization of the course of study, regular excursions abroad with international partners take place. The international excursion was part of the curriculum in the summer semester and led to Spain in 2018 and Iceland in 2019. Due to the COVID-19 pandemic, the excursion was suspended in 2020 and 2021.

In addition, students have the opportunity to complete an internship semester abroad or to write their final thesis in an international context. The Faculty of Management and Sales, where the study program "Sustainable Procurement" is located, has partnership agreements with universities in the USA, Canada, Mexico, Finland, France, Ireland, Croatia, the Netherlands, Poland, Spain, Ukraine, Hungary, South Korea, Taiwan and the Macao Autonomous Region (China).

13.3   Bachelor's Program Sustainable Procurement Management (SPM) Against the Background of the SDGs

International frameworks such as the UN Sustainable Development Goals (SDGs), which have been developed under the 2030 Agenda, try to highlight what is needed for a shift toward sustainability (United Nations, 2015). In addition, the Digital Economy and Society Index (DESI) shows that four out of ten adults in Europe lack basic digital skills. In this context, companies are seen as important drivers of sustainable development and digitization (European Commission, 2020). Therefore, companies need business change makers that bring along adequate skills, knowledge and mindsets to create sustainable digital business model innovations. Universities have a key role in preparing young people for the future and educating them on sustainability and digitization issues regardless of their study topic (Bauer et al., 2021; Sustainable Development Solutions Network (SDSN), 2020).

The program "Sustainable Procurement Management, SPM" provides in-depth knowledge of the entire area of business administration in combination with sustainable procurement and digitization specialist areas from the intersection of economic sciences (Hochschule Heilbronn, 2021b). It aims particularly at teaching the following basic competences: comprehensive business management competences, comprehensive specialist knowledge of procurement management and its interactions in global value-added processes, comprehensive specialist knowledge of sustainability management and digital transformation management. In detail, the following special topics are taught: sustainability law, world trade/foreign trade, business ethics, sustainability management, sustainable procurement management, sustainability control, risk management, green IT, information technology management, business informatics, technology and innovation management and IT systems in procurement. By focusing on the abovementioned management aspects, the study program especially contributes to SDG 12 ("Responsible consumption and production"), SDG 4 ("Quality Education") and SDG 9 ("Industry, innovation and infrastructure"). Table 13.1 shows in detail which courses were developed against the background of which SDGs and where a reference to sustainability and future digital skills requirements is made:

Table 13.1 Teaching courses against the background of the SDGs

Teaching courses/ SDG & digital transformation	4.7 Acquire knowledge/ skills needed to promote sustainable development	12 Responsible consumption/ production	12.6 Adopt sustainable practices/ integrate sustainability information into reporting cycle	12.7 Sustainable public procurement accordance with national policies and priorities	12.8 Ensure information/ awareness for sustainable development/ lifestyles in harmony with nature	12.a Strengthen scientific/ technological capacity toward more sustainable consumption and production	9.c Access to information and communications technology
H. 4.4. sustainability law	●	●	●	●	●		
H. 8.4. world trade/ foreign trade	●	●		●	●		
H. 9.3. business ethics	●	●	●	●	●		
H. 7.5. sustainability management	●	●		●	●		
H. 7.8. sustainable procurement management	●	●	●	●	●		
H. 1.5 sustainability controlling	●	●		●	●		
H. 7.4. risk management	●	●		●	●		

H. 1.7. Green IT

G. 5.4. information technology and management

G. 5.6. business Informatics

H. 2.4. technology and innovation management

H. 1.6. IT systems in procurement

Source: own compilation and presentation according to Hochschule Heilbronn (2018); United Nations, (2015)

13.4 Anchoring Sustainability and Digitization in the Strategy of Heilbronn University as Success Factors of the Bachelor's Program SPM

This paragraph delivers information and guidance for other educational professionals who like to adapt or renew their study trainings and integrate aspects of sustainability and digitization. Experiences can be shared on how to tackle barriers and challenges in curriculum development and implementation. First, this paragraph presents the connection of the bachelor's program "Sustainable Procurement Management, SPM" to other programs at Heilbronn University. Furthermore, it shows other supporting activities in sustainability and digitization of Heilbronn University.

In its mission statement, Heilbronn University is committed to making its contribution to sustainable development. In addition to being anchored in the mission statement, the topic is embedded in the university's internal organization (cf. Fig. 13.1).

The center of sustainability activities is the Council for Sustainable Development (RNE), which meets at regular intervals. It has an initiating, coordinating and advisory function. The Council for Sustainable

Fig. 13.1 Sustainability in, the organization of Heilbronn University. Source: Hochschule Heilbronn (2020a)

Development reports to the Senate and the Rectorate. It is authorized to make proposals to the Senate. The Council is composed as a representative of the Rectorate, the Ethics Officer, the Sustainability Officer, the Officer for Sustainable Development and the delegated representatives of each faculty, the administration and the technical operations, as well as a student officer for sustainability of the constituted student body. The council discusses current environmentally relevant issues and prepares draft decisions.

Through this institutionalization, Heilbronn University has permanent structures that enable it to introduce sustainability as a cross-cutting issue in the various areas of the university and to set impulses. This applies to both teaching and research. The integration of sustainability in studies and further education is an important strategic goal of Heilbronn University. Education for sustainability is implemented by anchoring sustainability content in the study and examination regulations. In addition to the bachelor's program presented here, Heilbronn University currently offers four other programs with an explicit reference to sustainability: Energy Management (Bachelor of Engineering), Environmental and Process Engineering (Bachelor of Science), Electromobility (Master of Engineering), and Sustainable Tourism Development (Master of Arts) (Hochschule Heilbronn, 2020a, p. 39 ff.).

In addition to the topic of sustainability, Heilbronn University is also committed to the topic of digitization in its strategy and would like to focus more strongly on this in the future. In view of the increasing importance of digitization in all its facets for various areas of life, the university considers it essential to continuously adapt teaching content in all of its degree programs and to develop new degree programs in this area (Hochschule Heilbronn, 2020a, p. 12). For example, the Faculty of Management and Sales, which is also home to the "Sustainable Procurement Management, SPM" program, has developed a master's program in Digital Business Psychology (diBsy), which explicitly addresses the trend toward digitization. In contrast to other master's programs in the field of business psychology, the megatrend of digitization is at the center of the study program. The program is deliberately designed to be open to students from all sectors and company sizes and to provide them with comprehensive qualifications. Thus, digital business psychology (diBsy) currently offers graduates of the study program "Sustainable Procurement Management, SPM" an opportunity to complete their studies with a master's degree at their own faculty (Hochschule Heilbronn, 2021a). In addition, the faculty will expand their commitment in the area of digitization and sustainability. Through an endowed professorship for digital management, a bachelor's degree program in "Management and Digitisation" will be established in the future. A master's degree program in "International Procurement" is also being considered and will provide a further link for graduates of the "Sustainable Procurement Management, SPM" program.

13.5 Recommendations for Establishing Responsible Management Education Integrating SDGs and Future Digital Skills Requirements

Based on the challenges identified for responsible management education and digital transformation, the "Sustainable Procurement Management, SPM" program was presented in detail as a best practice for responsible management education and digital transformation. The detailed elaboration of the SDGs focused on and addressed in teaching shows how requirements for sustainable development can be successfully operationalized in a degree program. Only in this way can a course of study claim to be responsible management education. Against this background, the special feature of the "Sustainable Procurement Management, SPM" program is that it also teaches future digital skills. The experience of the conceptual design of the study program in 2017 and 2018 shows that this narrow subject focus has only met with approval in the decision-making bodies of Heilbronn University (Faculty Council of the Faculty of Management and Sales, Senate Committee for Studies and Teaching, Senate, University Council) because it precisely addresses the strategic thrust of Heilbronn University. The anchoring of the topics of sustainability and digitization in the university's structural and development plan, as well as the traditional networking of the topic of sustainability at Heilbronn University, coupled with the university-wide development of the topic of digitization, are parameters for success.

References

Bauer, M., Rieckmann, M., Niedlich, S., & Bormann, I. (2021). Sustainability governance at higher education institutions: Equipped to transform? *Frontiers in Sustainability, 2,* Article 640458. https://doi.org/10.3389/frsus.2021.640458

BME Hochschulgruppe HHN. (2021). https://www.facebook.com/bme.hochschulgruppe.hhn

European Commission. (2020). *International Digital Economy and Society Index.* https://doi.org/10.2759/757411

García-Pérez, L., García-Garnica, M., & Olmedo-Moreno, E. M. (2021). Skills for a working future: how to bring about professional success from the educational setting. *Education Sciences, 11*(1), 27. https://doi.org/10.3390/educsci11010027

Hochschule Heilbronn. (2018). Studien- und Prüfungsordnung Nachhaltige Beschaffungswirtschaft (NBW), Heilbronn. https://cdn0.scrvt.com/5b9b bd140a15e188780a6244ebe572d4/f619f00cd31915c1/b1cc04bd7a06/f619f00cd31915c1-8a4407cf0e54-SPO01_NBW_SenEnt_2018-06-27_U.pdf

Hochschule Heilbronn. (2020a). Struktur- und Entwicklungsplan 2020-2025, Heilbronn. https://cdn0.scrvt.com/5b9bbd140a15e188780a6244ebe572d4/87b4e458a9bfb336/640ab4c8cfcf/2020-12-16_SEP-2020-2025-final.pdf

Hochschule Heilbronn. (2020b). https://www.hs-heilbronn.de/hhn-schliesst-sich-fuer-ihre-lehre-den-un-prinzipien-an-48dac0788ae59b6b

Hochschule Heilbronn. (2021a). https://www.hs-heilbronn.de/dibsy

Hochschule Heilbronn. (2021b). https://www.hs-heilbronn.de/nbw

Longoni, A., & Cagliano, R. (2018). Sustainable innovativeness and the triple bottom line: The role of organizational time perspective. *Journal of Business Ethics, 151*(4), 1097–1120. https://doi.org/10.1007/s10551-016-3239-y

Stifterverband für die Deutsche Wissenschaft e.V. (Ed.) (2018). Future skills: Which skills are lacking in Germany, Essen. https://www.stifterverband.org/medien/which-skills-are-lacking-in-germany

Stifterverband für die Deutsche Wissenschaft e.V. (Ed.) (2021). Die Zukunft der Qualifizierung in Unternehmen nach Corona, Essen. https://www.

stifterverband.org/medien/die-zukunft-der-qualifizierung-in-unternehmen-nach-corona

Sustainable Development Solutions Network (SDSN). (2020). Accelerating education for the SDGs in universities: A guide for universities, colleges, and tertiary and higher education institutions, New York. https://resources.unsdsn.org/accelerating-education-for-the-sdgs-in-universities-a-guide-for-universities-colleges-and-tertiary-and-higher-education-institutions

United Nations. (2015). Transforming our world: the 2030 agenda for sustainable development. Resolution adopted by the general assembly on 25 September 2015. https://undocs.org/A/RES/70/1

Wellbrock, W., & Ludin, D. (2019). *Nachhaltiges Beschaffungsmanagement. Strategien – Praxisbeispiele – Digitalisierung.*

Wellbrock, W., & Ludin, D. (2021). *Best Practices aus Wissenschaft, Unternehmenspraxis, Gesellschaft, Verwaltung und Politik.*

Yuan, Y., Lu, L. Y., Tian, G., & Yu, Y. (2018). Business strategy and corporate social responsibility. *Journal of Business Ethics, 162,* 359–377. https://doi.org/10.1007/s10551-018-3952-9

14

Adapting Legal Education for Technological Changes in Business

Lauren Traczykowski and Paul Dale

14.1 Introduction

We are experiencing a revolution in technology, which has resulted in innovations in all areas of life; legal practice has not escaped this phenomenon. Likewise, the reasons for and ways in which the commercial sector seeks legal advice are changing beyond recognition. Both sectors are increasingly reliant on the new technologies available.

The traditional practice of law is a reserved practice, which has always been regulated by statutes. The route to qualification has always been fiercely competitive, with only a handful of students practicing at the highest levels. In an effort to make the profession accessible and more diverse, regulatory bodies have made changes. The Legal Services Act 2007 eased traditional regulations on legal practice, allowing nonlawyers to own and manage law firms, which has resulted in a liberalization of the marketplace. More companies now recruit their own teams of in-house

L. Traczykowski (✉) • P. Dale
Aston University, Birmingham, UK
e-mail: l.traczykowski@aston.ac.uk

© The Author(s), under exclusive license to Springer Nature Switzerland AG 2023　**259**
C. Hauser, W. Amann (eds.), *The Future of Responsible Management Education*,
Humanism in Business Series, https://doi.org/10.1007/978-3-031-15632-8_14

lawyers instead of paying out expensive fees. As companies invest heavily to streamline workflows and reduce or eliminate risks, new technologies are emerging to aid the provision of legal advice.

These regulatory and technological changes within the legal profession have led to legal education providers innovating the way in which they deliver their training. Many providers are now revising and adapting their LLB degrees to make them more skills-based, within the framework of their own strategic directions, preparing students for the realities of the marketplace. Therefore, areas such as digitization and automation will become an integral aspect of new law degrees. The challenge for any forward thinking university is to grasp the advances made in technology, coupled with recent regulatory changes and innovative ways of teaching law that could not have been envisaged in the past (Susskind, 2017). These changes in practice are disruptive, as they do not always sit happily with the traditional methods of practicing law.

In regard to AI, issues—what to build, how to build it, who it serves, who it hurts and how it can be used ethically—are managed at the intersection of government regulation and business. The majority of research and publication on legal technology rely almost exclusively on the laws of the United States and Europe, which offer an interesting comparison. In the United States, market-based approaches are the driving force behind regulation, while in Europe, human rights concerns shape the legal response (Chesterman, 2021). In the past year alone, several hearings were held for governmental officials to consider the fair and just use of AI in the business, financial and insurance sector, among likely others (Eversheds Sutherland, 2021). For example, the United States House of Representatives has an Artificial Intelligence Task Force that recently (May 2021) held a hearing on "Equitable Algorithms: How Human-Centered AI can Address Systemic Racism and Racial Justice in Housing and Financial Services" (Eversheds Sutherland, 2021). In the United Kingdom, the Office for Artificial Intelligence drives "responsible and innovative uptake of AI technologies" (UK Gov, 2021). With that, this government body supports business and society (including "ethics, governance and future of work") and the enhancement of AI across all sectors (UK Gov, 2021). We can reasonably assume that the regulatory and business-related discussions on the use and integration of AI (for the above), however, were handled by lawyers.

In this chapter, we discuss training law students to adapt and prepare for advising clients about the ethical, social and legal implications of the use of artificial intelligence in the businesses with or for which they work. While interesting and important, we will not discuss the ways in which AI is being integrated into the day-to-day operations of legal practice, which is a different topic for a different audience. As with the thematic focus of this book, we are focused on the implications of AI on responsible management and leadership. To that end, we argue that training lawyers that advise businesses and organizations is just as important as training managers themselves. With this in mind we proceed in the following way. First, we consider that some of the skills legal professionals are taught during their formal education. Second, we explain how educating lawyers to adapt and advocate for ethical and legal innovations is imperative to ethical and legal innovations within businesses. Third, we explore the practicalities of teaching the regulation of technology and AI to future lawyers through a brief discussion of the content and development of our module at Aston University. We provide insight into the challenges we face and the opportunities provided through the development of a first-year, United Kingdom, undergraduate law module on the regulatory and ethical components of AI & technology.

14.2 Legal Education: Skills for Responsible Management

AI and technology more generally are not developed in silos; there is now constant regulatory oversight. Where these technologies push beyond existing laws and norms, it is lawyers and regulatory bodies that intervene to mitigate damage and ensure safe, continued use for society—be that as in-house lawyers or those working in public/private regulation. Consider, for example, that General Data Protection Regulation was introduced in 2018, when our personal data had been used (and abused) by companies for at least a decade previously (Quora, 2019). Even the most ethically minded businesses will make decisions based on furthering their own interests. While it may be argued that it is the business's social responsibility to self-regulate, the legality and ethicality of business structures must be publicly scrutinized and then regulated.

In this way, 'business people' do not make decisions about the future of their companies without first checking with their lawyers (or, at least they shouldn't) to make sure that no laws will be broken if they proceed as they choose. Furthermore, lawyers are there to advise on the regulatory, ethical and, sometimes, governance implications of any new product or process the business is introducing. Hence, responsible management requires insight from those outside of management, and as such, the concepts required for responsible management education should also be found in disciplines that advise businesses, such as law.

As legal educators, we must ensure that lawyers are trained to be AI savvy and ethically minded; with this training, they will be prepared to advise and support the development and integration of AI into future business and societal endeavors. Consider that there is increased demand for and use of legal technology for the drafting of legal documents, business contracts and the like (Hu & Lu, 2019). More importantly, lawyers are advocates, and with that, they must have skills to nurture the development and use of fair and just technology by businesses.

Furthermore, it is crucial that lawyers are educated for the future use/integration of AI into their work as well as the impact that technology will have on other professions related to or working with the legal field (finance, business, international relations, etc.) (Abdulrahman, 2020). In this section, we will first explain the current system for legal education (including recent developments), focused mainly on how it works in the United Kingdom (with some comparison to US legal education considering the influence of US regulation and business operations on the global market). We will then discuss the specific skills taught to law students that are relevant and valuable in the uncharted territory of AI development, use, regulation and advice to business and professional clients.

Legal Education System

According to the Solicitors Regulation Authority and Bar Standards Board (United Kingdom) Academic Stage Handbook, undergraduate law students must be taught certain transferable skills (2014).[1] These skills include the following ability:

- To apply knowledge in complex situations;
- To recognize potential alternative conclusions for particular situations and provide supporting reasons for them;
- To select key relevant issues for research and to formulate them with clarity;
- To use standard paper and electronic resources to produce up-to-date information;
- To make a personal and reasoned judgment based on an informed understanding of standard arguments in the area of law in question;
- To use the English language and legal terminology with care and accuracy;
- To conduct efficient searches of websites to locate relevant information; to exchange documents by email and manage information exchanges by email; to produce word-processed text and to preset it in an appropriate form (Bar Standards Board & Solicitors Regulation Authority, 2014, p. 18).

Future solicitors and barristers are taught the requirements of their profession upon these building blocks. Consider that any UK solicitor or barrister will have gone through further training and practical experience.

The route to legal practice in the United Kingdom has undergone profound change in the past 5 years. The Solicitors Regulation Authority introduced a new pathway route to becoming a solicitor from autumn 2021 onward: the Solicitors Qualifying Examination (SQE). Previously, the route involved studying foundations of legal knowledge within an undergraduate Qualifying Law Degree, before then moving onto a postgraduate Legal Practice Course, as part of the vocational training to become a solicitor. The new SQE sees two stages to practice for anyone with an undergraduate degree: SQE1, which focuses on legal knowledge, and SQE2, which focuses more on core skill requirements. The driving

---

[1] As we are developing and teaching law in the United Kingdom, we have taken a UK perspective on this topic. However, many of the skills and value-added from having lawyers advise and work for business on technology and AI issues will be similar globally.

force behind this change is to open up the legal profession to being more diverse and accessible, rather than the domain of the select few.

Likewise, in countries with similar legal systems (the United States and Australia, for example), it is postgraduate training (only) that provides individuals with the professional training necessary for advising clients, acting on behalf of a company and carrying out the intermediary role upon which business managers rely. For example, in the United States, prospective lawyers do not study law at the undergraduate level.[2] Instead, they pursue a degree—philosophy is always recommended if one eventually wants to go to 'law school', but any degree subject is acceptable. One's Juris Doctorate (JD) is the graduate-level education necessary to prepare for the 'Bar Exam' (Kowarski, 2019). The 'Bar' is a state-level administered test that prospective lawyers must pass to legally be allowed to practice law in their chosen state. Jurisdictionally managed exams are now one of the key qualifiers for lawyers in the United States and United Kingdom.

Skills Taught to Law Students

Indeed, through legal education ('Law School'—US; LLB + 'Legal Practice Course' or soon to be 'Solicitors Qualifying Exam/SQE'—UK), lawyers are trained to advise and support their clients. When these clients are businesses, law students must likewise be prepared to utilize leadership skills to ensure the best outcomes for clients. These skills include analytical rigor, persuasion, risk aversion, and the ability to 'think like a lawyer' (Sullivan et al., 2007). More specifically, written and verbal language skills focus on the ability to "critically analyze and communicate complex problems and ideas on the spot in the context of a broader, conceptual discussion of legal, ethical, and societal norms" (Westfahl, 2021). Lawyers are also encouraged to "adopt the viewpoint of a stakeholder", with that comes an ability to mediate and build bridges across

---

[2] With the UK SQE, prospective lawyers are similarly not required to study law at undergraduate level. Students may have a degree in any subject and then, as long as they have passed the exam and work experience requirements, may qualify as a solicitor.

departments, organizations, and, where necessary, multinational ventures (Westfahl, 2021).

A normal criticism of lawyers is that they deliberately elongate the process of decision making. As part of their training and an occupational hazard, lawyers read, consider responses to those in opposition, and form an argument based on an understanding their client's position in light of this reading and considering.[3]

One could argue that this deliberation is exactly what makes lawyers excellent support for a company's leadership. Regardless of any financial motivation, a lawyer's modus operandi is logic, rules and critical analysis; with that, the process of decision making is followed dispassionately (Westfahl, 2021). A focus on the rules and critical analysis helps lawyers advise clients and colleagues of what is possible within given parameters that govern the use of AI. Hopefully, this will also mean that lawyers are able to suggest which parameters should be questioned to improve technology regulation (Abdulrahman, 2020).

Consider the impact of these skills on any business team requesting support on AI and tech issues. For example, analysis is a skill learned early on in legal training—students must read, absorb, and synthesize a huge number of texts to provide responses (Gymer, 2019). Analytical rigor will mean that new lawyers are prepared to be agile responders to fast-paced changes in the tech industry (Gymer, 2019). Most law schools in the United Kingdom will have mooting, debate and/or negotiation competitions. Let us take, for example, moot competitions and the skills tested as an example of the skills developed within a legal education. According to Oxford University, mooting encourages deep thinking and improved advocacy, research and writing skills (University of Oxford, 2021). Importantly, mooting is an opportunity to showcase these skills, an opportunity "to demonstrate [their] interest in advocacy and competence as an advocate to prospective employers" (University of Oxford, 2021). Mooting plus legal education makes lawyers practiced practitioners of the

---

[3] Additionally, although, traditional legal billing is based on time spent and so some would argue that it is in the lawyer's best interest to elongate the process. If that is the case, then through the use of technology, legal advice, court rulings, and so on will be streamlined resulting in reduced costs charged to the business as client.

analysis and agility necessary for working with technological changes in the business sector.

While mooting is valuable, it highlights another criticism of the legal profession, which is that the lawyer personality often includes the need for achievement and/or competition (Westfahl, 2021). While this means that the lawyer will likely be a diligent and conscientious participant in management decision making, it can also inhibit cooperative and flexible working, particularly as is necessary in a high stakes situation (Westfahl, 2021). Working within a business gives a lawyer a chance to learn collaborative working (Westfahl, 2021).

Lawyers are also trained to consider the possible outcomes of a deal, venture, or opportunity and work backward (Westfahl, 2021). This is consistent with certain types of ethical analysis of situations, utilitarianism specifically, where we must determine whether the greatest good for the greatest number of people has been served. Mill's Utilitarianism, as applied to business situations, encourages decision makers to find the common good, long-term prosperity of society, and develop 'social concern' through the teaching of ethics itself (Gustafson, 2013, p. 330). Hence, a lawyer's training makes her ideally suited for working with and within businesses to advise, particularly in regard to issues that may have social and ethical implications as AI and technology do.

Additionally, and for obvious reasons, it is valuable to utilize the skills of a lawyer as part of a larger AI development team in regard to ensuring adherence to the law. There is already evidence of multinational corporations (MNCs) and small-to-medium enterprises (SMEs) using automation as a standard in their day-to-day legal activities (Flood, 2019). A law student's 'stakeholder viewpoint adoption' training will help them advise on how to translate the law to those practicing within that (legal) area and interpret insight from practitioners'—think: innovators, entrepreneurs, 'expert' witnesses—for the benefit of firms and government regulators (IE University, 2019).

Hence, lawyers are, in essence, advocates for their clients. 'Thinking like a lawyer' and being able to use those skills is the reason that so many firms hire in-house legal advisors and/or teams of external lawyers to support business ventures. This ability to translate skills across sectors, advocate for the needs of their employer, and advise on ethical, social and legal implications of decisions are exactly the reasons that lawyers are intricate components to responsible management of AI and tech moving forward.

14.3 Educating Lawyers for Future Management of AI & Tech

While lawyers are integrated into business operations, they are 'outside' the standard operations of the business. They have not been trained in the technology being discussed or the way a business is run. Broader members of the team may be highly skilled at things such as persuasion, risk aversion or critical engagement. In this case, it may not be necessary to engage a lawyer in AI/tech-related ventures. The learning achieved through legal education in Britain, for example, is quite narrow: students are not trained across disciplines as would be necessary to be a 'trusted advisor' in the machination age (Flood, 2019).

We hold, however, that legal education can and should teach traditional skills alongside the social, legal and ethical components of AI (Abdulrahman, 2020). There are particular components of legal education that make lawyers ideally suited to advise on such issues, and it makes sense to leverage these skills for use in the ongoing development and regulation of AI and technology. It is the role of a 'trusted advisor' that will stand lawyers in good stead as they face the technologically focused profession of the future. In that case, student lawyers must be prepared for and educated in the AI and tech world of the future.

Teaching law students about the regulation, ethics and governance of AI and tech is, therefore, imperative. In this section, we explain the bridge we are creating between traditional legal education (with the skills that offers) and the skills necessary to be a 'trusted advisor' for companies of the future. We begin with curricular aspects of this module and then move to content.

Curricular Aspects of the Module

The new module implemented in the new LLB for 2021 is entitled *The Future of Law: Introduction to Technology and its Regulation*. It is a core 15 credit undergraduate module in the first year of the LLB. In line with Aston University's strategic commercial direction and making use of the vital connections the school has with the business community, it will equip law students with necessary work-based skills. Aston Law School has a distinctive business and commercial edge on its LLB, which ensures that graduates are ready for the challenges of a legal career.

An important aspect of developing this module is to be able to 'dovetail' it into the rest of the LLB degree. The aim is for it to complement Aston's law degree, which has the distinctive business edge of developing employment skills of the students. To that end, it is designed to complement existing modules, demonstrating how technology can advance their practice.

The first learning outcome is to ensure that students apply a comprehensive understanding of the interaction of legal theory, regulation and ethics to the changing nature of technology, as it applies in a business scenario. The purpose of utilizing theory and ethics within technological advances ensures that students can identify the potential for gaps within the law. The law has been struggling to keep up with advances in technology, so if students were to learn the theory behind the application of law and ethics, inevitably it will make them better lawyers when advising their clients.

The second learning outcome is for students to understand the significance of technological change on future law making. The module team was mindful that many students would not be aware of the technological advancements as they relate to law. While technology has been an integral aspect of many 'young' lawyers' lives, its impact on the way in which law is practiced is both new and profound. It is important, therefore, to ensure that students obtain not only a good grasp of the law but also the technology itself as to how it relates to law-making.

The third learning outcome requires that students demonstrate their skills in legal research, making that research practical in its implication to technological advances. This is the skills-based stage of learning on the module. This will ensure that students will be equipped in their legal research and able to apply the previous two learning outcomes to a problem-based scenario around the development of new technologies.

This is particularly relevant to preparing law students to apply skills when advising business clients.

While the primary focus of the module will be on the legal frameworks within England and Wales, students will be encouraged to take a comparative approach to other jurisdictions. This means that the future lawyer can take more of a global perspective when advising clients in the commercial sector. Furthermore, taking this comparative approach can mean students can begin to take a critical path on the development of the law of England and Wales, thinking about ways in which gaps can be plugged, as technology inevitably advances. Therefore, students will need to be aware of both the theoretical and philosophical underpinnings of specific legal doctrines, as they apply on a global scale. This will nurture creative legal thinking when they contemplate questions, such as the possible regulation or promotion of technological change.

Content of the Module

Law students are taught from the outset of this module how to use technology during their studies as a way of complementing their assessments; if a student does not utilize the technological databases at the fingertips for legal research, such as LexisNexis or Westlaw, then inevitably it will result in a below par assignment. It should not be a stretch, therefore, for legal education to take on board further technological advances within the traditional degree structure. While these advances may well lead to interesting theoretical discussions among academics as to how far technology, or even robots, will replace the traditional tasks of the lawyer (Hawksworth et al., 2018), the main focus of this module will be to demonstrate how technology can complement and enhance future legal practice within a business.

Some of the technologies that we will refer to include advancements such as algorithms that predict the outcome of cases, chatbots that give clients legal advice, and the automatic generation of legal documents by artificial intelligence (Goodman, 2017). We will also examine the technological advances that are specific to our modules, such as the law on healthcare, intellectual property, commerce and taxation. This sits at the intersection of law and business, meaning that law graduates will have familiarity with the technologies used in the private sector. To enable students to critically evaluate technology, we will introduce students to human rights and ethical theory, encouraging students to 'think outside the box' and plug gaps in current regulations and legal propositions.

One of the main roles of lawyers has been the ability to be able to read the law from cases or statutes, apply it to a client's legal issue, and be able to predict the outcome. This will then inform a client's decision as to whether they wish to pursue a claim (or defense) or to settle before going to court. However, predictive analytics has made inroads into the way in which a lawyer will evaluate a case. For example, one US company, Lex Machina, is currently creating algorithms to predict the outcome of New York County Supreme Court cases (Huang, 2020). In Europe, one artificial intelligence system predicts the accuracy of cases at the European Court of Human Rights with 79% accuracy (Medvedeva, 2020). As these technologies advance, it will mean that future lawyers will be able to predict the outcome of cases at the click of a button and advise their clients to act accordingly. Inevitable questions arise on what this means for the way in which lawyers will advise clients but the intersection of law and tech must be taught regardless.

Every lawyer can tell a story on how they struggled at university to learn models to answer 'problem questions': a fictitious scenario where a client needs a legal problem solved. The IRAC model is the most familiar; students have been taught for decades to break a fictitious problem down into identifying the 'issue' (I), sourcing the relevant 'rule' (R), before then 'applying' (A) the said rule to facts of the problem, resulting in a 'conclusion' (C). However, introducing predictive analytics into the same said case will likely require the modern law degree to adapt.

One of the very real issues clients will face is that they will be hinging their legal rights to the decisions made by computers. However, machine learning is becoming advanced and created by vast teams so that computer programmers struggle to know how an AI code has predicted something. Hence, because we do not know how AI predicts something and we cannot predict what it will predict, AI causes ethical and, later, legal dilemmas that we have yet to even imagine. Future lawyers will need to adapt to the scenario where a client wants an explanation beyond the mantra 'computer says no', leaving the door open to still teach the traditional practical legal reasoning on law degrees but complementing it with the technological advance.

Another aspect of technological changes that we must account for in legal education is one that computer scientists address: bias. Consider, first, the elements of unconscious bias that exist in legal practice. Retired President of the Supreme Court states, Lady Hale, refers to the current judiciary as 'male, pale and stale'. She has often spoken of her desire to see a judiciary that is more representative of the society it serves, arguing in 2017, that judges 'bring our experiences of life, our values, our philosophies of judging, our inarticulate major premises, our unconscious biases' (Lady Hale, 2017).

On the technological plus side, judges may be fundamentally flawed in their decision making. Biases and prejudices exist at every level in society. The old adage coined by Jerome Frank, which says justice is 'what the judge ate for breakfast', may not be that far from the truth. Shai Danziger from Ben Gurion University conducted a study of over 1000 parole board hearings in Israel and found that judges were more favorable at the start of the morning than late morning and then back to the same leniency upon returning from lunch! The results sent shockwaves through the criminologists and social workers who sat on these boards (Yong, 2011). Therefore, it could be argued that technology is useful in relation to issues such as judicial sentencing and parole board hearings. We believe that highlighting these types of bias cases to students and showing how technology may help us reform our judicial system are vital aspects of technological and AI-aligned legal curriculum.

One of the effects of the COVID-19 pandemic has been a backlog of cases through the whole court system. With reports of many cases taking months and potentially years to resolve, this presents a huge barrier for the deliverance of justice. AI systems will prove useful to secure justice during these times. One of the most ambitious projects comes from Estonia, with the idea of the 'robot judge' to adjudicate on disputes and provide sentencing for criminals. Officials are hopeful of clearing a backlog of cases (Siboe, 2020). The problem is, however, that this technology is reliant on data, which in itself could be discriminatory (Angwin et al., 2016). This raises all sorts of concerns for the future lawyer. Inevitably taking on board such wider societal issues to law and technology can only broaden the minds of future lawyers.

Next, consider how legal decisions are amplified by machine learning. Therefore, for example, it is well documented that young black men are disproportionately more likely to be stopped and searched by the police than their white counterparts (Agnew-Pauley & Akintoye, 2021). If these data were used in a crime prevention algorithm, the result would be that a computer would instruct police officers to stop and search on the basis of racial prejudice. Therefore, the reliance on data amplifies existing prejudices within policing. It is therefore our job as legal educators to assist students so that they can grapple with such complex issues. While this example is not management/business-related, it demonstrates the importance of student learning to weigh up the pros and cons of technology, which makes decisions over people's lives simply on the basis of an algorithm. Students will need to learn the laws and how to interpret and apply them while also empowering them to evaluate how these technologies link to human rights and ethical issues.

Empowering students to evaluate the ethical implications of certain technologies has further advantages as well. Law is not always black and white with clear and distinct answers; it often takes into account society's principles, public morality, equitable outcomes, and matters of public policy, irrespective of how much legal practitioners object to such a notion. As the notable legal philosopher Ronald Dworkin states, principles are as much a part of judicial interpretation as are statutes or judicial precedents (Dworkin, 1967). Therefore, teaching tomorrow's lawyers the pros and cons of legal technology will inevitably lead to critical thinking on wider philosophical and sociological implications. Questions will need to be asked as to how far legal practice wants technology to infiltrate on matters that traditionally incorporate the 'human touch'.

With the changing nature of technology, no doubt rapid advances will be made even before graduation. Students will, therefore, need to develop a comprehensive understanding of the interaction between theory, ethics, human rights and regulation, applying these understandings to the changing nature of modern technology in the business context. This will mean that students will be able to understand the law's role in both challenging and promoting technological changes.

14.4   Conclusion

Having not yet delivered this new module (and new approach) to Law students, we do not have hard examples of how it is impacting students. Nor do we have examples of how the integration of this subject matter into legal education influences employment prospects and success. As recent coverage explains, "One thing remains certain: law students must actively engage with legal technology during their studies to ensure they are in the best possible position for future developments in their profession" (IE University, 2019). Universities are adapting: changes are already being made to law school curricula in the United Kingdom to account for these emerging and developing technological changes. The necessity for all students to engage with the changing nature of technology and AI is upon us.

To businesses we say, seek out graduates who can speak to their technology + regulation education. Business schools should partner with law schools to ensure the direct applicability of what is being taught. Short of partnered education, cooperative competitions or similar may help ensure that law students understand the true issues of tech; at the same time, business students will be prepared to work with their lawyer, who will be the best advocate and support for adherence to all regulatory issues.

In sum, teaching lawyers to be responsible and ethical and legal advocates for their business clients' technology interests is as important as teaching managers and businesspeople to be responsible managers. Legal education provides a niche set of skills that will be highly valued as AI and technology progress. The skills that legal professionals are taught during their formal education can and should be adapted and adaptable to changing innovations in business. In this chapter, we have explained changes we have made to our curriculum through the inclusion of a 'Future of Law: Regulating Tech and AI' module. This is included to prepare business clients of lawyers for what they can/should expect from their legal representatives. This kind of teaching and the world we are teaching for do not come without difficulties and challenges. However, preparing law students to advise and advocate on behalf of their business clients on the topic of tech will be an increasingly important aspect of legal education and should be championed.

References

Abdulrahman, N. (2020, June 19). *What are the most important skills for lawyers of the future?* Retrieved from The Lawyer. https://www.thelawyer.com/what-are-the-most-important-skills-for-lawyers-of-the-future/

Agnew-Pauley & Akintoye. (2021). *Stop and search disproportionately affects black communities – yet police powers are being extended.* The Conversation published 3 August 2021. https://theconversation.com/stop-and-search-disproportionately-affects-black-communities-yet-police-powers-are-being-extended-165477

Angwin, Larson, Mattu, & Kirchner. (2016). Machine Bias ProPublica 23 May 2016. https://www.propublica.org/article/machine-bias-risk-assessments-in-criminal-sentencing

Bar Standards Board & Solicitors Regulation Authority. (2014). *Academic stage handbook.*. BSB & SRA.

Chesterman, S. (2021). *We, the robots? regulating artificial intelligence and the limits of the law.* Cambridge University Press.

Dworkin. (1967). The Model of Rules. *University of Chicago Law Review, 35*(1), Article 3.

Eversheds Sutherland. (2021). *US House AI Task Force is the latest authority to address algorithms and racism.* Retrieved June 24, 2021, from https://us.eversheds-sutherland.com/mobile/NewsCommentary/Legal-Alerts/241756/US-House-AI-Task-Force-Is-the-latest-authority-to-address-algorithms-and-racism

Flood, J. (2019). Legal professionals of the future: their ethos, role and skills. In M. DeStefano & G. Dobrauz (Eds.), *New suits: Appetite for disruption in the legal world.* Stampfli.

Goodman, J. (2017). Legal technology: The rise of the chatbots. *The Law Gazette.* Retrieved July 2021, from https://www.lawgazette.co.uk/features/legal-technology-the-rise-of-the-chatbots/5060310.article

Gustafson, A. (2013). In defense of a utilitarian business ethic. *Business and Society Review, 118*(3), 325–360.

Gymer, S. (2019, November 18). *7 qualities every good lawyer should have.* Retrieved from All About Law: https://www.allaboutlaw.co.uk/school-leaver-law-careers/becoming-a-lawyer/7-qualities-every-good-lawyer-should-have

Hawksworth, J., Berriman, R, & Goel, S. (2018). *Will robots really steal our jobs? An International analysis of the potential long term impact of automation.*

PWC. Retrieved July 2021, from https://www.pwc.co.uk/economic-services/assets/international-impact-of-automation-feb-2018.pdf

Hu, T., & Lu, H. (2019). Study on the influence of artificial intelligence on legal profession. In B. a. Advances in Economics (Ed.), *5th International conference on economics, management, law and education (EMLE 2019). 110.* Atlantis Press.

Huang, G. (2020, October 22). Lex Machina launches legal analytics for New York County Supreme Court. https://lexmachina.com/blog/lex-machina-launches-legal-analytics-for-new-york-county-supreme-court/.

IE University. (2019, July 22). *It's clear that the law industry is undergoing a fundamental shift in the way firms work, with AI and machine learning leading the way for workflow and process optimization.* Retrieved from AI in the classroom: how artificial intelligence is changing law students' day-to-day lives: https://drivinginnovation.ie.edu/ai-in-the-classroom-how-artificial-intelligence-is-changing-law-students-day-to-day-lives/

Kowarski, I. (2019, June 24). What is a J.D. degree? *US News.* Retrieved August 14, 2021, from https://www.usnews.com/education/best-graduate-schools/top-law-schools/articles/2019-06-24/what-is-a-jd-degree

Lady Hale. (2017, August 11). *Judges, power and accountability: Constitutional implications of judicial selection.* Constitutional Law Summer School. Retrieved from https://www.supremecourt.uk/docs/speech-170811.pdf

Medvedeva, M. (2020). Using machine learning to predict decisions of the European Court of Human Rights. *Artificial Intelligence and Law,* 237–266.

Quora. (2019, July 1). What are the biggest regulatory issues facing the tech industry today? *Forbes.* Retrieved July 5, 2021, from https://www.forbes.com/sites/quora/2019/07/01/what-are-the-biggest-regulatory-issues-facing-the-tech-industry-today/?sh=7b14980b7ae9

Siboe, N. (2020, April). Use of artificial intelligence by the judiciary in the face of COVID-19. *Oxford Human Rights Hub.* https://ohrh.law.ox.ac.uk/use-of-artificial-intelligence-by-the-judiciary-in-the-face-of-covid-19/.

Sullivan, W., Colby, A, Wegner, J. W., Bond, L., & Shulman, L. (2007). *Educating lawyers (book summary).* The Carnegie Foundation for the Advancement of Teaching. Retrieved July 5, 2021, from http://archive.carnegiefoundation.org/publications/pdfs/elibrary/elibrary_pdf_632.pdf

Susskind, R. (2017). *Tomorrow's lawyers: An introduction to your future.* Oxford University Press.

UK Gov. (2021). *Office of Artificial Intelligence AI.* UK Gov.

University of Oxford. (2021). *Mooting: What is it and why take part?* Retrieved from Faculty of Law. https://www.law.ox.ac.uk/current-students/mooting-oxford/mooting-what-it-and-why-take-part#:~:text=A%20moot%20court%20competition%20simulates,submissions%2C%20and%20present%20oral%20argument

Westfahl, S. (2021). Leveraging lawyers' strengths and training them to support team problem-solving under crisis conditions. In R. Brescia & E. Stern (Eds.), *Crisis lawyering: Effective legal advocacy in emergency situations.* New York University Press.

Yong, E. (2011, April 11). Justice is served, but more so after lunch: how food-breaks sway the decisions of judges. *National Geographic*. Retrieved July 2021, from https://www.nationalgeographic.com/science/article/justice-is-served-but-more-so-after-lunch-how-food-breaks-sway-the-decisions-of-judges

15

PRME Principle Three, 15 Years Later: How Exponential Technologies Can Enhance the Quality of Impactful and Meaningful Business Education

Walter Baets

15.1 Introduction to the Context

Imagine 10 years further. The concept of a pandemic and of life-threatening viruses, both for humans and machines, has just become an everyday fact. We have also learned to live with the fact that we cannot truly fight this, but that we have to go with the flow and look for impactful innovations in the chaos created by the situation. Meanwhile, exponential technologies have taken a central place in our lives. The evident things are the self-steering car, the refrigerator that keeps track of its own inventory and automatically replenishes it, e-health devices (with health monitoring and immediate primary care), and sustainable and smart homes, everything controlled remotely from our smartphones. However,

W. Baets (✉)
Rotterdam University of Applied Sciences, Rotterdam, The Netherlands

Eindhoven Engine Academy, Eindhoven Engine, Eindhoven, Netherlands
e-mail: w.r.j.baets@hr.nl

more complex situations are also handled differently. We will have learned how to collaborate remotely, how this could improve our work-life balance (if we wanted that), and how we could make medical care and even education accessible to many more people, including in geographically (remote) areas where it truly matters.

What we will have understood is that it is neither the technology nor the uncontrollability that makes the difference. Those are just facts, a reality. While available technology allows us to do many innovative things, the question remains: what are we doing it for? How do we change the face of the economy and of society? Not as a slogan or aspiration, but practically, on the ground. What we will have seen by then is that the advancing technology is neutral but that ideally the guiding principle should be our search for meaning, for impact, for inclusiveness and ultimately for our existence as humanity: the community, the village, the tribe. Ubuntu (I am, because I belong to something bigger) is what we lost in our society, and we are searching for it intensely. The problem is of course not new. To bring it back to today: what do Bezos, Musk and Branson expect to contribute to society with their orbital aspirations? The acceleration that society lives through makes the need for this question, obviously, very invasive. Still the central question, which is already on the table since computers took forefront in our (business-)life is the following. How do we evolve from information (abundantly and freely available), to relevant (and correct) information, to knowledge (what can I do with it, not what has already been done with it), to wisdom (being impactful). Indeed, in 10 years, we will, even more than now, be looking for wisdom. That is why PRME has and remains to have a central place in business and management education.

Are our higher education institutes, today, designed to support young people (and employees) in this reflection? Or are we still training for professions, some of which already have no future, but where half of the professions that will exist in 10 years' time are not even known yet. Does our attention remain focused on what we have had (the past), what we know well (analysis of that past), or do we ask ourselves the question of what could have been done differently or should not have been done? Will we be able to adjust our teaching (and research) practice into a kind of compass that can guide people in their quest for wisdom? That is what principle three is concerned with.

The Principles of Responsible Management Education (PRME), the academic "chapter" of the UN Global Compact Program, has now been endorsed by hundreds of universities. However, has it truly had the impact it aimed to have? At the first Academic PRME Conference in New York in 2008, the contribution of the working group on the third principle made it clear that to shape the responsible citizens of the future, the approach, experimentation, systemic view of problems, multidisciplinarity, and an active approach to research (action research) are just as important as the content of curricula of universities.

More recently (2019), the World Economic Forum[1] shared a publication on what they see as the four biggest challenges facing higher education and how to deal with them. The four challenges they see are:

- Rising need for life-long learning in a nonlinear world
- Changing needs and expectations of the student/user
- Emerging technologies and business models
- Toward a "competence" over a "knowledge" model (focusing on the skills required in the future)

Let us zoom in on a few of those challenges and highlight the competencies that might help to deal with them.

15.2 Our World Seems a Little Sick, but from What?

We live in interesting times. Corona has profoundly disrupted economic life, and that disruption does not come from exponential technologies; we were expecting disruptions by exponential technologies and prepared for it. It is often said that a crisis brings up the things that matter and that we need a crisis to truly change things.

---

[1] https://www.weforum.org/agenda/2019/12/fourth-industrial-revolution-higher-education-challenges/

After times of worshiping the golden calf (economic growth, stock market values, financial optimization of our logistics chains, unbridled internationalization with little control over money flows), we suddenly rediscover, and rightly so, that the things that matter are close to home. It is about care, education, safety, about the people who are close to us. They are now receiving attention again and let us hope that this will continue to be a fundamental change in our way of doing and thinking. It is ultimately about the people, not the systems. We become aware that we have neglected the public good, often I favor of that golden calf, and now we see the consequences. Let us be careful with the social good, which in my view is one of the main achievements of Europe. However, as we rediscover our closeness to the immediate environment and perhaps even our togetherness within a region or country, cooperation beyond borders is necessary.

We have all underestimated the outbreak of coronavirus on several levels. We hoped it would stay "there" (we want the economic benefits of working with China, but the problems have to stay there). From a distance we watched what went wrong there. We thought we were at a safe distance. However, we thoroughly underestimated both the exponentiality of this epidemic and its mobility. We are suddenly shocked by the world we have created ourselves. The world has become a complex system (and not just complicated), which we can no longer control. The system has its own logic, while we think and preach that we can still control it. At what price? And with what success rate? Feike Sybesma (former CEO of DSM) sums it up well: how can you call yourself or your company successful, in a world that fails?

Hopefully, this crisis has made it clear to us that the world we live in is one of complexity, exponentiality, interaction between all kinds of networks, self-organizing, hence totally uncontrollable, and of course transdisciplinary. We are so hopelessly divided into silos, sectors, activities, and suddenly we see that Corona touches "everything." We were not ready for that. Everyone was ready to fight their war, but we are having a hard time overseeing the impact of Corona and living with it meaningfully. It is not a choice between health or economics, between education and security, or between whatever. It is a choice for the development of our communities, very locally, with respect to their natural habitat, but at the same time within a national and international framework. Borders, separatedness, are human inventions and not laws of nature.

The pandemic has forced us all into experimentation with virtual learning approaches. What was for years a lively debate whether to use (more) technology in education and define a different kind of environment, approach and learning experience suddenly became daily practice. It not only appeared possible but also caused a thorough rethinking of current practices. We have been teaching in the classroom for hundreds of years, and now overnight, we have to start thinking about how children learn, rather than how can we teach them. Let us hope that we have this dialog and experiments persevere and eventually come to the much-needed reform of education: from teaching to learning, from listening to doing, with the aim of developing the competencies needed to redefine oneself constantly. Indeed, education should be focused foremost on the development of competencies for the coming decades: values-based leadership, entrepreneurship, innovation, creativity, supporting networks of people (and communities), systems thinking, design thinking, human-centered management, and so on.

PRME also has a dimension of accessibility of education for all. Virtual education offers much potential for this, especially in emerging economies. Virtually assisted education (which we still need to define) could be a useful way to deliver education to many very flexible remote areas in the form of life-long learning that is totally adapted to each individual. It is possible, thanks to the potential of exponential technologies, we just have to do it right. In doing so, we begin to build another, more meaningful world.

The mind shift needed is not unknown. Ivan Illich, more than 50 years ago, pleaded for "Deschooling Society." It appeared difficult for many years, but the opportunities of technologies today could boost that goal. It is not about procedures, outcomes, learning objectives, testing; that is, the school dimension. It is about learning, doing, impact, inclusiveness, responsibility, community, and belonging, that is, the dimension of human development.

In earlier publications (e.g., Baets, 2020), this mindset is called value-driven innovation and analyzes the phenomenon of innovation from the perspective of systems thinking and complexity. This leads to a set of dimensions around which we must rethink education if we want to introduce meaningful technologies. Table 15.1 compares those dimensions to current practice.

15.3   The School Becomes a Living Lab?

Thanks to the availability of technology, it is easier today to rethink the school toward a Living Lab. The term Living Lab is used differently by different parties; everything that bears the name Living Lab does not always have the same intention. The Rathenau Institute[2] refers to four different types:

- Open scientific research facilities, several of which now exist at various universities;
- Field labs (sometimes also called fablabs) of the manufacturing industry;

Table 15.1 Key comparisons

Values-driven innovation	Procedure-driven innovation
(Massive) transformative purpose	Financial contribution
Driven by purpose and transformation	Driven by control and process
Success is measured by impact	Success is measured by margin
Holistic/a-causal	Causal/linear
Cooperation (open innovation)	Competition
Ubuntu (we belong)	I am
Sustainability focus	Short-term focus
Value added for the stakeholders	Value added for the shareholders
Humanoid management	Machine-like management
People are autonomous/take initiative	Structured and fixed procedures
Agile innovation	Planned (engineered) innovation
Minimum interaction rules	Detailed rules and regulations
Trial and error/experimentation	Analysis
Networked	Hierarchical
Shared purpose	Individual purpose
Leader	Bosses

---

[2] https://www.rathenau.nl/nl/vitale-kennisecosystemen/living-labs-nederland/faq#faq-item5

- Commercial urban testing facilities, experimenting with possible solutions;
- Living labs (what they call "real" living labs) are not only focused on technological innovation. Attention is also paid to the nontechnological aspects, government and policy, the involvement of the various problem owners, and the development of knowledge products.

It seems obvious that the approach we are looking for, to be an impactful university (of applied sciences), is realized in "real" Living Labs. Central to this is the focus on BMI: finding solutions that are impactful, scalable, and economically viable. The business model also includes the technical dimensions of what is offered, the (psychological) acceptance, and the ethical choices that one has to make. The business model is therefore certainly not limited to the business dimension of an innovation. Business model innovation is not what we currently pay the most attention to in business schools and universities. Cambridge University's IdeaSpace[3] uses the concept of "Founder." They are not interested in brilliant new ideas: there are plenty of them (output from scientific research). They are not interested in start-ups because they need all their time to start up. They are interested in "founders," those who can come up with creative successful business models. They can be high-tech, low-tech or no-tech, but they contribute to the solution of a real problem; they have an impact (and scale quickly and easily), and they are economically viable. PRME-based education should have this focus: practice-oriented, impactful, nonsense, and interdisciplinary.

Some of the most successful companies currently are examples of business model innovation and not technology innovation. Airbnb is a reversal of the logic in the hospitality industry: can you have a hotel without rooms? Can you turn your customers (who use rooms) into suppliers of rooms? Uber creates a taxi company without taxis: can you turn your customer into your driver? Even Facebook, and all companies use technology of course, is a digital news media without journalists. You are much more likely to fall into ethical questions: does Uber's approach more easily lead to the exploitation of drivers? As a reader of Facebook,

---

[3] https://www.ideaspace.cam.ac.uk/

how can you judge the quality of a contribution (or even the origin)? While these companies illustrate the role of BMI, they are certainly not examples of the innovative, value-driven use of technology.

A Living Lab is a flexible form of collaboration, in this case organized around a physical place, in which students, managers and employees, faculty and the public sector work together on open innovation with a clear intention to have a positive impact on the economy of the region (or the community). A short animation (https://youtu.be/82ey5Z5B_6o) brings this to life. For a more fundamental explanation, the following video may be interesting: https://youtu.be/WtlxxbwevUI. It is a place of creativity, colocation, and innovation. A Living Lab has a number of intentions that reinforce each other: the practical development of solutions (whereby we make use of the added value of all participants), guiding the innovation of the business community with a hands-on approach, learning from practice for students and employees, formulating lessons (research output) that we can learn from this and that can contribute to (policy) decisions (Baets, 2020). Technology can make this "space" a permanent and borderless experience.

A Living Lab therefore contains:

- Cocreation and innovation with and for the business community and thereby guiding the region toward the Next Economy
- Relevant practice-oriented research
- Learning-by-doing (action learning) for students (which gives them credits)
- Potential for employees to also define relevant learning pathways (which could lead to certificates and/or diplomas)

The key to success is that we are all committed to innovation in a different, more flexible way, making use of the diversity of knowledge and experience (collective intelligence) in the project groups. It is about transformation, rather than to keep doing what we have always done. This means that the participants must also dare to question themselves. Learning happens by doing, in a group of "peers," where everyone is expected to give feedback to everyone. In this way, we will succeed in activating the collective intelligence of groups: what comes out of a group is more than the sum of individual insights and capacities. Hence, we are going to be able to come up with innovations that go beyond what we could all do in isolation. Every participant must therefore be willing and able to take responsibility for his or her own learning path.

None of this is easy, so this process is supported by a meticulously thought-out and tested methodology, which is based on an integration of design thinking and systems thinking.

In summary, the expected outcome of PRME-based learning is a transformation to become a successful key player in the new economy for both the entrepreneur and the students (future entrepreneurial employees). Values and positive impact are the lighthouse on which we steer. The approach is based on design thinking, while the context is one of systems thinking. After all, we will only find sustainable solutions if we want to understand problems within its entire, interconnected environment.

In addition to the physical space, the Living Lab is a colocation in cocreation between entrepreneurs, companies, knowledge institutions, students and the government, and this is supervised by a multidisciplinary team of lecturers/coaches from various backgrounds. All parties play an active role, and faculty facilitate that process. The space is equipped for continuous group work and brainstorming, alongside spaces for quiet group and individual work. It becomes the home of the Living Lab, where creative work can be done outside the hustle and bustle of school or business.

This, of course, has quite a few consequences for the approach and structure of universities. First, we must make the switch from education to supervised learning. Although this is already happening sporadically, education remains the mainstream approach in universities and colleges. More responsibility will be transferred to the student, who will have to make more choices, take responsibility and initiative regarding his or her personal transformation but also pay more attention to what s/he wants to learn. Which competencies (managerial and others) do you want to develop, and in which way do you want to do that? The teacher transforms into a facilitator, colearner, and challenger. Business is taking a more active role in education, which at the same time creates real opportunities for life-long learning and on-the-job learning. The researcher obtains a dream environment for action research and practice-oriented research. University governance needs to refocus away from an organization that is too tightly organized around learning objectives, assessment criteria and citation indices to opting for measuring the impact of management (education and research). These are many challenges, but the potential gains are of course equally large.

These types of living labs are experimented with in various countries but often as part of a broader (more mainstream) curriculum or even within a course. Scandinavian countries pay attention to this approach, already during secondary education, which is reflected in how they deal with life-long-learning/executive education. The "Green Schools" around the world (secondary education) are pretty much in tune with what we call a Living Lab. Ecole 42, a programming school in Paris (with copies in other countries), consists of a 4-year sequence of assignments. No face-to-face lessons are organized. Assignments may be made individually or in groups. Students may ask for any help they can. It is highly self-organized. Reality is that most students do not complete the 4 years because they have already been bought out by the business community before graduation.

At the university level, it becomes slightly more difficult to find examples. The Masters in Inclusive Business Model Innovation of the Graduate School of Business at the University of Cape Town is possibly a good example. Students are selected based on a real problem they want to solve for and with a group of "real" people. Selection is based on the potential impact that the projects can have on society (the people involved). The entire year consists of working with the people (and not "for" the people) on a solution. There are still 3 weeks of course: agile innovation and design thinking; impact, values, meaning, systems thinking; how do I make a business plan. Evaluation is based on peer evaluation, whether the proposed solution (prototype) indeed offers a solution to the community of people involved (community evaluation), and an external examination. Approximately 75% of the projects continue after graduation, not led by the students but by the community involved.

15.4   What Do We Get in Return?

The purpose is not to organize the next field lab, fab lab, start-up village, coworking space, or accelerator. They exist, and while they are useful, they create neither that radically different economic model nor the fundamental turnaround necessary for our world in transition. We have seen successes abroad, especially in the technological field, where open innovation trajectories have given rise to completely new business models. Success stories are characterized by open innovation, diversity in the ecosystem, "entrepreneurial" students, and active participation (also for learning) of companies and entrepreneurs. In the Netherlands, the ecosystem that has developed around Wageningen University is probably also a good example and fertile ground for Living Labs.

Where can we reasonably expect to create added value? The goal of the Living Lab is to contribute to solving wicked problems, problems that transcend everyday management practice, require a systems approach, could have a slightly longer horizon, but that potentially have a major impact. These problems can be related to the challenges of the new technologies (and how they can contribute to the renewal of a company) but also have more of a system's dimensions, such as how innovation can contribute to reducing crime. A company, SME, start-up, or larger company, can put forward its own problems and tackle them in an innovative way in a team. For that, we need interdisciplinarity.

The Living Lab supports the development of the competencies that managers need to create more meaningful and responsible businesses. The Living Lab experience contributes to the necessary transformation from vertical, hierarchical thinking to thinking and acting that fits in with the new economy: working with small-scale networks and transcending disciplines with a view to solving major societal problems.

The Living Lab experience is an experiment in practice-oriented (action) research on issues that matter to corporations and society. The Living Lab experience directly defines the research agenda (for meaningful research), rather than academics defining what they feel would be interesting to research. It goes without saying that the Living Lab is a life experiment in pedagogical innovation, practicing action learning,

learning-by-doing and challenge-based learning. Is this perhaps the future of Business Schools?

Although for business the focus is on innovation of real problems, for them it is also a learning experiment. The Living Lab is an ideal and impactful experience in lifelong learning. Through a flexible organization of part-time courses at the university (the edu-badges), badges can be accumulated toward a certificate or degree. The Living Lab approach therefore offers great potential for the necessary upskilling of a region.

With the Living Lab, different things are catered for different groups. We integrate education and research in such a way that we not only contribute to both but also contribute to solving wicked problems. The Living Lab is transdisciplinary and therefore important as a contribution to further integration within the universities. For companies, added value not only works on their own innovation but can also contribute to the personal learning trajectory (certified or not).

15.5 Technology That Matters: Semantics to Support Learning and Learning Environments

Now that we know what we are doing, and what we are doing it for, the question emerges around how to do it and how technology could play an impactful and meaningful role. We have thoroughly analyzed and described the problem area; we can now search for meaningful supporting technology. By following this logic, we avoid developing technological solutions, searching for a problem.

Learning, (virtual) education, learning management systems, and knowledge management are struggling for years now with a huge availability of resources of varying quality, which are nevertheless difficult to access by learners. One must know where to find the information, and in particular in a learning situation, one often does not know what one does not know (yet) and hence what one is looking for, it is difficult to search meaningful and impactful. Recent developments in semantics and their use in learning by doing platforms are promising and powerful. For the last few years, we have developed such learning by doing virtual platforms, completely in line with the Living Lab approach, and have published the semantic approach in detail (Baets et al., 2019). For the less familiar reader, let us explore the challenge.

One of the big challenges for computers has always been their understanding of natural language and its interpretation. While commercial products are available such as Siri (digital assistant) or Dragon (speech recognition from voice to text), the theoretical potential of semantic analysis is still limited in business education. Semantics, however, has great potential in particular for bias-free automatic content curation in virtual learning by doing: content on demand, as needed and when needed.

We understand semantics as the linguistic and philosophical study of meaning in language, programming language, formal logic, and semiotics (meaning-making, sign processing, and meaningful communication). It deals with the relationship between signifiers (words, phrases, signs) and what they stand for, their denotation. The term semantics is often used while talking about Petri nets (Kurapati & Mengchu, 1999), semantic mapping and frame-based analysis (Fillmore & Baker, 2012). These approaches use semantics in reference to maps or webs of words or flows (graphic organizers), typologies, on which applications (programs) are based, and/or that describe such systems.

Semiotics studies the transmission and interpretation of meaning, represented symbolically in signs and messages, primarily in language (Mingers & Wilcocks, 2017). Semiotics analyses the manifest appearance of texts to reveal the underlying social and cultural structures that generate them. In semiotics, we focus attention on the form of representation itself, rather than on the message content, and the effects that the representation has on both the production and interpretation of the context. Semiotics is increasingly used in management to find meaning (Oswald & Mick, 2006, talking about the semiotic paradigm of meaning in the marketplace) and in marketing (Brannen, 2004) for a deeper understanding of recontextualization, semantic fit, and the semiotics of foreignness in particular brands.

The growing interest in semantics fits the discussion in the information systems community exploring more language interpretative approaches. Moving forward with IS research, Hassan et al. (2018)

suggest avoiding being overly logic. We should rely on language as a means of communications. Understanding important principles requires considerable background knowledge. However, coherence is the hallmark of scholarship. The "center" (according to Derida, in Hassan et al.) in IS is "positivism," which limits what can be researched and found. Myers and Klein (2011) suggest not using our principles too mechanically. Avital et al. (2017) argue for the use of more literary and narrative styles of research.

Rowe (2018) suggests that we too often neglect to develop our theoretical reasoning and conceptual reasoning based on intuition (Stahl, 2014). There is still a need for pure theory development papers (Te'eni et al., 2015), but at the same time, we should contribute to a better world. We need to go beyond specialized traditions to address these systemic challenges (Jean Louis Le Moigne in Eriksson, 1997). We should interrogate a problem in full richness. Can we construct an engine that is able to curate internet-based content based on relevance for the question at hand? (The theoretical background is described in Baets et al., 2019.)

15.6 Application in Automated Content Curation for Virtual Learning Platforms

To support the learning by doing the concept described before, it is interesting to make on-the-spot automated content curation for virtual learning platforms available. A pilot in a real-life application is developed and experimented on in a Masters level course.

The pilot was developed within a master's in general management program, and the particular course was titled Complexity, Exponential Organizations and Innovation. The project on which the participants worked was "The Business School of the next decade." Eventually, 32 students went through the full experiment and submitted all the assignments: a group project, an individual learning log, and daily group assignments. This particular course ran over a dedicated time period.

Participants leveraged a powerful toolkit of learning by doing through a hyperpractical online learning environment, which was then complimented with by face-to-face workshops. The platform is organized around two trajectories, both based on a combination of design thinking and systems thinking. They both go through several steps, with requested assignments, to support and structure the journey slightly, for those who would be in need of more structure. The learning path that each individual choses, however, is free. Each step in both journeys is supported by learning on demand modules. If you are asked, for instance, to realize an empathy map, then there are learning modules on demand (your decision to use them) on different levels about what an empathy map is and how to make one. Tools are provided in each step to realize the assignments.

While the platform is crucial, the pedagogical approach remains an important innovation. As developed before, it is based on concepts such as learning by doing, systemics, peer learning, self-evaluation/deep reflection, complexity, design thinking, and deep learning. While building a pedagogical approach around each of those concepts in themselves could have already been an impactful innovation, the integration of all of them in the approach makes it very powerful. It allows for agile innovation, including many dimensions, and even in a short period of time to come with very rich and creative innovations, as the final project presentations showed.

More relevant for this section is the integration of automated semantic content curation based on the principles described in Baets et al. (2019). While we have tested it in this particular course, there are multiple applications (see further). The "machine" can analyze any piece of text (an assignment given, a part of a group assignment made by someone else, a piece of text in a language that isn't yours, etc.) for the meaning of it. It is not the classical word search, where the exact words are searched for (classical Google search, prone to algorithmic manipulation), but this machine looks for concepts, meaning, understanding. It interprets the text and does not look for similarity. This machine has been developed specifically for automated content curation in this platform. In this version, it used free available content, that is, TedX and Wikipedia. Some student interviews speak for themselves (https://www.youtube.com/watch?v=oj5-nXNNavE&feature=youtu.be). The essentials of the feedback are:

- *The flexibility of the online platform truly enhances learning.*
- *The semantic engine is very exciting and helps us obtain quick and meaningful content.*
- *The methodology is very innovative, and all courses should include learning by doing.*
- *The platform is better than Brightspace (what is used as standard in that school), it is way more intuitive, and we had all the information we needed.*
- *We take responsibility for and get to cocreate meaningful learning experiences.*
- *The semantic idea is original and innovative; it was easy to use and adapted to the contents of the course, and the search site was better than Google.*

Figures 15.1, 15.2, and 15.3 are screen shots of the semantic machine in the platform. The first of the figures shows the input page. Participants can type or paste text into the square for semantic analysis. The outcome of the analysis is shown in the subsequent figure. In this case, some concepts are suggested that are the prevailing ones in the text. Some priority in those concepts is suggested (but can be overruled). If the participant accepts the priorities suggested or changes them, the machine is then going to curate the (public) content, in this case TedX and Wikipedia content. In the next figure, the Wikipedia-related content is already suggested. The participant can then either watch and/or read the

Semantic Engine

Semantics engine room   X

Salience: 0,01

Text to analyse

Analyse text   Reset all

Fig. 15.1 Input screen for the request or text to be analyzed

Fig. 15.2   The outcome of the machine in response to the request for analysis

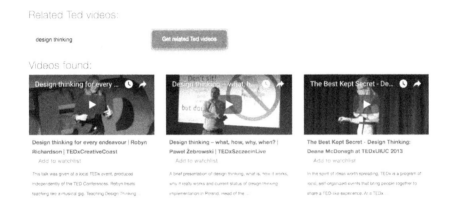

Fig. 15.3   Related TedX videos

suggested content or keep it in his or her private content library for possible later use or consultation. The subsequent figure shows the output of the machine in relation to the related TedX videos.

A final possible application is the use of this approach and platform for delivering an "affordable" (free?) education system in management and entrepreneurship for those who would never be able to follow a B-School (like in Africa and Asia, where the need is important). In a very cost-effective way, the platform could be offered free for all; those who want a certificate will have to pay a minimum fee and take part in a minimum test. From a PRME perspective, this technology would allow for affordable and meaningful basic business education where it matters.

15.7   Lessons Learned

Where principles one and two of PRME (what to teach and what to research) certainly have caused important revisions in many School's curricula since the inception of PRME 15 years ago, the third principle has received less attention but remains of paramount importance (if we want PRME to succeed). While currently available technology might suggest short and easy routes into the realization of PRME, the focus should not be on technology. Summarizing the lessons learned and suggesting a way forward, we adhere to following a design route with quick prototyping, testing, possibly failing and adapting. One can go fast but should certainly not jump into technology.

- The first step is to carefully consider the problem area: what are we doing it for? What is the eventual purpose, or do we just want to implement PRME? We need to understand the purpose of what schools do within the wider system (community, society, planet). That allows to define a vision.
- Next, we must decide what we would like to do. Are we interested in contributing impactful solutions to the world? Do we want to transform students and managers to act differently? Do we want to teach people and make material available for learning? While they are not completely exclusive, one cannot do everything.
- Now we are ready to think how to do things. We have suggested in this contribution to transform the concept of schooling into a concept of learning. We have suggested doing so on a wide scale, not only within the limits of a particular course or a degree. The approach that seems to work is based on learning by doing, open innovation, cocreation, collective intelligence, a curriculum from schooling to learning, based on personal transformation. This implies an impact on the pedagogical

model, and it would need courage and support to turn away from the school as a structure and focus on learning as a process.

- Once we know what we are doing and what we are doing it for, we can investigate ways to facilitate this, to make the student's experience more valuable and to reach markets that before could not be reached (emerging economies, rural areas, less privileged populations. Making supported learning available to people can be facilitated by an insightful combination of an electronic platform, digital resources (library), electronic brainstorm tools, virtual meeting facilities and semantics. The pace of learning can exponentially be improved if we are able to support the learner with content on demand, when needed, as needed on that moment, and rooted in many different disciplines. This kind of platform cannot be defined upfront but needs to be flexible and on demand. Semantic analysis seems to be the technology that can boost PRME-based learning.

References and Further Suggested Readings

Ackhoff, R. (1971). Toward a system of systems concepts. *Management Science, 17*(11), 661–671.

Avital, M., Mathiassen, L., & Schultze, U. (2017). Alternative genres in information systems research. *European Journal of Information Systems., 26*(3), 240–247.

Baets, W. (2017). *Une interpretation quantique de l'innovation*. Editions Universitaires Europeennes.

Baets, W. (2020). *Innovation through the lens of values*. Rotterdam University of Applied Sciences Publisher. www.hr.nl/openbareleswalterbaets.

Baets, W., Oldenboom, E., & Hosken, C. (2019, April 2). The potential of semantic analysis for business (education). Available at SSRN: https://ssrn.com/abstract=3364133

Baiyere, A. (2018). Fostering innovation ecosystems, Note on the 2017 ISPIM innovation forum. *Technovation, 69*, 1.

Brannen, M. (2004). When Mickey loses face: Recontextualization, semantic fit, and the semiotics of foreignness. *Academy of Management Review, 29*.

Carlsson, B., Jacobsson, S., Homen, M., & Rickne, A. (2002). Innovation systems: analytical and methodological issues. *Research Policy, 31*(2), 233–245.

Eriksson, D. (1997). A principle exposition of Jean Louis Le Moigne's systemic theory. *Cybernetics and Human Knowing, 4.*

Fillmore, C., & Baker, C. (2012). A frames approach to semantic analysis. In B. Heine & H. Narrog (Eds.), *The Oxford handbook of linguistic analysis.* Oxford Handbooks on Line.

Gomes, L., Facin, A., Salerno, M., & Ikenami, R. (2018). Unpacking the innovation ecosystem construct: evolution, gaps and trends. *Technological Forecasting Society Change, 136*, 30–48.

Grandstand, O., & Holgersson, M. (2020). Innovation ecosystems: a conceptual review and a new definition. *Technovation, 90–91*, 102098.

Hassan, N., Mingers, J., & Stahl, B. (2018). Philosophy and information systems: where we are and where we should go. *European Journal of Information Systems, 27*(3), 263–277.

Kurapati, V., & Mengchu, Z. (1999). *Modeling, simulation, and control of flexible manufacturing systems: A petri net approach.* World Scientific.

Lin, S. (2018). The structural characteristics of innovation ecosystems: a fashion case. *European Journal of Innovation Management, 21*(4), 620–635.

Mehta, D. (2019, April 8). *What attributes make an innovation ecosystem better and successful.* https://Yourstory.com.

Michael Page. (2016). The success factors for an innovation ecosystem. https://www.michaelpage.nl/advice/managementadvies/leiderschap/de-successfactors-voor-een-innovatie-ecosysteem

Millard, M. (2018, November 1). *What is an innovation ecosystem and how are they essential for startups?* MC, https://masschallenge.com.

Mingers, J., & Wilcocks, L. (2017). An integrative semiotic methodology for IS research. *Information and Organization, 27*(1), 17–36.

Myers, M., & Klein, H. (2011). A set of principles for conducting critical research in information systems. *MIS Quarterly, 35*(1), 17–36.

Oh, D., Phillips, F., Park, S., & Lee, E. (2016). Innovation ecosystems: a critical examination. *Technovision, 54*, 1–6.

Oswald, L., & Mick, D. (2006). The semiotics on meaning in the marketplace. In R. Belk (Ed.), *Handbook of qualitative research methods in marketing.* Edward Elger.

Ritala, P., & Almpanopoulou, A. (2017). In defense of 'eco' in innovation ecosystem. *Technovation, 60–61*(February), 39–42.

Rowe, F. (2018). Being critical is good, but better with philosophy: From digital transformation and values to the future of IS research. *European Journal of Information Systems., 27*(1), 1–14.

Seuillet E., & Lima, M. (2018, April 18). *7 Ways to develop innovative and living ecosystems*. https://medium.com.

Shaw, D., & Allen, T. (2018). *Natural ecosystems link*. Interconnection.

Smuts, J. (1926). *Holism and evolution*. MacMillan.

Stahl, B. (2014). Interpretive accounts and fairy tales: A critical polemic against the empiricist bias in interpretive IS research. *European Journal of Information Systems., 23*(1), 1–11.

Te'eni, D., Rowe, F., Agerfalk, P., & Lee, J. (2015). Publishing and getting published in EJIS: Marshaling contributions for a diversity of genres. *European Journal of Information Systems, 24*(6), 559–568.

Von Bertalanffy, L. (1968). *General systems theory*. George Braziler.

16

Pandemic, MOOCs, and Responsible Management Education

Sreerupa Sengupta and Divya Singhal

16.1   Introduction

The first reports of novel coronavirus (COVID-19) infection emerged from Wuhan city in Hubei Province, China, in December 2019. On March 11, 2020, the World Health Organization (WHO) declared the outbreak of novel coronavirus (COVID-19) disease caused by SARS-COV2 pandemic. This was not the first time that humanity faced a pandemic. In the last two decades, the world has witnessed several pandemics, such as SARS in 2002, Swine Flu in 2009, and Ebola in 2013. It may sound ironicity, but globalization, urbanization, environmental change, and greater mobility of people and animals have increased the potential for 'global transmission of epidemics' (Saunders-Hastings & Krewski, 2016). While the higher frequency of pandemics has contributed to an increase in human mortality and social apprehension, pandemics have

S. Sengupta • D. Singhal (✉)
Centre For Social Sensitivity and Action, Goa Institute of Management, Poriem, Sattari, Goa, India
e-mail: divyasinghal@gim.ac.in

© The Author(s), under exclusive license to Springer Nature Switzerland AG 2023
C. Hauser, W. Amann (eds.), *The Future of Responsible Management Education*,
Humanism in Business Series, https://doi.org/10.1007/978-3-031-15632-8_16

also led to transformational changes in environmental, societal, and health systems research (Hall et al., 2020). Therefore, pandemics have been disruptors but also our teachers. However, despite all the experiences of tackling the pandemic, the announcement of yet another pandemic in 2020 created chaos, uncertainty, ambiguity, and anxiety across the globe.

This pandemic has been referred to as a 'Black Swan Event' (Taleb, 2010), as it rapidly escalated from a health shock to a development crisis. The pandemic unleashed a systemic crisis that impacted societies and economies in unprecedented ways. Governments across the world have implemented a range of measures to contain the spread of the virus (ILO, 2020). Some of the major mitigation measures included lockdowns, mass screening and testing, restrictions on movement, bans on social gatherings, and physical distancing (Pokhrel & Chhetri, 2021). The purpose of these measures was to reduce interpersonal contact to minimize community transmission. Undoubtedly, the strategies helped save millions of lives but also came with a huge cost.

Undeniably, the pandemic was a catastrophe and caused major disruptions in many aspects of life. Education was definitely one area that was rocked by COVID-19 (Blankenberger & Williams, 2020). Overnight, the landscape of education changed drastically, and higher education was no exception. Universities worldwide had to close down their campuses to ensure the safety of their students, faculty, and support staff (Rashid & Yadav, 2020). According to the United Nations Educational, Scientific and Cultural Organization (UNESCO), education of over 220 billion students has been disrupted due to COVID-19 (UNESCO, 2021).

16.2   Online Learning: Panacea for Higher Education Institutions During the Pandemic

The acceleration of the pandemic necessitated a major shift in the pedagogy of higher education. Due to COVID-19, higher education institutions (HEIs) could no longer continue with their traditional mode of teaching and learning based on face-to-face interaction within the physical space of the classroom. To ensure undisrupted learning, the HEIs had to transform rapidly. Rashid and Yadav (2020) described how HEIs switched to online learning (with HEIs developing e-learning protocols) and embraced a virtual classroom as the new reality. Online learning and distance education are not new phenomena in many countries, yet the transition was not smooth for many HEIs. Owing to lack of experience, time, and human and financial resources, many institutions were not ready for such transformations; ultimately, all had to adjust to the process of increasing the digitalization of education (Schleicher, 2020). Several arguments are associated with online learning, including issues related to accessibility, affordability, learning pedagogy, and impact on the health of students, but during the crisis, online learning served as the panacea to ensure a safe and effective learning environment (Dhawan, 2020).

There is no singular definition of online learning.[1] Broadly, online learning refers to learning experienced through the internet where students interact with their instructors and other students from any location (Singh & Thurman, 2019). Online learning can be both synchronous and asynchronous. The exponential growth of technology over the years has made online learning extremely popular among students.

The pandemic can be given credit for changing perspectives toward online learning, establishing online learning as the main mode of regular learning in HEIs and thereby paving the way for the rapid digitization of the education sector.

16.3   MOOCs as a Tool for Online Learning

In the context of online learning, MOOCs or massive open online courses deserve special mention. MOOCs have played a vital role in popularizing online learning. MOOCs are defined as internet-based online environments that provide opportunities to students to learn online by

---

[1] The term online learning became popular in 1995 when a web-based learning system, WebCT, was developed as the Learning Management System, which later became Blackboard (Singh & Thurman, 2019).

using interactive tools such as videos, audio, discussion forums, and assignments (Kesim & Altınpulluk, 2015). According to Milman (2015), MOOCs are designed to support the 'Massive' participation of students, and 'Open' indicates that anyone can participate in these courses. Thus, MOOCs can be accessed by any one from anywhere (since MOOCs provide online learning), and the students do not need to be enrolled in or even affiliated with the sponsoring organization who is offering the MOOC. MOOCs are generally divided into two categories—cMOOCs based on connectivism (Downes, 2012) and xMOOCs—which follow the traditional behaviorist model (Kesim & Altınpulluk, 2015).

Canadian researchers George Siemens, Stephen Downes, and Dave Cormier created the first MOOC on 'connectivity and connected knowledge' in 2008 (Moe, 2015). This course was based on the theory of connectivity.[2] Although cMOOCs arrived early on the scene, the Stanford-based model of xMOOCs became more popular since their arrival in 2012. xMOOCs are based on the theory of behaviorism where content is specific and 'prepackaged', similar to the traditional in-class approach (Smith & Eng, 2013).[3] McLoughlin and Magnoni (2017) introduced a third category of MOOCs—a hybrid category—and named it Move-Me MOOCs. The hybrid category of MOOCs follows a linear structure and is divided into a number of sequential 'steps' (essentially follows the xMOOC model), but they also strongly support the development of digital and twenty-first-century skills (which, in turn, positions them within cMOOCs). In the last two decades, MOOCs, especially xMOOCs, have gained pre-eminence in the domain of higher education. MOOCs are now considered significant tools to enhance accessibility to higher education, reduce the inadequacies ingrained in our education systems (Hajdukiewicz & Pera, 2020), and achieve greater democratization of higher education (Dillahunt et al., 2014).

---

[2] The theory of connectivism states that each learner is responsible for their own learning and hence establishes their personal learning networks. cMOOCs denotes a similar personal learning environment, online—where the learners are free to determine their own learning goals.

[3] xMOOCs are basically systems in which the instructor provides video presentations to teach the course while each student follows their coursework at their own learning. The role of the faculty and the students is predefined like in a physical classroom and does not follow the essence of cocreation. Knowledge is imparted rather than cocreated. Some of the most well-known xMOOCs are sites such as Coursera, edX, Udacity, Udemy, and Khan Academy.

MOOCs were indeed novel, a decade ago. Today, MOOCs are a regular feature in many HEIs. Over the years, MOOCs have emerged as the most trustworthy tool for imparting broad and open access to knowledge in higher education. The rapid spread of the virus in 2020 provided fillip to the growth and popularity of MOOCs. In the absence of a physical classroom, MOOCs acquired center stage in the domain of higher education and are being hailed as having immense potential to solve the problems of accessibility to and availability of higher education.

16.4 Responsible Management Education: Journey from UNPRME to the Pandemic

Thus far, the chapter has discussed the transformations in the pedagogy of higher education ushered in by the pandemic. However, the content of higher education was not left unscathed. The scourge of the pandemic implored HEIs, especially business schools, to reflect on their interpretation of responsible management education. Discussions on Responsible Management Education have a long history. In the mid-2000 United Nations Global Compact, future managers played a crucial role in tackling sustainability-related challenges (Haertle et al., 2017). This realization by the United Nations led to the launch of the Principles for Responsible Management Education (PRME)[4] in 2007 with a mission to 'champion responsible management education, research and thought leadership globally' (Haertle et al., 2017; Sharma, 2017). Sharma (2017) observes that after a journey of over a decade, although PRME has firmly established its primacy in management education, challenges remain with regard to developing an appropriate curriculum for imparting management education on responsibility and sensibility. Notwithstanding challenges, PRME continues its journey and encourages all management schools to create a space in their curriculum to address issues related to sustainability, responsibility, diversity, inclusion, and human rights.

---

[4] The PRME initiative was launched by the UN Secretary General Ban Ki-moon in 2007 at the Global Compact Leaders Summit.

The discussions on responsibility were expanded with the declaration of the 17 Sustainable Development Goals (SDGs)[5] in 2015 by the United Nations. The motto of SDGs is to eradicate poverty, reduce all forms of inequalities, support economic growth, peace and justice, and tackle climate change by 2030. The achievement of this ambitious plan requires a multistakeholder approach and collaboration between various partners—and business leaders and managers can play a vital role. From 2015 onward, the focus of PRME was to create responsibility and sustainability mindsets among future managers for building inclusive and sustainable businesses and society. Business schools in both developed and developing countries have a wide reach through teaching, research and engagement. Thus, business/management schools, globally, emerged as prominent players empowering students and organizations to drive the agenda of sustainable development.

The current pandemic, once again, underscores the importance of discussions on responsibility and sustainability in management education. The world is currently trying to build a resilient future. This requires building individuals, organizations and societal resilience.[6] Managers, therefore, have to acquire the competency to address the ingrained grand challenges and systemic inequities of society and be able to act on them to avert the collapse of business and society during crises.

---

[5] Drawing on from the discussions in the United Nations Conference on Sustainable Development in 2012 (Rio +20) and building on the Millennium Development Goals (2000–2015), in 2015 the United Nations adopted the Agenda for Sustainable Development. The Agenda is underpinned by 17 Sustainable Development Goals (SDGs) and 169 targets. For details, refer to

https://council.science/wp-content/uploads/2017/05/SDGs-Guide-to-Interactions.pdf

[6] The American Psychological Association defines resilience as 'the process of adapting well in the face of adversity, trauma, tragedy, threats or even significant sources of stress'. There are various determinants of resilience such as biological, psychological, social, and cultural factors that interact with one another to determine how one responds to stressful experiences. Resilience can be seen a process which changes over time and as individuals interact with their environment (Southwick et al., 2014).

16.5 MOOCs: Key Player Toward Integrating Responsibility and Sustainability in Management Education

The launch of the PRME initiative led to the design of a plethora of courses, modules, programs on responsibility, empathy, sensitivity, business, and society. The proliferation of courses related to responsible management education was indeed a positive development. The development of such courses opened up new frontiers in management research. Such discussions also led to the creation of a forum for educators and facilitators of management programs to share experiences and deliberate on the framework and pedagogy for teaching responsibility to future managers. It was soon realized by the management institutes that to make future managers responsible, inculcate in them the values of empathy and sensitivity and to transform their mindset; a novel form of engagement is required.

MOOCs became the preferred tool for creating and sharing knowledge on social responsibility, inclusion, empathy and responsible management education. A study conducted by Zhan et al. (2015) identified the existence of fifty-one MOOCs dealing with issues of climate change, energy, ethics and sustainable development prior to the launch of SDGs. As discussed earlier, the UN Goals of Sustainable Development accelerated the pace of discussion on responsible management education. Since 2015, there has been a proliferation of MOOCs addressing responsibility and sustainability in management education.

The next section will discuss some of the most popular MOOCs offered on sustainability and responsible management after 2015. The aim of the section is twofold—(a) to illustrate the range of topics covered by MOOCs on sustainability and responsibility and (b) to highlight the varied players who are offering MOOCs. The authors have primarily chosen MOOCs on SDGs and responsible businesses that have had a higher subscription since the declaration of the Global Goals.

MOOCs Offered by HEIs on SDGs

The University of Michigan offers a Master Track Programme on the Coursera platform entitled 'Sustainability and Development'. The Master Track Programme is a six-course program. The program addresses sustainability and development challenges and provides actionable knowledge that empowers participants to develop solutions for the most pressing problems of the world.[7] The courses covered in this program are 'Beyond the Sustainable Development Goals' (SDGs); 'Addressing Sustainability and Development'; 'Methods/Skills in Sustainability and Development'; 'Pathways to Zero Hunger'; 'Good Health and Well-Being: Behaviors', 'Structures and Spillovers'; 'Gender and Quality Education for Sustainability'; 'Climate Change and Adaptation: Adaptive Development in a Changing World'; 'Conservation and Sustainable Development Conservation and Sustainable Development'; and Capstone Projects More than 13,000 participants have enrolled since 2015 in these courses.

Another popular course on SDGs (with special emphasis on SDG 13) is offered by the University of Copenhagen on Coursera. The course on 'Sustainable Development Goals—A global, transdisciplinary Vision for the Future' has enjoyed much popularity since its launch, post 2015. More than 59,000 participants benefited from this course. Similarly, a course designed by the Erasmus University Rotterdam on 'Driving business toward the Sustainable Development Goals' consists of seven units, each focusing on several aspects of sustainable development. This course received a 'MOOC Award of Excellence' by the Sustainable Development Solutions Network and the SDG Academy in September 2019. A course on 'Critical Development Perspectives' by the University of Queensland also received the 'MOOC Award of Excellence' in 2019 and focuses on what development is and how development can be achieved.

SDA Bocconi launched a course on 'Understanding and Seizing the Strategic Opportunity' after the announcement of SDGs. The course aimed to address the macroeconomic and microeconomic consequences

---

[7] To receive the Master Track program certificate, participants are required to complete six courses out of nine courses. The certificate is available only to learners who have paid for the program.

of climate change, poverty, hunger, gender, or race discriminations. The prime objective of the course was to highlight the role of businesses in tackling sustainability issues.

xMOOCs on SDGs and Responsible Management Education

In the last 6 years, there has been a commendable increase in xMOOCs related to corporate responsibility, sustainability, social responsibility, and ethics. For instance, the Edx platform offers several courses on ethics, social responsibility, sustainability and SDGs. Given the enhanced discussion on ethics, in recent years, the Edx platform has provided 176 courses related to ethics that range from ethics in bid data, bioethics, fintech and ethics, social responsibility and ethics. It is interesting to note that the global movement for the achievement of the 2030 Agenda has inspired Edx to push the boundaries of discussion and offer courses on inclusion, justice and human rights. The 'Justice' course on Edx explores the critical analysis of classical and contemporary theories of justice, including a discussion of the present-day application of theories of justice in making business inclusive and sustainable. The course, at present, has been subscribed by 467,468 participants. Pickard (2019) shared that Class Central, with the help of the SDG Academy, has identified a list of more than 100 courses on sustainable development that are offered by global universities, including Harvard, Oxford, Stanford, and MIT.

MOOCs Offered by the World Bank and UN Organizations

In the last few years, UN agencies have emerged as critical players in the landscape of MOOCs. Since 2015, there has been a gradual increase in the MOOCs developed by UN agencies. These MOOCs serve two purposes: (a) to raise awareness about sustainability, SDGs and the interdependence between the 17 goals of sustainable development and (b) to provide training with regard to the implementation of the SDGs at the ground level (Weybrecht, 2018).

World Bank Open Learning offers courses related to the environment, society, governance and economic sustainability. Since the outbreak of the pandemic in 2020, the platform has added many new courses largely focusing on health, inequalities, sustainable mobility, smart cities, climate action, and so on.

UNITAR offers various courses related to sustainable development goals that run throughout the year or several times in a year. These courses are free and open to the public. UNITAR courses are offered in six thematic areas—Peace, People, Planet, Prosperity, Multilateral Diplomacy and Accelerating SDG Implementation. UNICEF offers various open courses related to the interface between child rights and sustainable development through its free portal on Agora. The UN Women Training Centre offers MOOCs related to SDG 5 Gender equality and Women's Empowerment. Currently, 36 self-paced courses are offered on 'Women, Peace and Security', '2030 Agenda for Sustainable Development and Gender Equality', and 'Gender Equality in the World of Work'.

United Nations University (UNU) has also developed several MOOCs related to responsible management education. For instance, the UNU Land Restoration Training Programme (UNU-LRT) offers a unique course on 'Business Model Innovation for Sustainable Landscape Restoration'. This course addresses the challenges of large-scale landscape restoration with a partnership approach and reflects on the interconnections of nature, society, and economy in landscape management. Many of the courses offered by the UNU also target policy makers, and hence, a constant effort is made to introduce them to newer topics such as 'media, information and literacy' and 'gender and intersectionality'.

The SDG Academy is another platform that curates and offers free MOOCs and educational materials on sustainable development and the Sustainable Development Goals. These courses on the SDG Academy platform are taught by faculty from the United Nations, the World Bank, universities such as New York University, Harvard University, the University of Oxford, the Stockholm Resilience Centre, and other academic, government, and nonprofit institutions. The SDG Academy provides an opportunity to filter the courses by specific SDGs, as all courses are mapped with SDGs.

The One UN Climate Change Learning Partnership (UN CC:Learn) offers courses related to climate change action to help people, governments and businesses understand, adapt, and build resilience to climate change.

MOOCs: Facilitating and Expanding Discussions on RME During the Pandemic

Undeniably, the pandemic had been devastating, but it has also been a game changer in many ways. While many HEIs struggled to offer courses online, platforms such as Coursera and Edx announced free online learning during COVID-19 and provided free access to many of their courses, which are offered by their university partners. This resulted in 640% higher enrollment from mid-March 2020 to mid-April 2020 on the Coursera platform, and Udemy witnessed a 400% increase in the rate of enrollment (Impey, 2020). The pandemic exponentially increased enrollment in MOOCs. In short, MOOCs emerged as one of the most sought-after options to educate students and professionals about various aspects of disease control, risk communication, epidemiology, and the relationship between the environment and health. This sudden surge in the uptake of online courses motivated various stakeholders to offer new courses related to mental health and resilience. Figure 16.1 highlights the most followed topics on Class Central[8] (pre- and during the pandemic).

Rindlisbacher (2020), in a report that analyzed the 100 most popular courses of Class Central, pointed out that in 2020, between March 15 and May 15, there were approximately 11.7 million new enrollments during the pandemic. It is interesting to note that nearly 20% of those 11.7 million enrollments came from the course 'The Science of Well-Being' offered by Yale University. Discussions on well-being gained currency during the pandemic. Patra's (2020) compilation of the 100 Most Popular Free Online Courses of 2021 clearly shows that there has been a surge and greater uptake of the courses related to various aspects of the pandemic.

While COVID-19-related MOOCs ruled the charts, there was also interest in courses on critical thinking, mental health, and resilience. For instance, a course on 'critical thinking', offered by the AICTE and Shiv Nadar University on the Swayam platform in 2021, saw enrollment and was listed as the top 100 MOOCs of 2021. The University of Toronto launched a course on 'Mind Control: Managing Your Mental Health During COVID-19' on Coursera to help participants tackle the anxiety

---

[8] The Class Central is a search engine which reviews sites offering MOOCs.

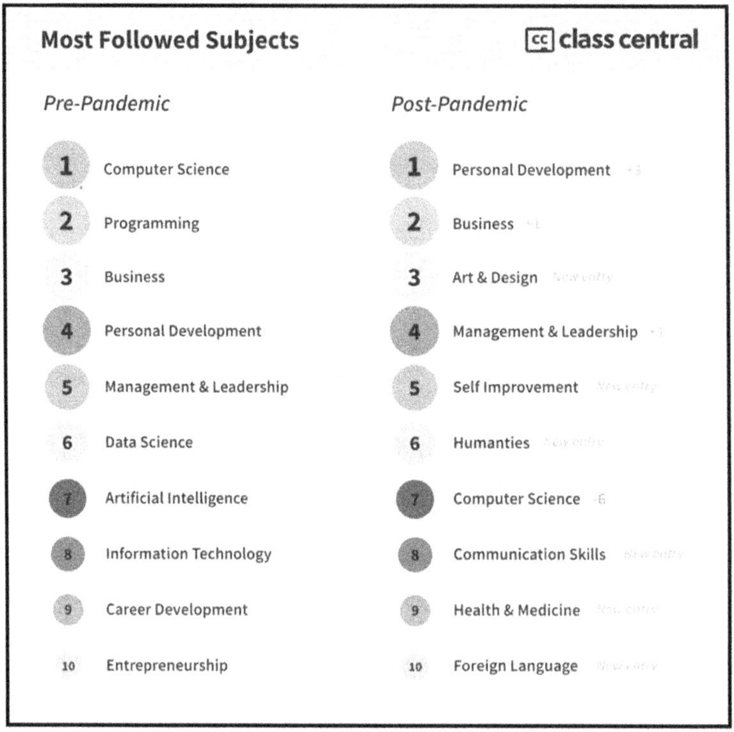

Fig. 16.1 Most followed topics on class central pre and during the pandemic. Source: Shah (2020)

related to COVID-19. University of Pennsylvania's course on 'Resilience Skills in a Time of Uncertainty' offered on Coursera intended to help students and professionals deal with uncertain times. The course shared strategies for practicing resilience, managing anxiety and increasing positive emotions such as gratitude. The course on 'Science Matters: Let us Talk About COVID-19' by Imperial College London at Coursera facilitated people to analyze COVID-19 better through the lens of public health, epidemiology, medicine, health economics, and social science. Another course on 'COVID-19: Psychological First Aid' offered by Public Health England was aimed at supporting people during emergencies and offering guidance on delivering psychosocial care in the immediate aftermath of the emergency event.

There were also new courses offered on diversity and inclusion. For example, the University of Glasgow offered a course on Coursera entitled 'Diversity and Inclusion in Education' with the aim of ensuring inclusive and equitable quality education and promoting lifelong learning opportunities for all.

16.6 Moving Ahead: New Framework

As countries recover from the pandemic, institutes of higher learning may open up face-to-face modes of teaching and learning, but online learning is here to stay. The world has realized the huge potential of online learning and has also witnessed the immense benefits of MOOCs. Business schools are often critiqued as being elitist, offering education to a certain social stratum and not reaching out to larger sections of society. MOOCs can solve this problem of HEIs and help them engage in responsible practices. MOOCs have surely emerged as a reliable, cost-effective way of imparting higher education to many students and can help extend the frontiers of higher education.

MOOCs have not only changed the landscape of teaching and learning but also significantly expanded the discussions on responsible management education and sustainable development. The increase in the enrollment of MOOCs on SDGs and responsibility is a clear indication that the world is gradually realizing the importance of addressing the three pillars of sustainability (social, economic, and environmental) in both business and society. The most important contribution of MOOCs has been to help future managers engage with discussions on sustainability, responsibility, and diversity at a more personal level—beyond the realms of the classroom.

As we move ahead, there is a need to rethink the framework of MOOCs on SDGs and responsible management education. We therefore propose a framework for MOOCs that is more inclusive in nature. MOOCs should represent voices, experiences, and expertise from both developed and developing countries. Currently, a large proportion of the content of MOOCs on SDGs and RMEs reflects the knowledge and experiences of the Global North. As countries respond to SDG 17, which reiterates forging global partnership for the realization of the goals of sustainable development, it is essential to make MOOCs more representative. The forces of globalization have changed the business landscape considerably. The pandemic has also brought out interdependence between developed and developing countries. Taking into account these realities, it is time that our future managers will be exposed to good practices from both developed and developing countries. MOOCs need to address these changed realities of business, society, and development and accordingly make a conscious effort to develop courses that incorporate management acumen as well as wisdom from developing countries. We need to nurture future managers who also become ambassadors for transnational corporations, and the new framework of MOOCs should address this need.

MOOCs should also incorporate the needs and wisdom of the community, which will help future managers be more sensitive to their environment and conduct their business with greater responsibility and empathy.

MOOCs have the power to make higher education a more inclusive space, and our focus should be to strategize for creating that environment.

References

Blankenberger, B., & Williams, A. M. (2020). COVID and the impact on higher education: The essential role of integrity and accountability. *Administrative Theory & Praxis, 42*, 404–423. https://doi.org/10.108 0/10841806.2020.1771907

COVID-19 courses curated by Coursera. (n.d.). Coursera. https://www.coursera.org/collections/covid-19

Dhawan, S. (2020). Online learning: A panacea in the time of COVID-19 crisis. *Journal of Educational Technology Systems, 49*(1), 5–22. https://doi.org/10.1177/0047239520934018

Dillahunt, T., Wang, Z., & Teasley, S. D. (2014). Democratizing higher education: Exploring MOOC use among those who cannot afford a formal education. *International Review of Research in Open and Distributed Learning, 15*(5), 177–196. https://doi.org/10.19173/irrodl.v15i5.1841

Downes, S. (2012, January 6). Creating the connectivist course. *Downes.* https://www.downes.ca/post/57750

George, G., Howard-Grenville, J., Joshi, A., & Tihanyi, L. (2016). Understanding and tackling societal grand challenges through management research. *Academy of Management Journal, 59*, 1880–1895. https://doi.org/10.5465/amj.2016.4007

Haertle, J., Parkes, C., Murray, A., & Hayes, R. (2017). PRME: Building a global movement on responsible management education. *The International Journal of Management Education, 15*(2), 66–72. https://doi.org/10.1016/j.ijme.2017.05.002

Hajdukiewicz, A., & Pera, B. (2020). Education for sustainable development—The case of massive open online courses. *Sustainability, 12*(20), 8542. MDPI AG. https://doi.org/10.3390/su12208542

Hall, C. M., Scott, D., & Gössling, S. (2020). Pandemics, transformations and tourism: be careful what you wish for. *Tourism Geographies, 22*(3), 577–598. https://doi.org/10.1080/14616688.2020.1759131

Impey, C. (2020, July 23). *Massive online open courses see exponential growth during COVID-19 pandemic.* The Conversation. https://theconversation.com/massive-online-open-courses-see-exponential-growth-during-covid-19-pandemic-141859

International Labor Organization (ILO). (2020). *An employer's Guide on working from home in response to the outbreak of COVID-19.* International Labor Organization. Retrieved from https://www.ilo.org/wcmsp5/groups/public/%2D%2D-ed_dialogue/%2D%2D-act_emp/documents/publication/wcms_745024.pdf

Kesim, M., & Altınpulluk, H. (2015). A theoretical analysis of MOOCs types from a perspective of learning theories. *Procedia-Social and Behavioral Sciences, 186*, 15–19. https://doi.org/10.1016/j.sbspro.2015.04.056

McLoughlin, L., & Magnoni, F. (2017). The Move-Me project: reflecting on xMOOC and cMOOC structure and pedagogical implementation. In Q. Kan & S. Bax (Eds.), *Beyond the language classroom: Researching MOOCs and other innovations* (pp. 59–69). Research-publishing.net. https://doi.org/10.14705/rpnet.2017.mooc2016.671

Milman, N. B. (2015). Distance education. In J. D. Wright (Ed.), *International encyclopedia of the social & behavioral sciences* (2nd ed., pp. 567–570). Elsevier. https://doi.org/10.1016/B978-0-08-097086-8.92001-4.

Moe, R. (2015). The brief & expansive history (and future) of the MOOC: Why two divergent models share the same name. *Current Issues in Emerging eLearning., 2*(1) https://scholarworks.umb.edu/ciee/vol2/iss1/2

Patra, S. (2020, November 30). The 100 most popular free online courses (2021 edition). *Class Central* https://www.classcentral.com/report/100-most-popular-online-courses-2021/

Pickard, L. (2019, September 3). 100+ free online courses to learn about the UN's Sustainable Development Goals. *Class Central.* https://www.classcentral.com/report/united-nations-sdg-courses/

Pokhrel, S., & Chhetri, R. (2021). A literature review on impact of COVID-19 pandemic on teaching and learning. *Higher Education for the Future, 8*(1), 133–141. https://doi.org/10.1177/2347631120983481

Rashid, S., & Yadav, S. S. (2020). Impact of Covid-19 pandemic on higher education and research. *Indian Journal of Human Development, 14*(2), 340–343. https://doi.org/10.1177/0973703020946700

Rindlisbacher, E. (2020, July 29). The 100 most popular courses during the pandemic. *Class Central.* https://www.classcentral.com/report/coronavirus-most-popular-courses/

Saunders-Hastings, P. R., & Krewski, D. (2016). Reviewing the history of pandemic influenza: Understanding patterns of emergence and transmission. *Pathogens (Basel, Switzerland), 5*(4), 66. https://doi.org/10.3390/pathogens5040066

Schleicher, A. (2020). *Impact of COVID-19 on education: Insights from education at a glance 2020.* OECD. Retrieved from https://www.oecd.org/education/the-impact-of-covid-19-on-education-insights-education-at-a-glance-2020.pdf

Shah, D. (2020, December 14). The second year of the MOOC: A review of MOOC stats and trends in 2020. *Class Central.* https://www.classcentral.com/report/the-second-year-of-the-mooc/

Sharma, R. R. (2017). A competency model for management education for sustainability. *Vision, 21*(2), 10–15. https://doi.org/10.1177/0972262917700970

Singh, V., & Thurman, A. (2019). How many ways can we define online learning? A systematic literature review of definitions of online learning (1988-2018). *American Journal of Distance Education, 33*(4), 289–306. https://doi.org/10.1080/08923647.2019.1663082

Smith, B., & Eng, M. (2013). MOOCs: A learning journey. In S. K. S. Cheung, J. Fong, W. Fong, F. L. Wang, & L. F. Kwok (Eds.), *Hybrid learning and con-*

tinuing education (ICHL 2013. Lecture notes in computer science) (Vol. 8038, pp. 244–255). Springer. https://doi.org/10.1007/978-3-642-39750-9_23

Southwick, S. M., Bonanno, G. A., Masten, A. S., Panter-Brick, C., & Yehuda, R. (2014). Resilience definitions, theory, and challenges: interdisciplinary perspectives. *European Journal of Psychotraumatology, 5*(1), 25338. https://doi.org/10.3402/ejpt.v5.25338

Taleb, N. (2010). *The black swan: The impact of the highly improbable* (2nd ed.). Penguin Book.

UNESCO. (2021). COVID-19: Reopening and reimagining universities survey on higher education through the UNESCO national commissions. https://unesdoc.unesco.org/ark:/48223/pf0000378174

Weybrecht, G. (2018, September 3). An overview of MOOCs offered by United Nations Agencies. *The PRME Blog.* https://primetime.unprme.org/2018/09/03/an-overview-of-moocs-offered-by-united-nations-agencies-part-1-of-3/

Zhan, Z., Fong, P., Mei, H., Chang, X., Liang, T., & Ma, Z. (2015). Sustainability education in massive open online courses: A content analysis approach. *Sustainability, 7*(3), 2274–2300. MDPI AG. Retrieved from https://doi.org/10.3390/su7032274

17

Transforming Academic Journal Assessment from "Quality" to "Impact": A Case Study of the SDG Impact Intensity Academic Journal Rating Artificial Intelligence System

David Steingard and Simon Linacre

17.1 Unpacking Academic Evaluative Assessments

Two large questions with fluctuating and elusive answers endure when assessing academic research[1]:

[1] This publication and research effort are made possible through the financial support of the Johnson & Johnson Foundation, the Haub School of Business at Saint Joseph's University, and Cabells. We especially thank Cabells for their full support and extensive collaboration on the development and deployment of this research. We gratefully acknowledge the faculty and staff of the Haub School SDG Dashboard Team for their innovative and invaluable contributions.

D. Steingard (✉)
Haub School of Business, Saint Joseph's University,
Philadelphia, PA, USA
e-mail: steingar@sju.edu

© The Author(s), under exclusive license to Springer Nature Switzerland AG 2023   **317**
C. Hauser, W. Amann (eds.), *The Future of Responsible Management Education*,
Humanism in Business Series, https://doi.org/10.1007/978-3-031-15632-8_17

What normative standards are employed to determine if academic research is valuable in terms of supporting the Common Good and environmental sustainability?
What explicit methodological rationales, unstated assumptions, and cultural forces determine the definition of value?

To address these questions, let us first examine the dominant conception of evaluating academic research loosely amalgamated in "good quality research" or "high quality research" (Joireman & Van Lange, 2015). One of the challenges with defining quality research is the sheer number of variations on the theme and the enduring dominance of existing perspectives. In the main, these perspectives offer a myopic and detached definition of quality, oftentimes irrelevant to advancing the larger movement of responsible management education to inspire positive social and environmental change. However, the promise of digital transformation as a tool to unseat tacit assumptions of academic cultural norms is very encouraging. We trust that our offering in this book chapter makes a direct contribution to this vital movement.

There are three overarching characteristics of existing conceptions of quality research that can ground our discussion of these questions. First, quality research should make a differentiating and additive contribution to existing knowledge, echoing Newton's famous adage: "If I have seen further it is by standing *on the shoulders of Giants*" (Chen, 2003: 135). Second, it should reflect communal standards of principle and method. Academic research is particularly focused on objectively expressing arguments, ideas, and solutions based on theoretical and empirical analyses that are not subjective opinions or cultural constructions. Third, while motivations for producing research vary, it is reasonable to assume that the production of research is intended to make some type of positive difference in its utilization. It is not just to stand on the shoulders of giants, but to leverage that elevated vantage point to offer some novel

S. Linacre
Digital Science, London, UK

innovations to make a meaningful contribution to society—to inspire and deliver *impact*.

For the purposes of our chapter, we will define impact as the degree to which research *demonstrably advances ethical and sustainable outcomes for humanity and the Earth through its dissemination, adoption, and outcomes.* We argue that this tripartite codification of research impact is not fully supported by conventional notions of quality. Why? First, the enormous proliferation of academic research (Bhattacharya & Kaul, 2015; Collyer, 2018; Delfanti, 2021; Gui et al., 2019; To & Yu, 2020) is not necessarily commensurate with an increase in quality. In fact, it is plausible to conjecture that the upswell of academic output is more a function of the need for academics to "publish or perish" (De Rond & Miller, 2005; Garfield, 1996) than the necessity of generating research that has an impact. Second, the emergence of a purported gold standard of impact in a variety of "impact factors" has defaulted into an exclusively quantitative and normatively bereft evaluation system of the type of impact we are outlining here. Impact, as mediated by bibliometric impact factors (Aksnes et al., 2019; Glänzel & Moed, 2002; Saha et al., 2003), devolves to a false sense of a comparable numeral metric that determines impact based on quantity of citations and not on the content, let alone real-world impacts, of those cited articles (Amin & Mabe, 2003; Bloch & Walter, 2001; Seglen, 1997a, 1997b).

Similarly, traditional and social media metrics deployed as proxies for impact, for example, the Altmetric Attention Score (Collyer, 2018), can be problematic and misleading (Bornmann et al., 2019; Davis, 2021; Sugimoto, 2020; Thelwall, 2020a, 2020b; Trueger et al., 2015; Xu, 2018). However, at least one study finds a "reasonable proxy" relationship between Altmetric scores and societal impact evaluated subjectively by a "panel of experts" (Wooldridge & King, 2019: p. 271). Third, academic impact determinations are significantly, albeit subjectively, influenced by academic and publishing cultures. Editorial boards and publishers are at best, principled stewards, at worst, indiscriminate gatekeepers, of what determines research impact. Likewise, academic elites and powerful publishers offer a barrage of ratings, rankings, and awards to acknowledge impact research (Locke & Spender, 2011). These assessments come with serious, problematic considerations. They are products of human communities that may or may not thoughtfully apply objective standards of impact to their assessments. A potpourri of biases (Cudd & Morris, 1988; Drieschová, 2020; Dunn, 2005) in academic publishing has been identified: gender bias (Cislak et al., 2018; Easterly & Ricard 2011); whiteness bias (Bates & Ng, 2021); elitist bias (Aarssen & Lortie, 2009; Ball, 2006; Zhang, 2021); first-language bias (Politzer-Ahles et al., 2016); and institutional affiliation bias (Reingewertz & Lutmar, 2018).

Praxis Model of Academic Evaluative Assessments

The preceding literature review established that quality research, as it is currently evaluated, can have varying degrees of impact. In offering our definition of *impact—the degree to which research demonstrably advances ethical and sustainable outcomes for humanity and the Earth through its capture, dissemination and adoption—*we submit a model for rethinking academic quality in terms of impact assessment (see Fig. 17.1). This model offers a framework to more comprehensively and systematically configure how academic research may be evaluated for impact. The operating foundation of the model is the construct of praxis: "the process of using a theory or something...learned in a practical way" (Cambridge Dictionary, 2021). The point or telos of praxis is to inspire "action oriented toward changing society" (McLellan, 1969, p. 10).

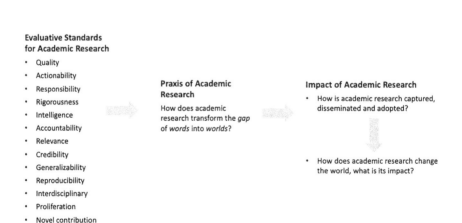

Evaluative Standards for Academic Research

- Quality
- Actionability
- Responsibility
- Rigorousness
- Intelligence
- Accountability
- Relevance
- Credibility
- Generalizability
- Reproducibility
- Interdisciplinary
- Proliferation
- Novel contribution

Praxis of Academic Research

How does academic research transform the *gap* of *words* into *worlds*?

Impact of Academic Research

- How is academic research captured, disseminated and adopted?

- How does academic research change the world, what is its impact?

Fig. 17.1 Praxis model for impact of academic research

Thus, the model aims to provide a conception of the process by which the written word of academic research has a material impact on the world: "the gap between theory and praxis, text and world" (Oxford University, 2021). A multiplicity of evaluative standards exists for academic research, as reflected in the incomplete list in the model. Given compliance (to varying degrees) with these standards, academic research is ultimately focused on its "words" influencing "worlds"—the praxis of academic research. The impact section of the model is a normative interrogation of the praxis: Does research, through its capture, dissemination, and adoption—turn "words" into "worlds" that are somehow *better* (and how is better construed and demonstrated) than if the research never existed?

Impact Evaluation in Business Schools

The model outlined above has been applied to business education and research for the pilot phase in the broader research project this chapter introduces. Business schools occupy a privileged position in higher education in some ways. They often bring diverse and substantial revenue streams into higher education institutions (HEIs) housing them and have a degree of autonomy, alongside law and medicine, that other subject disciplines do not enjoy. However, with this position also comes a degree of scrutiny, especially in regard to accreditation. Accreditation bodies such as AACSB, EFMD, and AMBA provide independent evaluations of business schools' operations to accredit them as meeting certain standards, which are in turn used by business schools to market themselves to the business school student market. With a vibrant research sector and industry looking ahead to how they can operate within a carbon neutral society that promotes human flourishing and equality, business education offers a rich opportunity to test impact assessment methodologies and metrics.

The business school accreditation bodies themselves have taken a progressive approach to impact engagement. In 2013, the AACSB updated its standards to include impact as one of the criteria it used to evaluate business schools, which was further enhanced in 2020 with one of its nine standards now focused on "societal impact" (AACSB, 2020). This position has been strengthened in marketing communications from various bodies.

In February 2021, AACSB published the article "Encouraging Business Scholars to Address Societal Impact" in its in-house online magazine (Berry et al., 2021), which suggested six lessons from history on how business schools can pivot their focus toward societal impact. Similarly, in the EFMD's in-house magazine Global Focus (EFMD, n.d.), there have been numerous articles highlighting the shift toward sustainability and adoption of the United Nations 17 Sustainable Development Goals or SDGs (United Nations, n.d.-b). These include utilizing the increased focus on sustainability in a business context (Aprea & Edinger-Schons, 2021), addressing a perceived existential crisis for business schools in how they first declare impact as part of their core mission, and then identifying what that mission entails (Kalika & Shenton, 2019).

Aligned to the shift in business school education toward impact, a number of actors have sought to cross the perceived divide between sustainability issues and the profit orientation of industry. Organizations such as the United Nations Principles for Responsible Management Education (PRME, n.d.) have reached out to business education to promote positive transformation, whereas the Responsible Research in Business & Management group (RRBM, n.d.) represents progressive academics who seek to move their colleagues and institutions toward global goals such as the UN SDGs. In the middle, there are also organizations such as Canadian Corporate Knights, which has created an MBA ranking that helps prospective students identify the greenest destination for their postgraduate business education (Corporate Knights, 2021). As we will see in the next section, this shift toward impact and sustainability in business education has been mirrored across higher education more broadly. Business schools offer an ideal proving ground for attempting to measure the intensity of impact that can be derived through academic research.

17.2   Global Academic Publishing's Paradigm Shift on Impact

In this section, we discuss the tectonic paradigm shift in academia and academic publishing—the quest for impact. Impact has become a catch-all mantra and evaluative objective: How does a piece of academic research get captured, disseminated, and adopted outside of academia and how is that empirically metricized? The simple notion of impact has been twisted and stretched over the years, not least because the first and main use of the word has been with the "Impact Factor." The brainchild of Eugene Garfield, this metric proposes that by counting citations from a journal article appearing in other journals, the relative impact of a journal could be determined. The more citations of an article, by extension, the better the journal (Garfield, 1955). Thus, citation counting indices feed "top" journal categorizations. However, as Singh et al. (2007) implore, such schemes bury meritorious individual journal articles not found in "top" journal lists to deleteriously "abdicate this responsibility [of assessing individual journal articles] by using journal ranking as a proxy for quality" (p. 319).

This proxy for quality existed almost unchallenged for decades until other similar measures, most notably from Scopus (n.d.), and the development of the H-Index metric (Hirsch, 2005) in the 2000s challenged the impact factor's primacy. However, the problem with the impact factor and other citation-based metrics is that while providing a convenient metric to judge articles and journals, they cannot tell the whole story in regard to impact. For example, an article in a journal might be cited frequently and the other articles published that year not at all, yet the impact factor looks at the overall output. In addition, one article might be cited as an example of terrible research, but the assumption is that all citations contribute to a positive evaluation—quantity without qualification, a "tyranny of metrics" (Muller, 2019). Numerous scholars have identified these and other problems with the impact factor formulation (Seglen, 1997a, 1997b). Recently, the San Francisco Declaration on Research Assessment (DORA) was set up to encourage academia to move away from using such metrics as the sole decision-making factor when judging quality and the impact of research (DORA, 2021). This is not to say that the impact factor and other citation-based metrics do not have a role in assessing the quality of research outputs, as they are capable of identifying and promoting quality in research—just not the *only* role in the process.

In the last several decades, impact, generally speaking (University of Illinois, n.d.), has become the paramount criterion for determining the overall quality, value, and goodness of academic outputs for at least three reasons. First, the proliferation of research and research outlets simply necessitates some type of mechanism to navigate the relevance of vast numbers of academic publications. Fewer publications and outlets in the past obviated the need for comprehensive approaches to quality assessment; what was available was, by default, largely considered good. Of course, a smaller set of outlets meant exclusion and elitism; clearly, the increase in publications has increased the diversity and access of academic publishing and consumption. However, like the explosion of broadcast channels in traditional television, the mushrooming of different networks, media, cables, internet, and so on provides an almost infinite variety and choices that cannot be sampled or evaluated thoughtfully. A process of determining goodness was needed: the advent of the move to impact metrics.

Second, funding for academic research is often tied to conditions regarding the wider impact of the research that is being supported. This can exist in different ways and has led to the broadening out of what impact means (see Bornmann, 2013 for a literature review of societal impact of research). Traditionally, both external funds and internal university support have required publication in top-ranked journals as a basis for supplying funding. More recently, they have mandated that research outputs be made available as open access articles or that research has a demonstrable impact in a specific community. In the UK, a large portion of government funding for research is distributed to universities through the Research Excellence Framework (REF) every 6 years or so. In the last round, which concluded in 2021, submissions were requested from each university department in the shape of a case study that summarized the most impactful research it had carried out in terms of its effect beyond academia, which in turn determines 25% of the total research funding awarded over the next cycle (REF, n.d.). The definition used by the REF is "...impact is defined as an effect on, change or benefit to the economy, society, culture, public policy or services, health, the environment or quality of life, beyond academia" (REF, 2020, p. 68; see also Ravenscroft et al., 2017)—transforming *words* into better *worlds*.

Third, the emergence of AI and big data analytics is a timely solution to the growth of academic publishing. It is now a manageable undertaking to take millions of articles, books, and other academic outputs and assign an almost unlimited number of metrics to evaluate their perfor-mance. Our subsequent case study offered in this chapter reflects an application of this movement to use AI and big data analytics to ascertain metrics of value for academic publications and outlets. For publishers, proxy metrics such as the impact factor were advantageous in identifying quality journals, and they in turn acted as value indicators for commer-cial publishers selling subscriptions to their journals to university librar-ies. Simply put, the higher the quality indicator, the greater the demand from researchers to access the content, and therefore, the higher the price publishers could place on their journal collections. As such, it was also in the interests of publishers—particularly the larger publishers with more higher ranked journals—to support citation-based metrics as they could drive up the commercial value of their product offerings.

Chiefly among these metrics, and as we will argue ominously over-shadowing other metrics, is the almost singular focus on *quantitative assessments of citation counting* as the normative benchmark, a proxy for an academic publication's worthiness. Thus, a simple calculus has emerged to adjudicate the value of an academic publication: *the more it is cited, the better it must be.*

From "Citation Intensity" to "Impact Intensity"

We call this construction of impact *citation intensity.* However, this unas-suming correlation between the frequency of citations and impact is highly problematic as a false proxy for impact. In the next section, we detail our concerns and offer a more encompassing and justifiable charac-terization of impact—moving from *citation intensity* to *impact intensity.* Citation-based metrics have been used as a proxy for quality for many years, and the existence of a convenient metric has led to a "tail wagging the dog" situation where funding, recruitment, tenure and decision-mak-ing in higher education have been driven by the pursuit of higher citation counts. However, this has occurred with very little attention to the impact of the research outside the impact on the metric itself moving higher or lower. This poses serious questions for our understanding of what the value of research is in the first place.

An example illuminating this problem is provided by former business school dean Roger Martin in his 2012 article *The Price of Actionability*

(Martin, 2012). He estimates business schools spent US\$600m funding academics to undertake and publish "nonactionable" research published in so-called "A-rated" journals represented by Financial Times' 45 journals (Financial Times, 2016, then used for its FT Research rankings, later expanded to 50 journals). While the calculations may lack sophistication, the point is clear: business schools were ignoring research that could be actioned by business itself to improve outcomes in the pursuit of theoretical purity and valorization through publication. This scenario was perpetuated by citation-based metrics and by being mirrored through the numerous business school and university rankings that developed through the late twentieth century and early twenty-first century, which have used these very same metrics. The result is a self-fulfilling prophecy where business schools push academics to publish in the same journals. This in turn reflects the same business schools in their authorship, producing a hegemony of institutions that has remained constant for decades, marginalizing others.

Our central thesis of the chapter revolves around a shift from traditional notions of quality to more beneficial norms of impact. If we define research impact as *research that demonstrably advances ethical and sustainable outcomes for humanity and the Earth through its dissemination, adoption, and outcomes*, it is clear that to the extent publications are measured toward an overall evaluation of impact, measuring purely citations can only be a small part of the solution. A much larger part can be gleaned by understanding the extent to which journal publications have engaged with the global challenges of our time. Hence, it is our contention that moving from citation intensity toward impact intensity will provide a much better tool for business schools, businesses, governments, academia and funders alike to assess the contributions journal publications make to real-world issues. However, it is important at this stage to underline that this should never be the whole solution as we have seen before but one key weapon in the armory for a fuller, more holistic understanding of how impactful research is determined.

This proposed shift from a focus on "citation intensity" to "impact intensity" is unassailably a necessary evolution. However, a further cautionary note is in order. Our earlier discussion of the praxis model for the impact of academic research (Fig. 2.1) forewarns that demonstrating the *words* of academic publications into *transformations in the world* is indeed daunting. How impact-intense scholarship is disseminated and adopted is still somewhat of a mysterious process for most academic research that is either not widely read and falls shy of substantive integration in government, business, civil society, and so on. However, in principle and by evidence, it is not inconceivable to cite specific examples of academic research "words" changing "worlds." Perhaps the most relevant contemporary example surrounds research that supports the understanding, treatment, vaccines, and prevention of the global pandemic fueled by the pernicious COVID-19 virus. For a different social science example, the advent of stakeholder theory pioneered by Ed Freeman (2010/1984) has incontrovertibly influenced the theory, practice, and outcomes of modern-day global corporate behavior and capitalism itself.

Moving Toward a Normative Model of Impact with the SDGs in Academic Publishing

We now turn to a discussion of how SDGs are emerging as a normative framework to understand impact intensity in academic publishing. We chose our analysis of SDG-intense evaluation in academic publishing because of an upswell of activity in this sector. Since ratification by 193 countries in 2015, academic interest in publishing about the SDGs continues to increase (Elsevier, n.d.; Linacre, 2021a, 2021b; Nakamura et al., 2019; Schemm, 2020). Evidence for this claim is provided by examining the sheer number of search engines and publisher portals that allow academic researchers to query academic research content through the lens of the SDGs.

A review of these SDG gateways produces a number of open source and commercial resources to query academic content and research vis-à-vis the SDGs: Digital Science & Research Solutions (n.d.); Elsevier (n.d.); Emerald Insights (n.d.); Emerald Publishing (n.d.-a); Linacre (2021b); RELX plc (n.d.); Rotterdam School of Management (n.d.); RRBM,[2] (n.d.); ScienceOpen (n.d.); Springer Nature (n.d.); Taylor &

---

[2] "UN SDG related issues for management" is a subgateway of the more encompassing Responsible Management Gateway.

Francis (n.d.). Additionally, as an important recent development through the United Nations, the SDG Publishers Compact now serves as an official signatory organization "designed to inspire action among publishers...to accelerate progress toward the Sustainable Development Goals (SDGs) by 2030" (United Nations, n.d.-c).

17.3   Artificial Intelligence as the Engine for Evaluating Research Impact

Centrality of Textual Analysis of AI

In keeping with the "words" in the "worlds" praxis model, this section contends that textual analysis—the fundamental epistemological ground of research—with AI and big data analytics is now the primary driver of determining impact. In reviewing methodological statements pertaining to the aforementioned publishing industry SDG-focused portals, search engines, classification schemes, and so on, it is apparent that all of these approaches are powered by some combination of human and machine (AI) intelligences (e.g., Elsevier, n.d.). Analyzing, cataloging, and adjudicating the "big data" of academic research is a formidable task that can only be handled effectively by AI. Fortunately, there is an emerging movement to purposefully align AI techniques with socially and environmentally positive outcomes, as well as a specific focus on SDGs. This movement will be detailed in the following section to provide context for our subsequent case study.

AI, Social Good, and the SDGs

As foreground to our case and its application, let us contextualize how socially and environmentally positive contributions are now embraced as popular domains to apply AI analytics and solutions to world problems. Broadly, the connection between AI and positive impact can be encapsulated into the emerging field of AI for "social good" or AI4SG (Floridi et al., 2020; see also AAAI, n.d.; AI and Society, 2021; AISOC, 2017;

Fig. 17.2 The 17 United Nations Sustainable Development Goals (SDGs) (United Nations, n.d.-b)

Chui et al., 2019; Gomes et al., 2019; Google AI, n.d.; Purdy, 2020; Tomašev et al., 2020). For the focus of our case study, we apply the 17 United Nations Sustainable Development Goals or SDGs (United Nations, n.d.-a; see Fig. 17.2) and accompanying Agenda 2030 (United Nations, n.d.-b) to the AI subfield of AI and the SDGs (Cowls et al., 2021; Di Vaio et al., 2020; Ensemble, 2021; Goralski and Tan, 2020; Hager et al., 2017; Kriebitz and Lütge, 2020: 85; Tsamados et al., 2021: 12; Vinuesa et al., 2020):

> Specifically, the aim is to understand whether this branch of computer science can influence production and consumption patterns to achieve sustainable resource management according to Sustainable Development Goals (SDGs) outlined in the UN 2030 Agenda. (Vinuesa et al., 2020, p. 7)

The SDGs comprise an ambitious and exigent plan to address some of the world's most vexing social and environmental issues. The SDGs reflect a morally normative framework based on human rights and sustainability that provides a roadmap for humanity and a methodological bulwark for our AI case study.

17.4   Case Study of SDG Impact Intensity Academic Journal Ratings

In this section, we look at a specific empirical case study of AI applied to the assessment of SDGs. In this example, we will apply AI to the particular domain of academic journal evaluation in terms of a move from "quality" to "impact" discussed previously. The objective here is to establish a model and algorithm that can make determinations about impact instead of quality assessments derived exclusively by counting citations. We have argued that conventional methods for assessing academic journal quality are fraught with subjectivity, institutional elitism, inconsistent rigor of applying standards, data deficits, and populistic biases. While these condemnations may appear harsh, the main issue at hand is the *lack of objective ethical and scientific standards* that underlie adjudications of impact. To avoid a similar fate for impact assessments, a more rationalized, transparent, reproducible, and predictive system of impact evaluation needs to be established. Our following case study will hopefully further open up the dialog about what such a system might resemble. We are inspired by Andrew Jack, publisher of the FT50 rankings (Jack, 2021):

> ...identify new metrics and weightings to reflect growing calls for change including a greater focus on sustainability and responsible business education. (p. 1)

Hypothesis

For background, this case study originates from the collaboration between Cabells (n.d.) and Saint Joseph's University on their SDG academic journal rating system entitled SDG Impact Intensity (Linacre, 2021; Steingard et al., 2022). The intent of SDG impact intensity is to generate an alternative journal evaluation system that departs from conventional notions of quality and assesses social and environmental impact. The SDGs are employed as a proxy for positive impact, although other normative frameworks could be utilized. A foundational assumption is made that conventionally defined quality journals and impact journals are disjunctive; we propose that quality journals, in the main, do not reflect standards of impact. Of course, if a quality journal does not uphold impact criteria, this does not mean its embodiment of quality criteria is somehow faulty. A journal may indeed be considered high quality by a given process (although that process might be flawed, as we have discussed), but this estimation of quality usually does not consider impact.

To test the viability of our SDG impact intensity system as a differentiated rating system focused on impact rather than quality, we first need to establish a data set containing substantive and consistent ratings across both quality and impact. The FT50 (Financial Times, 2016) is arguably the most well-known rating system of standard conceptions of quality for business and management journals and is not without critique (Christensen Hughes, 2020; Jack, 2021; Pontille & Torny, 2010). Thus, applying our SDG impact intensity system to the FT50 should generally rate the FT50 low on impact, as the FT50 is, in principle, not oriented explicitly toward impact. However, demonstrating that the FT50 journals are low in impact presents an incomplete picture. What does it mean for a journal to have a high impact rating? To address this question, we have complemented the FT50 journals with 50 business and management journals[3] that we predict will be highly rated with SDG Impact Intensity—the SDG50. To be clear, the SDG50 is not a ranking of the top SDG impact journals, but just a data set that will be rated for the sake of testing our hypothesis and experiment in this case study. In effect, we have used our expert knowledge to establish a theoretical "ground truth" (Guidotti, 2021) for what type of journals embody impact. Figure 17.3 provides a framework for hypothesis testing that will be elucidated in subsequent sections.

---

[3] Some of these journals would not be categorically considered business and management journals by traditional standards. However, these business-related journals are necessary to include because of the diversity and scope of the SDGs—achieving the SDGs is an interdisciplinary undertaking, so business scholars should and do frequently publish scholarship in these nontraditional journals. Outside the scope of this chapter, this move to be more inclusive of what even "counts" as a business- and management-related journal is also part of a paradigmatic upheaval of how we conceive of "proper" business and management research and journals.

Fig. 17.3 SDG Impact intensity predictive hypothesis test for FT50 and SDG50

Methodology

In keeping with the "words into worlds" praxis focus on textual-based analysis using AI algorithmic techniques, a baseline set of keywords is employed to assess the SDG content of the FT50 and SDG50. One thousand ninety-five SDG-related keywords from two different keyword banks (RELX, n.-d.; SDSN Australia, New Zealand & Pacific, 2021) provide the linguistic environment in which the SDGs come alive. Magnitudes of the presence or absence of these words in academic journals indicate varying degrees of alignment or misalignment with the impact outlined by the SDGs. The data itself for both the FT50 and SDG50 were drawn from the title and abstracts from all journal issues from 2016 to 2020 for a total of 13,600,000 words processed by the SDG impact intensity algorithm. The results are divided into four categories. The weighted algorithm produces an overall—across all 17 SDG composite ratings—in addition to the top three SDGs most often treated in the journals. A 0–5 SDG wheel rating is assigned for overall impact. Essentially, the SDG impact intensity technique provides a measure of SDG-related content contained in academic journals by analyzing SDG keyword content for frequency and concentrations.

17.5 Results

Tables 17.1, 17.2, 17.3, and 17.4 convey the results produced by applying the SDG impact intensity algorithm to the FT50 (in pink) and SDG50 (in green). Figure 17.4 summarizes the results. The results suggest very strong support for our hypothesis. Outcome measures generated by SDG impact intensity produce the anticipated bifurcation of the

Table 17.1 First quartile SDG Impact Intensity ratings for FT50 and SDG50

	Journal name	SDG Impact Intensity 5 Wheel Rating
1	Natural Resources Forum	5
2	Environment, Development and Sustainability	5
3	Globalization and Health	5
4	Smart and Sustainable Built Environment	5
5	International Journal of Sustainable Development and World Ecology	5
6	Gender in Management	5
7	The International Journal of Environmental Sustainability	4
8	The International Journal of Sustainability Policy and Practice	4
9	International Journal of Environment & Sustainable Development	4
10	Agronomy for Sustainable Development	4
11	International Journal of Water Resources Development	4
12	International Journal of Agricultural Sustainability	4
13	Current Opinion in Environmental Sustainability	4
14	Sustainability Science	4
15	Journal of Hunger & Environmental Nutrition	4
16	Sustainable Development	4
17	The Journal of Sustainability Education	4
18	Sustainability	4
19	Food Policy	4
20	Hydrology and Earth System Sciences	4
21	Journal of Renewable Energy	4
22	Sustainability: Science, Practice, & Policy	4
23	Journal of Sustainable Tourism	4
24	World Journal of Entrepreneurship, Management and Sustainable Development	4
25	International Journal of Sustainable Energy	4

Table 17.2 Second quartile SDG Impact Intensity ratings for FT50 and SDG50

Journal name	SDG Impact Intensity 5 Wheel Rating
26 Natural Resources Journal	4
27 Nature Sustainability	4
28 Sustainability Accounting, Management and Policy Journal	4
29 The International Journal of Social Sustainability in Economic, Social, and Cultural Context	4
30 Agroecology and Sustainable Food Systems	4
31 Landscape and Urban Planning	4
32 African Journal of Economic and Sustainable Development	4
33 Journal of Sustainable Finance & Investment	3
34 Business, Strategy and the Environment	3
35 Journal of Agricultural and Environmental Ethics	3
36 Sustainability: The Journal of Record	3
37 Environmental Progress & Sustainable Energy	3
38 International Food & Agribusiness Management Review	3
39 Environment: Science and Policy for Sustainable Development	2
40 Journal of Environmental Law	2
41 Organization & Environment	2
42 Research Policy	2
43 Process Safety and Environmental Protection	2
44 Ethics, Policy & Environment	2
45 Corporate Governance: The International Journal of Business & Society	2
46 Corporate Governance	2
47 Journal of Strategic Innovation and Sustainability	2
48 Business & Society	1
49 Social and Environmental Accountability Journal	1
50 Management Information Systems Quarterly	1

FT50 and SDG50 journal sets in terms of rating scores. Underlying FT50 standards of quality did not translate into any appreciable impact ratings. Our handpicked SDG50 journals scored consistently high and confirmed these choices for inclusion as high-scoring SDG impact intensity journals.

Additionally, each journal's preprocessed data are augmented by a word cloud (Heimerl et al., 2014; Kulevicz et al., 2020) that, through

Table 17.3 Third quartile SDG Impact Intensity ratings for FT50 and SDG50

Journal name	SDG Impact Intensity 5 Wheel Rating
51 Quarterly Journal of Economics	1
52 Journal of Business Ethics	1
53 Human Relations	1
54 Environmental Ethics	1
55 Administrative Science Quarterly	1
56 Review of Finance	1
57 Business Ethics, the Environment, and Responsibility	1
58 Information Systems Research	1
59 Manufacturing & Service Operations Management	1
60 Journal of International Business Studies	1
61 Strategic Entrepreneurship Journal	1
62 Journal of Applied Psychology	1
63 The Review of Economic Studies	1
64 Organization Science	1
65 Journal of Management	1
66 Human Resource Management	1
67 Journal of Business Venturing	1
68 Journal of Political Economy	1
69 American Economic Review	1
70 Entrepreneurship Theory and Practice	1
71 MIT Sloan Management Review	1
72 Academy of Management Journal	1
73 Accounting, Organizations and Society	1
74 Journal of Operations Management	1
75 Production and Operations Management	1

triangulation, offers more evidence to confirm or disconfirm the SDG impact intensity output. Figures 4.3 and 4.4 are two representative word cloud outputs from the top and bottom of the 100 combined journals. Clearly, the type of language vis-à-vis the SDGs is more intensely reflected in Figs. 17.5 and 17.6.

For the dissemination of the SDG impact intensity journal ratings, the numerical data will be converted to a 5 SDG wheel system and shared widely (Linacre, 2021d). It will also appear in individual records on the Cabells Journalytics subscription service (Cabells, n.d.) and is available as Open Access in a filterable table (Saint Joseph's University, n.d.).

Table 17.4 Fourth quartile SDG Impact Intensity ratings for FT50 and SDG50

	Journal name	SDG Impact Intensity 5 Wheel Rating
76	Journal of Management Studies	1
77	Journal of Management Information Systems	1
78	Organization Studies	1
79	Journal of Consumer Research	1
80	Strategic Management Journal	1
81	Harvard Business Review	1
82	Journal of the Academy of Marketing Science	1
83	Journal of Consumer Psychology	1
84	Econometrica	0
85	Journal of Marketing	0
86	Journal of Marketing Research	0
87	Management Science	0
88	Organizational Behavior and Human Decision Processes	0
89	Journal of Finance	0
90	Academy of Management Review	0
91	The Journal of Financial Economics	0
92	Contemporary Accounting Research	0
93	Review of Accounting Studies	0
94	Marketing Science	0
95	Journal of Financial & Quantitative Analysis	0
96	The Accounting Review	0
97	Journal of Accounting and Economics	0
98	Operations Research	0
99	Journal of Accounting Research	0
100	The Review of Financial Studies	0

Figure 17.7 is a partial snapshot of the published SDG impact intensity ratings.

The Future of SDG Impact in Business Schools

In light of the findings outlined in this chapter, perhaps the key question is for business schools and how they can facilitate a pivot toward a more SDG-focused research agenda for impact. As the performance of the FT50 journals by sustainability journals shows, any institution that seeks to identify the quality of research through publications in the FT50 may

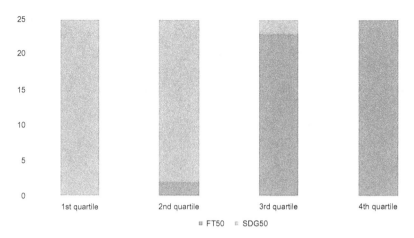

Fig. 17.4 Summary quartile SDG Impact Intensity ratings for FT50 and SDG50

Fig. 17.5 World cloud analysis from top-rated journal

be missing impact aspects related to the SDG agenda. Business schools are, of course, already aware that perceptions are changing, with traditional rankings such as those provided by the FT and US World & News

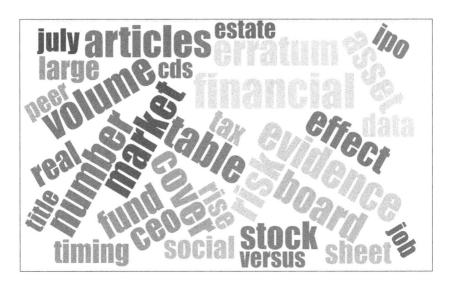

Fig. 17.6 World cloud analysis from lowest-rated journal

Report being joined by those championing engagement with sustainability and environmental concerns. As Linacre reports (Linacre, 2021e), business school students are looking at sustainability as a primary driver of their interest in a business school program in the UK, with SDG rankings now available from Times Higher Education (2021) and QS (n.d.) on universities and their sustainability credentials.

In addition to the developments in business school rankings and the findings of the research presented in this chapter, there are other forces at play in the business school firmament that either have an impact on their operations with regard to the SDGs or may well have in the near future. Accreditation bodies such as AACSB have changed their standards (AACSB, n.d.) and used their communications platforms to encourage members to follow an impact-focused agenda (Bisoux, 2019). Other approaches to ratings are emerging. Students joined the call with the first student-led SDG rating for business schools, the Positive Impact Rating (PIR, n.d.; see Rodenburg et al., 2021 for a helpful review), and publishers have also started following a mission-driven agenda to highlight the value of published research focused on SDG progress (Elsevier, n.d.). Given that business schools—like industry itself—are already facing huge

SUSTAINABLE
DEVELOPMENT
GOALS

SDG-Impact Journal Rating

Comparing the sustainability impact of the 50 journals used by the Financial Times to compile its FT Research rankings to Journalytics journals publishing in focused areas of sustainability

The Sustainable Development Goals (shown below) are the blueprint to achieve a better and more sustainable future for all. We've collected SDG data on the following 100 journals listed in Cabells Journalytics—including the 50 used by the Financial Times (FT) in compiling their FT Research rank and 50 publishing in the general area of sustainability. The SDG Impact Intensity ratings are calculated using AI-based textual analysis.

Title	SDG Impact Intensity™	Top SDG Goals	Publisher
Natural Resources Forum			Wiley-Blackwell Publishing
Environment, Development and Sustainability			Springer Nature
Globalization and Health			BioMed Central
Smart and Sustainable Built Environment			Emerald Group Publishing Limited
International Journal of Sustainable Development and World Ecology			Taylor & Francis, Ltd.
Gender in Management			Emerald Group Publishing Limited
International Journal of Environmental Sustainability, The			Common Ground Research Networks
International Journal of Sustainability Policy and Practice, The			Common Ground Research Networks
International Journal of Environment & Sustainable Development			Inderscience Publishers
Agronomy for Sustainable Development			Springer Nature
International Journal of Water Resources Development			Taylor & Francis, Ltd.
International Journal of Agricultural Sustainability			Taylor & Francis, Ltd.

Full list of individual goals referenced above

Fig. 17.7 Sample published ratings of SDG Impact Intensity for Cabells Journalytics (full ratings available here: SDGImpactIntensity)

uncertainty around their direction in relation to climate change and its impacts, many deans will feel stuck between the rock of tried-and-tested rankings and journal lists and the hard, yet transformative place of SDGs and sustainability-focused research. We hope that our research offers a clear way forward for business school and industry leaders alike to shift to impact in this chapter.

17.6   Future Research Directions and Challenges

In conclusion, we would like to offer two types of commentary. First, based on the research findings presented, we will suggest specific methodological innovations necessary to evolve the assessment and achievement of impact in academic publishing. Second, we will discuss the larger context of academic whole-system change (Arnold, 2016) in which our work is ensconced. Both types of commentary will be interwoven into the three sections below.

At this stage, however, we also need to state the research limitations of our study. First, a baseline for impact that can be agreed upon by most people is still elusive at best. Our contention—moving from "citation intensity" to "impact intensity" embodying a shift from quality to impact—can be regarded as a step in the right direction. However, this does not fully address the "words into worlds" progression we adopt as our proxy for intensity, as it essentially measures the textual concurrence of words and themes of the SDGs. As our results convincingly demonstrate, we are able to identify journal articles that address the SDGs. Perhaps this can be seen as the first stage of impact, with a second stage of impact actually identifying transformative "worlds." The UK's REF (n.d.) may be one such higher level example of impact assessment, although it too has several political and logistical issues to consider.

Second, it is important to acknowledge some basic methodological limitations of our case study. Although we are confident of the results, which concur with subject matter expertise predictions, this is a small-scale study that could evolve from continuing enhancements. Primarily, artificial intelligence algorithms can always benefit from fine-tuning, which is one of their key benefits. Therefore, some journals may improve or worsen if new data were fed into the system or if tweaks were made to the algorithm. In addition, the algorithm can be benchmarked against other techniques for determining SDG relevance in text-based analysis. Ideally, other researchers could access journal data, develop a new algorithm to produce ratings, and then compare the results. Currently, the project teams from Cabells and Saint Joseph's University are in discussions with academic and professional networks to pursue collaboration on this standardizing exercise. Finally, the data set for the case study consists of 100 journals—the analysis could be scaled across more journals and includes much more data. Presently, our teams are producing another 150 journal ratings to more deeply understand the nuances and variations in the ratings. Ultimately, there is a plan to undertake a much more sizable project by rating 3000 business- and business-related journals. At this scale, our algorithm should reveal in bold relief any distortions, coding errors, and methodological incongruence that could bias or invalidate ratings.

Third, following earlier comments on the necessity of a cultural shift in academia, specific attention needs to be focused on the systems-level change necessary to support such a fundamental shift from quality to impact, as we have outlined in this chapter—a shift that could perhaps threaten the status quo. While developing new approaches, standards, and tools to assess academic outputs for impact is critical, these efforts will fade into the margins if academic culture and academic publishing do not embrace and champion them. In particular, proponents of change in research and publishing behaviors have to be mindful of the larger picture affecting universities, publishing companies and research sponsors. For example: Will the funding be there to push forward SDG-intensive research? Will commercial publishers see value in publishing SDG-intensive research articles? Will universities recognize SDG-intensive research and support related programs? What key cultural shifts in the wider academic-commercial publishing ecosystem are critical to shifting focus to SDG-intensive research?

Counting vs. Impact: Transforming the Underlying Assumptions of What Makes "Quality" Academic Research

At perhaps the risk of oversimplification, one of the fundamental obstacles to reinventing assessment of quality research toward impact is an unspoken assumption that quality academic output—that output valued by academic culture—is valuable because it is cited and read most often. Aggregating citation indices such as the impact factor[4] (Garfield, 2006) and h-index (Hirsch, 2007) dominates contemporary academic culture, particularly as tools of adjudication for academic articles and journal quality. While such a purely quantitative evaluation of quality is most definitely necessary[5] while considering the positive social and environmental impacts of research, it is both incomplete and oftentimes dangerously misleading. Referencing our praxis model, simply having more eyes on "words" does not guarantee that these words will generate better "worlds." As we have outlined in this chapter, academic output that makes a meaningful difference needs standards and metrics that directly reflect constructs of impact. Merely counting citations (Singh & Chow, 2007) and social media hits (as a proxy for impact is methodologically indefensible and distracts from the shift to "real impact") (Emerald Publishing, n.d.-b):

> We refer to impact as the provable effects of research in the real world. It is not judged by traditional methods—such as citations—simply appraised by factors we can see and feel in wider society.

Moreover, frequently referenced articles may not only misrepresent impact but may also foster negative impacts. For example, it is frightfully too frequent that key articles influencing an entire discipline can be due to shoddy or nonreproducible results or outright fraud.[6] While academic culture is by and large capable of detecting weak or fully flawed academic outputs, and the preceding example may be an extreme example of how

---

[4] An important note disentangling differing ideas of impact. For Garfield and the impact factor phenomena that followed, impact is construed on the basis of quantitative counting of citations. The type of impact discussed in this chapter considers social and environmental impact, constructed from a different qualitative, normative set of operating principles sourced from the SDGs.

[5] Crawford (2020, p. 496) provides a helpful distinction of how adding considerations of impact is not "supplanting" traditional metrics, but "supplementing" them.

[6] Retraction Watch (https://retractionwatch.com) provides a curated and constantly updated collection of retractions and some ethics-related academic publishing violations.

outliers sneak through, it is not implausible to consider the current myopia on quantitative assessment of quality is eclipsing other considerations of impact. Herein lies the fundamental challenge for transforming quality to impact—the question of introducing *alternative impact metrics to augment quantitative standards of quality.*

Clearly, efforts such as SDG impact intensity and other more *qualitative, content-focused* schemas abruptly disrupt a singular focus on counting—introducing a qualitative dimension centered around impact is demonstrable evolution. However, even an interrogation of academic output content for impact-related words does not guarantee that those words will ultimately be consumed and reproduced in an influential manner that creates real change on pressing social and environmental issues. Effectively, academic content is an input for humanity to utilize, hopefully in the service of better outcomes for people and planet. This leap in understanding the pathway of "words" into "worlds" is perhaps the most pressing issue facing the academic-commercial publishing ecosystem today.

Our efforts in this chapter, aligning an impact-based assessment with the SDGs as a normative ethical framework for prescribing effective social and environmental impact, are a step in this direction. We are not unique in this approach, which is very encouraging. Recently, there have been a few key and concerted collaborative efforts to imagine and implement academic output quality parameters grounded in the SDGs. Mainly, the SDG Publishers Compact Fellows (https://www.sdgcompactfellows.org/, United Nations, n.d.-a), a United Nations sponsored signatory organization for the world's academic publishers, is making substantive progress toward infusing the SDGs into academic outputs. The United Nations Higher Education Sustainability Initiative (HESI, n.d.) has commissioned a rankings, ratings, and assessment working group where SDGs influence their recommendations for change. The Financial Times 50 (Financial Times, 2016) utilized in our research recently held a "Slow Hackathon on Rankings and Ratings in Business Schools" (Hinchliffe, 2021). The objective was to communally and critically reflect on the basic philosophical, methodological, and cultural assumptions that form the shibboleth of quality today, calling for "for fresh methods, metrics, and standards" (Jack, 2021). Finally, this paradigm shift of SDGs into academia is encouragingly heralded by the THE

Impact Ratings (Times Higher Education, 2021), which is gathering attention and legitimacy as a ranking of universities specifically oriented toward societal impact and environmental sustainability via the SDGs.

Quality and Impact as Cultural Productions of Academia: Challenges and Opportunities to Shift Norms

Targeting new standards and metrics for evaluating quality is central to the overall agenda of increasing the relevance of research for social and environmental impact. However, this more technical and bibliometric approach should be considered in the larger context of academia, as Fredric Jameson would construe as "cultural production" circumscribed in a larger "political economy" (Roberts, 2000). Because the value belying academic outputs is essentially a collective human cultural production and a sizable subsector of the global political economy, it is advisable to consider how academic culture establishes and maintains norms of quality and how it might evolve to embrace a more expansive definition of impact. The makeup of academic culture, the relevant stakeholders, might include these primary actors: publishers, academic institutions, research funders, academics, accrediting bodies, media, editors, professional societies, NGOs, and government. These actors interact to reproduce cultural expectations and, more importantly, have access to the levers of power that could inspire transformational and demonstrative change.

Everette Rogers' diffusion of innovation theory (García-Avilés, 2020) is an instructive framework to understand the cultural dynamics at play with respect to shifting academia from quality to impact. According to Rogers, innovativeness—in our case at hand, the move to impact—is divided into five adopter categories: innovators, early adopters, early majority, late majority, and laggards. Perhaps an even greater challenge than debating the veracity and methodological soundness of new metrics for impact is that the colossal shift required by academic culture is to intentionally move the impact revolution through Rogers' categories, perhaps captured most accurately as a "wicked problem" (Lönngren & Van Poeck, 2021). Clearly, enabling systems-level change in academic culture to empower more innovators is as daunting as it is exigent. Developing new metrics for impact, such as what we have proposed in this chapter with SDG impact intensity, may just be the proverbial tip of the iceberg. It may just be the massive academic cultural edifice under the surface that is the most effective lever for the type of whole-system change a pivot to impact demands.

Many Paths Up the Mountain of Impact: Pluralism or Singularism?
Based on the preceding discussion, it is reasonable to assert that a meaningful shift from narrow notions of quality to expanded horizons of impact in academic outputs is attainable. Focusing academic output evaluations of quality more on impact than counting, especially supported by an innovative shift in academic culture, is certainly conceivable. Crawford (2020) aptly identifies this shift in quality from "internal, peer review with narrow criteria of quality" to "socially accountable and reflexive—incorporates a diverse range of interests and uses a wide range of criteria in judging quality" (p. 496). However, a fundamental question remains unaddressed: Will there be one or several new standards adopted by academia to adjudicate impact? In our experience with SDG impact intensity, we have encountered a number of viable approaches to reformulate quality estimations into impact; not all of them are theorized and enacted from the SDGs as the benchmark of impact. In fact, there is a healthy heterogeneity of approaches being developed and implemented. Metaphorically speaking, there are "many paths up the mountain" of the transformation to impact.

However, a pluralism of approaches may be problematic, even when considering a particular approach to impact assessment such as the SDGs:

> Other assessments focused on the SDGs rely heavily on subjective, qualitative judgments by students and faculty. They are limited by reference to their own experiences and institutions, without an external benchmark. (Wilfred Mijnhardt quoted in Jack, 2020)

A plethora of subjective, idiosyncratic, and perhaps regionally and culturally influenced offerings of impact can suffer from being too limited in their scope, applicability, and power—simply not generalizable at scale. To illustrate this point by way of analogy, in pharmaceuticals, for the most part, universal standards exist about efficacy and safety. Similarly, in accounting, particularly public accounting, an agreed upon set of rules and guidelines conforms corporate reporting to comparable proforma.

Therefore, variegated approaches to impact assessment are less likely to galvanize a collective commitment to shift academic culture to impact. Furthermore, multiple approaches to impact developed in isolation miss the opportunity for multistakeholder input and collaborative research to improve them. In addition, a pluralism of impact approaches naturally engender competition and exclusion, which is very counterproductive to working together synergistically to improve the effectiveness of impact capturing assessments.

Paradoxically, a singular, perhaps even monolithic, "one right way" to assess impact can stultify innovation, silence needed voices, and ultimately deliver a universally acceptable platform that misses the mark on capturing impact. In the particular case of SDG impact intensity and related SDG bibliometric schemes and tools, there is a variety of differentiation. To attempt to resolve this challenging question, we propose that differing approaches to assessing a new version of academic quality that features impact could be collaboratively developed into what might be considered an international standard like those proffered by the International Standards Organization (www.iso.org). As a pertinent example, the ISO has promulgated Standard ISO 26000 as guidance for corporations interested in aligning themselves with "social responsibility" (ISO, 2021). However, even a concerted effort to elevate a singular standard in this well-developed field is not so simple; other worthy, competitive standards exist (e.g., SASB, www.sasb.org and GRI, globalreporting. org). Nonetheless, it is not that much of a stretch to conceive of a similar standard, or handful of standards, for academic outputs desiring to support positive social and environmental impact. More discussion and debate is warranted before choosing an admixture of pluralism and/or singularism as the way forward for the transformation to impact; there are possibilities and pitfalls with each.

Thus, we may consider two different tiers of impact for academic research. First is the shift of *academic content* reflective of social and environmental benefit; akin to the shift from "citation intensity" to "impact intensity." Second is the notion of how impact-intense research is actually incorporated into the policy, actions, practices, cultures, and so on of the world to make a tangible difference in advancing human and planetary conditions. This second notion of impact is worthy of a thorough inquiry of its own and outside the scope of this book chapter. This is not to say the first tier analysis predominates in this paper is problematic. There is still a great deal of work to be done in moving the needle from academic research subject matter aligned with conventional notions of impact (primarily, frequency of citations and other ungrounded notions of quality). Moreover, an outright dismissal of most academic research "words" not informing and changing "worlds" would be indefensible; academic research certainly is of real consequence, positively or negatively, and not an empty exercise or act of faith.

Digitally Transforming Responsible Management Education
Our chapter addresses the transformation from quality to impact, grounded in our case study of the SDG impact intensity rating system. We aimed to provide insight into how academic journal ratings powered by digital technologies can be rethought and redeployed in the context of the call to action, enlivening this book: "Responsible management education and the digital transformation challenge." We offer that digital transformation solutions such as SDG impact intensity will accelerate the proliferation, relevance, and impact of academic research supporting responsible management education for a better world. Digital technologies provide previously impossible opportunities to categorize and democratize the prolific global output of research. A new narrative on research, inspired by the insights provided by cutting-edge digital technologies, is now possible; one narrative reframes the basic purpose of research and reorients it to serve important real-world ends. Responsible management education can harness this new narrative, powering its world-leading role in reinventing management education and the practice of business for the better. We trust our chapter helps advance this urgent conversation about rethinking the fundamental issues surrounding the evaluation of academic published outputs—ultimately, for the Common Good and sustainability of the Earth.

17.7 Conflict of Interest

Marketing Director at Cabells from August 2018 to February 2022.

References

AAAI. (n.d.). *AI for Social Good*. AAAI 2017 Spring Symposia Registration. https://aaai.org/Symposia/Spring/sss17symposia.php#ss01

AACSB. (2020). *AACSB Business Accreditation Standards Comparison—2020 & 2013*. https://www.aacsb.edu/-/media/aacsb/docs/accreditation/business/standards-and-tables/2020%20proposed%20standards%20comparison%20chart.ashx?la=en&hash=EE49DA4ED72B3574F47465EA9AB2C5651E21724D

AACSB. (n.d.). Business standards. https://www.aacsb.edu/accreditation/standards/business

Aarssen, L. W., & Lortie, C. J. (2009). Ending elitism in peer-review publication. *Ideas in Ecology and Evolution, 2*, 18–20.

AI & Society. *(2021). Special issue on AI for People (with sponsored Best Paper Award)*. Springer. https://www.springer.com/journal/146/updates/18583616?error=cookies_not_supported&error=cookies_not_supported&code=b97d39db-75a5-4f36-aa87-1cf3f6cdae1e&code=44415b01-7edf-4834-9a3b-3ef34bbf2ed1

AISOC. (2017). *AI for social good (AISOC)*. University of Southern California. http://scf.usc.edu/%7Eamulyaya/AISOC17/index.html

Aksnes, D. W., Langfeldt, L., & Wouters, P. (2019). Citations, citation indicators, and research quality: An overview of basic concepts and theories. *Sage Open, 9*(1), 2158244019829575.

Amin, M., & Mabe, M. A. (2003). Impact factors: use and abuse. *Medicina (Buenos Aires), 63*(4), 347–354.

Aprea, C., & Edinger-Schons, L. M. (2021, June 10). *Sustainability games*. GlobalFocus. https://www.globalfocusmagazine.com/sustainability-games/

Arnold, M. (2016). *Systemic structural constellations and sustainability in academia: A new method for sustainable higher education*. Routledge.

Ball, P. (2006). Prestige is factored into journal ratings. *Nature, 439*(7078), 770–772.

Bates, K. A., & Ng, E. S. (2021). Whiteness in academia, time to listen, and moving beyond White fragility. *Equality, Diversity and Inclusion: An International Journal, 40*(1), 1–7. https://doi.org/10.1108/edi-02-2021-300

Berry, L. L., Reibstein, D. J., Wijen, F., Wassenhove, L., Voss, C., Gustafsson, A., Vereecke, A., & Bolton, R. (2021, February 9). *Encouraging business scholars to address societal impact | AACSB*. https://www.aacsb.edu/insights/2021/february/encouraging-business-scholars-to-address-societal-impact

Bhattacharya, S., & Kaul, A. (2015). Emerging countries assertion in the global publication landscape of science: A case study of India. *Scientometrics, 103*(2), 387–411.

Bisoux, T. (2019). A new era for business research. *BizEd—AACSB International.* https://bized.aacsb.edu/articles/2019/November/a-new-era-for-business-research

Bloch, S., & Walter, G. (2001). The impact factor: Time for change. *Australian & New Zealand Journal of Psychiatry, 35*(5), 563–568. https://doi.org/10.1080/0004867010060502

Bornmann, L. (2013). What is societal impact of research and how can it be assessed? A literature survey. *Journal of the American Society for Information Science and Technology, 64*(2), 217–233.

Bornmann, L., Haunschild, R., & Adams, J. (2019). Do altmetrics assess societal impact in a comparable way to case studies? An empirical test of the convergent validity of altmetrics based on data from the UK research excellence framework (REF). *Journal of Informetrics, 13*(1), 325–340.

Cabells. (n.d.). *Journalytics.* http://www2.cabells.com/journalytics

Cambridge Dictionary. (2021, August 25). *Praxis definition.* University of Cambridge. https://dictionary.cambridge.org/dictionary/english/praxis

Chen, C. (2003). On the shoulders of giants. In *Mapping scientific frontiers: The quest for knowledge visualization.* Springer. https://doi.org/10.1007/978-1-4471-0051-5_5

Christensen Hughes, J. (2020, April). *The future of business schools rankings & ratings—Davos 2020 Report.* Oikos. https://issuu.com/oikos-world/docs/davosrecapreport2020

Chui, M., Harrysson, M., Manyika, J., Roberts, R., Chung, R., Nel, P., & van Heteren, A. (2019, November 20). *Applying artificial intelligence for social good.* McKinsey & Company. https://www.mckinsey.com/featured-insights/artificial-intelligence/applying-artificial-intelligence-for-social-good#

Cislak, A., Formanowicz, M., & Saguy, T. (2018). Bias against research on gender bias. *Scientometrics, 115*(1), 189–200. https://doi.org/10.1007/s11192-018-2667-0

Collyer, F. M. (2018). Global patterns in the publishing of academic knowledge: Global North, Global South. *Current Sociology, 66*(1), 56–73.

Corporate Knights. (2021). *Better World MBA Ranking (2021).* Corporate Knights. https://www.corporateknights.com/reports/better-world/

Cowls, J., Tsamados, A., Taddeo, M., & Floridi, L. (2021). A definition, benchmark and database of AI for social good initiatives. *Nature Machine Intelligence, 3*(2), 111–115. https://doi.org/10.1038/s42256-021-00296-0

Crawford, A. (2020). Societal impact as 'rituals of verification' and the co-production of knowledge. *The British Journal of Criminology, 60*(3), 493–518.

Cudd, M., & Morris, J. (1988). Bias in journal ratings. *Financial Review, 23*(1), 117–125.

Davis, P. (2021, August 25). *Unpacking The Altmetric black box*. The Scholarly Kitchen. https://scholarlykitchen.sspnet.org/2021/08/24/unpacking-the-altmetric-black-box/

Delfanti, A. (2021). The financial market of ideas: A theory of academic social media. *Social Studies of Science, 51*(2), 259–276.

De Rond, M., & Miller, A. N. (2005). Publish or perish: Bane or boon of academic life? *Journal of Management Inquiry, 14*(4), 321–329.

Digital Science & Research Solutions. (n.d.). *Dimensions AI*. Dimensions AI. https://app.dimensions.ai/discover/publication

Di Vaio, A., Palladino, R., Hassan, R., & Escobar, O. (2020). Artificial intelligence and business models in the sustainable development goals perspective: A systematic literature review. *Journal of Business Research, 121*(December), 283–314. https://doi.org/10.1016/j.jbusres.2020.08.019

DORA. (2021, August 23). The Declaration on Research Assessment (DORA). https://sfdora.org/

Drieschová, A. (2020). Failure, persistence, luck and bias in academic publishing. *New Perspectives, 28*(2), 145–149. https://doi.org/10.1177/2336825X20911792

Dunn, Jr., R. (2005). The age bias in academic publishing. *Challenge, 48*(5), 5–11.

Easterly, D. M., & Ricard, C. S. (2011). Conscious efforts to end unconscious bias: Why women leave academic research. *Journal of Research Administration, 42*(1), 61–73.

EFMD. (n.d.). Global focus—The EFMD business magazine. https://www.globalfocusmagazine.com/sustainable-future/

Elsevier. (n.d.). SciVal—UN Sustainable Development Goals. https://scival.com/sdg

Emerald Insights. (n.d.). *Concise Guides to the United Nations Sustainable Development Goals*. https://www.emerald.com/insight/publication/acronym/SDG

Emerald Publishing. (n.d.-a). Our goals. https://www.emeraldgrouppublishing.com/our-goals

Emerald Publishing. (n.d.-b). Real impact awards. https://www.emeraldgrouppublishing.com/about/our-awards/real-impact-awards

Ensemble, G. (2021, August 29). *Tech B Corp prioritizes the well-being of people and planet.* Medium. https://bthechange.com/tech-b-corp-prioritizes-the-well-being-of-people-and-planet-73b35a83bdbf

Financial Times. (2016, September 12). *50 journals used in FT research rank.* https://www.ft.com/content/3405a512-5cbb-11e1-8f1f-00144feabdc0

Floridi, L., Cowls, J., King, T. C., & Taddeo, M. (2020). How to design AI for social good: Seven essential factors. *Science and Engineering Ethics, 26*(3), 1771–1796. https://doi.org/10.1007/s11948-020-00213-5

Freeman, R. E. (2010/1984). *Strategic management: A stakeholder approach.* Cambridge University Press.

García-Avilés, J. A. (2020). Diffusion of innovation. *The International Encyclopedia of Media Psychology*, 1–8.

Garfield, E. (1955). Citation indices for science. *Science, 122*(3159), 108–111.

Garfield, E. (1996, June 10). What is the primordial reference for the phrase 'publish or perish'. *The Scientist, 10*(12), 11.

Garfield, E. (2006). The history and meaning of the Journal Impact Factor. *JAMA, 295*(1), 90. https://doi.org/10.1001/jama.295.1.90

Glänzel, W., & Moed, H. F. (2002). Journal impact measures in bibliometric research. *Scientometrics, 53*(2), 171–193.

Gomes, C., Dietterich, T., Barrett, C., Conrad, J., Dilkina, B., Ermon, S., Fang, F., Farnsworth, A., Fern, A., Fern, X., Fink, D., Fisher, D., Flecker, A., Freund, D., Fuller, A., Gregoire, J., Hopcroft, J., Kelling, S., Kolter, Z ... Zeeman, M. L. (2019). Computational sustainability: computing for a better world and a sustainable future. *Communications of the ACM, 62*(9), 56–65. https://doi.org/10.1145/3339399

Google AI. (n.d.). *AI for social good—Applying AI to some of the world's biggest challenges.* https://ai.google/social-good/

Goralski, M. A., & Tan, T. K. (2020). Artificial intelligence and sustainable development. *The International Journal of Management Education, 18*(1). https://doi.org/10.1016/j.ijme.2019.100330

Gui, Q., Liu, C., Du, D., & Duan, D. (2019). The changing geography of global science. *Environment and Planning A: Economy and Space, 51*(8), 1615–1617.

Guidotti, R. (2021). Evaluating local explanation methods on ground truth. *Artificial Intelligence, 291*. https://doi.org/10.1016/j.artint.2020.103428

Hager, G., Drobnis, A., Fang, F., Ghani, R., Greenwald, A., Lyons, T., Parkes, D. C., Schultz, J., Saria, S., Smith, S. F., & Tambe, M. (2017, March). *Artificial intelligence for social good* (Grant no. 1136993). ArXiv.org. https://arxiv.org/ftp/arxiv/papers/1901/1901.05406.pdf

Heimerl, F., Lohmann, S., Lange, S., & Ertl, T. (2014, January). Word cloud explorer: Text analytics based on word clouds. In *2014—47th Hawaii international conference on system sciences, 1833–1842.* https://doi.org/10.1109/hicss.2014.231

HESI—Higher Education Sustainability Initiative | Department of Economic and Social Affairs. (n.d.). Rankings, ratings, and assessments. https://sdgs.un.org/topics/education/hesi

Hinchliffe, L. J. (2021, August 30). *Hacking a top journals list: A collective approach to developing metrics?* The Scholarly Kitchen. https://scholarlykitchen.sspnet.org/2021/08/31/hacking-a-top-journals-list-a-collective-approach-to-developing-metrics/

Hirsch, J. E. (2005). An index to quantify an individual's scientific research output. *Proceedings of the National Academy of Sciences, 102*(46), 16569–16572.

Hirsch, J. E. (2007). Does the h index have predictive power? *Proceedings of the National Academy of Sciences, 104*(49), 19193–19198.

ISO. (2021, August 30). ISO 26000:2010. https://www.iso.org/standard/42546.html

Jack, A. (2020, December 6). Weighing up business schools' work on sustainability. *Financial Times.* https://www.ft.com/content/6b499b5b-76fc-4fee-9684-f8055e52c46e

Jack, A. (2021). Business school rankings: The Financial Times' experience and evolutions. *Business & Society.* https://doi.org/10.1177/00076503211016783

Joireman, J., & Van Lange, P. A. (2015). *How to publish high-quality research.* American Psychological Association. https://www.researchgate.net/publication/269110626_How_to_Publish_High-Quality_Research

Kalika, M., & Shenton, G. (2019, February). Impact: Is it enough just to talk about it? *GlobalFocus.* https://www.globalfocusmagazine.com/impact-is-it-enough-just-to-talk-about-it/?utm_campaign=GF+shareaholic&utm_medium=email_this&utm_source=email%3CBR%3E%2D%2D%3CBR%3EShared

Kriebitz, A., & Lütge, C. (2020). Artificial intelligence and human rights: A business ethical assessment. *Business and Human Rights Journal, 5*(1), 84–104. https://doi.org/10.1017/bhj.2019.28

Kulevicz, R. A., Porfirio, G. E. D. O., de Oliveira, O. S., Zavala, A. A., Silva, B. A. D., & Constantino, M. (2020). Influence of sustainability reports on social and environmental issues: Bibliometric analysis and the word cloud approach. *Environmental Reviews, 28*(4), 380–386. https://doi.org/10.1139/er-2019-0075

Linacre, S. (2021a, March 17). The Source/Cabells launches new SDG Impact Intensity journal rating system in partnership with Saint Joseph's University's Haub School of Business. Cabells. https://blog.cabells.com/2021/03/17/

Linacre, S. (2021b, March 31). *The Source/Opening up the SDGs*. https://blog.cabells.com/2021/03/31/opening-up-the-sdgs/

Linacre, S. (2021c, April 28). *The Source/What truly counts for rankings?* https://blog.cabells.com/2021/04/28/what-really-counts-for-rankings/

Linacre, S. (2021d, September 15). *SDG-Impact Journal Rating*. https://blog.cabells.com/category/academic-journals/

Linacre, S. (2021e). *Global Focus—The EFMD Business Magazine, 15*(3). https://www.globalfocusmagazine.com

Locke, R. R., & Spender, J. C. (2011). *Confronting managerialism: How the business elite and their schools threw our lives out of balance*. Bloomsbury.

Lönngren, J., & Van Poeck, K. (2021). Wicked problems: A mapping review of the literature. *International Journal of Sustainable Development & World Ecology, 28*(6), 481–502.

Martin, R. (2012). The price of actionability. *Academy of Management Learning & Education, 11*(2), 293–299.

McLellan, D. (1969). *David McLellan, The Young Hegelians and Karl Marx—PhilPapers*. https://Philpapers.Org. https://philpapers.org/rec/MCLTYH

Muller, J. Z. (2019). *The tyranny of metrics*. Princeton University Press.

Nakamura, M., Pendlebury, D., Schnell, J., Szomszor, M., ISI Institute for Scientific Information, & Web of Science Group. (2019, April). *Navigating the structure of research on sustainable development goals*. Clarivate. https://clarivate.com/webofsciencegroup/campaigns/sustainable-development-goals/

Oxford University. (2021, July 20). *The Oxford English Dictionary | Oxford Languages*. https://Languages.Oup.Com/Research/Oxford-English-Dictionary/

PIR. (n.d.). Positive impact rating for business schools. https://www.positiveimpactrating.org

Politzer-Ahles, S., Holliday, J. J., Girolamo, T., Spychalska, M., & Berkson, K. H. (2016). Is linguistic injustice a myth? A response to Hyland (2016). *Journal of Second Language Writing, 34*, 3.

Pontille, D., & Torny, D. (2010). The controversial policies of journal ratings: Evaluating social sciences and humanities. *Research Evaluation, 19*(5), 347–360. https://doi.org/10.3152/095820210x12809191250889

PRME. (n.d.). A global movement transforming business and management education through research and leadership. https://www.unprme.org

Purdy, M. (2020). Unlocking AI's potential for social good. *Harvard Business Review, 2020*(October 27). https://hbr.org/2020/10/unlocking-ais-potential-for-social-good

QS. (n.d.). QS world university rankings: sustainable development goals. https://www.topuniversities.com/university-rankings/world-university-rankings/sustainable-development-goals

Ravenscroft, J., Liakata, M., Clare, A., & Duma, D. (2017). Measuring scientific impact beyond academia: An assessment of existing impact metrics and proposed improvements. *PLoS One, 12*(3), e0173152. https://doi.org/10.1371/journal.pone.0173152

REF. (2020, October). *Index of revisions to the 'guidance on submissions'*. https://www.ref.ac.uk/media/1447/ref-2019_01-guidance-on-submissions.pdf

REF. (n.d.). *About—REF 2021*. https://www.ref.ac.uk/about/

Reingewertz, Y., & Lutmar, C. (2018). Academic in-group bias: An empirical examination of the link between author and journal affiliation. *Journal of Informetrics, 12*(1), 74–86.

RELX. (n.d.). *SDG Resource Centre—Leading-edge information on the sustainable development goals*. https://sdgresources.relx.com/

Responsible Research in Business Management [RRBM]. (n.d.). *A vision for responsible research in business management*. RRBM Network. https://www.rrbm.network/

Roberts, A. (2000). *Fredric Jameson* (1st ed.). Routledge. https://doi.org/10.4324/9780203186008

Rodenburg, K., Rizwan, T., Liu, R., & Christensen Hughes, J. (2021). Enhancing the positive impact rating: A new business school rating in support of a sustainable future. *Sustainability, 13*(12), 6519.

Rotterdam School of Management. (n.d.). *SDG ranking*. https://rsmmetrics.nl/sustainable-development-goals/triple-crown-sdg/journals-3

Saha, S., Saint, S., & Christakis, D. A. (2003). Impact factor: A valid measure of journal quality? *Journal of the Medical Library Association, 91*(1), 42.

Saint Joseph's University. (n.d.). *SDG Impact Intensity Journal Rating*. SDG Dashboard. https://sdgdashboard.sju.edu/?page_id=8319

Schemm, Y. (2020, September). *Report: Mapping research to advance the SDGs*. Elsevier. https://www.elsevier.com/connect/sdg-report

ScienceOpen. (n.d.). *UN Sustainable Development Goals on ScienceOpen*. https://www.scienceopen.com/collection/e67a99d4-ef59-42f8-a498-18ec810fd9ac

Scopus. (n.d.). Welcome to SCOPUS Preview. https://www.scopus.com/home.uri

SDSN Australia, New Zealand & Pacific. (2021, March 5). *Resources*. https://ap-unsdsn.org/resources/

Seglen, P. O. (1997a). Citations and journal impact factors: Questionable indicators of research quality. *Allergy, 52*(11), 1050–1056.

Seglen, P. O. (1997b). Why the impact factor of journals should not be used for evaluating research. *BMJ, 314*(7079), 497.

Singh, G., Haddad, K. M., & Chow, C. W. (2007). Are articles in "top" management journals necessarily of higher quality? *Journal of Management Inquiry, 16*(4), 319–331.

Springer Nature. (n.d.). *The sustainable development goals programme*. https://www.springernature.com/gp/researchers/sdg-programme

Steingard, D., Balduccini, M., & Sinha, A. (2022). Applying AI for social good: Aligning academic journal ratings with the United Nations Sustainable Development Goals (SDGs). *AI & SOCIETY*, 1–17.

Sugimoto, C. (2020, September 16). *"Attention is not impact" and other challenges for Altmetrics*. https://www.wiley.com/network/researchers/promoting-your-article/attention-is-not-impact-and-other-challenges-for-altmetrics

Taylor & Francis. (n.d.). *Sustainable Development Goals online*. Informa. https://app.dimensions.ai/discover/publication

Thelwall, M. (2020a, May 12). *Scholarly assessment reports*. https://www.scholarlyassessmentreports.org/articles/10.29024/sar.10/

Thelwall, M. (2020b, June 24). Measuring societal impacts of research with altmetrics? Common problems and mistakes. *Journal of Economic Surveys*. https://doi.org/10.1111/joes.12381

Times Higher Education. (2021, September 9). Impact ranking. https://www.timeshighereducation.com/impactrankings#!/page/0/length/25/sort_by/rank/sort_order/asc/cols/undefined

To, W. M., & Yu, B. T. (2020). Rise in higher education researchers and academic publications. *Emerald Open Research, 2*, 3.

Tomašev, N., Cornebise, J., Hutter, F., Mohamed, S., Picciariello, A., Connelly, B., Belgrave, D. C. M., Ezer, D., van der Haert, F. C., Mugisha, F., Abila, G., Arai, H., Almiraat, H., Proskurnia, J., Snyder, K., Otake-Matsuura, M., Othman, M., Glasmachers, T., de Wever, W., ... Clopath, C. (2020). AI for social good: Unlocking the opportunity for positive impact. *Nature Communications, 11*(1), 1–6.

Trueger, N. S., Thoma, B., Hsu, C. H., Sullivan, D., Peters, L., & Lin, M. (2015). The altmetric score: A new measure for article-level dissemination and impact. *Annals of Emergency Medicine, 66*(5), 549–553.

Tsamados, A., Aggarwal, N., Cowls, J., Morley, J., Roberts, H., Taddeo, M., & Floridi, L. (2021, February 20). The ethics of algorithms: Key problems and solutions. *AI & Society*. https://doi.org/10.1007/s00146-021-01154-8

United Nations. (n.d.-a). *SDG Publishers Compact*. United Nations Sustainable Development. https://www.un.org/sustainabledevelopment/sdg-publishers-compact/

United Nations. (n.d.-b). *The 17 goals—Sustainable development*. https://sdgs.un.org/goals

United Nations. (n.d.-c). *Transforming our world: the 2030 Agenda for Sustainable Development*. Retrieved July 29, 2021, from https://sdgs.un.org/2030agenda

University of Illinois, Chicago. (n.d.). *Subject and course guides: Selecting publication venues: Journal Impact Factor (IF)*. https://Researchguides.Uic.Edu/c.Php?G=252603&p=1684747. Retrieved August 28, 2021, from. https://researchguides.uic.edu/c.php?g=252603&p=1684747

Vinuesa, R., Azizpour, H., Leite, I., Balaam, M., Dignum, V., Domisch, S., Felländer, A., Langhans, S. D., Tegmark, M., & Fuso Nerini, F. (2020). The role of artificial intelligence in achieving the sustainable development goals. *Nature Communications, 11*(1). https://doi.org/10.1038/s41467-019-14108-y

Wooldridge, J., & King, M. B. (2019). Altmetric scores: An early indicator of research impact. *Journal of the Association for Information Science and Technology, 70*(3), 271–282.

Xu, S. (2018). Issues in the Interpretation of "Altmetrics" digital traces: A review. *Frontiers*. https://www.frontiersin.org/articles/10.3389/frma.2018.00029/full

Zhang, T. (2021). Will the increase in publication volumes "dilute" prestigious journals' impact factors? A trend analysis of the FT50 journals. *Scientometrics, 126*(1), 863–869.

18

Giving Voice to Values as an Enabling Pedagogy for Digital Ethics

Adriana Krasniansky and Mary C. Gentile

18.1 Introduction

Over the past few decades, advances in technological capabilities, including artificial intelligence with algorithms for planning and prediction, rapid computation, tracking capabilities, and so on, have led to stunning new possibilities for communication and problem solving and have created numerous new business opportunities. Almost as soon as these new capabilities surfaced, practitioners, consumers, and policy makers began to identify the potential ethical challenges and value conflicts they would present. More than 30 years ago, faculty at Harvard Business School were already identifying the management and ethical/policy questions raised by new capabilities around data access, capture, speed, permanence/

A. Krasniansky
Petrie-Flom Center for Health Law Policy, Biotechnology, and Bioethics, Cambridge, MA, USA

M. C. Gentile (✉)
University of Virginia Darden School of Business, Charlottesville, VA, USA
e-mail: GentileM@darden.virginia.edu

storage, tracking, monitoring, and recombination (Sviokla & Gentile, 1990). [1] These capabilities and concomitant ethical questions have only increased since then, and given the scale of their impacts on the social fabric as well as business functioning, it is critical to prepare both business students and current practitioners to not only anticipate, recognize, and analyze these questions but also, and importantly, act effectively and responsibly when they arise.

As with other business ethics questions, educators and managers are far more likely to identify and create taxonomies of ethical issues and questions raised by technological capabilities than they are to prepare practitioners for action and positive solutions. For example, recent debates in the policy and ethical realms tend to raise questions of privacy and information security vs. market access; misinformation vs. free speech; bias and predictive accuracy vs. efficiency. While these are hugely important and thorny issues, there is little attention given to preparing managers to constructively discuss and resolve them or to share effective strategies employed by those who have done so.

In this chapter, the authors will share an innovative pedagogical approach for precisely developing this capacity for effective ethical action—Giving Voice To Values (GVV)—that has been widely adapted globally in business education, corporate settings, and other contexts. The discussion of GVV will be followed by a case example of potential bias in an algorithm-enabled product. Applying the GVV methodology, the authors will discuss possible ways that the executives could have more effectively dealt with this challenge. Finally, additional examples will be shared to illustrate beginnings of efforts to engage more deeply with the field of digital ethics through GVV frameworks.

---

[1] "Information Technology in Organizations: Emerging Issues in Ethics and Policy", John J. Sviokla and Mary Gentile, Harvard Business Publishing, # 9-190-130, February 15, 1990, page 12.

18.2 What Is Giving Voice to Values?

Giving Voice To Values[2] (GVV) is an innovative approach to value-driven leadership development and the preparation of managers and other professionals for ethical action. GVV has been piloted and/or shared in well over 1300 educational and organizational settings globally.

Drawing on actual experience and scholarship, *GVV* fills a long-standing critical gap in the development of value-centered leaders. GVV is not about persuading people to be more ethical. Rather, *GVV* starts from the premise that most of us already want to act on our values but that we also want to feel that we have a reasonable chance of doing so effectively and successfully. This pedagogy and curriculum are about raising those odds. Rather than a focus on ethical *analysis*, the *Giving Voice to Values (GVV)* curriculum focuses on ethical *implementation* and asks the question: "What if I were going to act on my values? What would I say and do? How could I be most effective?"

This shift to a new question—asking how to act ethically rather than asking what is ethical or whether it is possible?—is at the heart of the GVV reframe of ethical pedagogy. This approach grew out of frustration with the standard approaches to ethics education that positioned these discussions as intellectual puzzles, posing ethical challenges and then encouraging participants to engage in endless debates about what the "right thing" or even the ethically "permissible thing" to do might be. The focus was on presenting dilemmas and then applying models of ethical reasoning to the situation—consequentialist, duty-based, rights-based,

---

[2] *Giving Voice To Values* is based at University of Virginia-Darden School of Business, having been launched by Aspen Institute as Incubator & Founding Partner, with Yale School of Management; then supported at Babson College 2009–2016. The curriculum is available at http://store.darden. virginia.edu/giving-voice-to-values (or under the "Curriculum" tab at www.GivingVoiceToValues. org (most of it free to download). (Teaching notes and B cases are available to registered and approved faculty members. Register at https://store.darden.virginia.edu/login.)

The book from Yale University Press is *Giving Voice to Values: How to Speak Your Mind When You Know What's Right*, www.MaryGentile.com (available in Chinese and Korean). A series of 6 online interactive, social cohort-based customizable modules are also available: visit https://players.bright-cove.net/3326885378001/default_default/index.html?videoId=4134427723001 and Plans | Nomadic Learning. Additionally, a 4 week online course (MOOC) on "Ethical Leadership through Giving Voice To Values" is available from Darden in partnership with Coursera at https://www.coursera.org/learn/uva-darden-giving-voice-to-values

virtue-based approaches—to fully understand and try to determine how to respond. These discussions are inarguably useful and even essential because they develop the ability to think rigorously and consistently about value conflicts. However, they also most certainly do not determine what the ethical response should be because, in fact, the value of these various models of ethical reasoning is the fact that they conflict. That is, what one recognizes from a deontological vantage might be missed from a utilitarian vantage, and vice versa. By design, these approaches differ so that a more complete analysis can be achieved. Then, even if one decides what the "right thing" to do may be, there is little or no attention given to how to get it done successfully. We refer to this as the "preach and pretend" method: preach about what is right and then pretend we are able to do it.

GVV takes a different approach to ethics education and skill building. It still utilizes scenarios or case studies, but they are framed as "GVV Thought Experiments." That is, they feature a protagonist who has already determined the values that he or she holds dear and the decisions that support them, and then the focus of the discussion is to determine how best to enact that commitment. This is called a "thought experiment" because the cases are postdecision-making; they do not conclude with the question "what is the right thing to do?". Instead, they conclude with the following questions: "What if" you were this protagonist who wants to act on the values-driven choice they have made, how could you get it done effectively? What data would you need to gather? Whom would you talk to, in what sequence? What sorts of objections might you encounter, and then what would you say and do? And are you going to do this alone, or is this a situation where you need to build a set of allies? And is this a one-off decision, or is it a more systemic challenge that therefore requires a more systemic action plan? And so on.

By framing the discussion around this question of "what if" you were this protagonist who wants to act in this way—rather than "how would YOU act" in this situation—learners avoid the falling into the trap of arguing endlessly about whether the protagonist's choice is correct or even possible, and they circumvent the hesitancy to appear naive or uninformed about the complexities of organizational action. Instead, they are invited to demonstrate their cleverness and creativity by coming up with a strategy to achieve the end that is often assumed to be impossible or unrealistic.

GVV takes this approach for several reasons. First, we have learned from recent studies of behavioral ethics and social psychology that when we face value conflicts, we tend to react emotionally, automatically, and even unconsciously, based on what seems possible and then rationalize after the fact that our choice was the right one, or perhaps the only possible one to make.[3] Therefore, the "GVV Thought Experiment" is an attempt to rewire this automatic response to engage participants in literal prescripting, problem reframing, and action planning so that they can build a new habit, a sort of "moral muscle memory" whereby their automatic response to value conflicts is more capacious, allowing them to feel that there are more options available to them.

To build this new muscle, the GVV approach invites learners to respond to four questions in response to the GVV postdecision-making scenario or "thought experiment":

1. **What is the values-based position that the protagonist wants to take?**

    This is an opportunity for the learner to state the choice that the case protagonist has already made and to begin to place themselves in the "thought experiment": that is, what if they were this protagonist and wanted to take this action, how could they be successful?

2. **What is at STAKE or at RISK for all affected parties, including the protagonist?**

    This question is considered NOT to perform a stakeholder analysis because the protagonist has already decided what they believe is the right thing to do. Rather, this question is considered to identify all parties' motivations, fears, needs, impacts, and so on that may be useful in crafting the most effective action plan. For example, there may be ways to reframe an issue to minimize risk to the person(s) we are trying to influence or at least to acknowledge the impacts of what we are proposing.

---

[3] Jonathan Haidt, *The Happiness Hypothesis: Finding Modern Truth in Ancient Wisdom,* (New York: Basic Books, 2006), page 145–149.

3. What are the "Reasons & Rationalizations" that the protagonist is likely to encounter?

Reasons and rationalizations refer to the kinds of push back, the objections, the arguments that we think we will encounter or that we fear we will encounter when we try and express our values in the workplace. These rationalizations can be very powerful; they can be compelling, but they are, in fact, vulnerable to response. They're not bullet-proof. The idea behind giving voice to values is to give us a chance to anticipate them, to recognize them and to practice effective responses to them so that we will be ready when they come up in our conversations. Some of the most frequently encountered rationalizations[4] include the following:

(a) Standard Operating Procedure: It's the way we do things in this company, or this industry, or this part of the world.

Now, when you hear this rationalization, although it may be compelling, it is usually an exaggeration. So you might want to take a look and ask, "Can I look around and see if that is truly true?" Does everyone always do this? If that is true, why do we even have rules? These questions are a way to begin to question rationalization.

Another response is: if everyone truly did this, what would it actually mean for the functioning of this industry, of this company, for our relationships with customers, our relationships with the public sector, the government.

Or if it is truly true that everyone does this, would I be comfortable if someone knew we were doing this? Who would I be uncomfortable with having them know we were doing this?

So these are some of the questions that you can ask yourself, and you can begin to build into your response. You can also look for positive examples of folks who have found ways, either in your company or in other

---

[4] Examples of possible responses to these rationalizations can be found in *Giving Voice To Values: How To Speak Your Mind When You Know What's Right* by Mary C. Gentile (Yale University Press, 2010) and in "Ways of Thinking About Our Values in the Workplace" (OB-1126) by Mary C. Gentile in the GVV Curriculum Collection at Darden Business Publishing, http://store.darden.virginia.edu/giving-voice-to-values.

companies, to act according to the rules. In addition, then you can use those as counter arguments.

And finally, you can use the giving voice to values thought experiment, and simply say, "what if we wanted to do this differently? How might we do that?" In this way, we can trigger problem solving rather than a preaching or scolding approach.

(b) Materiality: It's not a big enough deal to worry about.

The problem with this one is that people usually use some sort of external metric to determine that a decision truly is not a big deal. These metrics are vulnerable to bad data, bad judgment, and even our own inherent biases and tendencies to want to diminish the size of the challenge. In addition, so when we're trying to respond to this, we can try and look for ways to question the assumption that it truly is not that big of deal.

Another thing that we can use in response to this rationalization is to remember that some things cannot just be a little wrong. Fraud is fraud; you cannot just be a little bit fraudulent.

Finally, a wonderfully powerful response to this one is to suggest "if it is truly not that big a deal, this is an easy time to address it. In addition, if we wait till it is a bigger deal it is going to be harder."

(c) Locus of Responsibility: It may be problematic but it is not my responsibility. It's above my pay grade.

If you're talking to someone who says that, you're in a good position because they're already admitting there is a challenge. In addition, so you do not need to argue that it is wrong or to preach to them. Instead, you can actually engage them in a problem solving conversation.

Start from the conclusion that you both share: that is, that "this is probably not the best thing to do," and then try to work with them to generate some options for alternate ways to proceed.

(d) Locus of Loyalty: It may be problematic, but I feel loyalty to my boss, my colleagues, my organization, etc.

In responding to this rationalization, you can point out that there are a couple of different ways to think about loyalty.

Therefore, for example, if you're working with a sales team who wants to inappropriately report a sale in this quarter, in order to enhance the bonus for the whole team, you might say, well, I want to be loyal to my team and increase the bonus. However, another way to be loyal to your team is to say, let us stick with the accurate reporting for this quarter, because otherwise we're putting ourselves in a more difficult situation next quarter. We're going to be under greater pressure, we're also risking our team's reputation, their productivity and their comfort level going forward. So you frame it as loyalty, but you redefine what loyalty means.

All of these rationalizations are likely to be encountered when questions of digitalization and ethics arise, but there are likely to be some additional ones as well. For example, as noted above, efforts to protect privacy may be countered with arguments around market access; efforts to prevent the dissemination of misinformation may be countered with arguments around free speech; and as we will see in the case example below, efforts to increase predictive accuracy by eliminating bias may be countered with arguments around efficiency and protecting intellectual property. The point here is that these are powerful objections, but they are not unassailable. However, it is often difficult to respond to them in the moment. Rather than simply rehearsing the pros and cons, it is important to anticipate the objections and literally prescript and rehearse effective ways to respond and/or reframe them.

4. **What is the most effective "Script" and "Action Plan" that the protagonist can take?**

What can he/she say? To whom? In what sequence? What data will be needed? What examples (positive and/or negative) will be useful? How can he/she respond effectively to the most likely "Reasons & Rationalizations" that may be encountered? Is this done alone or will allies be needed? Is this best done one-on-one or in a group? Can the challenge be reframed to reveal potential positive impacts of doing the right thing? Can the challenge be reframed to reveal potential negative impacts of doing the wrong thing? Is this a "one-off" situation/decision…or is this a "systemic" challenge that must be addressed systemically? If the latter, what sorts of steps will be required? And so on.

After learners have had the chance to work through these four questions and develop, rehearse, and peer coach around their scripts and action plans for values-driven solutions to GVV cases, the actual choices that were made by the case actors are shared. If the actual case protagonists found successful strategies for enacting their values, it is important to point out that every approach must be customized to the particular situation. If, however, the protagonist failed to act on the values-based decision effectively, the teaching objective was to consider how they might have done so more successfully. This is the pedagogical approach taken with the Northpointe case below.

18.3 GVV Case Example: Programming a "Fairer" System: Assessing Bias in Enterprise AI Products (A)

In the late 1980s, the University of Colorado professor Timothy Brennan researched the United States criminal justice system.[5,6] Brennan was interested in how an individual's psychological and social traits—such as intelligence, extroversion, and personal networks—correlated with recidivism or the likelihood that an individual would reoffend (commit another crime) after being released from custody. Historically, judges relied on their intuitions to forecast an individual's recidivism rate before making decisions such as assigning bail, probation, or parole, and such intuitions could be biased or otherwise inaccurate. Brennan wanted to build an enterprise artificial intelligence (AI) computer program trained

---

[5] This case (OB-1340) is part of the Copyright 2020 by the University of Virginia Darden School Foundation, Charlottesville, VA. All rights reserved. This (A) case, as well as the (B) case and Faculty-Only Teaching Note are available at the Giving Voice To Values Curriculum site from Darden Business Publishing: http://store.darden.virginia.edu/giving-voice-to-values

[6] This material is part of the *Giving Voice to Values* (GVV) curriculum. The Yale School of Management was the founding partner, along with the Aspen Institute, which also served as the incubator for GVV. From 2009 to 2015, GVV was hosted and supported by Babson College.

on years of criminal justice system data to provide a better "ground truth" recidivism risk assessment. Such a program was expected to be more efficient in its predictions than judges and less prone to human bias or error.

Brennan founded a private for-profit company, Northpointe, Inc. (Northpointe), to continue this mission. The team at Northpointe created a software product called the Correctional Offender Management Profiling for Alternative Sanctions (COMPAS). COMPAS used a proprietary AI algorithm to generate a series of risk assessment scores that would forecast the likelihood of a defendant reoffending. Because COMPAS was a closed software system, analysts, judges, and other stakeholders could read the COMPAS scores for each defendant, but they could not analyze the underlying data, test counterfactuals, walk through the decision process, or otherwise analyze in detail how COMPAS calculated its predictions. Judges were instructed to use the COMPAS AI scores to inform their sentences and rulings but not to base their decisions entirely upon them. The COMPAS software was marketed to courts as another information source to be used in the process of delivering efficient and uniform sentencing decisions.

COMPAS was launched in 1998; in the following years, criminal justice systems in New York, Wisconsin, and California adopted it, as did other municipalities across the country.[7] In August 2013, a Wisconsin judge cited COMPAS's impact on the sentencing decision for defendant Eric Loomis, saying that Loomis had been "identified, through the COMPAS assessment, as an individual who is at high risk to the community."[8] Loomis appealed the ruling on the grounds that, since the judge had considered an algorithm whose inner workings could not be examined, Loomis's due process had been violated. While Loomis lost the appeal, his case spurred national critique of recidivism risk–assessment algorithms. In 2016, inspired in part by Loomis's case, a public-interest journalism team at ProPublica conducted a comprehensive study of COMPAS results in Florida and concluded that the AI system was more

---

[7] "Practitioner's Guide to COMPAS," Northpointe, Inc., August 17, 2012, http://www.northpointeinc.com/files/technical_documents/FieldGuide2_081412.pdf (accessed Nov. 24, 2020).

[8] Julia Angwin, Jeff Larson, Surya Mattu, and Lauren Kirchner, "Machine Bias," ProPublica, May 23, 2016, https://www.propublica.org/article/machine-bias-risk-assessments-in-criminal-sentencing (accessed Apr. 19, 2020).

likely to overestimate recidivism risk for black citizens and underestimate risks for white citizens. COMPAS, ProPublica concluded, was exacerbating the same criminal justice bias historically present in the sentencing decisions.

Executive leaders within Northpointe faced the responsibility of responding to the ProPublica findings and allegations while continuing to maintain trust with clients and protecting the complexity and intellectual property of their COMPAS software product. How could Northpointe work to address bias within its COMPAS software while still growing its role as an emergent technology leader?

Background: AI, "Black Boxes," and Business Software

Developed in the 1950s, the field of artificial intelligence (AI) focused on designing and creating computer systems and machinery that could perform complex tasks as well as, or better than, humans. AI systems most often supported strategy, assessment, and reasoning processes, which had traditionally been viewed as beyond the scope of machines; example tasks undertaken by AI systems included language processing (e.g., translation services), image recognition (photo tagging), and situational planning (driving routes).[9]

There were several technical subfields within AI, one of which was machine learning (ML). By 2020, many AI business applications involved ML systems. ML used algorithms to sort data and draw predictive connections between certain data inputs and outputs. These predictions were based on patterns that the ML algorithm observed in the data. To locate these patterns, ML algorithms sifted through impossibly large datasets and analyzed them through complex computational processes, which could be difficult or impossible for humans to interpret. As a result, many AI systems were classified as "black box" software, meaning that there was no straightforward way for humans to trace the decision-making process of the program. Companies often further restricted access to their algorithms and statistical methods to prevent competitors from building similar software—compounding the secrecy surrounding these programs.

---

[9] Lizzie Turner, "Machine Learning: A Primer," *Medium*, May 27, 2018, https://medium.com/@lizziedotdev/lets-talk-about-machine-learning-ddca914e9dd1 (accessed Nov. 24, 2020).

For quality assurance, companies that produced and managed black box algorithms regularly compared algorithmic outputs to real-world data and calibrated the software to match real-world outcomes. While these calibration exercises aligned the algorithm's computations to real-world inputs and outputs, they did not reveal anything publicly about the inner workings of the software.[10]

Companies used black box ML software to optimize everyday processes: Uber employed such programs to streamline driving routes; Facebook used them to deliver the most relevant ads to users; and Amazon utilized them to match inventory to cost-effective packaging. A black box AI approach increased the potential sophistication of an ML program while also protecting a company's intellectual property—competitors were less likely to copy a product if they could not uncover how it worked. In examples such as Amazon's, the opacity of AI systems carried relatively low risk; there were minimal social consequences related to how Amazon's system chose packaging, as long as it reduced costs. However, there were higher considerations when black box AI systems were used to inform life-altering decisions, such as an individual's parole or probation terms.

Northpointe's COMPAS Software

Northpointe's COMPAS program was designed to streamline a complex human process—analysis for pretrial bail, parole, and probation decision-making. Historically, the criminal justice system required a judge to review and synthesize all a defendant's relevant information before issuing a bail, parole, or probation ruling. This human process was prone to error, bias, or inconsistency: judges might weigh certain factors—such as race—more heavily, make decisions based on their own life experiences, or issue rulings without complete information. Research indicated that there were wide sentencing and ruling disparities among judges who relied on their own decision-making for sentencing, even for similar defendants of near-identical crimes.

---

[10] Eugenie Jackson and Christina Mendoza, "Setting the Record Straight: What the COMPAS Core Risk and Need Assessment Is and Is Not," *Harvard Data Science Review* 2, no. 1 (March 31, 2020), https://doi.org/10.1162/99608f92.1b3dadaa (accessed June 25, 2020).

AI-based recidivism risk assessments were meant to standardize and streamline the analysis necessary for a judge to make a decision. COMPAS's AI program worked by scoring a defendant across several different psychological and social scales and combining these scales to generate composite risk scores designed to predict how likely an individual was to reoffend within the next 2 years. COMPAS gathered over 137 data points for each defendant, pulling information from previous criminal history and public records as well as a survey questionnaire. Data points captured behavioral tendencies (e.g., how often the defendant got into fights during school), social ties (how many of their friends were involved in illicit drug use), genealogical information (whether a parent was ever sent to jail or prison), and personal attitudes (whether they agreed or disagreed with the statement, "A hungry person has a right to steal").[11] Individuals' responses and data were scored against historical parole and reoffense data and adjusted to Northpointe-appointed norm groups (e.g., males, females, community, and regional populations).[12] The final COMPAS score report was passed along to judges before a defendant approached the bench to hear the sentencing decision. While judges and defendants could review the different data points that COMPAS analyzed as well as its final scores, the exact calculations that the black box AI software completed to generate the scores (i.e., the "guts" of the program) were not clear to either party.[13]

COMPAS Performance and Controversy

In the early 2010s, Northpointe's COMPAS program was not the only recidivism risk assessment tool on the market, but it was one of the most popular. When tested by independent researchers on historical criminal justice system data, COMPAS correctly predicted whether an individual

---

[11] https://www.propublica.org/article/machine-bias-risk-assessments-in-criminal-sentencing.

[12] "COMPAS Risk & Need Assessment System: Frequently Asked Questions," Northpointe, Inc., 2012, http://www.northpointeinc.com/files/downloads/FAQ_Document.pdf (accessed Nov. 24, 2020).

[13] Julia Dressel and Hany Farid, "The Accuracy, Fairness, and Limits of Predicting Recidivism," *Science Advances* 4, no. 1 (January 2018), https://advances.sciencemag.org/content/4/1/eaao5580.full (accessed Nov. 24, 2020).

was likely to recidivate 63.6% to 74% of the time; humans' informed predictions were correct only 64% of the time.[14] Northpointe's psychometric data were peer-reviewed in professional journals, and the company conducted several validation studies across the country.[15] Overall, Northpointe's COMPAS software seemed to perform as well as, if not slightly better than, human decision-makers—with less time invested and fewer opportunities for individual bias.

Northpointe marketed COMPAS as a neutral data-informed tool, whose only job was to "connect the dots" within defendant information.[16] This marketing language suggested to enterprise clients that COMPAS would be "amoral" and not apply the emotional or learned biases that human operators would.[17] However, because algorithms were created by humans and trained and tested on real-world data, their inner mechanics were likely to replicate or exacerbate biases that existed in real-world environments. There were several ways that algorithms could exhibit bias; for example, they could encode social norms that existed within real-world datasets, oversimplify social trends without acknowledging cultural or socioeconomic sensitivities or nuances, or amplify small differences into gross polarizations.[18] For developers and corporate stakeholders, it could be difficult to forecast or identify an AI software's bias traps before the program was released, at scale, in the real world.

In 2016, the independent journalism platform ProPublica published a report that analyzed bias within the COMPAS software. Using publicly available information, ProPublica compared COMPAS assessments for more than 7000 arrested individuals in Broward County, Florida, to their real recidivism outcomes several years later.[19] The report concluded that while the software correctly predicted recidivism in Black and White

---

[14] https://doi.org/10.1162/99608f92.1b3dadaa.

[15] http://www.northpointeinc.com/files/downloads/FAQ_Document.pdf.

[16] http://www.northpointeinc.com/files/downloads/FAQ_Document.pdf.

[17] Dana Casadei, "Predicting Prison Terms and Parole," *Downtown News Magazine*, March 24, 2020, https://www.downtownpublications.com/single-post/2020/03/24/Predicting-prison-terms-and-parole (accessed Nov. 24, 2020).

[18] Olivier Penel, "Algorithms, the Illusion of Neutrality: The Road to Trusted AI," *Toward Data Science*, April 10, 2019, https://towardsdatascience.com/algorithms-the-illusion-of-neutrality-8438f9ca8471 (accessed Nov. 24, 2020).

[19] https://www.propublica.org/article/machine-bias-risk-assessments-in-criminal-sentencing.

populations at similar rates, when the program was wrong, it was much more likely to mislabel Black individuals as higher risk (a false positive) and mislabel White individuals as lower risk (a false negative).[20] For example, among defendants who ultimately did not reoffend, COMPAS was almost twice as likely to label Black individuals as medium to high risk (42%) than it was to label White individuals as such (22%).[21] While COMPAS's accuracy rates looked good on paper, the patterning of its errors was highly discriminatory.

The ProPublica report highlighted an important oversight in the COMPAS design and review process: While the program's calculations adhered to one broad statistical definition of fairness (predicting likelihood to recidivate with the same accuracy), it grossly veered from another (systemically misclassifying black defendants as higher risk). Even though COMPAS's code was developed with "procedural fairness," it did not address the structural inequities encoded in its background data.

Bias was encoded within COMPAS's code in two ways. First, bias was incorporated within the data that COMPAS analyzed. COMPAS was trained and tested on historical data from the US criminal justice system, which had a historical bias of more closely policing black communities. As a result, in COMPAS training data, African Americans were overrepresented compared to other populations.[22] Second, while COMPAS did not explicitly consider a defendant's race during an assessment, other characteristics that it did evaluate acted as social proxies for race. Questions within COMPAS's assessment (e.g., whether a defendant's friends used drugs or a parent had been arrested) corresponded to socioeconomic factors, such as targeted policing or community trauma, that

---

[20] Ed Yong, "A Popular Algorithm Is No Better at Predicting Crimes than Random People," *Atlantic*, January 17, 2018, https://www.theatlantic.com/technology/archive/2018/01/equivant-compas-algorithm/550646/ (accessed Nov. 24, 2020).

[21] Sam Corbett-Davies, Emma Pierson, Avi Feller, and Sharad Goel, "A Computer Program Used for Bail and Sentencing Decisions Was Labeled Biased against Blacks. It's Actually Not That Clear," *Washington Post*, October 17, 2016, https://www.washingtonpost.com/news/monkey-cage/wp/2016/10/17/can-an-algorithm-be-racist-our-analysis-is-more-cautious-than-propublicas/ (accessed June 26, 2020).

[22] https://www.downtownpublications.com/single-post/2020/03/24/Predicting-prison-terms-and-parole.

disproportionately affected Black populations in the United States.[23] ProPublica argued that while COMPAS's assessments might have been in line with traditional sentencing trends in the United States, it exacerbated a negative bias toward Black defendants already prevalent in the US criminal justice system.

Decisions Moving Forward

Public response following the ProPublica report put pressure on Northpointe to grapple with the following challenges:

- Northpointe defined fairness as predicting recidivism with the same accuracy across different standard groups. Now, Northpointe was asked to consider whether, when COMPAS made a mistake, these mistakes were more likely to harm one racial group than another.
- Northpointe would need to address the negative effects that its software could induce—not only to the reputations of the software's state and municipal clients but ultimately to individual defendants' lives.
- Last, Northpointe would need to decide how to balance COMPAS's coding adjustments with competitive protection. Any decisions to disclose more information about COMPAS or to make the software more transparent would likely reduce the software's complexity or reveal sensitive information to competitors.

What if Brennan, Northpointe founder and CEO, wanted to make sure he was doing all he could to address any possibility of his COMPAS AI software exhibiting and amplifying biases within the US criminal justice system? Imagine you are Brennan. You are concerned about ProPublica's allegations against COMPAS. How would you go about organizing a Northpointe response to evaluate and address the fairness of the COMPAS software while still protecting customer and investor confidence, as well the intellectual property associated with your advanced AI product?

---

[23] https://www.propublica.org/article/machine-bias-risk-assessments-in-criminal-sentencing.

18.4   A GVV-Style Discussion of the COMPAS Case

Applying a GVV lens to this COMPAS case begins with the reminder that professionals in almost every field—including business, medicine, policy, law enforcement, and others—increasingly rely on advanced technological support to engage in their daily tasks and responsibilities. This reality motivates three perspective shifts. First, because technology is an increasingly ubiquitous component of work, managers in all disciplines must build confidence engaging with technology in a responsible manner. In other words, digital ethics is not simply a technologist's problem. Second, because technology increasingly underscores our workplace infrastructure, it is progressively more difficult for businesses to separate technology use from organizational values. In today's world, business values include digital values and vice versa. Third, because technology is constantly evolving, managers must prepare their teams to constantly reassess and adjust their digital value perspectives, just as they plan to iterate over their technologies themselves.

Private and public sector professionals will inevitably encounter value conflicts related to technology use between themselves, customers, stakeholders, and the norms of their environments. These conflicts could focus on data collection or application, the use of algorithms to inform corporate decision-making, or digital privacy and security protocols, just to name a few examples. In the GVV mindset, the best way to deal with these value conflicts is to have internal awareness of one's personal and organizational values and to practice relational skills to effectively voice them and problem-solve. As we have learned, GVV relational skills include identifying key stakeholders and their priorities, anticipating reasons or rationalizations that stakeholders might offer, and preparing scripts or action plans that find alignment between stakeholder interests and the values in question. Together, these skills help business leaders effectively address conflict in a way that speaks to everyone's best interests.

In the COMPAS case, Dr. Brennan faces a fundamental value conflict in deciding how Northpointe should respond to ProPublica's claims of bias within the COMPAS software while still protecting the complexity of the software and the company's algorithmic IP. While Northpointe did not publicly share their organizational values at the time of the case, we might imagine that, should Dr. Brennan have decided to engage in a values-first manner, he would have committed to uncovering and correcting for any racial bias present in the COMPAS system. Not only would he review bias claims stemming from the ProPublica investigation, but he would also thoroughly audit the COMPAS data pools and calculative processes to address structural inequities related to age, race, ethnicity, income, sexual orientation, gender identity, and other identity categories.

Next, Dr. Brennan would evaluate the different stakeholders in this situation and identify what is at risk for the affected parties. For example, one stakeholder group is COMPAS's enterprise customers: municipal and state courts that expect the software to increase the efficiency of sentencing trials and standardize sentencing appeals. They also expect the COMPAS software to improve their professional reputations by positioning them as fair and unbiased, innovative and data-informed organizations. Another stakeholder group includes COMPAS end users: sentencing judges who expect the software to be clear, easy-to-interpret, and consistent with historical sentencing trends. Because their sentencing decisions and subsequently their professional reputations are impacted by the performance of COMPAS as a professional aide, the software's consistency and reliability matter to them greatly. Additional stakeholder groups include defendants on trial, public interest organizations such as ProPublica, and Northpointe investors and employees. Because Northpointe investors and employees have financial outcomes tied to Northpointe's success, the company's profitability (in part affected by protection of the COMPAS algorithm's IP) is likely more important to them than it is to other stakeholders.

Brennan would then anticipate how these different stakeholder groups might respond to his intentions and prepare corresponding scripts and action plans. For example, Brennan might expect that Northpointe's customers would be concerned that changes to COMPAS's data pools and calculation procedures could reduce the technical complexity of the software's processes and thus diminish the value of the product. Using a GVV framework, learners would prepare a response for Brennan that acknowledges customers' concerns while also noting that, without making these changes, COMPAS carries the added risk of exacerbating racial bias within the courts, an outcome that could tarnish courts' reputations and incur a negative press or litigation. By making these values-first changes, Northpointe is in fact reducing product risk for COMPAS customers.

Brennan might also hypothesize that certain employees and investors would not want to involve themselves with a technology company that changes their product in response to racial injustice claims. They may argue that technology vendors should remain "neutral" to topics such as racial justice. Learners could prepare a response that explains how, when serving clients in the complex field of criminal justice, success is measured not only by how "accurately" a court predicts a recidivism outcome but also by whether the court offers all parties equal access to fair courtroom proceedings. By integrating bias analysis within its COMPAS work streams, Northpointe would be acting as an industry leader, aligning product development with client success and modeling best practices for industry competitors. Reframingly, addressing algorithmic bias becomes a key component of responsible vendor behavior.

In real life, Dr. Brennan chose not to enact a values-based approach in regard to the COMPAS case. Northpointe assembled an internal team of scientists and statisticians to scrutinize the findings within the ProPublica report and argue against them, effectively devolving ProPublica's ethical contestation into statistical nitpicking. Northpointe maintained its COMPAS software and later merged with two other risk assessment software companies under the new brand name Equivant, which is still in business today.[24]

However, by reviewing this case through a GVV lens, learners begin to recognize that a company's digital products and solutions are not designed or operated in a vacuum and therefore cannot be separated from the business's larger ethical challenges or commitments. GVV helps us learn to

---

[24] Equivant. "Equivant FAQ." Equivant.com, https://www.equivant.com/faq/. Accessed 4 Sept. 2020.

approach digital ethics conflicts as opportunities for constructive dialog and product development rather than as polarized spheres that foster corporate defensiveness. Technology development is an iterative process, and our digital ethics work must be as well.

18.5   Applying GVV to Other Digital Ethics Scenarios

Dr. Timothy Brennan and his company Northpointe sit at one extreme of the digital ethics conflict spectrum: There was strong evidence to suggest Northpointe's COMPAS algorithm applied bias in its computations, and these biased computations had destructive effects on a specific population—namely, Black defendants, who were more likely be systemically misclassified as being at higher risk for recidivism. However, not all digital ethics conflicts present strong evidence of bias (at least at the outset), and their effects on social equity may not be immediately apparent. These scenarios require us to be well attuned to relationships between technologies and the communities they serve and to be aware of how bias or other forms of injustice manifest in digital products. While the limitations of this chapter do not allow us to share a full taxonomy of present-day digital ethics challenges, we will use the following paragraphs to present a few common scenarios and introduce how GVV-minded approaches can be used to effectively voice value-based solutions.

As was the case in the Northpointe scenario, digital ethics challenges often originate within the datasets upon which technologies, particularly algorithms, are built and trained. Data bias presents in multiple forms, including sample bias (when a sample dataset does not represent the realities of the environment in which the technology operates), measurement bias (when a sample dataset is collected in one fashion, while real-world data are collected in another), or association bias (when a sample dataset reinforces certain stereotypes present within a culture). All of these biases can lead to ethical challenges, but thankfully, they can be addressed to improve the performance of digital products.

For example, a company developing an in-house resumes screening software to streamline hiring may inadvertently train the software's algorithms on a sample dataset with association bias, where male-identifying employees are represented in higher numbers in technical roles and female-identifying employees are represented more heavily in client service positions. Based on this sample dataset, the screening algorithm may "learn" to prioritize male applicants for technical roles and female applicants for client service roles. In fact, this exact association bias challenge occurred at Amazon, and the company ultimately disbanded its resumed screening tool in 2018.[25]

Using a GVV framework, we could brainstorm how the respective Amazon product team could have cataloged different stakeholder concerns and proposed product adjustments—specifically around rebalancing the training dataset—to make the resumed screening product more representative. They could have also proposed reevaluating how Amazon's recruitment teams use the software in tandem with other processes (e.g., targeted recruitment, interviews, onsite visits) and increased public awareness around the Amazon hiring process. In a highly optimistic scenario, this digital ethics challenge could have catalyzed Amazon's resume screening tool into the marketable digital product promoted by an equity-minded hiring team.

Not all digital ethics challenges stem from data bias. Other challenges relate to internet connectivity, affordability, design and accessibility, or data storage and privacy. For example, a web designer may need to negotiate with her team to prioritize making a client website ADA compliant,[26] despite already working under a strict deadline. A product manager at a health wearable company may need to persuade executives to pursue insurance reimbursement for their product to ensure that patients do not pay out-of-pocket for lifesaving digital services. Alternatively, a chief security officer at a cell phone manufacturer may need to convince her

---

[25] https://www.aclu.org/blog/womens-rights/womens-rights-workplace/why-amazons-automated-hiring-tool-discriminated-against

[26] That is, compliant with the Americans with Disabilities Act. Websites that are compliant with Title II of the ADA adhere to certain design standards in order to ensure website accessibility for people with disabilities.

C-Suite to pivot from selling user data to protect user data, positioning the move as a competitive advantage for the brand. In each of these cases, GVV can be used to identify stakeholder interests and craft compelling scripts or action plans that align values-oriented thinking with their key interests.

18.6   Conclusion

Obviously, new technologies offer varied and ever-growing opportunities for new products and services. However, just as obviously, the power of these technologies creates new ethical challenges, often unanticipated or even recognized until they begin to create unforeseen impacts. Thus, it is essential that technologists and business managers begin to frame these challenges as "normal"—an expected part of their professional operations. This "Normalization"[27]—one of the pillars of GVV—enables practitioners to anticipate the sorts of conversations and problem solving that will be required of them rather than to see such challenges as an unwanted interruption in their workdays. In so doing, it opens up the space for creative problem solving, prescripting, action planning, and peer coaching. It allows practitioners to see that they have more choices than they may have thought. Rather than framing these challenges as zero-sum decisions—address potential racial bias or remain profitable, for example—they begin to see that framing as a false dichotomy. Through rehearsal, they build "moral muscle memory," the habit of values-driven leadership. Applying the GVV approach to educational and training initiatives can lead not only to greater awareness of value conflicts in the digital space but also to more frequent and effective action to address these conflicts ethically.

---

[27] Mary C. Gentile, *Giving Voice to Values: How to Speak Your Mind When You Know What's Right* (New Haven, CT., Yale University Press, 2010), 72–85.

19

Society, Environment, Value, and Attitude: A Study on the Effectiveness of Digital Platforms in Enhancing the Sustainability Perspectives of Management Students

Arindam Das and Ishwar Haritas

19.1 Introduction

Businesses and communities have long realized that wider societal changes are needed to ensure a balance among economic growth, respect for the environment, and social justice. It is argued that while top-down policy implementations can help, these changes must start with individual action, knowledge, and the capacity and willingness to act, which is shaped by one's skills, values, and attitude (Napal et al., 2020). Toward this, the six principles of responsible management education (PRME), promoted by the UN Global Compact, encompass clearly defined purpose, values, method, research, partnership, and dialog in management education (Avelar et al., 2019; Haertle et al., 2017). PRME represents the single largest compact among management-related HEIs the world over

A. Das (✉) • I. Haritas
T. A. Pai Management Institute, Manipal Academy of Higher Education, Manipal, India

with a significant overlap with the institutions recognized by leading accreditation bodies and representation from across the globe. These principles help higher education institutes (HEIs) engage in management education to develop curricula and other interventions that commit to the development of necessary skills and capabilities in the future genera- tion of managerial workforces to develop an inclusive and sustainable global economy. However, critical assessment of PRME indicates that in its current form, PRME may not encourage critical reflexivity that is essential for an open-ended process of deliberations to generate social transformation (Millar & Koning, 2018; Millar & Price, 2018). Nonetheless, the broad principles of PRME allow HEIs to develop context-specific interventions. A recent survey of UN PRME signatory HEIs shows that institutes have taken vastly different approaches and demonstrate different levels of maturity in regard to implementing RME (de Assumpção & Neto, 2020). The pedagogical approaches adopted by HEIs range from project/problem-based learning (in an organization/ community) and apprenticeships with organizations to classroom-based case study discussions (Evans, 2019).

In this chapter, we present our findings on the effectiveness of digital delivery platforms for a field-based course, Society, Environment, Values, and Attitudes (SEVA). The course is offered to all management students at T A PAI Management Institute, an advanced signatory of the Principles for Responsible Management Education (PRME) forum, with extensive focus on sustainability-related education. In SEVA, the students, in groups of ten each and with dedicated faculty support, engage with dif- ferent types of external stakeholders in a variety of sustainability-related contexts, pilot limited solutions using a micro grant, and document and reflect on their own experience.

In the 2020–2021 academic year, due to the COVID-19-related lock- downs, all members of all SEVA project teams remained isolated in far- flung places across India, and they had to collaborate within the team, with their respective faculty advisors, with their external stakeholders and other key informants using digital platforms only. This case study utilizes the first-person experience of the authors of the study, who acted as fac- ulty advisors to different project teams, to assess the effectiveness and shortcomings of the digital format within which the engagements were conducted.

The chapter is organized as follows. We adopt a What—So What—Now What format: we start with a descriptive account of the SEVA course and the changes introduced for the digital platform version, highlighting the key facts about the course and expected outcome. Subsequently, we discuss the outcomes of the changes introduced, which are followed by our perspectives on how to develop leading practices in deploying experiential courses on sustainability using digital platforms.

19.2 Society, Environment, Value, and Attitude (SEVA): A Unique Experiential Learning in RME Initiatives

Society, Environment, Values, and Attitudes (SEVA[1]) is a 2-credit course at T A Pai Management Institute (TAPMI) that is entirely based on live projects. With active guidance through the Faculty Advisory System[2], SEVA introduces students to live, functioning government departments, NGOs, enterprises, and individuals who are creating or attempting to create superior societal or environmental value while maintaining or augmenting commercial gains. Every year nearly 400 students spend between 75 and 100 h on the ground, in class and self-learning mode, to devise solutions to management issues faced by small and microentrepreneurs, NGOs, the local administration, corporate entities, and other relevant actors. As part of these projects, SEVA students also actively explore opportunities to connect small-scale producers to mainstream value chains, to apply modern management principles in different functional areas to decrease operational inefficiencies, improve top-line management, introduce the use of information and communication technologies, and thus improve the overall business health of the beneficiary.

---

[1] While SEVA is an acronym here, in Sanskrit and other Indic languages, *Seva* means service.

[2] The Faculty Advisory System (FAS) consists of faculty mentors advising 10 students on academic and career matters for the duration of two years postgraduate management program.

This approach of involving industry partners as external facilitators in RMEs has been supported in the literature. Industry partners can act in the form of "legitimizers" in RMEs apart from playing the roles of being guides, monitors, enablers, and networkers in RME initiatives. Legitimizers provide necessary legitimacy and support to the academic institutions that designed the RME program (Borglund et al., 2019). In addition, an experiential approach that focuses on students' perspectives and involves external stakeholders not only improves students' understanding but also makes students find it transformative (Backman et al., 2019).

The course, in its sixth consecutive year as noncredited activity and third consecutive year (SEVA 3.0), as a credited course, continued since 2018 and met serious operational challenges when COVID-19 hit the world in 2020, limiting students' ability for in-person interaction among themselves, with their faculty mentor(s), and sponsoring/client organizations for whom the projects were to be executed. India witnessed strict lockdown conditions since the last week of March 2020 that prevented students from being on campus, with no access to the local communities and stakeholders in the Udupi-Manipal region where TAPMI and SEVA project sponsor organizations have traditionally been located.

Keeping this exigency in mind and taking advantage of the fact that all the students were residing in different parts of the country due to lockdown, TAPMI expanded the scope of SEVA to a national context with extensive use of digital platforms for collaboration and learning. It was believed that the problem statements and issues identified with the various stakeholders of SEVA in the Udupi-Manipal region are mirrored in similar sectors across the country. Hence, the extended scope of SEVA projects to a national focus would help understand the broader issues and challenges and identify possible solutions and innovations to common problem statements. The students would then be enabled to use this enhanced knowledge and learning to the specific problem statements in the Udupi-Manipal region. SEVA 3.0, thus, is divided into two phases: (a) Phase 1—National-level study and (b) Phase 2—Local problem statement addressal and implementation with insights from national-level learning.

Specific expectations from national-level Phase 1 activities included the following:

- Understanding the scale of the problem (figures, pictures, national and local level data)
- Identifying one government, one non-for-profit and two private players in at least two locations across the country to understand the depth of the problem; the possible locations would be the cities or villages where the SEVA project members were residing at the time of the project.
- Identifying possible impact of the gap in management—in terms of financial loss, environmental loss and possible negative social impact
- Identifying government initiatives and schemes to solve/address the issue
- Identifying solutions/innovations developed by private or other entities to address the issue
- Analyzing costs and feasibility of the solution at varied scales to achieve economic sustainability

All these activities were expected to be performed on digital platforms, with occasional and unavoidable visits to sites/offices of relevant organizations, by one of the members of the project team who lived in a nearby area at the time of the project. In essence, SEVA 3.0 at TAPMI attempted to promote a learner-driven approach in addition to being a learner-centered approach in sustainability education. Such a learner-driven approach has been well recognized in recent literature (Herranen et al., 2018).

Table 19.1 shows a representative sample of projects taken up by students in SEVA 3.0 from a total of 36 such projects carried out by teams of 10 students each in the 2020–2021 academic year. The extended scope at the national level not only augmented the volume and complexity of work but also opened new opportunities in students' learning.

Table 19.1 Representative sample of SEVA 3.0 projects with extended scope due to COVID-related lockdowns

#	Project title	Original local scope (direct interactions)	Extended national scope (primarily indirect interactions)
1	Conservation of Heritage Buildings and Structures	Understanding the impact of the COVID pandemic on the Manipal Heritage Village, its conservation initiatives, future marketing strategy, means to attract visitors and retaining staff in the near future	Working with designated conservationists and organizations involved in heritage buildings or traditional building conservation—focus on issues related to restoration activities and funding activities
2	Sewage Water Treatment for Small Scale Industries	Continuing the previous year's project, identifying the impact on the environment and preparing a Detailed Project Report for submission to the CEO of Zilla Parishad (the local administrative body)	Understanding the issues of wastewater management in small scale eateries in urban/rural locations across the country, legal requirements, impact on economy/environment, innovations, and cost structures
3	Value Chain Optimization for Vegetable, Fruits, Flowers and Other Agricultural Products	Working with local agricultural and horticultural product groups on product diversification, increasing market reach, finding larger markets and better storage for the produce	Identifying specific vegetables grown in the local area, understanding the value chain, secondary product innovations, and focus on preservation and market reach
4	Retail Management of Natural Fiber Garments (Khadi)	Working with a local Khadi clothes manufacturer to improve their market penetration and marketing of products	Working with natural fiber (khadi) retail shops to understand their marketing strategies, product diversification, and sales strategies

(*continued*)

Table 19.1 (continued)

#	Project title	Original local scope (direct interactions)	Extended national scope (primarily indirect interactions)
5	Improving Market Reach for Small-scale Pottery Business	Working with local potters for better market reach and creating portfolio of market-oriented products	Working with local potters, potter associations, and pottery retailers to understand issues with quality control, product diversification, market reach, and strategies for corporate connects
6	Management of Domestic Hazardous Waste	Working on the domestic hazardous waste/resource management issue in Udupi-Manipal area, identifying innovative ideas, and developing business plans for implementation	Working on domestic hazardous waste management at other localities, with focus on scale of the problem, innovations in the field, business plans to implement innovations, cost structures, and feasibility
7	Data Management of Bulk Waste Generators	Working on creation of an updated toolkit with information about bulk generators, their schemes, and regulations and innovations in management of waste	Understanding the practices of bulk generators at other locations across the nation, guidelines, issues, and innovations at policy and industry levels

(*continued*)

Table 19.1 (continued)

#	Project title	Original local scope (direct interactions)	Extended national scope (primarily indirect interactions)
8	Reuse of Construction Waste	Working with the local engineering college and individual architects on reuse of construction waste, identifying specific construction waste material, conducting materiality assessments, identifying ways of reuse, identifying players who are or can reuse, creating a business plan for specific material reuse	Identification of NGOs, construction houses, and private firms working on construction waste reduction and reuse—innovations in the field and business plans
9	Career Counseling for the Youth from Vulnerable Communities	Working with local tribal communities on career counseling, identifying systems for daily wage jobs and blue-collar jobs, suggesting means to make these systems more optimized, conducting/facilitating necessary career counseling sessions for the youth	Identifying career counseling services for vulnerable communities and for blue collar jobs, market-oriented trainings, market linkages and soft skills trainings
10	Management of Ocean Thermocol Waste	Understanding the unsustainable practices among the fishermen in Udupi area and looking for solutions for ocean thermocol waste	Working on impact of thermocol usage and waste across different economic activities, principal polluters, impact on economy and ecology, and identifying leading practices

19.3   Assessment of the Experience of Digital Platforms in Sustainability Training and Education

SEVA 3.0, on digital platforms in COVID times, was probably a unique approach among various initiatives taken up by PRME-signatory HEIs. The monitoring of student teams' progress during the course and evaluation involved obtaining stakeholders' feedback, assessments carried out by FAS mentors, evaluation of written reports and presentation by students, including online demonstration and models, if any, and most importantly, self-reflection reports written by students. The student reflection reports were expected to be metacognitive reflections to enable students to situate the meaning of what is learned relative to the self and the wider world. The emphasis of SEVA evaluation was not only on project outcomes and quality of education for sustainable development but also on the development of core competencies for managing sustainability in students. The development of these core competencies is a critical step for preparing management students to respond effectively to the many interconnected environmental, economic, moral, and societal challenges associated with improving quality of life for all (Glasser & Hirsh, 2016).

We adopt the sustainability core competence framework proposed by Evans (2019), which is an enhanced perspective of the propositions made by Wiek et al. (2015), on competencies required for transformative sustainability work. The framework involves five dimensions of competence: (a) system competence, (b) critical and normative competence, (c) interpersonal and communication competence, (d) creative and strategic competence, and (e) transdisciplinary competence. Each of these competencies is characterized through a specific set of knowledge, skills and attitudes (see Evans, 2019 for details). We provide brief definitions of these competencies in Table 4.1.

Based on formal assessments and informal feedback received on SEVA 3.0 projects and comparing these with the projects from the previous year (SEVA 2.0), we arrived at the overall evaluation of student competencies for both years. This comparison is presented in Table 19.2.

Table 19.2 Assessment of learners' competencies on a 5-point scale

# Competence	Explanation (Source: Evans, 2019)	SEVA 2.0	SEVA 3.0
1 System Competence	Ability to collectively analyze complex systems across multiple domains (cultural, environmental, economic, political, etc.) and at varying scales (local to global) through considering cascading effects, inertia, feedback loops, emergence and other systemic features in order to develop insights related to sustainability issues, challenges, and opportunities (past, present and future)	2/5	4/5
2 Critical and Normative Competence	Ability to collectively create, discover, experience, negotiate, communicate, and activate sustainability-oriented principles and goals	3/5	3/5
3 Interpersonal and Communication Competence	Ability to enable, facilitate, and motivate collaborative and participatory sustainability learning, thinking, and actions	4/5	3/5
4 Creative and Strategic Competence	Ability to collectively envision, develop, implement, and assess transformative interventions for sustainability	3/5	2/5
5 Transdisciplinary Competence	Ability to draw, in critical and imaginative ways, upon multiple disciplinary frameworks to inform sustainability-oriented thinking and action. Entails epistemological literacy, understanding multiple ways of knowing, including their respective methodologies, applications, benefits, and limitations. Additionally, entails collaboratively and inclusively applying sustainability competencies to foster social change	2/5	3/5

Our assessments reveal that SEVA 3.0, delivered on digital platforms, significantly enhanced the system competence of students. We find that Phase 1 of SEVA 3.0, that is, national-level engagement by students, which involved interactions with a large set of stakeholders through virtual interactions, helped students recognize interconnections, interdependencies, and relationships among various factors, appreciating the issue of scale and complexity in the system, focusing on reflexivity as system observers, and being sensitive to the context. We also find that students have demonstrated better performance in transdisciplinary competence. The shift from a learner-focused approach to a learner-driven approach in SEVA 3.0 ensured that the project team members leveraged each other's disciplinary knowledge more effectively, including the local contextual knowledge of each team member.

On the other hand, we see a dip in two competence areas: interpersonal and communication competence and creative and strategic competence. We observe that in several instances, a lack of uniformity in digital access, especially with stakeholder communities, affected the quality of communication, and trust-based relationships did not emerge. This limitation eventually affected collective envisioning and the development of transformative interventions to address the problems at hand.

Apart from evaluating students' competence development, we also assess how the outcomes of the SEVA 3.0 projects on digital platforms differed from those of the previous year. We use three parameters, Ideation, Implementation and Value Realization, to develop our overall comparative assessment of projects in 2 years. We observe that students, due to extensive desk research and online deliberations, were able to ideate better, bringing in diverse perspectives and viewpoints and triangulating the ideas toward a more mature conceptualization of solutions. However, on implementation and value realization parameters, we

Table 19.3 Assessment of projects' performance on a 5-point scale

#	Performance Parameter	Explanation	SEVA 2.0	SEVA 3.0
1	Ideation	Measures the extent to which new ideas are deliberated with stakeholders toward improving current operating model	3/5	4/5
2	Implementation	Measures the actual changes that have been implemented in stakeholders' processes	3/5	2/5
3	Value Realization	Measures the differential in value delivery and capture as a result of changes introduced by SEVA project teams	2/5	1/5

observe that the outcomes of SEVA 3.0 projects were inferior in comparison. This may be attributed to limited access to project sites, with a lack of connection and trust between the students and the local sponsor from the Udupi-Manipal region. Table 19.3 outlines the assessment of the overall project performance of SEVA 2.0 and 3.0.

19.4   Emergent Leading Practices in RME Through Experiential Learning

SEVA 3.0 on digital platform followed a learner-driven, project/problem-based learning (in an organization/community) pedagogy where the project team members, FAS mentors, local project sponsors and other national stakeholders connected on virtual platforms. The course was intended to not only address some of the sustainability-related issues of the project sponsors but also to instill critical sustainability core competencies in students as they progressed through their postgraduate management education. In other words, the objective of competency development was blended with implicitly addressing complex community problems through the development of solutions that could change the ways businesses and consumers relate to sustainability issues (Hermann & Bossle, 2020).

As outlined in the previous section, the adoption of digital platforms in conducting SEVA 3.0 produced mixed results. When we reflect on the outcomes of SEVA 3.0 projects, the competencies acquired by the students, we are able to identify three key propositions to improve the effectiveness of digital platforms while conducting experiential sustainability courses at HEIs. These are discussed below.

First, we observe that the uneven access to and familiarity of digital platforms in a situation where we have participants (including project sponsors and national stakeholders) from diverse backgrounds negatively affected the quality of engagement during the project as well as eventual outcomes through incomplete implementation of ideas generated in the project. Therefore, we make our first recommendations on digital infrastructure and individual/collective digital capabilities in collaboration.

Proposition 1: *Effective experiential learning through sustainability projects that involve diverse participants demands a level-playing field in access to digital infrastructure and uniform digital literacy.*

We further observe that a learner-driven pedagogy where learners deliberate, individually and collectively, on the issues at hand with a significant amount of desk research that substitutes in-person interactions fares better when team members come from diverse academic and social backgrounds. As students learn more by themselves, they are able to reflect on the issue based on their acquired knowledge and skills. Therefore, we posit:

Proposition 2: When students engage with each other in a learner-driven pedagogy on digital platforms, the diversity of student team members' academic and social backgrounds contributes significantly to the development of key sustainability core competences, especially in the areas of systems and transdisciplinary competences.

Last, we also observe that a 4- to 5-month duration for SEVA projects utilizing digital platforms may be too short a duration to introduce significant change in the sponsor's project and address the problem statement meaningfully. A short duration of virtual communication also does not help improve engagement quality. In addition, there is a risk that the acquired skills may not be sustained permanently in the students. Additionally, SEVA projects are carried out by students during the first year when they have relatively less exposure to managerial and business-level issues. Their critical thinking skills and ability to grasp and solutionize mature when they move to their second year of education as they learn advanced subjects. Considering the limited cost impact of carrying out the projects on digital platforms, we would recommend that these experiential projects be extended to about a year which would not only help student hone the sustainability core competences, but will also help them engage with their project sponsors and other stakeholders with higher level of trust and commitment, leading to significant outcomes through implementations of ideas generated by them. Therefore, we suggest,

Proposition 3: Longer duration experiential projects on digital platforms, with more integration with learning from other courses and superior engagement with stakeholders, improve retention of sustainability core skills and help implement new solutions, with greater chances of value realization.

19.5   Conclusions

As we have entered the decade of action to realize the UN SDGs, the emphasis on transformative changes in our society has become stronger and critically important. This heightened emphasis leads to exploring how education, especially management education at HEIs, can contribute to developing the skills and competencies required for the sustainable development of our society and the adaptation of economic activities for the greater good. While interventions offered by HEIs to inculcate these competencies vary in scope and approach, digital platforms play a salient role in the effectiveness of this capability-building process. In particular, since the COVID pandemic reduces our ability to interact with a broad range of stakeholders, it becomes critically important to leverage digital platforms to not only address the distance issue but also help students connect with sustainability-related issues across locations to develop richer perspectives and robust solutions.

In this paper, we have presented the case of SEVA 3.0, a core, project-based course for postgraduate management students for RME, delivered on digital platforms. We specifically study how students' ability to develop skills and capabilities and project performance have changed from the previous version of SEVA delivered in physical, in-person mode. We have used the framework proposed by Evans (2019) to study students' competencies. Our findings identify the crucial advantages digital platforms bring in RME and a few key deficiencies in the process. We develop our propositions based on these findings, suggesting more effective use of digital platforms in RME.

This study is important in two ways. First, it provides insights to all HEIs, especially HEIs who follow the principles of the UN PRME, in designing and delivering project-oriented sustainability-related courses that leverage digital platforms. Second, it recognizes the need for a robust framework for RME-related competencies and mechanisms to assess these competencies. While valuable work has been carried out by Wiek et al. (2015), Glasser and Hirsh (2016) and Evans (2019), we need to develop and adopt a unified framework for RME-related competencies across the board. Such a unified approach, akin to the way the UN SDGs are being promoted, has become a powerful rallying point, affecting transformative changes in the behavior and attitude of postgraduate management students. We believe further research can be carried out in these areas.

References

Avelar, A. B. A., da Silva-Oliveira, K. D., & da Silva Pereira, R. (2019). Education for advancing the implementation of the sustainable development goals: A systematic approach. *The International Journal of Management Education, 17*(3), 100322.

Backman, M., Pitt, H., Marsden, T., Mehmood, A., & Mathijs, E. (2019). Experiential approaches to sustainability education: toward learning landscapes. *International Journal of Sustainability in Higher Education, 20*(1), 139–156.

Borglund, T., Prenkert, F., Frostenson, M., Helin, S., & Du Rietz, S. (2019). External facilitators as 'Legitimizers' in designing a master's program in sustainable business at a Swedish business school—A typology of industry collaborator roles in RME. *The International Journal of Management Education, 17*(3), 100315.

de Assumpção, M. R., & Neto, M. P. M. (2020). State-of-the-art practices being reported by the PRME champions group: A reference to advance education for sustainable development. *The International Journal of Management Education, 18*(2), 100369.

Evans, T. L. (2019). Competencies and pedagogies for sustainability education: A roadmap for sustainability studies program development in colleges and universities. *Sustainability, 11*(19), 5526.

Glasser, H., & Hirsh, J. (2016). Toward the development of robust learning for sustainability core competencies. *Sustainability: The Journal of Record, 9*(3), 121–134.

Haertle, J., Parkes, C., Murray, A., & Hayes, R. (2017). PRME: Building a global movement on responsible management education. *The International Journal of Management Education, 15*(2), 66–72.

Hermann, R. R., & Bossle, M. B. (2020). Bringing an entrepreneurial focus to sustainability education: A teaching framework based on content analysis. *Journal of Cleaner Production, 246*, 119038.

Herranen, J., Vesterinen, V. M., & Aksela, M. (2018). From learner-centered to learner-driven sustainability education. *Sustainability, 10*(7), 2190.

Millar, J., & Koning, J. (2018). From capacity to capability? Rethinking the PRME agenda for inclusive development in management education. *African Journal of Business Ethics, 12*(1).

Millar, J., & Price, M. (2018). Imagining management education: A critique of the contribution of the United Nations PRME to critical reflexivity and rethinking management education. *Management Learning, 49*(3), 346–362.

Napal, M., Mendióroz-Lacambra, A. M., & Penalva, A. (2020). Sustainability teaching tools in the digital age. *Sustainability, 12*(8), 3366.

Wiek, A., Bernstein, M., Foley, R., Cohen, M., Forrest, N., Kuzdas, C., Kay, B., & Keeler, L. W. (2015). Operationalizing competencies in higher education for sustainable development. In *Handbook of higher education for sustainable development* (pp. 241–260). Routledge.

20

Conclusions

Wolfgang Amann and Christian Hauser

20.1 Summary of Emerging Insights

After covering challenges related to digital transformation, the overarching insight emerges that this phenomenon is neither simple, nor complicated. It is complex. In each of these three states, the role of guidelines and checklists, the role of experts and experts and expertise, and the repeatability of success diverge.

In a simple world, communicating clear guidelines and checklists is essential. In environments that are much more predictable, it is easier to draft them in the first place. If one has such lists, well-trained individuals should be able to repeatedly succeed in creating peak performance and

W. Amann (✉)
HEC Paris in Qatar, Doha, Qatar
e-mail: amann@hec.fr

C. Hauser (✉)
PRME Business Integrity Action Center, University of Applied Sciences of the Grisons, Chur, Switzerland
e-mail: christian.hauser@fhgr.ch

C. Hauser, W. Amann (eds.), *The Future of Responsible Management Education*,
Humanism in Business Series, https://doi.org/10.1007/978-3-031-15632-8_20

results. The situation changes, however, if environments either inside or outside of our organizations become more complicated. Checklists are still helpful in order to ensure compliance and minimizing risks. Experts become more and more required both when it comes to bringing guidelines to live and if need be go beyond. Success is surely not easily attainable or the norm anymore. The situation aggravates further if business and organizational environments become complex. The diversity of situations encountered in each organization, unit, and market renders it difficult to apply solutions. Technological options are diverse, too. System variables are interdependent, and being an expert in one area does not mean others can be mastered as well. A case in point is SAP—a company with tremendous experience in helping clients transform digitally. Yet, when it was time to introduce SAP to SAP, it failed horribly as internal communication was poor and top management suffered from complacency. In addition, there is flux. The speed of change and the overall number of dimensions on which change happens are breath-taking. Projects have every shorter amortization periods before the next wave of incremental or revolutionary change arrives. Such regular change across dimensions augments ambiguity. Cause and effect relations get blurrier, and sound data analysis becomes harder. Checklists or guidelines become less useful as each situation is so unique that they would merely create a false sense of certainty all is on track. Of course, experts are needed more than ever to cope with the challenges, yet only if they constantly update their expertise and keep on learning. We have outlined initial success rates of digital transformation projects at the beginning of the book. Only 16% seem to create sustainable success—in spite of major investments in numerous cases.

Our original assumption for this book seems to have been confirmed by the chapter authors. We started this book project by outlining that it is in business schools where current and future leaders as well as managers can 'download the latest mental software' and where fresh insights are created in order to help individuals and their organizations to succeed. We not only found a rich list of new content that is being woven into unique learning journeys but also technology for delivery is changing fast. We recommend applying a 'good-can-always-be-done-better' mentality. It takes substantial efforts and resources to innovate and work out functioning solutions. Yet, their life cycle will be short. It is essential not to fall in love with one's new creation and remain open to update more rapidly than this was the case ever before. Even if one's solution, be it in an organization or classroom, has proven to bear potential and reflect the latest technological possibilities, it is essential to honor the great progress made while continuing to disrupt. In turn, it is essential to grow a pool of innovation experts who can champion ideas and projects. Staff engagement, organizational energies, and cultures have been the foundation for success for a long time and receive even bigger roles in the age of digital transformation. Anticipating, designing, leading, optimizing, and in due time retiring solutions while retaining positive energies will be key for success in the future as well.

This brings our discussion to the crucial role of leadership and leadership talent available for digital transformation, which goes beyond the technological or project management skills. Organizational leaders see their demands increase as well. It starts with overcoming dated thinking in terms of maintaining a binary view of developments. Leaders are encouraged to not limit themselves to a traditional opportunity-threat view. Digital transformation offers both a list of pros and cons. Smart, capable leaders should also be able to even turn a threat into an opportunity and prevent a trend originally perceived as an opportunity into a value trap. Refraining from merely categorizing something in one way allows us to come up with a richer set of perspective and answers to challenges. For this to happen, we need to continue to regularly invest into learning on the levels of the individual, the team, the units, the organizations, and the industry. This book represents our resource for you to better understand the phenomenon of digital transformation and to ensure you have thought of many more perspectives as this may well otherwise have been the case.

20.2 The Crucial Role of the Addendum Principle

There is a key message here. It is not only for organization which turn to business schools for answers or for individuals who join learning institutions for the latest mental software or value compass. The United Nations Principles of Responsible Management Education initiative also comprises the so-called addendum principle. It is about creating a shared understanding in business schools (and related executive education institutions) that any organization in which management gets taught or researched we should become role models and serve as an example of the very values, attitudes, and practices communicated to course participants. It is essential to not only research or teach about digital transformation challenges but to 'walk the talk'. Therefore, this book contains as many insights for the professor active in research and classroom activities as it does for all those colleagues with leadership roles, be it as department chair, project leader, functional leader, or top management. This boils down to humanistic management principles being observed and used as moral compass for a business school's own activities when transforming digitally. Do budgets match project specifications? Is there psychological safety in place to openly talk about insufficiencies? Are enough experts recruited? Will learning journeys actually improve and how to we know? How to measure success holistically and have clear moments of truth predefined?

For example, COVID-19 made schools explore online delivery—often without the faculty being ready, the students having signed up for online programs, and without the proper technologies in place. It was pragmatic, yet often cheap while not a holistic solution. Rapid learning of what is working and what is not working continues to be essential. Humanistic management protects and fosters human dignity, which can be a conducive and simple point of orientation when designing and deciding on solutions. If business schools fully embrace all the responsibilities of the addendum principle, they ensure they can continue to add value, cement their own legitimacy, and enhance their credibility. What professors expect from organizations and their graduates, they should be willing to deliver as well. This book outlined a multitude of ways to do so, to add more value, and to build better business schools.

Index

Printed in the USA
CPSIA information can be obtained
at www.ICGtesting.com
CBHW051323120724
11513CB00004B/221

9 783031 156311